AMERICAN
INDIANS
&
NATIONAL
PARKS

AMERICAN

INDIANS

&

NATIONAL

PARKS

ROBERT H. KELLER   MICHAEL F. TUREK

THE UNIVERSITY OF ARIZONA PRESS   TUCSON

Dedicated to everyone who volunteers time, energy, and personal resources
to protect the wildlife habitat and natural heritage of North America.

The University of Arizona Press
© 1998 The Arizona Board of Regents
First Printing
All rights reserved

☺ This book is printed on acid-free, archival-quality paper.
Manufactured in the United States of America

03   02   01   00   99   98   6   5   4   3   2   1

Library of Congress Cataloging-in-Publication Data
Keller, Robert H.
American Indians and national parks /
Robert H. Keller and Michael F. Turek.
p. cm.
Includes bibliographical references and index.
ISBN 0-8165-1372-4 (cloth : acid-free paper)
1. Indians of North America—Government relations.
2. National parks and reserves—United States.
I. Turek, Michael F. (Michael Francis), 1950–   II. Title.
E93.K25 1998   98-9013   973—ddc21   CIP
British Library Cataloguing-in-Publication Data

A catalogue record for this book is available from the British Library.
Publication of this book is made possible in part by the proceeds of a
permanent endowment created with the assistance of a Challenge Grant
from the National Endowment for the Humanities, a federal agency.

All royalties will be donated to the Whatcom Land Trust and the
Native American Rights Fund.

*The greatest and most troubling conflicts
are not between good and evil,
but between good
and good.*

—West and Brechin
Resident Peoples and National Parks, 1991

CONTENTS

ILLUSTRATIONS

Photographs

Maps

PREFACE

In late August of 1877, five years after President Ulysses S. Grant signed legislation creating Yellowstone as America's first national park, two small parties from Radersburg and Helena, Montana, journeyed through the area. Each group encountered Chief Joseph's band of Nez Percé Indians, who were retreating before the U.S. Army. A confrontation on the Firehole River resulted in the wounding of two Radersburg tourists; others were held overnight and then released unharmed. Two days later a small force of young Nez Percé warriors intercepted the Helena party near Yellowstone Falls, wounding several and killing two. The events marked an ill-omened beginning for the relationship between the national parks and American Indians.[1]

Various people have heard of the Nez Percé adventure. But few realize that in 1877 the Nez Percé, like the citizens of Helena and Radersburg, were also "tourists," a foreign tribe passing through country much more familiar to Bannock, Shoshone, Crow, and Sheepeater Indians. Likewise, most tourists in modern California have no idea that by the time Abraham Lincoln signed the Yosemite Valley Act in 1864, the park's aboriginal people had been brutally removed, or that a different tribe, the Paiute, remained inside the park for another sixty years. Nor do many of us recall that in 1832, when George Catlin conceived the idea of preserving the West in its "pristine beauty and wildness" by creating "a Nation's Park," he had hoped to protect the culture of Plains Indians as well as to preserve grasslands, wolves, and buffalo. In *North American Indians* (1832) he wrote, "One imagines . . . by some great protecting policy of government . . . a *magnificent park*, where the world could see for ages to come, the native Indian in his classic attire, galloping his wild horse, with sinewy bow, and shield and lance, amid the fleeting herds of elk and buffalo."

National parks and Indians have much in common besides Catlin's proposal.

In the late nineteenth century, Indians, like the original landscape and wildlife, seemed destined to vanish—a prospect that finally motivated reform and protection in both cases. As a result, tribes today retain fifty million acres; the Park Service controls approximately eighty million. Many parks and monuments, as was true of many reservations, were created not by acts of Congress but by presidential executive orders. Indians and parks are both supervised by complex but weak federal bureaucracies: the Bureau of Indian Affairs (BIA) and the National Park Service (NPS), located in the same branch of the federal government, the Department of the Interior.

Being situated under Interior would place Indians and parks at risk whenever they tried to resist dams, mines, irrigation projects, cattle grazing, or other developments favored by that department. Early parks and Indian reservations were originally created out of "worthless lands" seemingly devoid of commercial value; when those areas later rose in value, parks and reservations faced economic pressures that overrode "inviolable" promises and earlier "misguided generosity." Both were also deeply affected by immediate and external threats, and both face serious problems today. The members of Indian tribes have the shortest life expectancy in the United States and the highest rates of violence, poverty, unemployment, alcoholism, and suicide, including youth suicide. National parks suffer from political impotence, confused management philosophies, commercialism, too many humans, far too many autos, and growing pollution from outside.[2]

In resisting threats to their well-being, parks and tribes alike have relatively little power in Congress: Indians constitute less than 1 percent of the total U.S. population; the Park Service receives an even smaller percentage of the federal budget than do Indians. In reality, Congress ultimately governs both parks and Indians, even though the national parks are protected "forever" and the tribes consider themselves "sovereign." Lastly, a special landscape distinguishes America from Europe, allowing the West's great scenic wonders at Yosemite, Yellowstone, Grand Canyon, Glacier, and the Grand Tetons to occupy a central place in the romantic imagination of many white Americans. The same is so for Indians.[3]

Although in Yellowstone, Yosemite, Glacier, and elsewhere a relationship between parks and Indians may seem obvious, the story remains untold. One can find thousands of books about American Indians, a considerable body of literature about national parks, but almost nothing linking the two. The two monumental works on government Indian policy, Felix Cohen's *Federal Indian*

Law and Francis Paul Prucha's *The Great Father,* between them contain one passing reference to national parks. The Smithsonian's *Handbook* on Indian/white relations does not mention parks. Similarly, John Ise's lengthy 1961 study, *Our National Park Policy,* had only two references to the BIA and one comment on the Nez Percé in Yellowstone; Ise mentioned Navajo Mountain, Navajo Bridge, and Navajo National Monument, but not the Navajo Indians.[4] Books published since 1990 continue the pattern.[5]

This neglected story gradually became apparent to the authors of this volume as we hiked and worked at Glacier, Olympic, and Mt. Rainier. Our previous knowledge of American Indian history, which had alerted us to nearby tribal communities, also made us aware that park rangers and superintendents could be oblivious to native history and culture. When conflicts arose, the Park Service, caught by surprise, often reacted in a patronizing or defensive manner. Indians, on the other hand, usually identified the NPS as just another cog in the federal bureaucracy. It was those negative attitudes, along with the surprising lack of information on park/tribal relations, that prompted this book.

In the beginning we knew about Mt. Rainier, Olympic, and the Little Big Horn, about the Nez Percé in Yellowstone and at the Big Hole, the Sioux in the Badlands, and the Havasupai at the Grand Canyon. We had heard of tiny Pipestone Quarry in Minnesota. But we knew nothing about Seminoles in the Everglades, Shoshone in Death Valley, Sheepeaters in Yellowstone, Papagos at Organ Pipe, Paiutes at Yosemite and Pipe Spring, Cherokees in the Great Smokies, Navajo at Chaco Canyon and Rainbow Bridge, or Zuni at the Grand Canyon. We certainly did not know about sacred sites in the Channel Islands or Chippewas fighting to retain land on Lake Superior.

As we investigated, the scope and variety of relationships became apparent. Of the 367 Park Service units in 1992, at least 85 had some relationship with Indian tribes. If one subtracts the Civil War sites, fossil beds, presidential homes, famous buildings, malls, and parkways, the ratio becomes much higher; look only at the "crown jewels" of the system and the figure reaches 100 percent. We found parks totally inside Indian reservations and Indian reservations totally inside parks. There are parks sharing a common border with one tribe, parks surrounded by a half-dozen or more different tribes, and tribes encircled by the NPS. In places, a tribe may have title to park land. Elsewhere Indians may lease land to the NPS, or the service may lease land to Indians. Sometimes Indians manage park facilities; elsewhere the NPS trains rangers for tribal parks.

The list of Indian/Park Service conflicts and disputes is long: boundary lines, land claims, rights-of-way, hunting and wildlife management, grazing permits, water rights, employment preference, craft sales, cultural interpretation, sacred sites and the disposition of cultural artifacts, entrance fees, dams, the promotion of tourism, commercial regulation, "squatting" in parks, relations with tribal parks, and resentment over past injustices. The scope of contact was reflected in NPS director Russell Dickenson's comment that he did not know "of a single major national park or monument today in the western part of the United States that doesn't have some sort of Indian sacred area."[6] In addition, we have encountered ill-informed attitudes that environmentalists may bring to park/Indian issues—either that true wilderness should show no human presence, or that natives living near parks should exist "in harmony with nature," meaning that they must not disturb or change ecological systems.[7]

The scope of the subject has forced us to set aside important tribes, parks, and issues. First eliminated was Alaska—where President Jimmy Carter doubled the size of the park system with the stroke of a pen in 1980—a story so different and enormous as to merit a book of its own.[8] We also reluctantly dropped chapters on the Badlands, Yosemite, Nez Percé National Historic Park, Death Valley, Snaketown, Mt. Rainier, and Canada. With so much left out of it, this book should inspire more study. To future scholars, we guarantee this much: The fieldwork is marvelous.

We ultimately selected parks and tribes that illustrate a variety of relationships that have changed over time. The story here begins with Apostle Islands National Lakeshore because its creation in the 1960s marked a historic shift— Indians at last moved away from a passive approach to Congress and the NPS. After the Apostle Islands story we provide a brief overview, beginning with the creation of Yosemite and Yellowstone, moving then to the founding of the NPS in 1916, and ending at Zuni-Cibola in 1990. Subsequent chapters describe how policy and practice evolved in specific parks, from early Mesa Verde and Glacier to modern Olympic, Grand Canyon, and the Everglades.

Comparisons beyond the United States can provide a needed perspective. In a rare scholarly book addressing the history of parks and native populations, *Resident Peoples and National Parks*, editors Patrick West and Steven Brechin analyze the international nature of this subject. We share many of their conclusions, but, more important, we believe they asked sound questions:

- What obligations, if any, do others owe to people displaced by parks?

- Do aboriginal people have special rights to their former resources

and homeland? to self-determination? If so, how is this exercised and
regulated?

- Are resource preservation and native economic development always
  incompatible?

- What is the role of human culture in natural ecosystems?

- Will preservation of nature enhance and protect local cultures?

- Who plans? Who decides? Who has political power?

- Does an assumption that native people live in harmony with nature fit
  reality? Do environmentalists have an overly romantic view of natives
  and ecology "before the white man came"?

- What is the role of national parks in cultural preservation and historical interpretation?[9]

Specific questions may help the reader sort through the complex relationships in our book. Between 1864 and 1994, how did the relative power held by
the NPS, local governments, Indian tribes, and conservationists change? When
and why? Do morality and holding power affect environmental tactics, and
how do politics and ethics influence governmental decisions, regulations, and
obligations? In what areas are Indians and the general public in agreement over
common interests? Where do they face inherent conflicts? What ideals and
imperatives drive the NPS, tribes, and environmentalists? For example, many
Indians live in poverty whereas most national park visitors belong to the American middle class. What attitudes, myths, and stereotypes influence our values
about land, government, and ethnic minorities? Who is an ethnic minority, and
what makes a bureaucracy tick?

"The American national park ideal," West and Brechin conclude in *Resident
Peoples and National Parks*, "has become the model system of conservation for a
large part of the world, enthusiastically imported by many countries. Unfortunately, the American ideal carries implicit meanings, political mandates, and
management objectives that do not always fit circumstances elsewhere." We
agree, but would add that these ideals do not always fit circumstances in American parks either, as Nez Percé and Radersburg tourists discovered in 1877. In
ways that George Catlin could never have foreseen, national park conflicts and
dilemmas have perplexed the government and native people in North America
for well over a century. We begin that story on the shores of Lake Superior.

ACKNOWLEDGMENTS

Research for this book required extensive travel that allowed us to engage landscapes and people at such places as Window Rock, Peach Springs, Moccasin, Shi Shi, Taholah, Red Cliff, Supai, La Push, Wupatki, and Lake Okeechobee. A mechanic named Jess Barnes in Cortez, Colorado, repaired a 1972 Datsun fuel pump that broke on Chapin Mesa; a roadside cafe gave directions during a blizzard in Babb, Montana; and friends in Chevy Chase, Maryland, provided lodging and encouragement after long summer days in the National Archives.

We recorded 235 interviews, and many people were helpful far beyond giving factual information. Marian Albright Schenck and her husband shared an entire day of table talk and family records; Michael Harrison, who celebrated his 100th birthday in 1998, offered enthusiastic support drawn from a remarkable memory. Others who stand out for their special insights and assistance are Charles and Edna Heaton, Donna Chapman, David Brugge, Fred White, Art White, Bill Byler, Billy Cypress, Bruce Hoffman, Steve Terry, George Kicking Woman, Wallace Stegner, Joseph Sax, Clarence Gorman, Stewart Udall, Mark Rother, Clay Bravo, Clay Butler, Howard Chapman, Ed Ladd, Emil Haury, Charles Voll, Barbara Sutteer, Ed Natay, Vicky Santana, and Jeff Ingram.

Institutions as well as individuals merit gratitude. The Washington Commission for the Humanities Inquiring Mind program provided a two-year, statewide forum for testing our ideas. Virtually everyone in the NPS and tribal governments cooperated with the two nosey outsiders who arrived at their doorstep; Gary Hasty, Reid Jarvis, Jim Tuck, Muriel Crespi, and the NPS Southwest Regional Office deserve special mention. Western Washington University in Bellingham, Washington, awarded one of us a full year's sabbatical; its bureau for faculty research provided two summer study grants and a grant toward publication expenses. The Arizona State Museum donated office and staff support during the sabbatical; its former director, Raymond Thompson, also delivered stimulating lectures on the history of antiquities in North America. Dewey Schwalenberg and Patty Brown-Schwalenberg of the Native American Fish and Wildlife Society supported work out of their Denver office.

Few people deserve more kudos from historians than librarians and archivists, such as Janet Collins, Peter Smith, Dorothy Sherwood, and Evelyn Darrow at Wilson Library, Western Washington University. Valerie Meyers at the Grand Canyon, besides being a delightful person, could locate any document immediately. Tom DuRant of the NPS photo center at Harpers Ferry went out of his way to help, as did Mary Davis and Michael Oakleaf at Pipe Spring. Others include Bruce Craig and Mary Mousseau at the archives of the National Parks and Conservation Association, Bill Simon with the Ziontz/Pirtle legal records in Seattle, staff at the Native American Rights Fund library in Boulder, David Shaul and Peter Steere in special collections at the University of Arizona library, Susan Schultz at Olympic National Park, Francis Mason and Pauline Capoeman at the Quinault Historical Foundation, Mary Morrow at the National Archives, and Mary Graham at the Arizona State Museum library.

For the onerous task of transcribing audio tapes, we thank Susan Ruiz, Tanna Chattin, and Phyllis Olson. Bob Lindquist of Bellingham designed all the maps.

This project began in 1986. The subsequent years brought dips, depressions, and desperations. We therefore appreciate friends who offered their encouragement at the beginning and along the way: Jim Officer, Bernard Fontana, Alvin Josephy, Charles Wilkinson, Luke Jones, Jan Balsom, Francis Paul Prucha, John Miles, Juanita Jefferson, Dana and Darby Jack, Bill Dietrich, Donna House, Mark Heckert, Beth Searcy, Bob Schroeder, and Ginny Mulle. Barbara Morehouse generously shared her Grand Canyon field notes and her insights.

A number of people commented on parts or all of the manuscript: Russell Dickinson, Rand Jack, Patricia Karlberg (only a wife would read it six times!), Jan Balsom, Kenyon Fields, Chris and North Moench, Jenny Hahn, Dennis Liu, Gerald "Buzz" Cobell, Joanne O'Hare, and Teresa Mitchell. Three classes at Fairhaven College—Grand Canyon, Olympic Peninsula, and National Park History—endured this book's evolution. Readers can be especially grateful to Martin Hanft for expert copyediting and to Evelyn VandenDolder for her devotion to last-minute details. We alone, however, are responsible for errors in fact, grammar, or interpretation.

Stephen Cox, director of the University of Arizona Press, immediately gave an enthusiastic endorsement. Later he provided timely direct assistance and sound judgments in the publication process. We hope the book merits his confidence.

ABBREVIATIONS

In Text and Notes

AIM	American Indian Movement
AINL	Apostle Islands National Lakeshore
APA	Arizona Power Authority
BIA	Bureau of Indian Affairs
CCC	Civilian Conservation Corps
CCF	Central Classified File
CF	Central File
CIA	Commissioner of Indian Affairs
CRM	Cultural Resources Management
FERC	Federal Energy Regulatory Commission
GAO	General Accounting Office
GCL	Grand Canyon Library
GNP	Glacier National Park
ICC	Indian Claims Commission
LA	Legislative Assistant Files
LC	Legislative Correspondence
LDS	Church of Jesus Christ of Latter-day Saints

MKU	Morris K. Udall Papers, University of Arizona
NA	National Archives of the United States
NARF	Native American Rights Fund
NCAI	National Congress of American Indians
NPCA	National Parks and Conservation Association
NPS	National Park Service
ONP	Olympic National Park
OPA	Olympic Park Associates
PM	Pirtle Morisset Files, Seattle
PSL	Pipe Spring National Monument Library, Arizona
RG	Record Group (National Archives)
SU	Stewart Udall Papers, University of Arizona
USFS	U.S. Forest Service
USFWS	U.S. Fish and Wildlife Service

AMERICAN

INDIANS

&

NATIONAL

PARKS

"A LUCKY COMPROMISE"

Apostle Islands and the Chippewa

We as a tribe of Indians in the past have ceded large areas of
land to the United States government, and what we reserve
for ourselves under treaty, we aim to keep.
—Albert Whitebird, Bad River, 1965

We leaned over backwards to make it fair and get the tribes
involved. . . . If we could have passed the bill three years earlier,
it would have been fine.
—Gaylord Nelson, 1991

In the cold, clear waters above Wisconsin's northern mainland, a chain of
twenty-two forested islands can be seen from the Bayfield Peninsula. Clustered
close to the mainland, this Lake Superior archipelago covers 720 square miles,
its islands ranging in size from three-acre Gull to ten-thousand-acre Stockton.
Each sandstone island has something special, whether the sea caves and weirdly
eroded coasts of Sand Island, subarctic boreal forest on Devil's Island, or gull
rookeries and eagle aeries elsewhere. On September 26, 1970, after ten years of
legislative wrangling, twenty of the islands and twenty-five hundred mainland
acres were designated as the Apostle Islands National Lakeshore. Long Island
was added in 1986.

Dating back two hundred years, the Apostle Islands had belonged to Lake Superior's Ojibwa people. Each island, Madeline and Long in particular, occupied

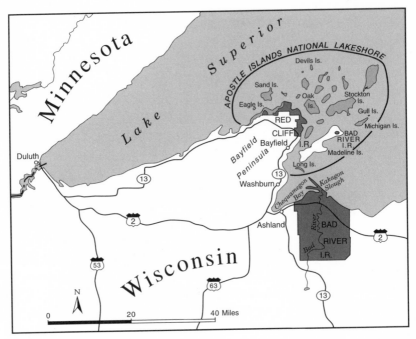

Apostle Islands National Lakeshore on Lake Superior in northern Wisconsin.

a special place in the culture, history, and religion of the Ojibwa (Chippewa) before white contact. Prior to the arrival of the French, Chippewas had migrated westward along Lake Superior's southern shore, a gradual process lasting nearly two centuries. Sacred birch-bark scrolls and origin songs of the Chippewa tell of the Islands.[1] In the early 1700s, as French explorers reached the coast of western Lake Superior, voyageurs christened this archipelago the "Apostle Islands."

Western migration by the Ojibwa had displaced the Fox and Santee (Eastern) Sioux Indians, forcing those tribes out of Michigan's upper peninsula and northern Wisconsin into Minnesota and then onto the prairies. The Apostle Islands, Chequamegon Bay, and the Bayfield Peninsula acquired special meaning for the newcomers. Long Island, the site of a key battle with the Sioux, is cited in Ojibwa migration legends as an important resting point; on Madeline Island, Mitewiwin ceremonies reached their zenith.[2] The cold and often treacherous waters around the islands, like the clear rivers and inland lakes of northern Wisconsin, teemed with fish. Wild rice marshes, such as Kakagon Slough southeast of the Apostles, produced nutritious grain. Maple sugar sweetened the native diet, while birch trees yielded material for baskets, wigwams, and canoes. Abundant deer, elk, bear, and beaver provided food, hides, bone, sinew, and fur—fur in such abundance that it eventually enticed the French from Montreal to western Superior.

As had other woodland tribes, the Chippewa became fur-trade partners with Europeans. In exchange for skins, canoes, snowshoes, and native knowledge of the land, the French offered guns, alcohol, metal goods, and woolen blankets. The voyageurs sought mainly pelts. Attempts by Catholic missionaries to "civilize" the Indians were limited and, for the most part, ineffective. After the defeat of France in 1763, the Canadian trade fell under British control. Not until Americans arrived in Chippewa country a generation later did copper, timber, and fish become motives for taking Indian land.

Although the Chippewas never waged sustained warfare against Americans, they nonetheless lost most of their land. The federal government, unable or unwilling to move the tribes from Michigan, Wisconsin, and Minnesota west of the Mississippi, established small reservations. One treaty followed another from 1795 until 1863, resulting in loss of land, resources, and power for the Indians. This process did not threaten the natives of northern Wisconsin until 1842, yet by 1900, after further "agreements," the tiny Red Cliff and Bad River Reservations were all that remained of the Chippewa homeland.[3]

Anticipating the first Earth Day, in 1970, Senator Gaylord Nelson traveled across the nation speaking on college campuses. A former governor and one of the early supporters of Earth Day, Nelson had established an admirable conservation record. As governor of Wisconsin (1958–1962), Nelson had initiated legislation and policies at the forefront of environmental conservation. Thirty-five years later, Wisconsin and its citizens still benefit from the results of his farsighted administration.

One of Gaylord Nelson's longest and most taxing projects involved the creation of Apostle Islands National Lakeshore. For a decade after 1960, from the state capitol in Madison to the halls of Congress, Nelson led a campaign to preserve and protect the islands. During 1970, that campaign brought a mixed reception in his own state. Indians in Madison and Milwaukee confronted the senator, claiming that Apostle Islands legislation was but another attempt to take Chippewa land. When Nelson extolled the virtues of Earth Day, demonstrators threw cans and trash on the stage. Defending his plan, Nelson promised audiences that inclusion of Red Cliff and Bad River lands into a national lakeshore must have Indian consent—but he failed to add that tribal decisions could be vetoed by the secretary of the interior.[4]

Non-Indian efforts to protect the Apostle Islands had begun in the early 1930s, when U.S. representative William Lafollette recommended the islands for inclusion into the national park system. After an initial survey, the Park Service concluded that because of extensive logging the islands did not meet its standards. In the mid-1950s conservationists made another attempt. As second-growth forests matured, the islands again looked like jewels in Lake Superior. Wisconsin established an Apostle Islands State Forest consisting of Stockton, Oak, and Basswood Islands, and in 1963 negotiations for three more islands began. By that time Nelson had realized that protection of the Apostles was too much for state government: If the entire archipelago deserved protection, the federal government must assume responsibility.

To conservationists, time was running out on the Apostles. They anticipated more clear-cutting when island timber matured, but proliferation of summer homes posed an even greater threat. Individuals in Chicago, Detroit, Cleveland, Milwaukee, and the Twin Cities now owned extensive recreation land around the Great Lakes, effectively closing much frontage to public access. In early May 1962, the Bad River Band of Lake Superior Chippewa gave conservationists a boost when a tribal council resolution requested study of Lake Superior shoreline and marshes as a potential wildlife refuge. The Chippewa sought to preserve the land and waters "for all times [which] should contribute now and in the future to the economic well-being of the Tribe."[5] The tribal resolution, directed to Secretary of the Interior Stewart Udall, opened a door for federal involvement.

By the mid-twentieth century Chippewa Indians retained only a remnant of their Wisconsin lands. Established by treaty in 1854, the Red Cliff and Bad River Reservations served as the Chippewa homeland in western Lake Superior. In the late 1930s, many logged and burned-over reservation allotments (individual tracts) had been sold to non-Indians. In 1960 the Bad River and Red Cliff Reservations encompassed 125,000 and 18,000 acres, respectively, each with approximately eight hundred tribal members. Red Cliff consisted of a narrow strip along the northern tip of the Bayfield Peninsula's spectacular Lake Superior coast. Bad River, seven times larger than Red Cliff and east of Ashland, Wisconsin, included the ten-thousand-acre Kakagon Slough. Kakagon, "home of the walleyed pike" and an angler's paradise, contained wild rice and fur-bearing animals. Both reservations once boasted forests, but by the 1960s all marketable timber had been harvested, leaving the tribes with extensive unemployment and poverty.

One possible solution to poverty on Indian reservations was tourism. With that in mind, on May 22, 1962, Governor Nelson presented his Apostle Islands proposal to BIA commissioner Phileo Nash, Secretary Udall, and Edward Crafts, director of the Bureau of Recreation. Nelson's plan included all of the Apostle Islands, with the exception of privately owned and heavily developed Madeline, and it incorporated a twenty-thousand-acre Kakagon/Bad River slough tract on Indian land. The unit would be a national shoreline-recreation area, with Indian and non-Indian hunting, fishing, trapping, and wild rice harvesting permitted. Nelson called for giving the Chippewa preference in employment and guide services. The Apostles would retain their wilderness character while the federal government protected the environment and contributed to the local economy through promotion of tourism.[6]

Edward Crafts visited Wisconsin in June 1962, and, on the advice of environmentalist Harold Jordahl, added the sloughs, the islands, and Bayfield Peninsula to his tour. What he saw convinced Crafts of the entire area's value.[7] The Apostles fit federal lakeshore requirements perfectly: They offered excellent scenery and recreation only 250 miles north of Minneapolis and St. Paul. A role for the federal government in managing the islands seemed assured.[8]

In the early 1960s, northern Wisconsin suffered from economic recession, adrift in an otherwise healthy economy. Economic carcasses littered the area: Logging had dwindled; farming had never taken root in poor soils with a short growing season; water pollution, excessive catches, construction of locks and dams, and an invasion of sea lampreys had all but destroyed the rich Lake Superior fisheries. Yet the northern waters and forests retained a measure of their natural beauty and abundance. On Superior's coastline, one still sensed the mystery and power of Kitchigami (big sea).

Although no longer alive with elk, ancient white pines, and old-growth hardwoods, Lake Superior woodlands remained vast and awesome. Deer and bear, while not as diverse or numerous as in the past, still roamed in forests. Bald eagles floated on thermals above lakes that contained northern pike, walleye, muskellunge, and bass. Northern Wisconsin remained a sportsman's paradise where tourism seemed an excellent option for solving economic problems, a region in which a national park marketed to Midwestern cities could bring in millions of dollars. One study of the Apostles predicted a million people spending

$7 million annually.[9] Lakeshore supporters used Yellowstone, Yosemite, and Glacier as examples of profit to be made from "worthless" lands. The Park Service, some hoped, could transform the Apostles into another Yosemite.

Legislation for creation of a national lakeshore began to inch forward late in 1962. Meetings were held with state and federal officials, local citizens, and members of the two reservations. Gaylord Nelson and his supporters believed that combining reservation lands with the islands would ensure a better economic future for the tribes: "For years, the Bad River Indians and the Red Cliff Indians living in the area have had to exist on what is left of the economy. With the project's approval, they will be able to seize new opportunities both inside and outside the national lakeshore."[10] The area under consideration included all of the Apostle Islands except Madeline, Bad River's Kakagon Slough, and all lakeshore on the Red Cliff Indian Reservation, including Red Cliff Bay, Frog Bay, Raspberry Bay, Point Detour, Sand Bay, and a narrow forest south of State Highway 13. Non-Indian lands on the Bayfield Peninsula within the Chequamegon National Forest and the Bayfield County Forest were also targeted.[11]

Drafts of enabling legislation provided for acquisition and transfer of tribal and individually allotted lands from the Red Cliff and Bad River Chippewa Bands. At the same time it provided for Bad River and Red Cliff hunting, fishing, and trapping rights on Interior lands south of U.S. Highways 2 and 13, land that the Chippewa would receive in exchange for shoreline. Some Indian land would be traded for federal land, other sections would be purchased by the government, and yet other tribal land would be leased. The legislation established exclusive native rights to wild rice in Kakagon Slough, gave Chippewas free access to the recreation area and any docks, and reserved rights to harvest timber in the recreation area as well as preference for employment and concessions to the Indians.[12]

As work continued on draft legislation, Chippewa support began to erode. In August 1964, Wisconsin game wardens arrested a number of Bad River Chippewas for illegally harvesting wild rice in the Kakagon Slough. The conflict arose because Bad River had adopted rules for harvesting reservation wild rice that differed from state regulations. The tribal council insisted that Wisconsin had no jurisdiction over Indian wild rice, and the arrests raised concern about how transfer of Kakagon to the NPS might affect harvest rights.[13]

Harold Jordahl, who drafted the Apostle Islands National Lakeshore bill, understood the importance of wild rice to the Chippewas; he likewise realized the threat this issue posed to retaining Indian support for his legislation. In

September Jordahl suggested that Secretary of the Interior Udall enter the wild rice case as a "friend of the court" in support of the Chippewa, because such an action by the federal government would demonstrate good faith and concern for the tribe's welfare while at the same time enhancing relations between Indians and other lakeshore supporters.[14]

Gus Whitebird of Bad River also worried about Chippewa rights, but from a different perspective. In a resolution of May 14, 1965, Whitebird chastised his tribal council for failing to inform tribal members of lakeshore negotiations. Whitebird, whose allotment extended into Kakagon Slough, insisted that any loss of reservation land required majority consent from the tribe. The council, Whitebird claimed, lacked authority to sell or exchange allotted lands: "[The Kakagon Slough] is noted [as] one of the best fishing and hunting area[s] in the Northern part of Wisconsin. . . . For the past hundred years the Indians reserved this area for their livelihood; the Indians harvest wild rice and cranberries for their winter supply, trap, hunt and fish for their maintenance."[15] Bad River opponents of the lakeshore proposal had found a spokesman.

Within a year after the arrest of Bad River Chippewas for harvesting wild rice, state game officers apprehended another tribal member, Mike Neveaux, for illegally netting Lake Superior fish. Neveaux's defense, based upon treaty rights not yet clearly defined, was rejected by the court.[16] The Neveaux conviction provoked a sharp response from the Bad River council:

> WHEREAS, the creation of the Apostle Islands National Lakeshore now pending before Congress, appears to be another step by the Government to acquire Indian Lands and destroy Indian hunting, fishing and gathering wild rice rights without just compensation,
>
> NOW THEREFORE BE IT RESOLVED, that the Bad River Band of Lake Superior Chippewa Indians do hereby oppose any and all bills introduced in Congress or any acts of Congress to create within the original boundaries of the Bad River Reservation any part or parcel of the so-called Apostle Islands National Lake Shore.[17]

The resolution passed on October 7, 1965. In an interview with the *Ashland Daily Press*, Councilman Albert Whitebird insisted that his tribe would never again surrender a foot of land.

Despite adverse developments on the reservation, supporters of the lakeshore did not give up. In late October, Martin Hanson, a close friend of Gaylord Nelson, met with BIA superintendent Emmett Riley. The two leaked the idea that Bad River members would lose all benefits from the lakeshore if the tribal council persisted in opposition. Hanson and Riley also planned to circulate a petition among the band in support of a park. With enough signatures, they could bring the issue directly to tribal members.[18]

Meanwhile, at Red Cliff the council had unanimously endorsed the lakeshore proposal, an endorsement that Hanson put in Nelson's congressional newsletter, where he also reproduced a photograph of Red Cliff's float in the Bayfield Apple Festival. The float featured a large map of the Bayfield Peninsula showing boundaries of the proposed lakeshore: "Red Cliff—Gateway to National Lakeshore Park." Four young tribal members rode on the float in buckskin and feathers. Distribution of the newsletter at Odanah village would underscore the price of being left out.[19]

Throughout 1966 drafts of bills to establish a lakeshore came under review at Interior, with Chippewa land a major concern. At the same time, startling changes emerged in Indian country with a new generation of leaders. College-educated and politically active, these men and women had been influenced by the civil rights movement and had witnessed social upheaval in mainstream America. Political groups, from the well-established National Congress of American Indians (NCAI) to the more militant National Indian Youth Council and the American Indian Movement, began to influence tribal leadership. As "Red Power" spread across America's reservations and through urban communities, young, dynamic, and outspoken leaders stepped forward. Indian voices such as Vine DeLoria, Jr., Hank Adams, Clyde Warrior, and Russell Means caught the attention of the news media. Lake Superior Chippewa heard the rhetoric and responded.

In July of 1967 a referendum was held at Red Cliff, and, following the example at Bad River two years earlier, Red Cliff now voted against participating in a national lakeshore. Both bands now agreed that a new park, if created, must not infringe on Indian lands or tribal rights.[20] Conservationists, oblivious to these developments, continued to underestimate the influence of national Indian organizations. Twenty years later, William Bechtel, Nelson's administrative assistant, would recall that Indian resistance had caught him by surprise, as conservationists failed to appreciate the importance of land and resources to the Chippewa: "In a way," Bechtel reflected, "we were babes in the woods. . . . It was probably unrealistic to introduce a bill that had that degree of impact on Indian reservations without an awful lot of very high level negotiating and counseling."[21] Bechtel, Nelson, and others had hoped that changes in language covering Chippewa land might pacify native opponents; yet not until 1970, and then over protests by the Park Service and the Department of the Interior, were significant compromises introduced. By then the conflict had become a national issue, a precursor to the bitter struggle of environmentalists with the Havasupai in the Grand Canyon.

As Apostle Island legislation progressed, the NCAI came to the aid of the Chippewas. John Belindo, a Kiowa-Navajo and NCAI executive director, claimed that Indians did not oppose the general idea of a national park but did reject loss of tribal lands. The NCAI requested that the park boundary be redefined to exclude Red Cliff, whereas Bad River would contribute some land through leases. Belindo warned that leaving the boundary issue open, with the possibility of obtaining land from Indian allottees in the future, was unacceptable because the tribes did "not desire to be subjected to continuous pressure from the Federal government or any of its agencies, attempting to beg, borrow or steal their lands." The Red Cliff Band and NCAI also addressed hunting and fishing rights, urging an amendment that read: "Nothing in this Act shall affect the existing rights of members of the Bad River or Red Cliff Band to hunt, fish, trap, or gather wild rice, and the Secretary shall grant to such Indians the same rights with respect to lands acquired by him within portions of the lakeshore that are applicable within the Bad River and Red Cliff Indian Reservations."

The NCAI next requested a hearing at Bad River on hunting, fishing, wild rice, and boundary issues. The band was especially upset over giving Udall the right to act as tribal spokesman, a vestige of Indian wardship and trust status that would come under increasing attack in the 1970s. Belindo's testimony pinpointed the roots of Chippewa dissatisfaction:

[The Apostle Islands Bill] represents a classic illustration of why the Department of the Interior, whose primary responsibility is Federal land and resource management, has totally failed in its responsibility to administer Indian Affairs and serve the needs of the Indians under its jurisdiction. Simply stated, it is because the two interests are in continual conflict, as they are in this bill, and the needs of the Indian have always come second to the other purposes of the Department.[22]

Others besides the NCAI supported the Chippewa. Professor Howard D. Paap, a social consultant at Red Cliff, bluntly wrote Nelson that he and Udall seemed unwilling or unable to hear native concerns: "Many Red Cliff people are in favor of maintaining their land in a wilderness state. These people are just now adjusting to the values that you have—they are realizing the material value of this shoreline. These people are beginning to talk about developing their own park—by themselves. Has it ever occurred to you that this could be the answer to your problem?"[23]

Another vocal group of Chippewa supporters were non-Indian cottage owners and potential inholders who feared losing their land. William C. Brewer, chairman of the South Shore Property Owners Association, testified at a congressional hearing: "We, the Indians and the owners, feel that our land is too valuable for a 'price tag.' Our feeling for our land renders it priceless. . . . The culture of the American Indian and his land are inseparable as life is to the body. We owners have been taught well by the Indians and also are inseparable from our land."[24] Some conservationists accused cottage owners of supporting the Chippewa to serve their own interests, but other environmentalists, such as the Apostle Islands Wilderness Council, supported the position of Red Cliff and Bad River.[25] Matters had become quite confused.

By 1970 it was clear to Gaylord Nelson that the Chippewa would not yield. Even though the Senate had passed S.621 in 1967, providing for a park of fifty-six thousand acres with thirty miles of peninsula lakefront, success in the House seemed unlikely. The bill provided for bringing tribal lands into the park "voluntarily" within five years. Nelson and backers of S.621 believed that leaving the final decision to tribal members was fair, reasonable, and democratic.

Others disagreed. In 1970, John Belindo told the Senate subcommittee why Indians distrusted voluntary provisions: "There are too many ways in which these agencies can exercise unfair leverage, and too many precedents for the application of this kind of pressure for the Red Cliff Band to accept the assurances of white men, even distinguished Senators, that no land will be taken without the consent of the Indians."[26] Nelson later conceded that he had exerted pressure at Bad River: "We sought those resolutions. . . . We got the federal government involved; we got a study going. . . . I dealt with the representatives of the tribes and [they] became persuaded that including their land on a long-term lease would have benefits for the tribe. . . . They were finally persuaded to agree."[27]

Nevertheless, the House questioned Nelson's bill. Even Colorado's Wayne N. Aspinall, seldom an advocate of Indian rights, expressed doubt. Aspinall's committee considered reducing Nelson's bill from fifty-six thousand acres and thirty miles of lakefront to forty-two thousand acres and fifteen miles, eliminating all Chippewa land.[28] By the summer of 1970, letters of support for the

Chippewa flowed into the committee. Nez Percé chairman Richard A. Half-moon, whose tribe had recently donated land to the government for the Nez Percé National Historic Park, telegraphed support of the Chippewas who "remain opposed to these bills despite outside persuasion and harassment. . . . We join them in their opposition. All of these bills . . . are unacceptable to Indian People."[29]

By March of 1970, Gaylord Nelson, along with Wisconsin congressmen Robert W. Kastenmeier and Alvin E. O'Konski, sponsors of the companion bill, were ready to surrender. The Department of the Interior and Park Service were not: The agencies said that a Wisconsin national lakeshore must include Indian land. Interior claimed such land was essential to the "integrity" of the park unit; the NPS needed land at Red Cliff for construction of a scenic coastal highway and visitor center.[30] Nelson, Kastenmeier, and O'Konski countered that the Apostle Islands were of national park quality even without Chippewa land. Nelson believed that although reservation land would enhance a national lakeshore, the islands were its heart and soul.

NPS director George Hartzog disagreed, standing firm in his high assessment of Chippewa land. When later asked about his involvement in the Apostle Islands debate, Hartzog quickly recalled the Indian issue: "[My] argument was not so much with the Indians but with the white brothers who are advising them and exploiting them. . . . The speculators and promoters were what hurt the Apostle Islands project and caused all the trouble over Indian lands. . . . The Park Service had little to do with the proposal itself. It was Jordahl's proposal."[31] Asked about words exchanged with Nelson over inclusion of Indian land, Hartzog laughed. "You might call it . . . a negotiating position. . . . You take what you get."

William Bechtel's view of Indian opposition differed from Hartzog's. Bechtel recognized that the national Indian organizations, as well as some senators and congressmen on the committees, were more experienced in Indian affairs and understood the complex issues better than either the Park Service or Nelson. During congressional hearings, Hartzog acknowledged little awareness of Chippewa treaties; he evidently had limited understanding of Great Lakes Indian history as well. And his detailed knowledge of the proposed lakeshore made his weakness in Indian affairs even more glaring.[32] In the end, he lost the arguments and took what he could get.

On September 26, 1970, Congress finally passed and President Richard Nixon signed legislation creating an Apostle Islands National Lakeshore that included twenty islands and twenty-five hundred acres of shoreline. Section 2 provided: "No lands held in trust by the United States for either the Red Cliff Band or Bad River Band of the Lake Superior Chippewa Indians, or allottees thereof, shall be acquired or included within the boundaries of the lakeshore established by this Act." An exception to section 2 were two Red Cliff allotments on Sand Bay that could be acquired by the secretary of the interior if Indian owners agreed to sell. The final legislation did not mention employment of Chippewas or cooperative arrangements with the Park Service. Indian benefits had been tied to the land; when the land transfer failed, the benefits disappeared.[33] Bad River did not lose Kakagon Slough, making it unnecessary to protect wild rice rights. Hunting, trapping, and fishing were allowed in all national lakeshores irrespective of treaty rights.[34]

In 1986, Congress added Long Island. At the southern limit of the chain, Long Island is a narrow two-and-one-half-acre sandy spit that forms the northern limit of Chequamegon Bay. Chippewa refer to the island as "the sandy point where the water breaks." Its addition was justified, once again, on economic grounds. As the park stimulated business in Bayfield, supporters of Long Island claimed that expansion would bring tourists to nearby Ashland and Washburn. As a breeding ground for the endangered piping plover, Long Island had the endorsement of the National Audubon Society, Sierra Club, and Wilderness Society.

Bad River Chippewa opposed inclusion of Long Island for several reasons. They cited the island's cultural, historical, and spiritual significance for Indians, and the island's inclusion would require faith in NPS ability to manage sacred sites. Ecological and economic factors also concerned the band because Long Island shelters Kakagon Slough, creating concerns that lakeshore status might stimulate more boat traffic, threatening rice harvests through outboard wash and water pollution. Chippewas, unfortunately, did not attend the hearings, and no one raised their concerns.[35]

Twenty years after the establishment of Apostle Islands National Lakeshore, a visitor to the NPS information center in Bayfield learns little about Lake Superior Chippewa; the Park Service depends on a presentation at the Red Cliff Band's own cultural center.[36] In 1991, however, the Red Cliff center closed for lack of funds. Here, as at Pipe Spring, Montezuma's Castle, Canyon de Chelly, Bandelier, and elsewhere, a tribe has been unable to fully interpret its history and culture to park visitors without direct NPS help.

The Apostle Islands' official handbook mentions the Ojibwa only briefly. An interpretive slide program at the Bayfield center includes less than a minute on a people who have lived in the area for more than two hundred years. In the early 1990s, the park's bookstore stocked one book on Chippewa Indians. No information appeared about the 1842 Treaty of LaPointe or other cessions, about the LaPointe Indian agency, or about its remarkable nineteenth-century agent, the Reverend Alfred Brunson. Lack of historical and ethnographic interpretation left Apostle Islands visitors with a distorted view of the region's history and Indian/white relations.

During the 1970 congressional hearings, Harold Jordahl spoke about the potential benefits that a lakeshore park offered the Chippewa. Jordahl, Gaylord Nelson, and others believed that Indians would benefit through employment opportunities with the Park Service and concessionaires. While Jordahl expected a Chippewa superintendent, others predicted only menial jobs for native people. Since 1970 there has been no Chippewa superintendent and, up to 1991, no permanent Chippewa ranger. Tribal members do work on campground maintenance and as administrative assistants.[37]

Today the Chippewa believe that lack of NPS outreach and poor communications signify indifference. Requests by both bands for technical assistance in archaeological surveys receive little response. Because poorly funded park managers seem to show little interest in cooperative interpretation, Indians consider employment of tribal members a token effort.[38]

In contrast to the attitudes of the Chippewa, the creation of Apostle Islands National Lakeshore brought rejoicing among Wisconsin environmentalists. They had struggled diligently for a decade to preserve a remnant of the wild north woods. William Bechtel, supporter of the lakeshore, a senate staff member and property owner in the region, holds a special perspective on the Apostles:

> We didn't fully appreciate what we were proposing in terms of the impact on Indian lands. . . . I would rather see it as the kind of park it is today than the type of park we originally proposed. . . . In terms of preserving the environmental situation and preserving the Indian lands, it probably is a better long range compromise than the original proposal. . . . We ended up not doing violence to Indian lands and traditions. . . . I think it is almost a lucky compromise we made.[39]

Yet as part of the compromise Bad River must deal with increased motor traffic in Kakagon Slough. At Red Cliff, the band purchases ancestral lands whenever possible, but once the NPS acquired the Apostles, the dream of recovering those islands ended.

Nevertheless, the Chippewa did successfully protect their reservations against park expansion. That victory of 1970 marked a watershed in relations between American Indians and national parks. For a century the government had pursued reservation lands needed for parks, and in doing so it had treated living Indians as a passive if not invisible presence—at Mesa Verde, Olympic, and Canyon de Chelly, at Glacier, Grand Canyon, and Mt. Rainier. After 1970, the NPS could no longer ignore resident Indians. The Park Service and environmentalists learned a lesson on Lake Superior, and they were soon to learn it again in the Grand Canyon. In the larger context of national park history, the magnitude of a Chippewa victory at Apostle Islands will become apparent.

2

FROM YOSEMITE TO ZUNI

Parks and Native People, 1864–1994

The fundamental purpose [of national parks] is to conserve the
scenery and the natural and historic objects and the wildlife
therein and to provide for the enjoyment of same in such
manner . . . as will leave them unimpaired for the enjoyment of
future generations.

—U.S. Congress, August 25, 1916

One hundred years from now, as people look back on our use of
this continent, we shall not be praised for our reckless use of its
oil, nor the weakening of our watershed values through overgrazing, nor the loss of our forests; we shall be heartily damned
for all these things. But we may take comfort in the knowledge
that we shall certainly be thanked for the national parks.

—Ray Lyman Wilbur, Secretary of the Interior, 1931

In 1832, when the artist George Catlin proposed "some great protecting policy
of government" to be called a national park, he imagined a sanctuary for Plains
Indian culture as well as wildlife. A century and a half later, after America had
created hundreds of park units on eighty million acres of land, the government
would finally adopt an official park policy toward native people. As a special
statement about a specific topic, that 1987 document survived just one year before being disassembled and scattered by seemingly endless NPS management

directives. Thus, even after the Wisconsin Chippewa and a few other tribes had successfully resisted park initiatives, inbred habits of thought continued on.

The oldest habit of conservationist and Park Service thinking had been to overlook tribal welfare, yet despite repeated if unintentional oversights, Indian relations with national parks have been intimate, just as Catlin had anticipated. National parks had already existed for fifty-two years when Congress created the NPS in 1916 and placed it within the Department of the Interior. With the BIA next door, by then lodged in Interior for sixty-seven years, the Park Service and Indians could not avoid each other. That was nothing new. For context, it is helpful to review federal Indian policy and then outline the early growth of America's park system before examining specific stories at Mesa Verde, Glacier, Olympic, Grand Canyon, and elsewhere.

The Evolution of U.S. Indian Policy

When Congress transferred the Indian Office from the War Department to Interior in 1849, the government's approach to native people had shifted from an emphasis on promoting domestic trade and preventing foreign alliances to seeking complete removal of Indians from the path of national expansion. This led to the creation of reservations, a policy begun shortly before 1849. While the language of some Americans, including a few in the Office of Indian Affairs, could be racist and genocidal, the official policy of Congress and the U.S. Supreme Court endeavored to protect Indians and promote their welfare. With John Marshall's landmark Cherokee decisions of the 1830s, the Court assumed its role as defender of Indian rights. Congress in turn promised to provide protection, schools, religion, and material aid. Most important, Congress had decreed that all negotiation with tribes be a federal monopoly; by using treaties to achieve its ends, the federal government conferred a legal status on Indians enjoyed by no other group in America.

A flurry of treaties in the 1850s acquired vast tracts of Indian land on the plains and in the Pacific Northwest. Because of geography, the Civil War, and determined native resistance, matters did not proceed smoothly over the next decades as railroads, cattlemen, loggers, and miners occupied the Great Plains, the Rocky Mountains, the deserts of the Southwest, and the Pacific Coast. The names Little Crow, Sitting Bull, Crazy Horse, Sand Creek, Bozeman Trail, Beecher Island, Adobe Wells, Cochise, Geronimo, Little Big Horn, Kit Carson, Custer, Canyon de Chelly, Bear Paw, and Chief Joseph reflect the bloodshed and military conquest of the 1860s and 1870s. That violent era brought about the end of treaty-making, although "agreements" continued to be made for another three decades. The 1880s and 1890s saw determined governmental and humanitarian efforts to assimilate Indians into Euro-American society through schools, Christian missions, and industrial training. The General Allotment Act of 1887 imposed individual land title in lieu of communal tribal lands. Over the next forty years land allotment in private tracts would reduce tribal territory from 138 million acres to under 47 million; some tribes lost over 90 percent of their reserves.

Their cultures scorned, ridiculed, or romanticized, their treaty rights often ignored, bewildered by defeat and dispossession, suffering from epidemic diseases, American Indians watched their population decline toward extinction. In the era in which the nation laid the foundation for its national park system, native people suffered immensely. The "crown jewels" of Yosemite, Yellowstone, Mt. Rainier, Crater Lake, Mesa Verde, Olympic, Grand Canyon, Glacier, and Rocky Mountain had been "Indian country" in 1850.

In 1934 Franklin Roosevelt's Indian New Deal abolished the allotment policy, reversed tribal land loss, and, however imperfectly, sought to restore native self-government and self-esteem. After a setback during the Truman-Eisenhower years, the 1960s policy of tribal self-determination, supported by favorable federal court decisions that guaranteed legal rights, began to show results such as those seen in the Apostle Islands story. By 1990 the BIA had lost its liaison position between tribes and Congress. Indians now spoke openly about "nationhood" and "sovereignty," and the Park Service approached tribal government with a deference formerly reserved for state agencies.[1]

The Birth of the National Parks

National parks inherited a small yet significant fraction of Indian land surrendered between 1850 and 1920. The first acquisitions came at Yosemite in California and Yellowstone in Montana, official birthplaces of the world's park system. What had inspired this American idea? As usual with innovations, different factors coincided: nostalgia for the wild, as experienced by George Catlin; a sense of loss created by settlement; commercial tourism promoted by railroad companies; a patriotic need to display canyons and mountains as monuments superior to Europe's cathedrals and museums; a growing realization that industrial-urban civilization had the potential to subdue, diminish, and even

destroy such spectacular natural features as Niagara Falls; and a dawning awareness that the resource cornucopia called North America had limits and that
"moving west" could no longer expand those limits. In addition, in the minds of
a small but increasing number of people, especially scientists, a respect for
nature itself began to emerge.

Whatever their reasons, Americans decided to set aside and protect large
natural areas called "parks." Historian Simon Schama has observed that wilderness "does not locate itself, does not name itself. . . . Nor could the wilderness
venerate itself." The creation of national parks first of all required a dramatic
shift in human consciousness.[2]

Except for Catlin's nostalgia, the reasons for creating parks did not take
Indians into account. With newcomers believing that the land was virgin or
that native populations would soon disappear, early park experience seemed to
confirm this bias. Yosemite Valley had a long indigenous history and probably
owed much of its pastoral beauty to Indian land use, while Yellowstone had an
even more complex human history. Yet to John Muir and others the land
seemed vacant, gardenlike, unspoiled, ripe for the taking—or saving.

At Yosemite, created by Abraham Lincoln in 1864 and assigned to California
for management, a virgin land illusion seemed true because twelve years earlier
miners had driven out or killed the original Miwok/Ahwahneechee inhabitants.
Indeed, this first national park provided the worst possible scenario for Indian/
white relations: prior occupation with extensive horticulture by Indians; brutal
military conquest of the land; a park created with no regard for past or present
native claims; an Indian petition for redress of grievances; the ignoring of the
petition by Congress; repeated efforts by park rangers to evict remnant villages;
Park Service neglect of ethnographic interpretation; and belated NPS recognition that Yosemite was, and is, important to aboriginal people. It would be
difficult for any park to build a worse record.[3]

During the century preceding creation of Yosemite, California's native population had declined over 80 percent after contact with Spanish, Mexican, and
American settlers. The 1849 gold rush accelerated a fatal process previously
driven by disease and Hispanic slavery. In the 1850s the native population
dropped by another 100,000. In Yosemite Valley, settlers called this onslaught
the Mariposa Indian War. Grim details of invasion, trumped-up charges, lynching, the slaughter of the Ahwahneechee, and their forced expulsion are recorded by participant LaFayette Bunnell in his *Discovery of the Yosemite and the
Indian War of 1851*. Writing thirty years afterward, Bunnell was unreliable on

facts and causes, but his candid attitudes reveal a nineteenth-century mentality that supported the creation of parks in the West.

LaFayette Bunnell, a physician, marched into Yosemite Valley with the Mariposa Battalion, the first Americans to enter the homeland of a Miwok group called the Ahwahneechee, who had intermarried with Paiutes from east of the Sierra. The beauty of Yosemite ignited Bunnell into a frenzy of clichés: The land was "awe-inspiring," "exhalted [sic]," a "sublime vision." By 1880 he had become convinced that "this wonderful land," still controlled by California, must become a national park open to all people. Bunnell considered himself humane and sympathetic toward Indian victims of government policy, but the doctor's bland description of a lynching betrayed him. At best, an old "squaw [was] a peculiar living ethnological curiosity"; at worst, "redskins" plundered, murdered, and committed atrocities. They were superstitious, treacherous, cunning marauders, "yelling demons [and] savages . . . overgrown vicious children" on whom moral teaching had no effect.

Bunnell accepted the need "to sweep the territory of any scattered bands that might infest it." The tactic of burning villages to starve or freeze the Miwoks into submission apparently did not disturb him. In one encounter Bunnell boasted that the Battalion suffered no casualties while killing twenty-three Miwoks: "No prisoners were taken," he calmly reported. This from a lover of nature who, as he later gazed at El Capitan, "found [his] eyes in tears with emotion."[4]

With such a beginning it is not surprising that the administrators of a park run for fifty years by the state of California and the U.S. Army could fall into thinking that the Indians had conveniently disappeared, and that sylvan meadows had just occurred as a product of nature. Neither belief was true. Indian horticulture had created the open valley that transfixed Bunnell. The people, although forced out in 1851–52, would escape captivity and return to Yosemite's Indian Canyon.

Bunnell may have considered them superstitious and ignorant, but his Ahwahneechee contemporaries knew exactly what had happened to their parents. An 1890 petition to Congress from fifty-two Indians asked for a million dollars in gold in compensation for ancestors victimized by "the overbearing tyranny and oppression of the white gold hunters." Forty years after the Mariposa War, Indians still wandered the valley, "poorly-clad and unwelcome guests, silently the objects of curiosity or contemptuous pity to the throngs of strangers." Inside Yosemite, the petition claimed, white men strung fences, grazed horses and cattle, felled trees, and destroyed fish: "The valley is cut up completely by dusty, sandy roads, leading from the hotels of whites in every direction. . . . All seem to come only to hunt money. . . . This is not the way in which we treated this park when we had it. . . . This valley was taken away from us [for] a pleasure ground. . . . Yosemite is no longer a National Park, but merely a hay-farm and cattle range."[5]

Nothing came of the Ahwahneechee petition. A century later the Indian Council of Mariposa County still sought recognition, and as late as 1990 a few Miwoks remained in Yosemite, the last two being park employees Jay Johnson and Ralph Parker. While the government failed to evict the Havasupai at Grand Canyon Village in the 1960s, it succeeded at Yosemite: "It was the fourth era of village destruction," writes Rebecca Solnit. "The army had done the job in 1851 and 1906; the Park Service in 1929 and 1969."[6] Although Yosemite built one of the first park museums, early curators interpreted Indians as relics or not at all. Today Indians at Yosemite demand that their story be told accurately and their culture be recognized.[7]

Compared with Yosemite, Yellowstone saw a gentler and less violent removal process. The first whites came as trappers, hunters, and campers, not as soldiers. Resident Sheepeaters consisted of small, scattered bands. Other Indians—Lakota, Shoshone, Crow, Bannock, Nez Percé, Flathead, Blackfeet—used the area often enough to inspire Philetus Norris, the second superintendent, to call for their expulsion shortly after the park's creation in 1872. Yellowstone also differed from Yosemite in having a treaty history and in having seen limited armed conflict.

Nevertheless, Yellowstone resembled Yosemite in having a long history of aboriginal use and in the decision that natives were no longer welcome. Prior human occupation left evidence of ancient campsites, hunting, a wide-ranging obsidian trade, and a trail system (which modern park highways follow) that dated back at least seventy-five hundred years. Yellowstone's average elevation of eight thousand feet and its status as a boundary area for the Great Plains, Basin, and Plateau cultures probably made year-round residence rare. This, coupled with drastic reductions of native population by disease, gave support to the white perception of vacant wilderness. The unratified Fort Laramie Treaty of 1851 did recognize Blackfeet and Crow claims to the area, but the government extinguished those claims in subsequent treaties and agreements.[8]

Negotiations for a major Crow cession in 1880, with Yellowstone getting a small segment, reveal prevalent nineteenth-century attitudes about reservation and park land. Of the 1.7 million acres obtained by the government at a Washington meeting, Crows on the reservation refused to sell the easternmost 115,000 acres. "The portion ceded," the commissioner of Indian affairs reported to Interior, "is chiefly valuable for its mineral resources and its occupation has long been desired by the whites . . . the strip of land which the Crows refused to sell not being considered of any special advantage to the whites, if indeed it is of any particular value to the Indians."[9] Likewise, a small northern strip added to Yellowstone from the Crow cession probably seemed of no advantage to anyone.

The idea of making Yellowstone a national park allegedly had occurred a decade earlier, when nine campers, two packers, and two cooks explored the area for a month. Astonished and stunned by an "unlimited grandeur and beauty" that they felt surpassed that of Niagara and Yosemite, the men at their final campfire supposedly pondered how to preempt superior lands for themselves. A lawyer named Cornelius Hedges spoke out, saying that he opposed all such plans, "that there ought to be no private ownership of any portion of this region, but that the whole of it ought to be set apart as a great National Park." His proposal, reported in Nathaniel Pitt Langford's journal of the expedition, "met with an instantaneous and favorable response."[10] Following their adventure, Hedges, Langford, and the others devoted themselves to establishing a park, and they managed to achieve their goal in less than two years. On March 1, 1872, the Congress and President Ulysses S. Grant created the first national park in the history of the world.[11]

Yellowstone Indians, despite a long association with the land, offered little resistance. Shoshone Sheepeaters, relatively recent occupants, retreated from contact and, at the request of superintendent Philetus Norris, were relocated to the Wind River and Fort Hall Reservations. After the Nez Percé incident in 1877 and skirmishes with the Bannock a year later, Norris decreed that all Indians must leave Yellowstone.[12] His reasoning persisted for years:

Yellowstone is not Indian country and no natives lived in the park; any that did were "harmless hermits." Like others before it, the 1870 Washburn expedition armed itself fully, fearing ambush, and on its second day of travel believed it saw a hundred Indians; at the same time whites insisted that Indians feared the region and stayed away. Norris considered firearms necessary for defense and built a fort; Indians posed a threat even though he claimed that few of them lived there. For him, the "pigmy tribe of timid and harmless Sheepeater Indians" were also "dexterous thieves and dangerous cliff fighters" who attacked miners. Later the Army would report that Indians set fires in the park, raided, poached game, and could not be controlled by the BIA.[13]

Indian fear of geysers kept them out of the park. This idea ignored campsites, artifacts, and trail routes. As with Yosemite, this myth denied the human activity that made Yellowstone appear parklike to early visitors, a management factor that the NPS would overlook with disastrous results.[14]

Yellowstone is for the use and enjoyment of all Americans. But the people who had used it the longest were driven away. Even in 1935, when Crow Indians sought free access, the government rejected their request. NPS critic Alston Chase saves his harshest words for such irony: "Created for the benefit and enjoyment of the people, [Yellowstone] destroyed a people. Dedicated to preservation, it evicted those who had preserved it. Touted as pristine, the policy required that we forget those whose absence diminished it. Denied its Indian past, it deprived us of the knowledge to keep it pristine."[15]

The widespread misconception that Indians feared national park areas and had not used the land merits further comment. Even though native traditions indicated otherwise, whites claimed that supposed fear of spirits prevented Pacific Northwest tribes from climbing Mt. Rainier or using the interior Olympic Peninsula. In the Southwest, "superstition" kept Navajos and Utes away from Anasazi ruins, while in Utah, according to one NPS official, "the red man held the tinted walls of Zion in fearsome awe." Similar stories explained an imagined absence of natives at Canada's Banff and Riding Mountain National Parks.[16]

Nowhere, however, did a myth of fearful Indians become as deeply entrenched as at Yellowstone. Very likely originating in fur trapper tales, including those of Jim Bridger, and then recorded by Jesuit missionary Pierre-Jean DeSmet, the idea of a native geyser taboo has persisted into the present. Philetus Norris quoted a Shoshone who called the geysers "heap, heap bad," and Norris claimed that other tribes stayed away because of "a superstitious awe concerning the rumbling and hissing sulfur fumes of the spouting geysers and other hot springs, which they imagined to be the wails and groans of departed Indian warriors who were suffering punishment for their early sins."[17] Park guidebooks repeated such beliefs, as did Yellowstone superintendent Horace Albright in 1928 and Secretary of the Interior Stewart Udall in 1966. Scholars such as Ake Hultkrantz likewise promoted the idea that the geysers frightened Plains tribes.[18]

At Yellowstone, as elsewhere, the geyser taboo helped justify a national park that excluded natives. It also illustrates how ideas about Indians often possessed more power than reality. The same was true about nature. Wilderness does not locate or define itself, as Simon Schama observes; rather, "all our landscapes, from the city park to the mountain hike, are imprinted with our tenacious, inescapable obsessions."[19] Stewart Udall once called the creation of Yellowstone "a fluke." Not so. Yellowstone resulted in part from an obsession with beauty, remarkable landscape, and natural wonders that inspired Cornelius Hedges, Henry Washburn, and Nathaniel Pitt Langford to reject the convention of private ownership and work toward the creation of a park available to everyone.

Twenty-seven years later the same emotions would make Mt. Rainier in Washington state a national park. One author of this book grew up in the shadow of Rainier, has climbed it a number of times, and has hiked hundreds of miles on its trails; the other author worked there for several seasons. Between us, we have traveled almost every road and path in a park that for nearly a century after its birth neglected native history.

Living in Tacoma, one learned that the peak's true name is "Tahoma." Hiking the trails, one came upon Sluskin Falls, Mowich Lake, Little Tahoma, Yakima Park, Indian Henry's Hunting Ground, Indian Bar, Naches Peak, and Ohanapecosh Creek, yet the Park Service provided little or no information on what the names meant or their origin. Nor did tourists learn that Indians had hunted game, gathered berries, and guided early white men to the mountain; Indians may have assisted in the first ascent of the 14,400-foot summit. In 1960 at Rainier a visitor would find less Indian history than had been available in the colorful stories published by John H. Williams in *The Mountain that Was God* (1910). Few modern guests were told that place names like Yakima, Cayuse, Muckleshoot, Puyallup, and Nisqually are also names of living people and modern communities. Few park rangers knew about early controversies over the confiscation of native weapons, nor did they realize that past conflicts at Rainier had resulted in attempts to legally define Indian hunting and fishing rights for all parks. Even fewer NPS staff knew that the Rainier National Park

Company once imported Yakamas to perform for tourists and sell goods, a project that eventually failed because the Indians preferred to race their horses and pick berries.[20]

A Service and a System

When Congress created the NPS in 1916 to operate the national parks, it bequeathed distortions and ignorance about native history at Rainier, Yosemite, Yellowstone, and many other of the thirty-six existing units. The Service would do little to rectify the situation until late in the century, partly because the new agency faced problems of its own.

From its beginning the NPS lacked the power and prestige of other land management agencies in Washington. Thanks to the dedication of Stephen Mather and Horace Albright it developed the "founder's myth" necessary for esprit de corps. More than most federal agencies, it pursued an idealistic mission that led to exceptional public trust. But the NPS, although victorious in initial turf battles, could not compete in Congress with the Bureau of Reclamation, the Army Corps of Engineers, or the U.S. Forest Service (USFS). Considered a luxury, the Park Service lacked scientific or military prestige; its programs did not produce dollars or protect potential wealth—instead, they cost dollars and could limit wealth. In the iron triangle between agency, lobby, and Congress, the NPS never had enough support to solve its budget problems. As for a lobby, few among the millions of park visitors provided political backing. Until the mid-sixties the strongest NPS lobby was the National Parks and Conservation Association (NPCA), a group that at times harshly criticized the service. Jeanne Clarke and Daniel McCool in their comparative study conclude that the Army Corps and USFS became federal "superstars," with the NPS not even attaining "shooting star" status.[21]

Compared with the BIA, however, the NPS indeed looked like a superstar. The BIA had no founder's myth, no lobby, no public popularity, few avid supporters in Congress, no tourist industry, and no upper-class professional elite. It did not even produce wealth of the spirit. Representative Louis Cramton, who strongly supported Mather and the NPS in the twenties, was an outspoken, persistent critic of the BIA during the same period. The Bureau had no power brokers like Henry M. Jackson, Gaylord Nelson, or Wayne Aspinall inside Congress, nor advocates like David Brower of the Sierra Club or Anthony Wayne Smith of the NPCA outside it.

At the birth of the Park Service, BIA reform groups such as the Board of Indian Commissioners and the Indian Rights Association had become ineffectual, in part because they had embraced assimilation and land allotment as the solution to the Indians' plight. In 1916 the program of massive tribal land transfers progressed under the Allotment Act, a process endorsed by the U.S. Supreme Court in its *Lone Wolf v. Hitchcock* decision, which confirmed absolute congressional control of native land. Opening of reservations for settlement compensated for millions of acres withdrawn from the public domain by national forests and parks, while inside the BIA Indians had iron-fisted "friends" like James McLaughlin, who believed that surrender of excess land was in a tribe's best interest. Secretary of the Interior Franklin Lane, a Western land developer with oil interests, supported parks, allotment, and assimilation; his Commissioner of Indian Affairs, Cato Sells, shared his views. Lane would be succeeded by Albert Fall, and Sells by Charles Burke, both of whom made Lane and Sells seem benign. The Park Service appeared during a grim era for Indians.[22]

Congress created the NPS because early parks, along with national monuments, which the president could create at will under the American Antiquities Act of 1906, had grown into this "hodgepodge of areas inconsistently managed and inadequately protected." Stirred into the hodgepodge were former Indian lands at Yellowstone, Mesa Verde, and Glacier, as well as odd places like Sully's Hill and Platte. Condemned as "the most worthless national park ever created," Sully's Hill had been carved out of the Devil's Lake reservation of the Wahpeton Sioux in 1904; the NPS cheerfully turned it over to Agriculture in 1931. The nine hundred acres at Platt National Park in Oklahoma had been purchased from the Chickasaw and Choctaws in 1902. Featuring hot springs polluted by sewage from the town of Sulphur, it became the most ridiculed park in the system, the butt of "give it back to the Indians" jokes.[23]

In the years before 1916, park advocates did not find it funny that Hetch Hetchy Valley had been drowned in Yosemite, that the Wilson administration favored the USFS and development interests over preservation, or that five unrelated federal agencies, which included the Army, the USFS, and the General Land Office, managed the parks. Whether creating a new bureau could streamline and rationalize matters, whether a National Park Service meant a national park system, became a debate that continues today.

Whatever its successes or failures, the service marked a final step in the Far West's "bureaucratic revolution" that had begun thirty years earlier. Westerners and corporations had first applauded placing the public domain under federal agencies to provide subsidies and services; the West later came to resent the NPS, USFS, U.S. Fish and Wildlife Service (USFWS), Bureau of Land Management, and U.S. Geological Survey, all run by a college-educated managerial elite who imposed regulations and restraints.[24] Unlike Canada, in the twentieth-century American West federal control of land and water did not disappear, nor have sagebrush rebellions and bitter arguments about "wise use" ceased. The NPS may be the most admired and trusted of all federal agencies, but when one talks to loggers, ranchers, or Indians, that feeling proves to be far from universal.

Although the service's first two directors, Mather and Albright, plus many of the superintendents, had a genuine interest in archaeology and native artifacts, their knowledge of living Indians was superficial and naive. Albright's chapter devoted to "Indians!" in *Oh, Ranger!* and Superintendent Miner Tillotson's *Grand Canyon Country* reveal early NPS attitudes. Both men recognized that tribes had a historic, inherent relationship with parks, a relationship far older and deeper than that of other Americans. But for "dudes," as Albright called tourists, romantic stereotypes loomed more real than life. And since "picturesque" misconceptions added drama to parks, he was not eager to dismantle the myths.

Although Albright and Tillotson rightly considered themselves more knowledgeable than the average American, at the time they lacked anthropological knowledge and, like all of us, they accepted cultural myths: Albright could assert that the most distinct elements in Navajo culture were colorful costumes and headbands. He described Sheepeaters as "diggers . . . a timid people . . . lacking in brains and initiative"; natives around Mt. Rainier were "short, flat-faced, unattractive." Tillotson considered the Hopi and Navajo to be "fascinating lures" to the Grand Canyon: "The red man [is] primitive but happy, contented, unchanged by the white man's civilization." Native legends were "childish."

Despite their shaky knowledge, Tillotson and Albright had a genuine concern for Indians and could defend native interests as they understood them. Albright, an honorary member of the Salish-Kootenai, understood the religious significance of landforms and avidly collected native crafts. He favored keeping Indian place-names, appreciated cultural diversity among tribes, and knew that not only Yellowstone, Yosemite, and Glacier but also Lassen, Zion, Crater Lake, Rocky Mountain, and Mt. Rainier had extensive native histories. Unlike other NPS directors, Albright had enough sensitivity never to pose for photos in Indian garb, and unlike many in the NPS, he also perceived that parks and reservations shared the distinction of being considered America's "worthless lands."[25]

NPS history after 1916 is extensive and complex, forcing us to select a few specific parks that best illustrate what happened. Lack of space forces omission of fascinating stories, such as that of the dispute in 1923 between Mather, Albright, and Secretary of the Interior Albert Fall over a park that would have involved Fall's own land in New Mexico as well as land of the Mescalero Apache.[26] Omitted are the careers of Indian park superintendents, including Indian women.[27] Not included are relations with fifteen Pueblo reservations near Bandelier, or the story of the Sioux and Chippewa at Pipestone Quarry, the Sioux and Crow at the Little Big Horn, or the Sioux in the Badlands. The NPS manages a recreation area behind Grand Coulee dam, which flooded Colville lands, and another behind Yellowtail dam on Crow land. Native people have relations with Acadia in Maine, Organ Pipe and Saguaro in Arizona, Kaloko-Honokohau in Hawaii. They obviously claim a common history with NPS historic sites at Forts Vancouver, Bowie, Smith, Larned, and Laramie, with missions such as Marcus Whitman's at Walla Walla and Father Kino's at Tumacacori.

We regretfully pass by the model "partnership park" managed by the Nez Percé tribe since 1965, as well as failed attempts to create similar partnerships with the Gila River Pima at Snaketown in Arizona and the Zuni at Cibola in New Mexico. Snaketown and Cibola, like Apostle Islands, mark a modern era in park/Indian relations. Congress authorized the parks in 1971 and 1988 respectively, only to have the Pima and Zuni people block the process.[28] Similar native resistance early in this century at Mesa Verde, Glacier, Canyon de Chelly, and the Grand Canyon did not succeed.

Writers often refer to national parks and Indian reservations as islands: Parks are called "islands under siege" or "islands of hope"; reservations appear as islands of poverty and islands of despair. But whereas the concept of an ecological island may help us understand biology, insular analogies will mislead anyone studying the history of native people and parks. The word "island" implies some degree of autonomy and isolation, of geographic separation with distinct borders. Except for a few parks such as Isle Royale, the Channel Islands, and Apostle Islands, however, that is not physically, politically, or culturally true of national parks. Parks, like reservations, border other lands defined by artificial and often controversial boundaries that change over time, borders that seldom coincide with rivers, wind currents, animal migration routes, toxic waste pollution, highways—or with the cultural heritage of native people. As we shall learn, the island metaphor does not apply. Or at the very least, it requires a half-dozen sturdy bridges for every mile of waterfront.

THE UTES, THE ANASAZI, AND MESA VERDE

Never in the history of the Ute Indians has the government
made such a liberal proposition.

—Frederick H. Abbott
Assistant Commissioner of Indian Affairs, 1911

The commissioner stole that land from the Utes. . . . They
wanted to keep it.

—Chief Jack House, 1967

The Four Corners, a land of red rock canyons, distant snow-capped mountains, green mesas, and dry arroyos, is a place of Indian reservations, pueblos, and national parks. Native Americans have lived for centuries in this rugged, arid southwestern landscape where the borders of Colorado, Utah, New Mexico, and Arizona intersect. New Mexican pueblos of adobe line the rivers, while Arizona's Navajo Reservation and isolated Hopi mesas are considered by many to be the heart of Indian country. Southern Utes and Ute Mountain Utes, who once traversed the Rockies, Utah, and southern Wyoming, now live on two reservations in southwest Colorado, a land once occupied by cliff-dwelling Anasazis, the Ancient Ones. In turn, the best-known Anasazi ruin, Mesa Verde National Park, was once part of the Ute Mountain Ute Indian Reservation.

For centuries bands of Utes had lived in the mountain basins. Prior to 1700, they fished, gathered plants, and hunted rabbits, antelope, deer, and elk; hunters occasionally brought home bison meat from alpine parks. Shortly after the Pueblo Revolt in 1688, in which the Indians temporarily drove the Spanish out of the Rio Grande country, Utes acquired the horse. Larger bands formed under headmen who took greater authority over raiding and big game. Mounted hunters seeking elk now expanded into remote Rocky Mountain meadows and then onto the plains in search of buffalo. Utes developed buckskin clothing, elaborate ceremonial regalia, and large tepees made of buffalo hide. Their warriors raided pueblos for booty and hostages. Horses stimulated rapid cultural change, and they became the measure of wealth.[1]

By 1800 Utes hunted and raided as far west as southern California. They skirmished with the Arapaho, Cheyenne, and Sioux to the east, harassed the Hopi mesas, and fought with Navajos over game in the Four Corners. Ute raiders ventured as far south as Chihuahua, Mexico, their increased mobility opening a lucrative slave trade in which Paiute and Pueblo women and children were exchanged for Spanish horses and silver. Yet the horse had a negative impact: Cheyenne and Arapaho hunters now began entering Colorado's high mountain parks from the east, while mounted Navajos challenged the Utes in Arizona, Utah, and southern Colorado.

Despite pressure from other tribes and from Mexico, the Utes controlled their mountain hunting grounds well into the nineteenth century. Prior to 1850, American homesteaders had shown little interest in the high plains and Rocky Mountains, where imposing peaks, windswept flats, subzero winters, and alkaline basins diverted settlers toward friendlier climates in Oregon and California. Still, overland routes to the north and south eventually eroded Ute hegemony. In 1847 Mormons settled at Salt Lake, followed by other Americans seeking quick fortunes in Colorado and eastern Utah. The Utes would soon succumb to cataclysmic events beyond their control: gold rushes, disease, warfare, and starvation. As miners and settlers arrived in Colorado, Indian hunting grounds and winter village sites saw conflict and atrocities on both sides. Treaties ceded the land and brought an end to the freedom to gather plants, to fish, to hunt and raid. The Utes became wards of the United States within a generation. The "Meeker Massacre" of 1879, in which the Utes murdered their Indian agent and kidnapped his daughter, fueled hatred of the Indians and white reprisals. "Unless removed by the government," Governor Frederic Pitkin announced, "[the Utes] must be necessarily exterminated."[2]

Pitkin notwithstanding, Utes in Colorado and southeast Utah were neither exterminated nor removed. Reduced to living upon a fifteen-mile-wide strip that ran for 110 miles along the Colorado and New Mexico border, Wiminuche and Capote bands retained a homeland. Eventually the government divided the reserve into individual allotments, opening surplus land to settlement. A hamlet called Ignacio became the Southern Ute agency for the Muwach and Capote people. The Wiminuche, resisting encroachment and loss of territory, rejected allotment and retreated to a remote, broken area near Ute Mountain and Mesa Verde. A half-century later Wiminuche land became the Ute Mountain Ute Indian Reservation, with an agency at Navajo Springs.[3]

Mesa Verde

In 1873 a new style of invasion had begun in Ute country. John Moss, a wandering New Englander searching for gold, led a party of California miners to the Mancos River. The affable Moss soon became acquainted with Utes, learning their language and negotiating an agreement for land in La Plata Canyon. Continuing to look for gold, Moss came across Anasazi ruins. The next summer in the San Juan Mountains, Moss and his partner, Tom Cooper, met William Henry Jackson, a photographer with the Hayden Survey. Three years earlier Jackson had joined Hayden in Yellowstone to record geysers and mudpots; a portfolio made Jackson famous and helped gain congressional approval for Yellowstone National Park. Reaching the fantastic ruins on the Mancos, Jackson photographed several ancient sites and, through his work, the world quickly learned of Mesa Verde.[4]

Jackson's photos brought a stream of visitors to the plateau, but not until 1881 did a new railway turn the stream into a flood that caught Mancos cattlemen as unprepared as the Utes. One family in particular, the Wetherills, would become synonymous with Mesa Verde. A Ute named Acowitz had told local rancher Richard Wetherill that ruins of the "ancient ones" existed in Cliff Canyon but that Utes never went there because if spirits of the dead were disturbed, "then you die too." Wetherill, having no such fear, explored the ruins and began bringing along guests. His Mesa Verde tales sparked the interest of tourists, scientists, pot hunters, and grave diggers.[5]

Early visitors, whether coming to find an artifact, plunder a grave, or merely examine a cliff house, were asked to leave by the Utes. As early as 1881 the Wetherills complained about difficulties on the reservation; Virginia Donaghe, a correspondent for the *New York Graphic,* likewise reported a wonderful time at Mesa Verde "despite some Ute troubles." Soon the tribe demanded tolls. Even Richard Wetherill and Frederick Chapin, archaeologist author of *The Land of the Cliff-Dwellers,* were expected to pay when entering Wiminuche land. Attempting to control illegal entry, the Indians protested that trespassers had uncovered Anasazi graves: "White man dig up Moquis, make Ute sick."[6]

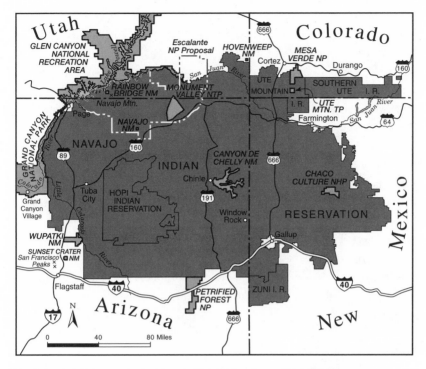

Navajoland and Ute country in Arizona, Utah, Colorado, and New Mexico.

As more people visited the ruins, protection efforts increased. Virginia Donaghe McClurg organized a group of determined Colorado women who sought to halt vandalism and attract tourists. McClurg recommended that Utes police the ruins, a suggestion never pursued by the government. The *Denver Republican* admitted that Ute rangers might be "practical and economical" but unpopular in Colorado.[7]

In her crusade for a park, McClurg and a friend, Alice Bishop, visited the Southern Ute Reservation in 1899. After a dusty ride from Durango to Mancos Canyon, McClurg and Bishop met with tribal leaders Ignacio and Acowitz at Navajo Springs. The Utes listened to McClurg's proposal for a thirty-year lease at $300 a year, a plan that would have had the tribe police the park. Ignacio demanded that the entire $9,000 be "plunked down at one pop." Startled by the demand and lacking money, McClurg and Bishop left the agency disappointed.

In 1900 Alice Bishop and four other Durango women returned to Navajo Springs and reached a tentative agreement only to have their lease declared illegal by Secretary of the Interior Ethan Hitchcock because private citizens had no authority to negotiate agreements with a tribe. The women submitted another lease agreement in 1901. Rejected once again and now calling themselves the Cliff Dwelling Association, the women next received permission from Congress to negotiate with the Wiminuches. The Utes refused to sell or trade Mesa Verde; not until 1906 did they and the federal government reach the understanding that would result in Mesa Verde National Park.[8]

As popular support for conservation and national parks began to grow at the turn of the century, loss of archaeological resources also had become a public concern. Representative John Lacey of Iowa, an avid conservationist and supporter of historic preservation, introduced an antiquities bill in Congress to protect ruins on federal land; at the same time, Representative Herschel Hogg and Senator Thomas Patterson of Colorado presented park bills for Mesa Verde. Both concepts had previously died in committee, but a new political climate forced the issue. Scholars, politicians, businessmen, even the governor of Colorado, called for protection of the cliff dwellings. Edgar Hewlett, an archaeologist, college president, and writer who had worked for years to protect southwestern ruins, endorsed the legislation, as did President Theodore Roosevelt.

The congressional bills brought together two groups: Colorado supporters of Mesa Verde and national antiquities advocates. Despite in-fighting over whether Mesa Verde should be a state or national park, support coalesced in the spring of 1906. As committee chair for public lands, Lacey ensured quick action. Roosevelt signed the American Antiquities Act on June 8; on June 29 he signed a Mesa Verde National Park bill.

The 1906 Mesa Verde legislation included 42,000 acres of Indian land. Unfortunately, because of a faulty survey, almost none of the ruins were included. To redress this error, an amendment to the bill placed all unpatented prehistoric ruins on Indian and federal land located within five miles of the park boundary under control of Interior, to be "administered by the same service that is established for the custodianship of the park." Thus an additional 175,000 acres, much of it on an Indian reservation, fell under jurisdiction of Mesa Verde National Park.[9]

In October 1906, Secretary Hitchcock appointed Southern Ute agent William Leonard as acting superintendent of the new park. After Hitchcock requested the Smithsonian to conduct an archaeological survey to determine if ruins on Ute land needed protection, Edgar Hewett led a team of scientists

from Denver and Harvard and also hired an eager young photographer named
Jesse Nusbaum. The survey found many remarkable cliff dwellings on Ute
land—outside the park.

At first the Utes seemed willing to exchange land at the south end of Mesa
Verde for a nearby national forest tract. A five-mile strip that contained Spruce
Tree House, Cliff Palace, Balcony House, the Sun Temple, and other dwellings
would be traded for summer range on Ute Mountain, land the USFS considered
costly to administer and of no commercial value. Although observing that the
tribe already had a claim to Ute mountain, the BIA endorsed the trade. BIA
superintendent John Spear cautioned in 1905 that future negotiations would
require an excellent interpreter because two Ute chiefs took "delight in opposing anything proposed by the authorities, and it would be easy to block the
whole matter by a very slight wrong move." Spear's concern proved prophetic.
A Ute council refused to negotiate, and Navajo Springs agent U.L. Clardy
reported that the tribe "positively and persistently refused to make the exchange of lands. . . . They are wise in this refusal in as much as the mesa affords
excellent winter grazing and Ute Mountain, I am informed, has little grass at
any time." The Utes also decided to terminate leases to non-Indians.[10]

In spite of such setbacks, the government persisted. The BIA's Frederick
Abbott believed that the Utes held "some of the very best ruins" in the Southwest. Faced with stubborn Wiminuche resistance, the iron fist slipped into a
velvet glove when Abbott asked James McLaughlin to help with negotiations.[11]

"The Major Knows How to Make Indians Understand"

James McLaughlin, after serving more than twenty-five years as agent to the
Sioux, had been appointed a special inspector by Interior in 1909. Tough,
honest, and intelligent, "Major" McLaughlin was the Indian Office's favorite
troubleshooter. If a tribe balked at giving up land or traditions, the BIA would
dispatch McLaughlin, knowing that he would deal firmly and fairly with Indians. He drove hard bargains, usually convincing a tribe to see matters the
government's way. Until his death in 1923, McLaughlin traversed the West negotiating complicated agreements, mediating disputes, adjusting claims, com-
piling tribal census rolls, pressing for assimilation, and promoting land allotment. Years of experience on the Dakota plains had made him a formidable
opponent, and one with a keen dislike for the "unwhipped" Ute Indians.[12]

On May 5, 1911, James McLaughlin arrived at the Southern Ute Agency to negotiate Mesa Verde with the Wiminuche Band. Forty-eight Utes attended the council, including interpreters Nathan Wing and Antonio Buck. Frederick Abbott, who joined McLaughlin, opened the Saturday meeting with assurances that they came as Ute allies, the major being "friend of the Indian for nearly fifty years." Abbott said that both men wished to speak "about a matter of great importance. . . . If you agree with us, your reservation will be made larger." He explained how Congress sought to preserve Mesa Verde for future generations, but that a number of cliff dwellings had been mistakenly excluded from the park. Abbott assured the Wiminuches that he needed only a five-mile parcel: "If you will give up this small piece, the government will give you a larger piece of land on the Mesa Verde where the grass is just as good. . . . It will be a good trade for you, and I know you will want to trade when you understand it fully."

Abbott then introduced McLaughlin as a man who had "talked to Indians for many years and knows better than I how to make you understand."[13] McLaughlin told the Utes that he came to assist them, in the first two minutes using the words "friend" and "friendly" six times. He mentioned Uintah, Uncompaghre, and White River Utes to assure the Wiminuche that Indians trusted him: "I have made it one rule throughout my service with the Indians to always tell the truth . . . so that, after having transacted business with them, I never am ashamed to return to their reservation and look them in the face." McLaughlin turned to a map and indicated the area in question: "This little piece of land down here we wish to obtain, 3 & 1/2 miles wide and 5 & 1/2 miles in length." For the cession, he offered a portion of the original park plus other land, which meant the tribe stood to gain six thousand acres more than it surrendered. Instead of their reservation shrinking, he explained, it would grow.[14]

Nathan Wing, the Ute interpreter, found McLaughlin's offer too good to be true. Wing pointed out that three of the canyons sought by the government contained springs, then he claimed that the tribe already owned the new land on Ute Mountain: "This Ute Mountain we thought was in our reservation. The line came down to the west and comes down here [pointing to the map] and we never knew that it did not belong to us." McLaughlin brushed Wing's objections aside and turned to concerns about bringing government crews onto the reservation. Surveyors and geologists, the major claimed, did not change boundary lines but only examined ruins. Disagreeing, Wing retorted that "we thought they cheated us."

Nathan Wing was not the only Ute to question the government's motives. Mariano, a Ute, expressed disbelief over McLaughlin's claim that Congress wanted ruins solely for their historical value. "The government gave us this reservation long ago," Mariano wondered. "Now why do they want to take some back again?" John Hay also opposed the swap: "There is no use in you trying to buy [the ruins] from me. . . . I think you are only joshing us." Utes like Hay could not comprehend why white men wanted "old houses." Jawa insisted that the Anasazi must be left alone and refused to believe that ruins were the BIA's main interest: "I know why you want those old houses . . . gold mines and coal mines and coal oil there. . . . That is why you want them. . . . You cheat us all the time."

When Wing said that Utes seldom went near cliff dwellings and never collected artifacts, McLaughlin responded that looting and vandalism by others had to stop. A park, he promised, would accomplish that goal and belong to everyone in the United States, including the Indians.[15] For the remainder of the day McLaughlin repeatedly assured the Utes that he sought nothing more than friendship. He insisted on the agreements being clear; he would not rush or pressure them, and everyone who wished to speak would be given an opportunity. Finally, he suggested that the Utes select a committee to visit the sites with Abbott and himself.

Tribal members Asa House, Juan Tobias, John Miller, and John Ayers joined Wing, McLaughlin, and Abbott on the overnight inspection of Five Mile Strip. When negotiations resumed on Tuesday, Wing and the other Utes confirmed that the land included three springs: "You want to trade for the best land we have." At first McLaughlin dismissed the three springs, then promised that the Utes could retain water rights. To illustrate government generosity, he asked the Indians to consider: "If you gave two horses to us and we gave you three of equal value, that is one-third more land than we ask from you." Wing answered that "we don't want to trade these old ruins. We know you offer a good trade but we don't want it." Mariano added, "We often try to buy another fellow's horse. We offer two horses for one horse but if the fellow don't want to trade we can't trade, so that is all I have to say."[16]

With the meeting approaching a stalemate, Abbott took over as chief negotiator. Castigating the Indians for not improving their land, he presented an ultimatum: "The government is stronger than the Utes. . . . When the government finds old ruins on land that it wants to take for public purposes, it has the right to take it. . . . The government is strong enough to take land away from the Ute Indians that it wants for a National Park. . . . We want you people to understand all about the proposition we have made to you. . . . Congress is going to have that land."[17] Given little choice, the Utes agreed to a transfer. On May 10, 1911, sixty-five members of the Wiminuche band approved trading 10,000 acres on Chapin Mesa for 19,500 acres on Ute Mountain.

Mesa Verde and the National Park Service

On May 19 the *Mancos Times Tribune* reported "Government Secures Ruins for Park—Exchange Effected after Years of Unsuccessful Effort." The *Tribune* described new boundaries set by the "treaty" negotiations, a feat accomplished "only by the firmest persuasion and most persistent effort of these gentlemen [Abbott and McLaughlin] the Indians being very reluctant to relinquish their claim to the land in question which they knew to be valuable. Since before the creation of the park the Government has been trying to secure possession of this land but the Indians have persistently refused to consider every proposition the Government has urged upon them, and the exchange was effected this time only by refusing to consider a number of grievances the Indians had, until they should consent to the exchange."[18]

After the tribe had signed the agreement, yet another emergency arose, when the Geological Survey discovered that the proposed park boundary still ran north of Balcony House. Without notifying the Utes, the legislation was amended to add 1,320 acres. Congress passed that bill on June 20, 1913.[19]

When Stephen Mather's new NPS inherited Mesa Verde in 1916, it also inherited the grievances reported in the *Mancos Times Tribune.* Jesse Nusbaum, superintendent from 1921 to 1931 and acting superintendent from 1942 to 1946, encountered familiar problems: Utes hunted, grazed livestock, cut timber, and left untended campfires. In 1926 he put "a scare into them," expecting his action to make Utes more cautious about fire and hunting.[20]

Besides Ute resentment over the 1911 land swap, the NPS faced animosity between the tribe and the Navajos. The two tribes had competed for centuries in the Four Corners, and after creation of the park they clashed over reservation boundaries. When a federal court awarded a disputed area to the Navajo, it added to Ute bitterness.

NPS hiring practices also stung the tribe. Nusbaum erected hogans, hired Navajos for 90 percent of his labor force, and encouraged his wife to welcome seasonal Navajo families to Mesa Verde. Enthusiastic and skillful workers, Navajo craftsmen who trained under Nusbaum eventually became NPS experts in ruins stabilization for the entire Southwest. Navajo laborers and their families also performed for tourists, with evening "sings" of sixty or more Indians becoming popular during the 1920s. The casual sings and dances gradually evolved into shows by outstanding performers. Dressed in white cotton pants, velveteen shirts, brilliant silk headbands, and handcrafted silver, the Navajo added exciting entertainment on summer nights as tourists witnessed a Yebeichai dance ceremony or circle sing. Other singers delighted park visitors with impromptu concerts in Spruce Tree House amphitheater.[21]

While Navajos became favorites at Mesa Verde, relations with the Wiminuches deteriorated. Rangers chased away poachers or cited hunters for trespass. Ute backlash appeared in many forms. In 1925, when the NPS tried to clear a landslide from Knife Edge Road, Utes blocked the route down Mancos Canyon to impede repairs. Yet despite a growing rift, the NPS pressed for more tribal land along the river. The service knew that purchase would be impossible but once again hoped to trade public lands. Ute agent E.J. Peacore was sympathetic to the NPS because the land sought had little value for the tribe "but would be of immense value to the park." In a confidential 1931 memo the park superintendent assured Arno Cammerer that Peacore would help the NPS, that a local congressman was cooperative, and that state government supported land transfer. The NPS wildlife division also urged acquiring Mancos land. Division director George Wright knew that once reservation cattle were removed, the river's wooded banks could support beaver and songbirds.[22]

A new BIA agent, D. H. Watson, agreed that adding tribal land along the Mancos would benefit the park, but he knew that lack of comparable acreage made an exchange impossible. The agent told Commissioner John Collier that it was local cattle ranchers who had overgrazed the range, not Indians, who seldom entered the area. Watson promised to use "every influence . . . to bear down on our Utes" to protect wildlife, yet he warned Collier that the problem really lay with whites and the Navajo: "The Mesa Verde Park has for a number of years employed Navajo Indians on labor projects to the exclusion of Utes. [Navajos] are constantly encroaching upon our lands with their sheep and horses. They establish regular hunting camps on the Ute reservation in the fall and winter for the accumulation of venison and buckskin [while] not more than six or eight Utes make a practice of hunting in this area."[23]

BIA resistance did not deter the Park Service. In 1935 Mesa Verde superintendent Ernest Leavitt asked for a western extension onto Ute land "rich in cliff dwellings and archaeological material [and] a few good springs." Leavitt recommended regaining land traded in the 1911 agreement because the lost area would make the park "a complete geographical unit" in archaeology and biota. Park officials also tried to halt BIA plans for a road through Mancos Canyon by acquiring the land; they knew that a road would open the river to grazing, poaching, and pot-hunting.[24]

In spite of NPS efforts, the Wiminuche adamantly refused to surrender more territory. They knew that Mancos Canyon had grass and water, and a road would make access easier. Furthermore, the Utes still insisted that the 1911 trade was a trick. In response, Collier's BIA conducted a thorough search of the records and indeed found an error. The 1911 trade, Jesse Nusbaum confessed to his superiors, involved "deed lands of the Wiminuche Band that had been temporarily withdrawn for some purpose or other," which meant that the Utes had made "a contribution of 10,080 acres, more or less, of their deeded lands to Mesa Verde National Park for the privilege of reclaiming 20,160 acres, more or less, of their own deeded lands."[25] That is, in return for every acre the tribe gave the park, they were awarded two acres of their own property. Nathan Wing had been right all along: "This Ute Mountain we thought was in our reservation . . . and we never knew that it did not belong to us."

A Bitter Past and Poisoned Present

As World War II ended, superintendent Jesse Nusbaum sought to make Mesa Verde "100% United States owned land." He planned to eliminate Farm Security Administration land and private inholdings while acquiring Ute land on Chapin Mesa and in lower Mancos Canyon. Nusbaum, however, was not sanguine about the Indians. "If you know the Indian manner of dealing as well as I do," he told his superiors, "and the antipathy towards us which still survives among the Utes as a result of the land exchange effected with them in 1913 . . . you will understand why . . . an acceptable exchange probably will be a long and painful procedure."

Besides the original exchange, the Wiminuches remembered and resented the extra 1,320 acres that Congress had unilaterally taken for the park—land included in a 1947 claim against the government after the Court of Claims in 1942 had awarded the Utes $32 million for the loss of 14,500 acres, including Mesa Verde lands. During this period the tribe and park negotiated over Chapin, Moccasin, Long, and Wetherill mesas, with the NPS in 1955 offering to trade approximately 10,000 acres. Rumors of oil and gas reserves ended discussion.[26]

By the mid-sixties, the NPS despaired of enlarging Mesa Verde. When Director George Hartzog met with tribal members in 1966 to discuss a master plan for archaeological sites in the park and on Ute lands, the tribe grew skeptical and uncooperative. Then the service made a brilliant move: Hartzog appointed Meredith Guillet as superintendent. No more qualified person could have been found. Raised in Montezuma County of southwest Colorado, Guillet had grown up at his family's Navajo/Ute trading posts. After working at Mesa Verde for the Civilian Conservation Corps in the 1930s, he had decided on an NPS career and spent much of it on the Navajo reservation. Fluent in Ute and Navajo since childhood, Guillet brought to the job a deep knowledge and informed cultural understanding of Indians. Even he could not undo Mesa Verde's past, yet his superintendency remains a bright spot in NPS/Ute relations.[27]

When Guillet and his staff urged the Utes to comanage Mancos Canyon, the Wiminuches refused to sign any agreements. Nevertheless, Guillet developed cordial relations that led to a growing awareness among tribal leaders that ruins have value. As land claim awards dwindled, the tribe needed new economic opportunities, and, despite opposition from elders, Chief Jack House began to press for a Ute tribal park in Mancos Canyon. House had lived in the canyon and believed that his people could at once protect the ruins and profit from them. Before he died in 1971, Jack House had repealed the area's status as a reservation roadless area and had convinced the council to establish a park.[28]

As a result of House's vision, the Utes opened a 125,000-acre park in 1981. By 1991, twenty-five hundred people were visiting annually, using native guides to explore the canyon. The tribal park's rich prehistory and low number of visitors offered an alternative to bustling Mesa Verde immediately north. While not lucrative, the tribal park provides employment and, perhaps most important, a sense of pride to the Wiminuches.

The NPS dropped its long quest for Ute land after 1970, but other conflicts and resentments continued to fester. The service still does not employ many Utes, even though it recruits at community colleges and native fairs. In 1994, of 120 seasonal and permanent positions, Indians held one of each. Looking to the future, the park has invited tribal members to training sessions and has had favorable responses.[29] One conflict involves yet another improper survey. The Soda Point road winds from the park onto the reservation and back into the park, and at the point a gift shop, fry bread stand, and helicopter pad provided Utes an opportunity to profit from tourism. The NPS considered the enterprises an eyesore and the chopper flights a safety hazard, while preservationists worried that engine vibrations might damage the ruins.[30]

Helicopter tours from Soda Point proved unprofitable, ending in 1990; it is doubtful they will resume. Despite protests and threats of a Ute lawsuit, the NPS moved ahead with realignment of the Soda Point loop in 1987, claiming that improving a dirt road and diverting traffic off the reservation would benefit visitors. Only after Congressman Ben Nighthorse Campbell intervened did the Utes and Park Service reach an agreement, one that left hard feelings. The Utes added Soda Point to a long list of grievances.[31]

Among the grievances is cultural interpretation. Recent legislation has shut down the public display of human remains, but Mesa Verde's program continues to neglect Ute history, instead emphasizing Anasazi, Pueblo, and Navajo cultures. The park's gift shop is filled with books about other tribes and about archaeologists, with only a handful of items on the Wiminuche. Nor until recently has the park promoted the Ute Tribal Park. Most rangers seem to know little about native culture, past or present. Interpretation of modern Indian life has been "an afterthought," a condition that the ranger in charge of interpretation, Sarah Craighead, hopes to remedy.[32]

Utes remember. At Ute Mountain, the Wiminuche recall that they once traded ten thousand acres and received their own land in return, and that Congress took another thirteen hundred acres without their consent. "The commissioner stole that land from the Utes," Chief Jack House complained in 1967, "and [the Utes] wanted to keep it because it was theirs, their own land, and they were living there."[33] In return, Mesa Verde National Park—a World Heritage Site, the world's first archaeological park—set high standards for managing ruins. Other southwestern parks followed its lead, preserving artifacts and interpreting aboriginal prehistory while ignoring resident peoples. The world gained a treasure at Mesa Verde, yet the Ute Mountain Utes profited little.

The Navajo had a different experience. Jesse Nusbaum welcomed their crews to Mesa Verde, where they learned about ruins stabilization and performed for tourists. But on their reservation, as we shall see, the Navajo had their own vexing encounters with the Park Service.

4

THE BLACKFEET AND GLACIER NATIONAL PARK

Chief Mountain is my head. Now my head is cut off.
The mountains have been my last refuge.

—White Calf, Piegan headman, 1895

It is a happy circumstance that this fine nation of Plains Indians
should live still on the border of Glacier National Park.

—Horace Albright, 1928

We only sold them the rocks.

—Earl Old Person, Blackfeet chairman, August 1991

Along the continental divide, mountains rise into the Montana sky to split
Glacier National Park in half. Entering from the west, a visitor will see yet
another spectacular northwest range, but coming from the east after a thousand
miles of prairie and plain, one can appreciate the awe of the Blackfeet for this
Backbone-of-the-World. The western big sky ends after Great Falls. Here the
earth rises up—a horizontal world becomes vertical. In a land still home to
grizzly and wolf, grass and butte are replaced by snowfields, glaciers, forests,
and alpine meadows. Outside of Alaska, Glacier National Park and its adjacent
national forests remain the premier habitat in the United States for bald eagles,
bighorn sheep, cougar, lynx, deer, ptarmigan, trout, whitefish, wolverines,
and moose.

Designated a world biosphere preserve, Canada's Waterton Lakes and America's Glacier National Parks join at the border to form a single international park
related to three governments: those of the United States, Canada, and the

Blackfeet. The United States purchased its portion from the Blackfeet in 1895, paying $1.5 million for 800,000 acres. This "mineral strip" ran twenty miles east from the divide to the present border of the Blackfeet Reservation, and eighty-five miles from the Canadian line south to Birch Creek. The southern strip, now known as the Badger-Two-Medicine Wilderness, eventually became part of Lewis and Clark National Forest. In 1910 the northern section became the eastern half of Glacier National Park.

The 1895 purchase was not the first time this land had changed hands. Early in the 1700s, Algonquian-speaking Blackfeet Indians migrated south to Montana from the Saskatchewan River, driving Kootenai and Shoshone people across the continental divide.[1] According to a Blackfeet creation myth, Na'pi (Old Man) told his people, "Here I will mark you off a piece of ground." Na'pi's boundary began at a point on the summit of the Rockies west of Edmonton, Alberta, then traveled south "taking in the country to the east," which included the Porcupine Hills, Cypress Hills, and Little Rocky Mountains. At the Yellowstone River's confluence with the Missouri, the territory curved west until it reached a peak above the Beaverhead Valley, then returned north to its starting point. Na'pi told the Blackfeet that this land was theirs, and until the middle of the nineteenth century a Blackfeet confederacy maintained firm control of Old Man's vast domain.[2]

The confederacy contained three tribes: the Pikuni, or Piegan (pronounced pay-GAN); the Kainah, or Blood; and the Siksika, or Blackfeet. All spoke the same language, shared customs, intermarried, and fought common enemies. Until disease reduced its numbers in the 1830s, the Blackfeet Confederacy was the strongest military power on the northern plains, feared by other Indians, the British, and Americans. At their zenith, the Blackfeet controlled the plains of Montana, Alberta, and Saskatchewan; war parties raided south to Santa Fe, east to the mouth of the Knife River in present North Dakota, and west onto the Great Columbia Plain. Primarily buffalo hunters, the Piegans, Bloods, and Blackfeet controlled mountain passes in northern Montana and southern Alberta. Even after they suffered smallpox, measles, and influenza, the Blackfeet continued to harass Euro-American fur trappers in the northern Rockies.[3]

Blackfeet relations with the American government began at the Treaty of Fort Laramie in 1851, where the United States included them in its division of territory across the northern plains, even though no Blackfeet attended the council. Four years later Americans and Blackfeet did meet for treaty negotiations with Isaac I. Stevens at Judith River. The 1855 treaty reserved several million acres from the continental divide east to the confluence of the Milk and Missouri, and north from the Missouri to the Canadian border. Beginning at Fort Benton in 1868, a succession of agreements transferred extensive tribal land and resources to the United States. More executive orders and congressional acts further reduced Blackfeet lands, a process that continued into the twentieth century, including the creation of Glacier National Park on May 11, 1910.

The Blackfeet Agreement of 1895 and the Mineral Strip

In 1877 James Willard Schultz left his New York home for the Far West. The lean, chain-smoking, whiskey-drinking, yarn-spinning easterner fit in well with a crowd of rough men on the Upper Missouri. Beginning a long career as trapper, hunter, and Indian trader, Schultz profited from the Canadian whiskey trade via Montana's Whoop Up Trail. With the disappearance of wildlife and the establishment of law and order by the Northwest Mounted Police, Schultz found himself out of business. Deciding to remain in Montana, "Apikuni," as he became known to the Blackfeet, turned to guiding wealthy hunters.

After marrying a Piegan woman, Schultz became intimately involved in reservation politics as a "squaw man." Still after gold, "Apikuni" tried his luck with pick and shovel, gaining little more than thick calluses. Striking a mother lode eluded Schultz until an eastern client named George Bird Grinnell suggested that his guide turn campfire yarns into popular fiction. After 1900 Schultz supported himself by writing articles and books about the Montana Blackfeet. Meantime, he had set forces in motion that would take much of their land.[4]

In the early 1880s Schultz had noticed prospectors in the hills near St. Mary Lake. A decade passed before he paid attention to rumors of gold, but by 1893 he wrote to W.H. Morrell, a fellow New Yorker with political connections in Washington, to ask for help in opening the Blackfeet reserve to white settlers. Schultz assured Morrell about the likelihood of wealth in the mountains; furthermore, the Indian agency's chief clerk and a half-Indian trader named Joe Kipp, with whom Schultz had collaborated in the whiskey trade, would welcome prospectors. In exchange Schultz offered Morrell a share of the profits. According to "Apikuni," the Indians were willing sellers with little need for mountains.

Morrell responded immediately. He wrote to the Commissioner of Indian Affairs requesting cession of the reservation's "mineral strip." Morrell insisted that "so rich a strip of mineral territory [must] be thrown open to development," that the Indians favored opening it, and that the land was worthless for any purpose other than mining. Secretary of the Interior Hoke Smith had doubts and wrote to George Bird Grinnell, a recognized authority on the Blackfeet. Grinnell believed that the odds of a mineral strike on the reservation were low and that logging or mining would result in erosion and loss of irrigation. Recommending that tribal land remain closed, Grinnell worried that a "loose and lawless mining population" would corrupt the Blackfeet.

Schultz and the miners were stymied, not stopped. In August 1894, Montana Senator Thomas C. Power, himself involved in illegal prospecting on Indian land, asked Hoke Smith to open the mineral strip. Despite Power's demand, Smith stood firm. Power then convinced Congress to add a special provision to the Indian appropriations act requiring negotiations with the Gros Ventres, Blackfeet, and Assiniboines for mineral lands in Montana.[5]

The 1895 Blackfeet land cession was related to unsuccessful government attempts to convert the tribe into farmers and cattle ranchers. For the previous twenty years, Midwestern farming techniques had not succeeded on the semi-arid northern plains. The Blackfeet, traditionally warriors and hunters, showed little interest in sod busting; they disliked monotonous, back-breaking labor, and they objected to "turning Mother Earth wrong side up."[6] Although it had not yet shown a profit, cattle ranching held more promise. Livestock required grass and horsemanship, both of which the tribe had in abundance. But the herds did not require mountains, and until cattle ranching could support the people, the tribe needed money to survive.

In 1886 the Blackfeet had sold the Sweet Grass Hills, a small mountain range east of the Rockies near the Canadian border. With that money they purchased cattle and farm implements, then ate the cattle and ignored the tools. By 1895, once again penniless and on the verge of starvation, the tribe faced parting with more land just as William Pollock, George Bird Grinnell, and Walter Clements arrived to negotiate.[7] If the commissioners thought that purchasing mountains would be simple, it must have surprised them to discover "the Indians considerably excited and holding what we believed to be exaggerated ideas of the value of their mountain lands for mineral purposes." Little Dog, convinced that his people had been swindled at the Sweet Grass Hills, told the commissioners that "there are many things in which the Great Father has cheated us. Therefore we ask Three Million Dollars. . . . Those mountains will last forever; the money will not."[8]

William Pollock and George B. Grinnell, both experienced land negotiators, would make the government's case. As a BIA official, Pollock knew federal policy. Grinnell, who had hunted on the reservation and collected ethnographic data since the 1880s, knew the country and its people. When asked by Hoke Smith to join the commission, Grinnell had hesitated. "The Indians will growl," he warned, "and accuse me of not looking out for their interests." After receiving requests from tribal members, however, Grinnell reluctantly consented.[9]

Contemporaries considered George Bird Grinnell a "friend of the Indians." Writer, naturalist, ethnographer, trophy hunter, conservationist, founder of the Audubon Society and of Glacier National Park, Grinnell was born in 1849 to wealthy and influential New York parents. He spent much of his youth on the estate of John James Audubon, tutored by Audubon's widow, Lucy, from whom Grinnell acquired values of wildlife conservation. Following graduation from Yale in 1870, Grinnell had visited the West as a paleontologist. Four years later he rode with George Armstrong Custer into the Black Hills as the expedition's naturalist. Custer enjoyed Grinnell's companionship enough to invite him to accompany the Seventh Cavalry in 1876 to the Little Big Horn. Other commitments led Grinnell to decline.

Fascinated by the Far West, George Bird Grinnell repeatedly came back to the plains and mountains for the next thirty summers. The naturalist from Audubon Park was a close friend to Theodore Roosevelt and Gifford Pinchot, sharing their concern over the waste of America's resources. A prolific writer, Grinnell published books and articles on the Pawnee, Cheyenne, and Blackfeet; as editor of *Forest and Stream*, he influenced public opinion on conservation.

Indebted to Grinnell for assistance during the winter of 1883–84, when nearly six hundred Blackfeet had starved to death, the tribe adopted him as Pinotu'yi Iszu'mokan (Fisher's Cap). Many Blackfeet, especially Christian elders, looked upon Grinnell as friend and advisor. Genuinely concerned with the tribe's welfare, Grinnell also embraced a nineteenth-century attitude that Native Americans had "the mind of a child in the body of an adult." Because "vanishing Americans" were destined to be swept aside by Progress, Grinnell, like other humanitarians, argued that the only way to "civilize" and save Indians involved breaking up communal lands that sustained traditional culture. He saw no contradiction in destroying the Indian to save the individual.[10]

Unlike everyone else involved in the 1895 negotiations, Grinnell believed that the mountains contained few if any valuable minerals. For him, the Backbone-of-the-World provided another kind of wealth. He had explored and hunted in the reservation mountains with his friend and guide, James Willard

Schultz, and as early as 1891 the idea of creating Glacier National Park had occurred to him. It required nineteen years to realize his dream; one step in that direction was the 1895 cession.[11]

The motives of the other Blackfeet advisors in 1895 were more transparent. The "agency ring" of Schultz, Garrett, Kipp, and former agent Lorenzo Cook, all of whom illegally prospected on the reserve, recommended that the tribe sell the strip. The Indian agent, a Texas cattleman named "Diamond R" George Steell, was also suspected of illegal prospecting. Two other tribal friends, A.B. Hamilton and Charles Conrad, Montana businessmen and associates of railroad baron James J. Hill, stood to gain from opening the land. All these advisors claimed that the Blackfeet wanted to sell the mountains.[12] Negotiation records reveal a more complex story. Although the Indians were divided over selling, they were in agreement that they wanted hunting, fishing, grazing, and timber rights on any land they ceded. Besides that, they had feelings that they could not share.

Before 1895 the Blackfeet not only hunted, fished, gathered plants, and cut timber but also conducted religious ceremonies in the mountains. The high country was and still is part of the tribe's mythology and religion. In the crags and caves of the Rockies lived "Thunder" and other "powers." Young men went to mountains on vision quests. There a powerful deity possessing great power, grizzly or "Real Bear," could be propitiated.[13] But if the Rocky Mountain wilderness was essential to native traditions, why did the Blackfeet fail to discuss spiritual values in 1895? Context provides an answer. At the end of the nineteenth century the United States and Canada sought to suppress traditional Indian beliefs and ceremonies. Both governments had declared the Sun Dance, Potlatch, Ghost Dance, and other rites illegal. Indian agents considered "medicine men" threats and sought to turn tribal people against their religious leaders, while the government promoted Christian missions.[14]

Although the Blackfeet at the 1895 negotiating table remained silent about their religion, they insisted on retaining access to nonmineral resources. Three Suns used horses to illustrate his point: "You have said that the mountains are poor. No, they are rich. . . . We want to reserve part of the mountains, as when a man is selling his horses, he keeps one for himself." At first the tribe offered land north of Cut Bank Creek, desiring to retain the Two Medicine wilderness. But when the government demanded more, the Blackfeet reluctantly agreed to land above Birch Creek. Next came disagreement over price: The commissioners offered $1.5 million, whereas the tribe wanted twice as much. On the afternoon of September 23, negotiations broke off after two days of wrangling. That evening agent Steell and trader Kipp met with Little Plume, Tail Feathers, Curly Bear, and Eagle Ribs; at midnight news reached the commission that they would sell the mineral strip for $1.5 million.[15]

Reluctantly agreeing to the sale, White Calf spoke for the Piegan: "Chief Mountain is my head. Now my head is cut off. . . . [This] is what I now give you. I want the timber because in the future my children will need it. . . . I would like to have the right to hunt game and fish in the mountains. . . . We will sell you the mountain lands from Birch Creek to the boundary, reserving the timber and grazing land." After Blackfeet leaders and the commission signed an agreement, 357 out of 381 Indian men decided to accept the deal. As the council ended, White Calf told the commissioners that "we don't want our Great Father to ask for anything more. . . . If you come for any more land, we will have to send you away."[16]

George Bird Grinnell would later claim that his only motive for serving on the commission had been concern for the Blackfeet, yet he hoped the cession could lead to a national park. Greeted by three dozen Blackfeet when he arrived before the meeting, Grinnell refused to talk and headed into the mountains. Returning from Swiftcurrent Creek, Grinnell joined a group of Blackfeet for "a long and tiresome council." After complaining that their slow progress toward assimilation disappointed him and that the excuses from White Calf, Siyeh, and others bored him, Grinnell abruptly ended the meeting. On September 2 he and Pollock had another informal session with two hundred Blackfeet, from among whom Grinnell selected eight men to accompany him on a tour of the strip. Two weeks later Grinnell returned to the agency to face tribal protests. Amused and upset by the confusion, he claimed he could see "both sides of the game." Once official talks began, he offered little advice other than saying that the tribe's $3 million demand was absurd and foolish.[17]

Congress approved the Blackfeet Agreement on June 10, 1896. Article I reserved the rights that White Calf had demanded:

Provided, That said Indians shall have, and do hereby reserve for them-selves, the right to go upon any portion of the lands hereby conveyed so long as the same shall remain public lands of the United States, and to cut and remove therefrom wood and timber for agency and school purposes, and for their personal uses for houses, fences, and all other domestic purposes; And provided further, that the said Indians hereby reserve and

retain the right to hunt upon said lands and to fish in the streams thereof
so long as the same shall remain public lands of the United States under
and in accordance with the provisions of the game and fish laws of the
State of Montana.[18]

In 1898, the strip opened to mining; by 1902, the boom was a bust. After
miners left, the federal government placed the cession under control of the
fledgling U.S. Forest Service, bringing Grinnell's dream a step closer to reality.[19]

Glacier National Park

In September 1901, George Bird Grinnell's *Century Magazine* eloquently described the mountains and wildlife surrounding St. Mary Lake as "the Crown of
the Continent." Grinnell called for a campaign to preserve the region as a
national park. As editor of *Forest and Stream,* Grinnell published articles by Emerson Hough favoring protection of the northern Rockies. James Willard Schultz
added "Apikuni's" voice to the chorus. Grinnell directed a news blitz while
lobbying Montana's Senator Thomas Carter and other politicians for a park.
Even so, it took ten more years to convince Congress. On May 11, 1910,
President William Howard Taft signed legislation making a reality of the idea
that Grinnell had jotted down in his diary twenty years earlier: Glacier National Park.

Encompassing two thousand square miles, our eleventh national park rises
out of lush, green forests on the North Fork of the Flathead River in the west,
spans the continental divide, and then drops to a windswept eastern border
with the northern plains. The mineral strip, east from the divide to the Blackfeet line, forms half of the park and creates a hundred-mile common border
with the tribe. Despite this, the enabling legislation contained no reference to
Blackfeet Indians, their hunting, fishing, or timber rights, nor had the tribe been
invited to the congressional hearings. Opposition to a park from west-side non-
Indian landowners led to a provision on inholders' rights; the Blackfeet, with
much more at stake, were ignored, as were the Kootenai and Salish tribes on the
western Flathead Reservation.[20]

The legislation had serious consequences for Indians. Later the federal government would claim at Olympic and Rainier that once land became a park it
no longer resided in the public domain. Jurisdiction also remained unclear. The
first article of the Glacier legislation provided that management of fish and

wildlife belonged to Montana. In 1911 the Montana legislature ceded exclusive jurisdiction over Glacier's fish and wildlife to the United States, a concession Congress finally accepted in 1914. The 1914 law declared that the federal government had "sole and exclusive" control of a park in which "all hunting or killing, wounding, or capturing at any time of any bird or wild animal . . . is prohibited within the limits of said park; nor shall any fish be taken out of the waters of the park in any other way than hook and line, and then only at such seasons and in such times and manners as may be directed by the Secretary of the Interior."[21]

While creation of Glacier terminated Blackfeet rights, it sustained those of non-Indians. In 1911, a west-side inholder named Paul Schoenberg wrote to Interior requesting clarification: "We were here before the Park and killed deer on our places during the open season and I want to know can [we] still do so?" Glacier's first superintendent, William R. Logan, responded by approving hunting on homestead sites.[22] If Logan noticed any difference between Indians and inholders, it apparently did not bother him. Previous to his appointment, "Major" Logan had served as Indian agent for the Blackfeet. Like "Diamond R" Steell, Logan was a cattleman who came to Montana from Texas seeking free grass. An energetic reformer with the BIA, he sought to run the Blackfeet Reservation on a sound economic basis, which meant cutting rations and annuities. When this upset the tribe, Logan developed a dislike for his job and the people. "The Indian is a natural begger [sic] and bummer," he concluded, "and if they were in possession of the earth and all things on it, they would still beg for more."[23] Fortunately, others in the BIA would respond aggressively on the tribe's behalf in opposition to Logan.[24]

Besides an unfriendly superintendent, the Blackfeet had other problems with Glacier. While visiting Washington in 1915, a delegation that included Curly Bear and Wolf Plume met with Stephen Mather and Horace Albright a few months prior to the establishment of the NPS. The Indians protested renaming lakes, mountains, glaciers, and rivers in the park. Tail-Feathers-Coming-Over-The-Hill complained that white men used "foolish names of no meaning whatever!" The Indians wanted Blackfeet names, and Mather promised that in the future only the Indian language or translations would be employed. If the problem of Indian hunting was discussed, no record exists.[25]

In Logan's era and for many years thereafter, controlling poachers, preventing forest fires, and destroying predators were a park ranger's primary duties. A national park protected desirable animals like elk, deer, bighorn sheep, and

A Blackfeet delegation visits Washington, D.C., in January 1915 to request that native place names be used in Glacier National Park. Seated: Stephen T. Mather, who would later become the first NPS director. Standing, left to right: Bird Rattlers, Curly Bear, Wolf Plume, an interpreter, Horace Albright, and two unidentified government officials. (Courtesy of Marian Albright Schenck)

mountain goats from undesirables like coyotes, wolves, mountain lions, and poachers. Bears, a prime tourist attraction, were desirable enough to be fed garbage on hotel lawns, while rangers and bounty hunters poisoned wolves and coyotes, hunted lions and cougars with hounds, and systematically destroyed mink, weasels, and marten. Human predators were arrested or escorted out of the park. On the east, or Blackfeet side of the divide, Indian hunters posed a major threat to wildlife: "Unless the Indians are curbed in their desire to kill everything in sight," one ranger declared, "Glacier Park will soon have no game."[26] Indian hunters were either jailed or removed. Sometimes rangers confiscated guns, traps, and game; at other times they did not. In February 1912, a park ranger arrested two Indians and took their firearms, traps, and hides. Interior then instructed Glacier to return the gear and to warn the Indians that "they will no longer be permitted in the Glacier National Park, and if found within the [park] they will be summarily ejected."[27]

Three years after Interior's warning, Peter Oscar Little Chief appealed to Franklin Lane. Little Chief, hearing of Lane's "kindness toward Indians," requested the secretary's help in acquiring a permit to kill two bighorn rams. Lane refused, yet asked for a solicitor's opinion. Upon receiving it, Lane learned that the Blackfeet held no rights in Glacier National Park other than those enjoyed by the general public. The government counsel based his opinion on section 2 of Glacier's enabling legislation, which authorized regulations "for the care and protection of the fish and game within the boundaries thereof." The opinion also cited the 1914 law which, in accepting Montana's cession of jurisdiction, gave park officials sole authority over fish and wildlife. Blackfeet poaching, the NPS decided, must cease.[28]

Mather, Albright, and their Glacier rangers next realized that enforcement limited to the park would not fully protect game. Deer and elk browsed in Glacier until winter storms drove them to lower elevations on the reservation. An obvious way to protect animals from being "ruthlessly slaughtered" was to extend the park boundary six miles to the east, a Blackfeet buffer strip that would be actively pursued by the NPS for the next thirty years.[29]

The Blackfeet Extension

In attempting to limit hunting on the Blackfeet Reservation, Mather and Albright first sought cooperation. They suggested a joint wildlife program managed by the NPS, Montana, and the BIA. The tribe, holding that the service and state had no jurisdiction, rejected the plan. Mather then decided to expand the park eastward by purchasing land.[30]

After an exceptionally severe winter followed by a long drought threatened the Blackfeet with starvation in 1919, it seemed "an opportune time" to acquire land. Prices plummeted, but Mather had to act quickly because the BIA was allotting tribal holdings to individual members. For once, Stephen Mather missed his chance; by the time he was ready, the western rim of the reserve had been split into small parcels.[31]

Even with individual allotments greatly complicating his task, Mather did not quit. In 1921 he suggested to the BIA's Cato Sells that Glacier's east line extend to the Blackfeet Highway, from there to lower St. Mary Lake, and then along St. Mary River to Canada. After enlisting the aid of George Bird Grinnell in an effort to acquire this large block purchase, Mather asked Sells to halt allotment procedures. The NPS director pointed out that the area was "valueless except for scenery, or for game refuge . . . or for the protection of Glacier National Park." Mather assured Sells that the NPS would allow tribal members to collect firewood for personal use and to graze cattle and horses without charge.[32] Sells rejected the proposal: The rights of Indians, he told Interior, must be protected "to the fullest extent possible." Anticipating BIA disapproval, Mather had included other options in his proposal, and the two agencies finally agreed to Park Service jurisdiction over the Blackfeet Highway.[33]

The NPS rationale for pushing its boundary into the reservation, or at least managing the highway, addressed more than protection of wildlife. Indian cattle that wandered across the road created traffic hazards, competed with wildlife for grazing, and carried exotic plant seeds into Glacier on their hide or in their dung. In addition, tacky tourist attractions and Indian homes along the Blackfeet Highway struck the NPS as "unsightly filling stations, hot dog stands, and shacks [that are] springing up along this highway like mushrooms."[34]

Park control of the highway in the 1920s had little effect on hunting as Indians continued to kill game on the reservation and in the park. Rangers and state wardens worked closely with the BIA to arrest Blackfeet, Cree, and "Breed" hunters. Believing the tribe subject to state law, the BIA ordered Indians not to kill wildlife near the ceded strip and urged a ban on all hunting west of the highway. These efforts foundered amid confusion over who had what jurisdiction in parks and on Indian reservations. Non-Indians questioned the legal authority of rangers; the BIA, non-Indian hunters, and conservationists supported state control on the reserve; Indians claimed the tribe had jurisdiction over wildlife on their reservation. When wardens arrested Blackfeet member Henry Moore and several Cree for killing five elk a mile east of the park boundary, a judge released the men and allowed them to keep the elk. Angry state officials demanded further prosecution to make an example of Moore.[35] In 1923 the Park Service tried a new approach when it advised an Indian agent in Browning, the Blackfeet capitol, that Glacier's elk were not native but had been imported from Yellowstone; consequently local Indians had no right to them in or outside the park. George Bird Grinnell, who supported NPS efforts against Blackfeet hunting, correctly predicted the tribe's reaction: "The Indians will laugh," he said. The arrests continued.[36]

Despite efforts of the NPS, the state, conservationists, and the BIA, Blackfeet persisted in hunting. Peter Oscar Little Chief circulated a petition in 1924 calling for recognition of Indian rights in Glacier. Crisscrossing the reservation by car and horseback to collect signature marks in Browning, Heart Butte, Babb, and elsewhere, patiently explaining his document to those who could not read, Little Chief claimed that the Blackfeet retained their 1895 rights:

We sold to the U.S. Government nothing but rocks only. We still control timber, grass, water, and all big or small game or all the animals living in this [*sic*] mountains. The treaty reads that as long as the mountains stand we got right to hunt and fishing so long as the [land] shall remain public lands of the U.S. . . . And now we are all known as the Glacier National Park [Indians] of Montana [but we] can't hunt there. . . . And you all know that the game belong[s] to us Indians. Now I want every man and woman to sign it so we can hunt in the Park when the season opens.

Little Chief submitted his petition to the BIA, waiting in vain four years before he complained to Senator Thomas Walsh. Walsh mentioned the letter to Commissioner of Indian Affairs Charles Burke, who knew nothing of the petition. The BIA informed Walsh that Indians retained no special rights in the park.[37]

Confident of its authority to arrest trespassers, the NPS developed another eastern extension plan. In March of 1929, Arthur Demaray drafted a proposal to enlarge Glacier. Demaray explained to Horace Albright how the government had acquired Blackfeet land in 1895 and recommended the same procedure for a new extension, provided that "such a contract not reserve any rights within the area to the Indians." Albright asked the BIA for help and also enlisted General Hugh L. Scott, an Indian expert and member of the Board of Indian Commissioners. When Scott visited the reservation in 1920, he had become friends with influential Piegans and thus, in Albright's view, had extraordinary influence with the tribe.[38]

Albright had other powerful allies. Louis C. Cramton, the Michigan congressman and avid park supporter, toured Glacier and the reserve during the summer of 1929. The visit convinced Cramton that tribal forests and individual allotments on the western reservation belonged in the park, but he also realized that the Blackfeet had no desire to sell because Indians knew that the western lands contained their only timber. "The Blackfeet," their agent wrote to Washington, "will not give up this area for a money consideration. . . . [They] also prize their Treaty rights as to hunting, trapping and fishing." The BIA informed Cramton that Indians opposed any plan to expand the park.[39]

During this same summer, Albright lobbied the Audubon Society's Gilbert Pearson by inviting him to Glacier as a Park Service guest. Albright instructed his superintendent to provide Pearson "all practicable courtesies. . . . Take him in a Government car all the way to [Waterton Lakes] showing the entire boundary problem." Albright likewise aligned the Great Northern Railroad firmly behind park expansion. Armed with support from politicians, business-men, Indian experts, and conservationists, Albright again asked for an eastern extension. He told the new BIA commissioner, Charles Rhoads, that Blackfeet land "is by topography, juxtaposition and character logically a part of Glacier National Park." Rhoads replied that the Blackfeet opposed park annexation, then forwarded Albright's correspondence to the tribe.[40]

The NPS, realizing that it had ignored the Blackfeet while seeking to acquire their land, feared that the Indians would reject any extension. Even without reading Albright's letters and in spite of NPS "missionary work," the tribal coun-cil resisted his efforts. Equally determined, the service pursued eastward expan-sion for two more decades.[41]

"Some Good Type Indians"

In managing Glacier National Park, the NPS not only had to interact with the BIA and the Blackfeet but it also had to work with the Bureau of Reclamation, as well as a major concessionaire and lodge owner in the park, Louis Hill's Great Northern Railroad.

The 1910 act establishing Glacier allowed the Bureau of Reclamation to maintain and develop water projects that had existed before that date. Irriga-tion systems on tribal land at eastern Lake Sherburne, the Swiftcurrent River, lower St. Mary Lake, and lower Two Medicine Lake all bordered the park. Earlier, the BIA had relinquished Blackfeet land to Reclamation, which in turn leased large sections to the Park Saddle Horse Company, a Great Northern subsidiary.

When Senator Burton Wheeler conducted hearings in Browning during the summer of 1929, he inquired about the land leased to the company—why had Reclamation allowed the Great Northern to build tourist chalets on land set aside for irrigation projects? When the bureau responded that they had orig-inally leased the land to the Park Saddle Horse Company for grazing, Wheeler pointed out that the terrain was too steep and rocky for grazing. The lease, he concluded, apparently served to keep Indians from using or leasing their own land.[42]

By 1929 Great Northern and its subsidiaries had become an integral part of Glacier. Louis Hill cultivated close relations with NPS directors and Glacier superintendents as his hotels and chalets became the park's primary tourist facilities. Efforts to control Hill, whether inside Glacier, on Reclamation lands, or on the Blackfeet Reservation meant delicate politics for the NPS. A passionate supporter of parks, a concessionaire and promoter, and president of the Great Northern, Louis Hill viewed passengers differently than his father had. James J. Hill had once remarked that train passengers were "like the male teat—neither useful nor ornamental." His son believed just the opposite and proceeded to turn Glacier into a major tourist destination.

In doing so, Louis Hill employed Blackfeet Indians as official hosts at his chalets and hotels. The tribe became known, even to themselves, as "the Glacier Park Indians." Hill promoted a Plains Indian warrior mystique on the railway's advertisements, calendars, and resort decor. To a lesser extent, the NPS also took advantage of this romantic-savage-in-a-pristine-wilderness motif. Both Great Northern and the park preferred "some good type Indians . . . who do not have too large of families." The natives should be friendly, "have good costumes, put on a good show, and live in peace and harmony."[43]

Other advocates of national parks utilized fascination with Indians. Horace Albright's chapter, "Indians!" for example, unwittingly fell into noble redman imagery. For Albright, the Blackfeet were "bound together by a strong racial pride . . . warlike, predatory, and inconsiderate of their neighbors . . . handsome and noble in appearance, their features more finely carved. . . . Their complexions were lighter than those of other Indians, the men being almost tan, the women often so fair they were very nearly white."[44]

Albright's bleached Blackfeet in buckskin and feathers, once the most respected warriors on the northern plains, now greeted new arrivals at the park train depot, drove tourist buses, and welcomed guests to the hotels. At resorts decorated in quasi-Indian art, tourists shook hands with Blackfeet "chiefs" and flirted with "Indian door girls." The tribe drummed, danced, and signed postcards on the sprawling estate of a hotel, then conducted naming ceremonies in the crowded lobby. Indians "passed the tom-tom" for tips and sold miniature bows, arrows, and tepees. Between 1914 and 1919 hardier tourists slept in real tepees on the lawn of East Glacier Hotel. When the popularity of such camping declined, the railroad hired Blackfeet to live on display in tepees.[45]

Not everyone approved. The BIA in particular objected to Blackfeet exploitation. When Wallace Streeter asked for eleven Indians "for exhibition purposes" in 1915, the Bureau's E. B. Meritt denied the request. "It is desired to have the Indians settle on their allotments and become active in the improvement of

A Northern Plains Indian camp in front of East Glacier Lodge did not happen by chance. In the 1920s, the Great Northern Railroad hired Blackfeet families to greet tourists and provide local color. (Courtesy of Fred Des Rosier)

their economic conditions. . . . Their employment for exhibition by circuses, wild west shows, and the like, tends to influence them to continue their no-madic habits. . . . The employment of Indians for such purposes is strongly discouraged." If Meritt disapproved of employing showcase Indians, he could not halt the practice. Thus the BIA set conditions: a written agreement approved by the local agent and the D.C. office; the Indians must receive medical care, food, transportation, and salary; the employer must take "necessary precaution to guard [the Indians] from improper influences, and to see that they are not furnished with intoxicating liquor."[46]

BIA employment regulations were not always followed. At Glacier in 1923 Blackfeet agent Frank Campbell complained that the tribe was "doomed to furnish cheap amusement to the white man for many years to come. . . . Another annual opening of the Park must have attention, and this probably cannot be done without a delegation of Blackfeet. . . . These people have been exploited in this way for so many years that they have been looked upon as professional celebrators." Campbell was not alone. After hearing rumors about Indians at the Great Northern hotels, federal investigator Walter W. Liggett submitted a negative report entitled "Indians Exploited by Hill Hotel," which claimed that Blackfeet were paid with handouts and "the leavings of the hotel kitchen."[47]

Regarding food, menus at Great Northern lodges featured another native attraction: Glacier Park whitefish. The fish were caught with gill nets in upper St. Mary Lake and Lake McDonald during the winter by hotel employees. One lodge took up to two hundred fish a night until the Park Service limited daily catches to forty. Although the park's enabling legislation outlawed net fishing, whitefish remained on Louis Hill's menu for years. As early as 1933 NPS attorneys recommended that the netting stop, but Albright asked for new regulations to legalize the practice. The service allowed net fishing until 1939, finally banning it on ecological grounds.[48]

Indian Hunting Rights

The NPS allowed Louis Hill to fish commercially in Glacier Park until 1939, yet the service refused to tolerate Indian hunting. Peter Oscar Little Chief continued to insist that Blackfeet could take fish, game, and timber. Little Chief's protest in 1932 evoked another solicitor's opinion that tribal hunting, fishing, and tree cutting inside Glacier had ended with the creation of the park.[49]

Shortly after Glacier officials received this opinion, rangers arrested four armed Indians for trespassing. U.S. attorney Arthur P. Archer expected a dispute over "an old Indian treaty" to reach the U.S. Supreme Court. After a lower court conviction, the four Indians appealed to the U.S. District Court in Great Falls. Barely able to raise the five-dollar filing fee, the Blackfeet had difficulty finding a lawyer. Eventually Superintendent Eivind Scoyen arranged a meeting between the government attorney and a local lawyer who had taken the case. Although Blackfeet continued to assert treaty rights, the four men agreed to plead guilty. Judge Charles N. Pray fined the Indians $150 each, suspended their convictions, and placed them on probation. Scoyen reported that his policy of arresting Indians had been vindicated.[50]

Throughout the 1930s the NPS and the tribe continued to quarrel over hunting, a dispute compounded by the park's quest for an eastern "Blackfeet extension." Expansion or tribal cooperation was essential for the park's new bison herd plan. First proposed in 1933, the buffalo program required winter range on the reservation. Scoyen realized that Indians suspected park motives, and he conceded that entertaining visitors was his primary goal. The Blackfeet refused to cooperate, leaving the NPS with the sole option of expanding its borders.[51]

Game management ranked high on the service's agenda, and during the New Deal it gained BIA support. In 1934, John Collier launched a conservation plan that called for introducing wildlife into Indian territory. Collier, who considered all Indians to be conservationists, argued that reservations were perfect game preserves because "the Indian . . . kills animals and catches fish only for food. One never hears of him indulging in slaughter." After the Blackfeet responded positively to the commissioner's proposal to establish fish and game regulations, Scoyen believed the new rules would finally settle Glacier's controversy over hunting. That would not be the case.[52]

During the 1930s, NPS biologist George Wright had developed a farsighted wildlife management program that resulted in profound changes. By 1945 Glacier had stopped feeding deer and had abolished predator extermination programs. The deer rebounded quickly, but solving the predator situation was not so simple. Fifty years of systematic killing had eliminated wolves from Glacier; they would not return until the 1980s, which left the deer population out of balance.[53]

Eventually park staff recognized the role of Blackfeet hunters in controlling deer and elk. At the same time, Glacier began to reassess its desire for more Blackfeet land, realizing that a "Blackfeet extension" would remove the tribe's only timber while not stopping poachers.[54] Park officials and conservationists who previously had claimed that Blackfeet hunters decimated elk herds now studied new research pointing to overpopulation. By eliminating large predators while feeding elk and deer in the winter, the NPS had unwittingly increased the ungulate population beyond the area's capacity. Rangers had to kill many animals in 1955 and 1956 or drive them onto the reservation. Despite this, the service still refused to allow Blackfeet hunters inside the park for fear of setting a precedent.[55]

In the 1940s and 1950s the Blackfeet and other tribes neglected to lobby for hunting in national parks. Could they have succeeded? Perhaps. Wyoming sportsmen, backed by national outdoor organizations and by U.S. Senators Joseph O'Mahoney and Lester Hunt, managed to open Grand Teton to elk hunters. Deputized by the NPS, sportsmen "harvested" elk in the Tetons, thereby creating the precedent feared in Glacier.[56]

When Indian activists began to pursue treaty rights in the 1970s, the Blackfeet pressed the park issue. On September 15, 1973, after Woodrow L. Kipp refused to pay an entrance fee, a ranger cited him. The case went to a federal court in Missoula, which, relying on the 1895 agreement, acquitted Kipp. The judge warned that his decision covered only the right of entry. A few months later tribal member Darrell R. Momberg was arrested for tree cutting inside the park. Momberg lost, the court concluding that he had not cut the wood for personal use as specified in the 1895 agreement. This decision, based on a 1935 Court of Claims ruling, failed to persuade the Blackfeet.[57]

In 1975 the tribe, assisted by the Native American Rights Fund (NARF), petitioned Secretary of the Interior Rogers Morton on the basis that they retained rights on the ceded strip and that Morton as trustee was responsible for upholding those rights. Reacting to the petition, environmentalists condemned Blackfeet claims as a major threat to Glacier: "Indian attempts to penetrate national park lands for exploitative purposes, like the successful efforts by the Havasupai Indians [at] the Grand Canyon . . . represent another sad commentary in Native American History. . . . Indians may destroy something of value to both themselves and the rest of the nation."[58] Interior rejected the Blackfeet proposal, leaving ill feelings over hunting that have simmered into the present. Tribal chairman Earl Old Person spoke for most Blackfeet in 1991 when he referred to taking game in Glacier: "We only sold them the rocks."[59]

Indians as Entertainment

Glacier officials had another reason for eastward expansion besides the protection of game—namely, the protection of tourists from the reality of modern Indian life. If Indians wore ceremonial dress and appeared on cue, the Park Service considered them an asset. Accurately interpreting native culture or observing actual living conditions along the park border was another matter.

A need to patrol the Blackfeet Highway and prevent "further intrusion of undesirable features, signs, stores, and other unsightly shacks destroying the sides of the highway" was an NPS motive for moving east in 1940. The service also opposed tree cutting along St. Mary Lake, therefore seeking to lease Bureau of Reclamation land. Reclamation supported the request, joined by the Indian agent in Browning who privately told the NPS that he endorsed a land transfer.[60]

The service next considered asking Congress for help. New legislation would have allowed Indians to gather wood, establish craft shops, obtain surplus bison and fish, and retain certain grazing rights. When the NPS realized that any land transfer would face "vigorous opposition by Blackfeet Indians, white residents, and the Breed Indians," it countered with a Blackfeet National Highway proposal. Beginning at East Glacier, passing through St. Mary and Babb, the route would meet Chief Mountain International Highway north of

Kennedy Creek. The plan included one-hundred-foot NPS easements on each side of the road to impede construction of shacks and "reprehensible slums." The plan went nowhere.[61]

If shacks along a road offended tourists, the Park Service obviated that risk in the summer of 1933 when it opened Going to the Sun Highway. Here Glacier's "good type Indian" entertainment reached a new high as large camps of colorful Blackfeet and Kootenai tepees straddled Logan Pass, and Indians in buckskin added to the mountain grandeur. Standing on the continental divide, scores of native men, women, and children posed for photographers. The area's largest gathering of Indians since the early nineteenth century included a Blackfeet brass band.

Since Glacier's founding, tourists had always taken home postcards, posters, ashtrays, and coffee mugs with Blackfeet motifs. Blackfeet appeared in the park's promotional films, in magazine articles, and on Great Northern calendars. Hollywood shot films in the park and brought Indian actors back to California. Following World War II, however, the tribe began questioning its role as park curio, and younger Indians lost interest in amusing tourists. Great Northern officials also criticized the staged ceremonies, finding the performances "more or less hokum" and native garb "pretty much worn out." The railroad complained that older Indians steeped in the culture were "rapidly dying off, and the younger generation are too modern in their habits . . . are hard to handle, and would not be suitable for entertainment purposes."[62]

Hoping to economize, Great Northern left the 1951 summer arrangement up to the tribe, because "by doing so, the Indians may be more cooperative and accept a more reasonable deal." When the Blackfeet did not respond, company officials realized that ending Glacier's native programs affected tourism and would cut deeply into profits from souvenirs: "We have definitely got to get the Indians back to Glacier Park. . . . I realize it is something of a problem to handle them [but] guest after guest inquires . . . why don't we have them. People even detraining for a few minutes inquire as to why [the Indians] are not on the platform. . . . The Indians are considered part of Glacier Park. . . . We definitely have to have the Indians back."[63]

Other than catering to fantasies, posing for photographs, and selling trinkets, few jobs for Blackfeet existed in a park where eastern college students took summer jobs in hotels and with the NPS. Although some Indians worked in Glacier as truck drivers, garbage collectors, camp tenders, maids, janitors, and fire fighters, no program trained Blackfeet to operate concessions. A few have

From Navajo rugs to juniper beads, native crafts and pseudo-Indian trinkets have fascinated park visitors. Here Medicine Boss Ribs, a Blackfeet, sells mock tepees while posing for
photos in Glacier National Park. (Courtesy of Special Collections, Montana State University, Bozeman, Mont.)

been park rangers. In 1932 Glacier hired Francis X. Guardipee, a much-admired
tribal member who stayed on the staff until 1947. Gerald Cobell, a Blackfeet,
began as a seasonal worker in 1975. Helped by BIA scholarships, Cobell gradu-
ated from Utah State University with a masters degree in wildlife management,
later becoming a resource ranger at Glacier. In 1991, Cobell and Ted Hall,
another Blackfeet, applied for the assistant superintendent opening. When
neither succeeded, Hall contested the decision.[64]

On a more positive note, the park has recently increased Blackfeet involvement. Tribal members Curly Bear Wagner, Earl Kipp, and Jack Gladstone visit
hotel lobbies and campgrounds to offer summer programs on Blackfeet culture.
Wagner conducts cultural workshops for non-Indian staff. Genuine efforts at
historical awareness, however, may not make the NPS comfortable. Many modern Blackfeet believe that these lands were stolen from them. George Kicking
Woman recalls his mother being told, "Don't ever give away this beautiful land,"
and about how it was taken through confusing language, incorrect surveys, false
promises, and whiskey. Vicky Santana agrees: The park resulted from fraud.
George Bird Grinnell, she adds, died insane, "partly driven crazy" by guilt over
stealing Blackfeet lands.[65]

In addition to conflicts over land, hunting, fishing, boundaries, employment, and timber rights, the Blackfeet and the NPS have disagreed on many other issues since 1910. Cattle trespass led the Park Service to begin fencing the eastern border until Blackfeet ranchers protested. Conflict arose over management of sacred sites. For instance, the park-reservation boundary bisects Chief Mountain, a peak important not only for Blackfeet but also for Kootenais, Canadian bands, and Plains tribes. The NPS has rejected requests to curtail non-Indian access.[66]

Although modern managers at Glacier conscientiously seek to improve relations with the Blackfeet, the message may not reach park staff. During a campfire program in 1991, a ranger described how he had led Indian children on a hike around Lake McDonald. When he told the children to make noise to alert bears, a little girl reacted literally, singing out "Noise, Noise, Noise . . . ." Other children told her to be quiet, to no avail; then a little boy threatened to scalp her. At this point the ranger doffed his hat to reveal a glistening bald head: "The boy meant it, folks," he exclaimed. "Look what happened to me in Browning down on the Blackfeet Reservation!"

PAIUTES, MORMONS, AND WATER

One element in Mormon settlement is invariable: water.
Mormonism flowed down the rivers and the irrigable valleys.
— Wallace Stegner, *Mormon Country*, 1942

We start very early this morning. . . . Climbing out of the valley
of the Rio Virgin, we . . . come out at the foot of the Vermillion
Cliffs. All day we follow this Indian trail toward the east, and at
night camp at a great spring, known to the Indians as Yellow
Rock Spring, but to the Mormons as Pipe Spring.
— John Wesley Powell, September 13, 1870

Logic, geography, and culture dictate that Pipe Spring National Monument
belongs in Utah; politics places it inside the borders of Arizona. Pipe Spring's
state capitol should be three hundred miles north in Salt Lake City instead of
three hundred miles south in Phoenix. At different times, the spring has been in
one state or the other, and in three different counties. Since 1923, when the
Park Service obtained the site, these forty acres of federal property have been
entirely within a 120,000-acre Indian reservation belonging to the Kaibab
Paiutes. At the monument, park and tribal headquarters face each other across a
country road, separated by hardly more than one hundred yards.

These odd political metes and bounds do not diminish Pipe Spring's second
most valuable asset, an awesome sense of distance and empty space on the
Kanab Plateau. The Vermillion Cliffs block the view north; otherwise one looks
in all directions over the Arizona Strip as far as the eye can see. Fifty miles due
south is the Havasupai Reservation, separated from Pipe Spring by the Grand

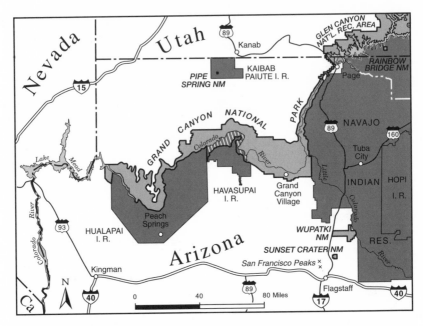

The Arizona Strip and Grand Canyon National Park in northern Arizona.

Canyon. Mount Trumbull breaks the horizon to the southwest, a sixty-mile view that looks like twenty. East beyond Kanab Creek, the forested Kaibab Plateau fosters the same illusion of proximity. This expanse rises north from the Grand Canyon in a broken jumble of mesas, plateaus, buttes, canyons, rocks, and endless cliffs. Even the terrace between the Canyon and Pipe Spring turns into washes and gullies when one travels across it. Elevations vary between twenty-three hundred and nine thousand feet; temperatures range from zero to one hundred degrees. John Wesley Powell called this the Plateau Province. His biographer, Wallace Stegner, has described it as being "scenically the most spectacular and humanly the least usable of all our regions . . . the strangest and newest, last to be opened and last known."

> The tiny oases huddle in their pockets in the rock, surrounded on all sides
> by as terrible and beautiful wasteland as the world can show. . . .In the
> Plateau Country the eye is not merely invited but compelled to notice the
> large things. From any point of vantage the view . . . is often fifty and
> sometimes even seventy-five miles—and that is a long way to look, espe-

cially if there is nothing human in sight. The villages are hidden in the canyons and under the cliffs; there is nothing visible but the torn and slashed and windworn beauty of absolute wasteland.[1]

Wasteland never intimidated one of the most determined and successful pioneer vanguards in American history, the Church of Jesus Christ of Latter-day Saints (LDS). After founding Salt Lake City in the 1840s, the Mormons sought to expand north to Canada, south to Mexico, and as far west as San Diego. Within a decade, Brigham Young had dispatched exploring parties to the Shivwits, Kanab, Kaibab, and Paria Plateaus along this corridor of land south of Utah and north of the Grand Canyon called the Arizona Strip. His followers would eventually settle as far east as the Little Colorado, Marble Canyon, and Lee's Ferry. By the 1860s, discovery of water sources and fertile grassland led to the establishment of Mormon cattle ranches and towns on the Virgin River, Short Creek, Kanab Creek, Pipe Spring, and Moccasin Springs.

As at Salt Lake and Las Vegas, the Mormons strove to occupy remote, desolate regions that no one else wanted, or would want. The Colorado River Plateau was such country. Stegner again: "Its distances were terrifying, its cloudbursts catastrophic, its beauty flamboyant and bizarre and allied with death. Its droughts and its heat were withering. . . . In the teeth of that—perhaps because of that—it may have seemed close to God. It was Sanctuary, it was Refuge. Nobody else wanted it, nobody but a determined and God-supported people could live in it."[2]

Not quite. Nearly a thousand years earlier a resolute, civilized people we call the Anasazi moved into the Plateau Province and survived there longer than the Mormons have. At about the same time, Numic-speaking people, ancestors of the modern Southern Paiutes, migrated east from the Great Basin onto the Colorado Plateau. Here they and Anasazi cultures coexisted for several centuries before the latter, for reasons unknown, left their cliff dwellings. The Southern Paiutes remained, six centuries later becoming the "aboriginal" people in the minds of white explorers, traders, miners, and Mormon settlers.

Although whites often expressed even more contempt for Paiutes—"digger Indians," "lizard eaters"—than other Indian cultures, considering them dishonest, thieving, and barbaric, the five thousand Southern Paiutes living north of the Grand Canyon before contact with Europeans had developed a way of life that allowed them to survive in what Stegner calls "as terrible a wasteland as the world can show." In their three-million-acre territory between the Paria River and the Unikaret Plateau, the original Kaibab Paiute hunted deer and dried venison for lean winter months; birds and small animals such as quail, squirrels, ducks, gophers, and especially rabbits provided a year-round source of meat. The Paiute also moved frequently in search of seeds, berries, roots, and flowers, which women collected in finely made burden baskets. As with all native people of basin and range, piñon nuts, often harvested by both men and women, added a nutritious staple to their diet.

The Paiute, however, were not simply nomads. Where possible, they irrigated fertile land to raise corn, melons, squash, pumpkins, beans, amaranth, and, in the nineteenth century, wheat. Agriculture depended on a consistent water supply; springs, small water pockets, and streams were also the most likely places to find game. As John Wesley Powell learned, flowing streams and creeks were virtually nonexistent east of the Virgin River. "We discharged a number of Indians," Powell recorded, "but take two with us for the purpose of showing us the springs, for they are very scarce, very small, and not easily found. Half a dozen are not known in a district of country large enough to make as many good-sized counties in Illinois. There are no running streams, and these springs and water pockets are our sole dependence."[3]

Powell had returned to Paiute country in 1870 to continue his geologic charting and to satisfy himself about the fate of three men who had deserted his epic Grand Canyon exploration the previous summer. He traveled unarmed, ate and slept in native camps a hundred miles from the nearest white settlement, and entrusted his life to Paiute guides. Indian knowledge of the terrain astounded Powell, himself one of the great western explorers: "There is not a trail but what they know; every gulch and every rock seems familiar. I have prided myself on being able to grasp and retain in my mind the topography of a country; but these Indians put me to shame. My knowledge is only general, embracing the more important features of a region that remains as a map engraved on my mind; but theirs is particular. They know every rock and every ledge, every gulch and canyon, and just where to wind among these to find a pass; and their knowledge is unerring."[4]

In 1870, Kaibab Paiute independence and mastery of their land were about to collapse under a Mormon invasion that had begun ten years earlier. The church's settlement of the Arizona Strip had three disastrous results for native people: disease, destruction of vegetation, and loss of water sources. Sickness such as mumps, cholera, whooping cough, malaria, and measles decimated the

Kaibab Paiute Indians gather near Pipe Spring on the Arizona Strip, ca. 1910. (Courtesy of the National Park Service, Pipe Spring National Monument)

Paiute population. At the same time, settlers cut down piñon trees, their domestic sheep and cattle foraged grasses and plants, and wildlife disappeared. Finally, the Mormons and their livestock soon occupied all scarce water sources, including Mu-tum-wa-va (Dripping Rock)—also known as Yellow Rock Spring, or by its Mormon name, Pipe Spring.

In 1863, a Mormon convert and former Texas cattleman named James M. Whitmore with his wife and three children had ridden out of an LDS settlement on the Virgin River in southern Utah and turned east in search of rangeland. After ascending the Hurricane Cliffs and crossing thirty miles of open country beneath the Vermillion Cliffs, Whitmore found Pipe Spring, built a crude shelter, and obtained title to 160 acres that he planned to turn into a townsite. After building fences and corrals, planting grapevines, apple, and peach trees, Whitmore moved back to St. George, leaving his cattle and sheep to roam the vicinity of the spring. Meanwhile, Navajo Indians who had escaped capture and forced removal by the U.S. Army in 1864 began crossing the Colorado River to raid domestic stock near Mormon settlements.

Just after Christmas, 1865, Whitmore heard rumors of Indian raids. He left St. George for Pipe Spring with his son and a brother-in-law, Robert McIntyre, to check his livestock. On January 9, 1866, as two of the men tracked stolen sheep across fresh snow, they encountered Navajo raiders at Bull Wash, four miles southeast of Pipe Spring. Both whites were killed. Whitmore's son reported his father's disappearance, and ten days later a thirty-man Mormon militia found stolen goods in a Paiute camp. In a surprise attack the posse killed two Indians and captured five others whom the volunteers interrogated and then executed on the spot. In April the Paiute sought revenge by killing two Mormon brothers and a woman near Short Creek. With Navajo raids continuing and with settlers planning retaliation, Brigham Young in Salt Lake City invoked the church's traditional policy of peace with the Indians: In May he ordered withdrawal from Paiute lands at Long Valley and Kanab.[5]

The ebb of white settlement was brief. After Navajo raiding ceased in 1869, the church quickly moved to secure its earlier occupation of the Arizona Strip. In 1870 Brigham Young visited Kanab twice, in April creating the Canaan Cooperative Stock Company, then coming back in September to consecrate the settlement.[6] On his return to Salt Lake, Young stopped at Pipe Spring to establish a fort and cattle ranch under the supervision of Anson P. Winsor. September 13, 1870, proved a memorable day for Mu-tum-wa-va. Besides Brigham Young, those camped at the spring included Jacob Hamblin, the missionary; John Wesley Powell; and Chuarumpeak, a Paiute and Powell's guide. A Mormon fort called Winsor Castle two years later became the first telegraph station in Arizona, but it was never needed to protect pioneers from Indians. Native resistance and raiding ceased after the federal government created a Navajo reservation in 1868, with peace-making efforts by Hamblin also contributing to pacification of Navajo and Southern Paiutes.

The church, through its cattle subsidiary, held Pipe Spring for twenty years before selling Winsor Castle to a private owner. As overgrazing and the white population increased on the Kanab Plateau, the Kaibab Paiutes shrank in numbers. As a result of disease, starvation, and limited access to water their population plunged from an estimated seventeen hundred in 1863 to a low of eighty-one in 1909. Jacob Hamblin, who had first explored Pipe Spring in 1858, clearly understood what was happening. When Hamblin wrote to John Wesley Powell for help in 1880, he, like the Paiutes, relied on Powell's promise of aid made ten years earlier:

Dear Sir:
The Kanab or Kaibab Indians are in very destitute circumstances; fertile places are now being occupied by the white population, thus cutting off all their means of subsistence except game, which you are aware is quite limited. . . .
The foothills that yielded hundreds of acres of sunflowers which pro-

duced quantities of rich seed, the grass also that grew so luxuriantly when
you were here, the seed of which was gathered with little labor, and many
other plants that produced food for the natives is all eat out [sic] by stock.

As cold winter is now approaching and seeing them gathering around
their campfires, and hearing them talk over their suffering, I felt that it is
no more than humanity requires, of me to communicate this to you. . . . I
should esteem it a great favor if you could secure some surplus merchandise for the immediate relief of their utter destitution.

> Jacob Hamblin
> Nov. 1, 1880

Three and a half months later Powell sent his greetings. No help was possible. If the Kaibab Paiutes wanted to survive, they must move to Indian agencies
in Nevada or central Utah and learn subsistence farming. Powell, busily building a career based on his Paiute fieldwork, had become an eastern administrator
who found it impossible to help a small group of starving people in the Plateau
Province.[7]

Not until 1907, five years after Powell's death, did the federal government
create a reservation for the Kaibab Paiutes. The reserve was eighteen miles long
and twelve miles wide, its boundary beginning south of Kanab, Utah, and west
of Fredonia, Arizona. It included Yellow Rock Spring.

Pipe Spring National Monument

After Stephen Mather dedicated Zion National Park in September 1920, he
drove south to visit other southwestern monuments. During his tour, Mather
passed a deserted Mormon fort at Pipe Spring. Once back in Washington,
Mather informed the Indian Office that he had found "a very interesting old
homestead" on the Kaibab reservation that he wished to acquire for the park
system.[8] A year later, as Mather again drove from Utah to the Grand Canyon,
his Packard had trouble west of Pipe Spring. During the delay the director and
his party stayed with the Heaton family, Mormon ranchers at Moccasin Springs
who owned "Winsor Castle." Mather, sympathetic to the church and fascinated
by its history, listened carefully as Charles Heaton explained the pioneer past
of the ruins. When Heaton suggested a historic monument, Mather with char-
acteristic decisiveness offered to buy the forty-acre site for the Park Service.
Heaton agreed to sell for five thousand dollars.

Steve Mather returned to Washington pondering Pipe Spring. During the winter he convinced Warren G. Harding that the five thousand dollars could be raised privately and that a historical monument in southern Utah would add an important link to the national park system. Harding, noticing the site's location inside the Kaibab reserve, checked with his commissioner of Indian affairs, Charles Burke. On May 31, 1923, shortly before leaving on his own tour of the Far West and Alaska, Harding, under authority of the 1906 Antiquities Act, created Pipe Spring National Monument. The antiquities in this instance dated back to 1863, when Whitmore's bunker provided, in the words of the presidential proclamation, "a place of refuge from hostile Indians by early settlers." The monument thus would "serve as a memorial of western pioneer life."

Further settlement was prohibited, but the land remained "subject to all prior valid claims." With one exception, the NPS would manage and control the site. That exception, soon to be a source of prolonged controversy, lay in the final sentence of Harding's proclamation: "Provided, that in the administration of this Monument, the Indians of the Kaibab Reservation, shall have the privilege of utilizing waters from Pipe Spring for irrigation, stock watering and other purposes, under regulations to be prescribed by the Secretary of the Interior."[9]

Before the water rights dispute that arose among the BIA, the Park Service, the Indians, and local cattlemen after 1923 is described, more background is necessary. By 1900 the Paiutes of the Arizona Strip numbered less than a hundred, most of them dependent on begging or menial jobs at Mormon farms around Kanab. Given the depleted wildlife and the loss of native plants, both the church and the Indian Office agreed that the only hope for Paiute survival lay in agriculture at some permanent site. In the early 1900s the church ordered that one-third of the flow from Moccasin Springs be diverted to the Indians. Congress in 1906 appropriated $10,500 to purchase farm equipment, cattle, land, and water for the Kaibab Paiute. The next year a Paiute tract was withdrawn from public lands by the secretary of the interior, who also purportedly reserved water rights.[10]

Access to water brought Indian families from Kanab to Moccasin Springs, where a native village and BIA day school were established after 1907, both located near Mormon homes and serviced with a water pipe from Moccasin. The local whites, according to the Indian agent, opposed admission of Paiute children into the public school.

Meanwhile, three miles south of Moccasin at deserted Pipe Spring, the water had become a privately owned, quasi-public "commons" resource. Cowboys on the Arizona Strip corraled herds at several water holes fed by the spring. Increasing auto traffic between Zion and the Grand Canyon used the abandoned fort as a stopover point. To avoid conflict, Woodrow Wilson in 1916 declared all land within a quarter mile of the spring a public water reserve. Secretary of the Interior Albert Fall adjusted the boundaries of the water reserve on May 31, 1922, exactly one year before Harding created the monument.

To summarize, by the end of 1923 the United States had proclaimed Pipe Spring a national monument—inside an Indian reservation and at a public water source. The federal government at this point had no title, had not paid for the land, had appropriated no funds for purchase or maintenance, and probably had little idea even of where the site was. Mormons had lived in the area for sixty years before the creation of the monument and for forty-five years before the creation of the reservation. The Indian reserve, according to a 1917 executive order, did not affect "any existing rights of any person to any of the lands . . . therein." Mormon cattlemen had been sharing the spring in common for decades before 1923, having learned "by revelation and accident and adaptation . . . what the cliff-dwellers had discovered centuries before: that the only way to be a farmer on the desert plateaus of the Colorado watershed was to be a group farmer."[11]

After 1916, that common understanding at Pipe Spring had the legal title of a "public water reserve." But when Harding created the monument, very likely the local cattlemen, Charles Heaton, Stephen Mather, and Horace Albright had never heard of another legal principle, called the Winters Doctrine. Yet someone in the Indian Office knew about it, therefore the Paiute "privilege of utilizing water . . . for irrigation . . . and other purposes" was written into the monument's charter.

Water: 1924–1933

Months before the federal government finally obtained a quit-claim deed for Pipe Spring from Charles Heaton on April 28, 1924, the Park Service realized that it faced a water rights battle. In February, after Heaton had insisted that cattlemen have access to the spring, Mather promised to retain the public water reserve. Because this required changing the presidential proclamation and gaining the cooperation of the BIA, he cautioned Heaton that "it may take a little time to accomplish." For months after he had received the quit-claim deed, Mather assured Heaton that local cattlemen would retain access to water. On

October 30, 1924, the director wrote that prior rights would be "fully recognized" by Interior. If the BIA did not renew grazing permits, he promised
Charles Heaton, water could be piped off the reserve: "There should be no
reason to worry about this as at the proper time it will be taken care of."

Mather then urged Commissioner of Indian Affairs Burke to approve a public water reserve on grounds that it would somehow benefit the tribe. The Park
Service director either did not know about, or ignored, existing Indian use of
Pipe Spring through a system built by Kaibab agent Dr. E. A. Farrow. Through
it, Farrow supplied Indian stock and that of whites who held tribal grazing
permits. Hope for BIA cooperation faded when the agent forcefully spoke out
against Mather's plan.[12]

Faced with disagreement between its agent and a director of the Park Service, the BIA sent hydraulic engineer C. A. Engle from Idaho to investigate the
situation. Engle agreed with Farrow, reporting that "under no circumstances
should public access to tribal water be allowed":

> In the past there has been considerable trouble between the Indians, the
> Agency employees, and the stockmen of the vicinity who claim the right
> to pasture their horses within the reservation where water is available. . . .
>
> More than 4,000 acres, constituting the most valuable portion of the
> reservation, and including practically all of the springs, which are the
> only source of water supply in this country, are already claimed and used
> and virtually owned by white people. To take from the Indians any
> additional land, and especially any of the water supply that has been
> developed on land not claimed by whites, would constitute a grave in-
> justice and would only lead to endless friction and trouble and possibly
> end in violence between the whites and the Indians. . . . Any proposal to
> further decrease the size of this reservation and especially to surrender a
> drop of water originating on the reservation, [must] be firmly rejected.

If water were sold to cattlemen, Engle insisted, it should be piped at least a mile
off the reservation, with all construction and maintenance paid for by stock
growers, who must also buy all water "at a price fixed by the Agent of Kaibab
Reservation, the proceeds to go to the Indians of the reservation."[13]

Caught between Mormon cattlemen and Indians, Mather immediately dispatched his strongest man in the Southwest to Pipe Spring—Frank "Boss" Pinkley of Casa Grande. From Washington, D.C., the BIA sent its chief engineer,
William Reed. Meeting at the monument in early June with Reed, Pinkley,

Charles Heaton, and a local citizen named Randall Jones, agent Farrow found himself a minority of one when Reed unexpectedly sided with Pinkley and the cattle growers. Pinkley, who shared Mather's respect for Mormons, disagreed with Farrow's claim that local whites had exploited the Indians, and he felt that the stockmen possessed prior-use rights dating back to 1861—nearly forty years before the first Paiute herd. Farrow, who had originally opposed the monument, eventually gave in and signed the first in a series of agreements dividing the Pipe Spring waters. The document recognized that local cattlemen had "ownership" of one-third of the spring. The agreement further stipulated that if their grazing permits were not renewed by the tribe in 1928, the cattlemen's share of water could be diverted off the reservation.[14]

By the end of 1924, Mather held title to Pipe Spring and apparently had resolved the water rights question. However, he had no congressional appropriation for protection, much less development, of the monument, and he was paying the caretaker out of his own pocket. In 1926 he solved the last problem by hiring Charles Heaton's son Leonard for a dollar a month. During the same year, another change favored the Park Service when Farrow left Kaibab for Cedar City.

Leonard Heaton was twenty-four years old when he took control of Pipe Spring as caretaker and manager, a position that he would hold for the next thirty-seven years. He and his eighteen-year-old wife, Edna, accepted the position with the understanding that they could move into the old fort, and then operate a gas station and store in exchange for custodial work and greeting visitors. Heaton worked for a dollar a month until 1933. His family lived in the "castle" until 1936, and he had no full-time help until 1954. During those years he was a jack-of-all-trades: carpenter, plumber, electrician, irrigator, farmer, tour guide, administrator, historian, bird-watcher, ranger, auto mechanic. "Sept. 20, 1944," Heaton jotted in his diary. "Worked all day putting the transmission back into the truck one heck of a job [without] the right tools."

Heaton spent his free time crisscrossing southern Utah and the Strip in search of relics with which to refurbish the pillaged monument that he had inherited. After years of sheep corrals and stock-watering, the earth around the spring resembled a wallow, so Leonard Heaton planted grass, roses, a vegetable garden, willows, and poplar trees to make it a Mormon oasis once again, thereby placing a large demand on the water supply.[15]

Heaton had grown up with Indian playmates and considered them his friends, although he never learned more than a few words of their language. As park custodian he employed Ray Mose, a Paiute, for seven years; he also gave talks and published short articles on native history. Paiutes invited him to their funerals, at times even asking him to officiate. But Leonard was also the son of Charles Heaton, and Charles had sold Pipe Spring water for years to fifteen or twenty cattle outfits using the Strip, men whom Leonard knew and admired, men still entitled to their share of the spring. That placed a second, continuous demand on the water supply.[16] Given his loyalties and plans for the monument, meeting a third demand, that of an Indian "right" to more than the surplus, would not come easily for Leonard Heaton.

As soon as Leonard and Edna moved onto the monument in 1926, they planted trees and a garden, to which Heaton channeled water from the spring. When the BIA demanded the Indian share, Heaton talked about diversion systems but did nothing. His inaction had the tacit and at times explicit support of his superiors, Horace Albright and Frank Pinkley. The Park Service argued that Heaton, being paid only twelve dollars a year, needed the garden to survive. Furthermore, the Paiutes had no claim because the spring was on park land. Frank Pinkley, from his experience with Pima claims to the Gila River at Casa Grande, had vague knowledge of "a certain case in Montana" which, he felt, did not apply to Pipe Spring.[17]

Fort Belknap Indian Reservation in eastern Montana is over nine hundred miles north of the Kanab Plateau. Its Gros Ventres and Assiniboins differ from Paiutes in many ways but had one circumstance in common: arid land. When the federal government created the Fort Belknap reserve in 1888, its purpose was to transform nomadic plainsmen into farmers, yet most of the water in the Milk River that bordered the reserve had already been diverted by white settlers and cattle companies. In 1908, after a twenty-year struggle to regain a share of the water, the BIA, on behalf of the tribes in *Winters v. U.S.*, won the legal contest.

The U.S. Supreme Court ruled that although the 1888 agreement with the tribe did not mention water, access to it was a "reserved right" implicit in setting aside land for the purpose of making the Gros Ventre and Assiniboin "a pastoral and civilized people." Without irrigation, the court reasoned, arid land remained "practically valueless." Such a condition violated common sense as well as principles of Indian law; neither the government nor the Indians in 1888 could possibly have had such a worthless reservation in mind. In other words, the traditional western legal doctrine that guaranteed prior appropriation of water—the settler who comes first gets and keeps whatever he needs—did not apply in Indian country.[18] In regard to water, conditions on the Kaibab reservation were identical to those at Fort Belknap.

Frank "Boss" Pinkley specialized in preserving ancient ruins, not water law. He and others in the Park Service spoke of "some recollection" that a Montana case might give the Paiute a very strong claim, but the service did not seek a legal opinion until the crisis erupted in the 1930s. In regard to Pipe Spring, Pinkley conjectured that *Winters* applied only to rivers and flowing streams, not groundwater. Lack of traditional Paiute irrigation, the late creation of the reserve, and previous private ownership of the water source, in the opinion of Pinkley and Mather, would exempt the monument from sharing its water with Paiutes.[19]

Dr. E. A. Farrow, although he had left the reservation school, still served as Kaibab agent from Cedar City, and he continued to demand water. While Farrow was away during the summer of 1928, his wife had two guests from the East. One was Mary Vaux Walcott of the Board of Indian Commissioners, an advisory committee created by President Ulysses S. Grant in 1869. Accompanying her was John Collier, who, five years later, would begin his career as perhaps the most radical commissioner of Indian affairs in American history. In 1928 Collier already had the reputation of being a tough, zealous, and idealistic crusader for native rights. He had heard that the monument shorted Paiute water. If this proved true, he assured Farrow's wife, he planned to launch "a press campaign in Washington which would show up . . . the Park Service." By 1933 Collier would be exerting much more direct influence on Pipe Spring.[20]

Pushed by John Collier in 1929, the BIA in turn pressured the Park Service to develop water-sharing procedures. Albright, who had replaced Mather as director, stalled. In April of 1930, Indian Commissioner Charles Rhoads at first mildly protested the inaction, then Rhoads followed with a sterner letter, insisting that the dispute be resolved. Albright responded on June 21 with a bureaucratic shuffle. He asked park staff to meet with BIA officials in Arizona: "Perhaps some way can be found to let the Indians have more water although I do not [know] how the present situation can be changed to any extent." Albright referred the matter to Associate Director Cammerer, who referred it to George Moskey, an assistant director.[21]

In Arizona the arguments grew more emotional as Superintendent Pinkley defended Heaton's refusal to divert water. Pinkley contended that the water clause had been slipped into Harding's proclamation because the BIA knew it lacked any title to the land:

What prior use of the waters of Pipe Spring for irrigation on behalf of the Indians can the Indian Service show? . . . I know of no usage by modern Indians for irrigation. . . . If the Park Service were a private corporation owning that land I don't believe the Indian Service would have a leg to stand on in bringing suit to take the water over our boundaries and give it to the Indians. . . . The water being ours legally, like the roads and the stones and the trees and the houses, why should we have to state that we are going to use it and what use we are going to put it to? . . . [Farrow] is going to allow us to use enough water to supply the needs of only one family and he takes the remainder for the Indians! . . . If they can take the irrigation water after 40 years or so of use on the land, they will be back next year after the drinking water and tell us to catch rainwater for our Custodian! . . .

Why cripple ourselves by giving away the water which means so much to us and can be of no great benefit to them? They have never used it for irrigation, have worried along thus far without it, and what great need can they show which now makes the demand so serious?[22]

Leonard Heaton, Pinkley retorted, needed water for trees and for landscaping the monument, for sheep, geese, chickens, and for tourists. If the service somehow did decide to surrender water, Pinkley said that no ditches should be built or pipes installed, but Indians must come to the monument to receive their share. That would protect the greenery planted by Heaton "as part of the little oasis in the desert which we now have and [it] would keep the water right on our reservation where it belongs."[23]

During the next four years the BIA and NPS sparred over Pipe Spring. The Indian Office insisted on a share of the water while the Park Service either ignored the demands or found reasons for delay. In 1931 both parties requested a solicitor's opinion to settle matters. To the dismay of the NPS, the response ignored prior rights, concluding only that Leonard Heaton could not use any water for his family. Horace Albright then convinced the BIA to allow Heaton to draw water through the summer.[24]

By early 1933 NPS officials in Washington had given up. In January, Arno Cammerer told Heaton that blocking Indian access appeared hopeless. The next month, with his custodian still refusing to release water, Albright sent a telegram ordering Heaton to do so "immediately." Nothing happened. Perhaps hoping that a new commissioner of Indian affairs would be more flexible than Charles Rhoads, Albright again explained to the BIA that diverting the Indian share would reduce Pipe Spring to "a barren desert." To avoid that, he proposed another investigation by NPS and BIA hydraulic engineers. At this point, Horace Albright ran directly into John Collier.[25]

Collier had been Indian commissioner for less than a week, but his answer to Albright was unequivocal. A conference of engineers would only delay allocation of "all of the waters of these springs" to the Paiutes. The monument, he said, could retain enough water for stock and tourists, but, as Dr. Farrow had insisted, Indian subsistence was "of much greater importance" than trees and monument landscaping, however desirable. Albright, a lawyer, now faced a formidable adversary. Under the New Deal, time was no longer on his side, and within a few months Collier's staff had outlined its legal arguments for Paiute rights. Besides digging out the 1931 solicitor's opinion, Collier used the "all prior valid claims" language of Harding's proclamation to mean protection of an Indian prior water right "as of at least October 16, 1907." The stockmen's agreement of June 9, 1924, Collier pointed out, may have been approved by the NPS and BIA, but not officially by the secretary of the interior, and therefore it lacked legal status.[26]

Albright's telegram had left Leonard Heaton in despair. He argued that his father had had a bitter fight with E.A. Farrow after 1920 and had sold Pipe Spring to Mather in order only to protect water for cattle against Indian claims. Now the Park Service appeared ready to surrender its legitimate rights, and Farrow himself was at the monument driving cattle away from the ponds.[27] Even after receiving the telegram ordering compliance, Heaton told Farrow that trees and plants came before Indian needs and that everyone must stop acting on selfish motives.[28]

Under pressure, the NPS began to disagree internally. Frank Kittredge in the San Francisco regional office supported the Indian claim. An assistant superintendent at Zion, Thomas Parker, investigated Pipe Spring and reported that the root of the problem was a vicious feud between the Heaton family and Farrow, and that the Heatons had tricked the Park Service into taking their side of the quarrel. The monument itself had been turned into a barnyard for Leonard Heaton's "calves, sheep, chickens, ducks and geese. . . . I saw dead poultry, sheep pelts and litter all over the little meadow." Parker concluded that Pipe Spring "is a disgrace to our service," a condition, along with the Indian water dispute, that could be solved only by firing Heaton.[29]

Parker's memo evoked a response from "Boss" Pinkley. Apologizing for his rancor, Pinkley told Albright that Heaton had every reason to be angry with

Farrow for trying to steal family water and destroy a cattle business established sixty years earlier—"What would you do with [Farrow]? Kiss him?" Leonard Heaton might not be the perfect custodian, much of the monument certainly was ugly, "but until we get something besides cigar bands to use for money up there," nothing could be helped. As for water division, Thomas Parker had been swayed by Farrow and did not understand hydraulic systems. Parker also ignored Mather's promise to the Mormons as well as the needs of the Park Service: "I am sorry for Dr. Farrow's Indians, but if the President had wanted them to have 99 percent of the water of our spring . . . he had better have stated his intention. . . . They are welcome to 'surplus' water but they are not welcome to say how much water is surplus; some place in our organization we ought to have some engineers and landscapers who can do that for us."[30]

Pinkley's remonstrance was supported by a fifty-four page report from his assistant, Robert Rose. Besides putting forth arguments about legal jurisdiction, flow rates at the spring, Indian waste of water, alternative sources, and Heaton's stewardship, Rose introduced additional rationales for Park Service appropriation: future tourism, the purpose of the monument, and the NPS obligation to the Mormon Church.

The need for expanded tourist facilities, Rose correctly predicted, seemed inevitable. In accepting the site, the NPS also committed itself to restore the nineteenth-century setting: "Irrigated trees, orchards, gardens, and a meadow were all a part of the history of the Monument . . . as the Mormons once had things developed." Maintaining such conditions, Rose argued, was a historic trust, one that involved keeping faith with the LDS Church when it approved the transfer in 1923:

> Our Service should, it seems, remember that the Heads of the Mormon Church—not merely Heatons—are interested in the complete historical restoration of Winsor Castle and its setting of trees, orchards, meadows, and gardens. Mr. Mather's dream was to carry out this beautiful restoration. . . . To fall short . . . would mean breaking the faith of the whole Mormon Church in the National Park Service and Mr. Mather. We must realize the magnitude of this intense interest in the Pipe Spring. It is the whole Mormon Church and its leaders.[31]

In light of these considerations, Rose declared, no more than surplus water at Pipe Spring should be given to the Paiutes.

Rose and Pinkley could not prevail over John Collier. On November 2, 1933, ten years after Harding's proclamation, regulations "to be prescribed by the Secretary of the Interior" were officially published. In that document, cattlemen, the Paiutes, and the monument were each entitled to one-third of the water. Each party had to pay for installation and maintenance of meters at the spring head and at various outlets; delinquent payment resulted in no water. Each party had access to all records of water diversion. Finally, the regulations did not prejudice any other rights or claims.[32]

After years of wrangling, avoidance, and Park Service stalling, the earlier Mormon Church principle of defining an Indian right to one-third of Moccasin Spring flow had become official government policy at Pipe Spring. Whether the policy would be implemented, and whether the amount was sufficient, remained to be seen.

Water: 1934–1972

Leonard Heaton retained control of Pipe Spring for thirty years after Interior issued its water regulations. He and his wife, Edna, moved out of the fort and, with the Zion/Grand Canyon tourist route now bypassing the monument, they no longer operated a gas station to help support a family that eventually included ten children. As caretaker of a Mormon desert oasis, Heaton never stopped planting and watering trees. Forced to supply the tribe with water, he had few problems with the Paiutes. He collected their artifacts, took Indian school children on Easter outings, and entertained them at the monument. When the BIA school caught on fire in 1948, he helped fight the blaze, as he did another fire in the Indian village two years later. Paiute youngsters sometimes left graffiti on the fort, and they fished in the pools below the building—in 1946 they raided a meadow pond and escaped with every fish, "including the old carp I had here since the spring of 1926, weighing about 17 lbs and 30 inches long."

Much more troublesome than Paiutes was the Civilian Conservation Corps (CCC). They came during the Depression to help restore Pipe Spring, but did more damage to the monument than Indians ever had. Heaton disliked the military officer in charge, a commander who also issued cleanup orders to the park custodian, insisting "how the monument should look like a dance floor." The Army officer would not or could not control the "CCC boys," who shot birds, snakes, and lizards when they were not destroying cacti or catching fish in the ponds. They "kill for the pleasure of killing," Heaton recorded in his diary. By June of 1937 he had had enough: "DAM [sic] it I wish this camp would leave soon." "DAM [sic] IT" he repeated in his diary two months later, after "the boys" had defaced buildings, stolen relics, cut down more trees, and defecated in public areas. Fifty years later Leonard Heaton would recall the CCC years as among his most trying.[33]

The Conservation Corps required grass, trees, and, at the insistence of the commander, a swimming pool. Even more irritating than these demands on water was a squandering of the ten thousand gallons a day allocated to the CCC while some of Heaton's trees were dying: "I [did] all I could to keep them from wasting it, but they would not listen to me." In addition to the CCC, a drought on the Arizona Strip in 1936 brought additional cattlemen and the Wildlife Service to the spring. During the crisis, a dozen families living to the west also depended on Pipe Spring. These pressures led an NPS attorney in 1937 to argue that the service should protect itself legally by filing a water rights claim with the State of Arizona. The BIA successfully halted the process, but the proposal resurfaced during World War II as the Park Service saw a way to double its share of the spring. An NPS hydraulic engineer calculated that the seventy-six hundred gallons a day that the Paiute "wasted" might be appropriated for the monument because the BIA could not justify the one-third allocation. Nothing came of the effort, but throughout the negotiations it was again clear that Park Service engineers and attorneys had little understanding of the Winters Doctrine.[34]

During the 1950s, when the NPS made an inventory of Pipe Spring water in response to a lawsuit between Arizona and California over the Colorado River, the agency once more concluded that the Paiute did not need or use their third. In the mid-1960s, after Leonard Heaton had retired, the service also opposed efforts of other Heatons in Moccasin to claim a share of Pipe Spring. The Park Service, however, soon faced a more serious challenge.

Lyndon Johnson's "War on Poverty" programs provided financial support to encourage tribal business enterprise and to establish Indian Development Districts for Havasupai, Ute, Apache, Navajo, Makah, and many other Indian tribes. For the Paiutes, a $7,253,000 Indian Claims Commission (ICC) award in 1965, much of it set aside for tribal development, had already provided impetus to change. One day in mid-1969, NPS staff at Pipe Spring noticed survey crews staking reservation land across the road. The dismayed rangers soon learned that the Kaibab Paiute planned a large business complex that would include not only a tribal office building but also a motel with swimming pool, trailer court, gas station, curio shop, store, and museum. By 1969, increased tourism and more employees had sharply raised the Park Service's own water consumption. With the Paiute project scheduled to begin in 1970, its magnitude and the determined attitude of BIA officials convinced park staff that the tribe would use the Winters Doctrine to demand the entire spring flow.[35]

Negotiations in August and September "bought a little time," during which park historian Raymond Geerdes assembled extensive evidence to show that the NPS had a full and complete title to Pipe Spring that could be traced back to James M. Whitmore in 1863. That title, Geerdes reasoned, overrode *Winters* and placed the monument under the Arizona law of prior appropriation, which in turn meant that the NPS owned the entire spring flow. Geerdes did not, however, comprehend the power that *Winters* gave to Indians, and his argument did not prevail. This left the Park Service with a single option: to drill for more water. When tests proved successful, and after Paiute development plans faltered, the service began to negotiate another water-sharing agreement with the tribe. The new well was on Kaibab land, two miles north of the monument, which meant that the process was negotiated, not dictated.

It required nearly two years before the monument and tribe reached an agreement, in 1972. A new division of the waters at Pipe Spring obligated the NPS to construct and maintain a pumping station, treatment plant, and storage tank, plus a supply and metering system capable of providing the Paiutes with nearly eight million gallons of water a year for twenty-five years, renewable for another twenty-five years at the tribe's option. Any NPS water drawn from the well would be purchased from the tribe at $33 per acre foot. In exchange, the Park Service acquired the Paiute third of the original spring flow. The entire cost of the project fell to the NPS, which also agreed to transfer any surplus water from the monument into the tribal storage system. Cattlemen retained their share.[36]

That the tribe and BIA drove a hard bargain is obvious from comparing early NPS drafts with the final document. "The agreement," wrote Utah superintendent Karl Gilbert, "should not indicate that the Indians are *giving* us anything or that we are *selling* them water from their own reservation. Now is not the time to think of the NPS acquiring any additional water rights from the spring. This agreement is urgent; we can't mark time and still keep in good stead with the Paiutes. They want to move, and *will* move if we sit idly by."[37] Fifty years after Stephen Mather decided to buy Pipe Spring, the NPS finally understood the Winters Doctrine.

A Joint Venture

The 1972 water-sharing agreement at Pipe Spring has apparently succeeded. Efforts of the Reagan administration in the 1980s to recast western water law did not reach *Winters*, thus leaving the Paiutes in a strong position. The service, for its part, has touted Pipe Spring as a model of federal/tribal cooperation, one that "forged a lasting friendship" between government and Indians. In 1983, when the Kaibab-Paiute used in excess of nine million gallons, the monument superintendent asked them to desist but did not charge the tribe for extra water. The water-sharing contract was not renewed in April 1997, but Superintendent John Hiscock was confident that an agreement would be reached in early 1998. Meanwhile, the tribe and NPS have cooperated in improving the supply system and in building a new line to service tribal cattle.[38]

Despite the solution in 1972 of the water problem, Kaibab-Paiute remained one of America's most impoverished Indian reservations. In 1975 the annual family income was three thousand dollars, compared with fifteen thousand dollars nationally.[39] In 1990 the tribe alarmed the Park Service and citizens of Kanab and Fredonia by discussing construction of a hazardous waste incineration plant with Waste-Tech Services, a Colorado subsidiary of Amoco Oil. Kaibab's isolation, exemption from certain environmental laws, and access to water made the reservation an attractive site for toxic waste disposal. When the tribe terminated negotiations with Waste-Tech in 1991, the question of whether the 1972 NPS agreement covered industrial water use became moot. "Water resources have dictated what has happened here on the Arizona Strip for the last thousand years," observed monument superintendent Gary Hasty, "and it's still going on today."[40]

Another Paiute involvement with the Park Service began soon after the water agreement was reached. The NPS, needing offices and a modern visitor center, negotiated with the tribe to build a structure on reservation land immediately adjacent to the monument. The service provided architects and engineers; the tribe contributed funds, labor, and materials. When finished, the building would be shared, with the NPS renting half of it and the Paiutes operating a curio shop, cafe, and museum in the remaining space. The new building would complement a commercial tribal campground with interpretive trails built nearby. On paper the project looked ideal: The Park Service managed its monument and attracted tourists; the tribe prospered by selling goods, food, and campsites at the only services available for twenty miles.[41]

The venture failed. Today the NPS still leases half of the center for its purposes, but the gift shop and cafe are managed by the Zion Natural History Association. Instead of hiring native guides on the trails, tourists conduct themselves to sites after purchasing a two-dollar booklet, *Kaibab Paiute Educational Hiking Trails*. The campground, a half mile from the visitor center, commands a sweeping view of the Arizona Strip, from Mt. Trumbell to the Kaibab Plateau. The facility, which provided water, sewage disposal, and power to forty-eight RV sites, until recently was poorly advertised and haphazardly operated. A laundry, recreation room, office, showers, and toilets fell into disrepair and were randomly used by tribal members until the building was converted to a casino in 1994.

When asked about campground customers, a caretaker vaguely replied that business was "fair to middlin'." Tribal leaders accept responsibility for the failure: "Well, it's our fault in a way," reflected Chairwoman Gloria Bulletts Benson in 1991. "We built the camp and trailer park with the hopes that we were going to make money on it, and then the tribe just hasn't done our part. . . . We've had bad management people in there."[42]

A tribal museum at the visitor center was never constructed, while poor management, bickering, and undependable employees sabotaged the tribal coffee shop and gift sales. Eventually the monument superintendent convinced the tribe to lease its business to the natural history association. Visiting Pipe Spring before 1994, the average tourist would seldom meet or even see a Paiute. Within two years the casino had changed that, until the gambling hall closed in 1996. The building is now being used for natural resources management.[43]

Mormons and Paiutes

In 1933 the Utah Pioneer Trails Association and Citizens of Kanab Stake offered to donate a bronze plaque for Pipe Spring. The proposed text began: "Occupied in 1863 by Dr. James M. Whitmore, who, with Robert McIntyre was killed four miles south east of here January 8, 1866 by Navajo and Paiute Indians. The Washington County Militia recovered their bodies and seven Indians were killed."

When the NPS in Washington and Frank Pinkley at Casa Grande reviewed the original design and wording, someone in the Park Service removed the last sentence, but left the story of Whitmore's and McIntyre's murder as a rationale for celebrating the fort as "a frontier refuge from Indians." Following an

Protectors of Pipe Spring meet at the monument's gate in 1928. Left to right: Heber Grant, LDS bishop; Stephen Mather, NPS; Carl Grey, president of the Union Pacific; U.S. Senator William King (Utah); Harry Chandler, publisher of the *Los Angeles Times;* and Jonathan(?) Heaton, previous owner of the spring. (National Park Service photograph, courtesy of Harpers Ferry Center, Charles Town, W. Va.)

autumn ceremony, the bronze marker was installed at Winsor Castle, where it remains today.

In 1992, interpretive and cultural questions at Pipe Spring have replaced the dispute between Mormons and Indians over water. LDS members at Kanab, Moccasin, and Colorado City believe that the monument should reflect their history on the Strip because it is their monument. They have solid reasons for their possessiveness. Mormons have lived on or near the site for 130 years. It was their church, not the government, that allocated to Indians one-third of the water thirty years before the NPS and BIA signed the 1933 contract. The LDS and its members helped Mather purchase Pipe Spring in 1923; without the support of Mormon president Heber Grant, the deal would have collapsed. Leonard Heaton, whose parents sold the spring, worked there for the NPS for thirty-seven years at a miserable salary. His care and labor restored the castle, garden, trees, and ponds, as they are seen today.

For half a century, the NPS at Pipe Spring honored Mormon history to the near exclusion of other values. A 1954 master plan unequivocally asserted what was significant at the monument: "The story is primarily historic, with geology and biology secondary." Nineteenth-century agriculture, the master plan announced, should be demonstrated to visitors, with Indian culture "presented briefly." Conflict with Navajo and Paiutes, it was said, took place "despite the Mormon policy of friendship." In this 1954 document, Pipe Spring existed primarily as a monument to Manifest Destiny:

> [It is] dedicated to memorialize the early Mormon pioneers and their struggle to maintain an outpost for the exploration, colonization and development of this part of the great Southwest. The spirit of these pioneers, their courage, vigor, persistence and faith, lives in the old stone fort, and its furnishings. Here, in the Arizona Strip, the visitor may understand the home life, the agriculture, and the measures to defend their homes and families which were common to all pioneers who took part in the Westward movement. . . . [Pipe Spring] is a concrete reminder epitomizing the development of a great state by a courageous people. In a measure, the history of Pipe Spring is the tale of the ideals, the sufferings, the ambitions and the perseverance of a determined band of men and women who sought religious and economic freedom in an inhospitable land and who won out against great odds. Pipe Spring may well interpret the story of Utah and the fighting spirit of the Mormon pioneers.[44]

Park Service sympathy for Mormons and local cattlemen continued into the 1960s and 1970s as the Kaibab Paiute planned economic projects. Park historian Raymond Geerdes stressed that Mormon stock growers had a legal right to one-third of the spring flow. Honoring past agreements with the cattlemen could, Geerdes urged, provide the NPS with strong support against Indian claims: "[Mormons] are our strongest allies. . . . Their rights are but a lien or obligation against ours. They are and will be our staunch friendly allies. . . . As the only National Park Service area directly related to Mormon History and the Mormon Frontier the L.D.S. Church has and retains a vital interest and as such is our friend and ally."[45]

Modern Paiutes do not accept this interpretation of history and their place in it. Despite growing up with local whites, to Indians the community at Moccasin is "Mormon Moccasin" and it lies "behind the Zion Curtain." Kaibab Paiutes tell stories of whites in Kanab offering bounties for Indian scalps as late as 1903. The volunteer guides and interpreters at the monument, in the tribe's view, have been "Mormon ladies" whose mission was to evangelize tourists. All park superintendents, the Kaibab say, have supported the Mormons, until the appointment of Gary Hasty in 1989. The original purpose of Winsor Castle, they say, was to protect polygamists from the U.S. government, not from Indian attack. According to the late Ralph Castro, grandson of Powell's guide, Chuarumpeak, visitors to Pipe Spring heard a one-sided, sugar-coated story and saw a distorted picture that Castro tried to correct:

> When I was giving talks over there, I told [visitors], here at the park we've got three different versions, which one do you want to hear? We've got the Park Service version, we've got the Mormon version, and we've got the Indian version. And you know, I'd get those people riled up by telling the Indian version of it. . . . And in 1923 [a settler] told Watermelon Jake that they were holding an election on whether to do away with the remainder of the Indians. It was to wipe them all out over the water. And if he rode through on his black horse they would take the women and children and head for the hills. But if he rode through on his grey horse it would be safe to stay. . . .
>
> Well, to the victor belong the spoils, they can make their own history. Mormons say, "We were friends to the Indians and we were the only ones who paid them to work," and stuff like that. This is their version. What actually happened is two different things. . . . And I used to tell them, "Well, our history says that the settlers weren't exactly the up and up people that you claim. So whose version are you going by? They say, "Well, our church tells us this and that." And I say, "Well, I'm sorry ma'am, but our version is different than yours."[46]

After 1980, and especially after the arrival of Hasty, who had worked at Canyon de Chelly, the Park Service sought to expand the scope of interpretation at the monument, a goal that causes some resentment in Moccasin. Hasty and his chief ranger, Mary Davis, saw the spring as a national, not local, resource, and they believed that the interpretation should be much broader than its history since 1863, or even since Paiute occupation. An Anasazi ruin lies buried beneath park maintenance sheds on the NPS/Kaibab boundary. Its excavation, Hasty feels, would balance and enlarge the monument's interpretation of the Arizona Strip by giving the fort a full historical context.

As for the Paiutes, Indians still work on the grounds crew, their history now recognized in visitor center displays, although the 1990 tourist pamphlet tells only the story of cattle and cowboys threatened by Navajo "marauders." The gift shop sells a selection of native crafts, together with many books on Indian culture and history.

These innovations go far beyond Harding's proclamation of 1923, which called for Pipe Spring "to serve as a memorial of western pioneer life." Such changes, as Gary Hasty realized, evoke strong emotions: "This site, you know, for forty acres generates a lot of intense feelings from everyone. We're dealing with church history, issues of polygamy. That's one whole area of concern. There are conflicts between Paiute and Navajo; Paiute, Navajo and Anglo, there's another whole story. Grazing on the Arizona Strip, on public lands. John Wesley Powell, that's another whole issue. So we are venturing into uncharted waters."[47]

A monument asking visitors to confront such questions may not be a soothing oasis, but it will better serve the purposes of history. If the Park Service can expand its message to include the 110-year struggle between Indians and Mormons over water in an arid land, a visitor's view of the human condition may become more complex and thus more relevant. The story on the Arizona Strip involves not only Indians and cattlemen but also ethical differences between a church hierarchy that urged humane policies and the lay people who sought new lands. Pipe Spring presently celebrates Mormon conquest of the Plateau Province, but it could celebrate the Mormon conscience as well, a conscience that has led LDS historians to condemn as "vengeful and wanton" the lynching of five Paiutes accused of Whitmore's murder.[48] That same conscience spoke clearly in Brigham Young's Indian policy: "This is the land they and their fathers have walked over and called their own," he wrote in 1864,

> and they have just as good a right to call it theirs today as any people have to call any land their own. They have buried their fathers and mothers and children here; this is their home and we have taken possession of it and occupy the land where they used to hunt. But now their game is gone and they are left to starve. It is our duty to feed them. The Lord has given us ability to cultivate the ground and reap bountiful harvests; we have an abundance for ourselves and for the stranger. It is our duty to feed these poor ignorant Indians. We are living on their possessions and at their homes.[49]

Placing a bronze tablet with those words next to the present plaque, which tells of Whitmore's murder, would give all who visit Pipe Spring National Monument pause for thought.

6

"A GREAT PLEASURE GROUND FOR THE NATION"

My heart is not bad but I do not wish to leave all my land. I am
willing you should have half, but I want the other half myself.
You know my country, I want part for my villages. It is very
good. I want the places where the stream comes in.

—Ke-bach-sat (Makah), Treaty Council, 1855

[Olympic Park . . .] conceived in controversy, born of
compromise, and developed amidst constant conflict.

—Congressman Don Bonker, House Hearings, 1976

One morning in March of 1982 Gregory Hicks and Steven Shale, both Quinault Indians, slipped into Olympic National Park. In violation of federal regulations, they began to hunt in the Queets River valley. Hicks and Shale were
later arrested for killing three elk. In court their attorney argued that the
Quinault through an 1855 treaty with the federal government had retained a
right to hunt on any traditional land that remained "open and unclaimed." After
a lower court agreed, an appeals court at first concurred, then, under public
pressure, reversed itself and upheld Park Service regulations. The ultimate
conviction of Hicks and Shale muted the shock that had spread through the
NPS and the environmental community after the Indians' initial acquittal. An
irony missed in most reports of the case was that ranger Clay Butler, the
investigating officer, was also a Quinault.

The elk kill, more than any previous event, awoke Olympic National Park
officials to a fact of life: They were surrounded by Indian tribes. A new political

reality also dawned: Tribal members no longer would act like wards of the BIA, nor would they necessarily obey laws protecting the park passed by their own tribal councils. If, in the past, Olympic National Park had largely been unconcerned about the Indians living on its borders, after the 1982 hunting incident that was no longer possible. Ten years later, Olympic's seventy-year unofficial policy of ignoring its tribal neighbors had changed to one of recognition and interaction.

Mesa Verde, Organ Pipe, Glacier, the Badlands, and many other parks share a common border with a single tribe. Some, like Navajo National Monument, Canyon de Chelly, Pipe Spring, and Custer Battlefield, lie totally inside a reservation. At the other extreme, Canadian bands at Pacific Rim and the Havasupai at Grand Canyon have been completely surrounded by a park. But the most complex arrangement involves parks surrounded by many separate Indian groups, as is also true at the Grand Canyon. Olympic, with eleven reservations nearby, falls into the last category. These reservations—the Makah, Ozette, Lower Elwha, Skokomish, Jamestown Klallam, Quileute, Quinault, Hoh, Port Madison, Port Gamble, Squaxin Island—vary in location, size, wealth, population, language, interest in the park, and political power. No single park policy can possibly meet all circumstances.

Geography contributes to disparate tribal interests. The Olympic Peninsula, forming the northwest corner of Washington state, is nearly sixty miles across its southern base and ninety miles wide, east to west along the Strait of Juan de Fuca on the north. The peninsula has one hundred miles of Pacific Ocean beach to the west, while Hood Canal and Puget Sound separate it from Tacoma, Seattle, and Everett to the east. No road crosses the rugged interior, with glaciated alpine peaks rising to nearly eight thousand feet. Out of a confusion of jagged ridges, rivers flow in every direction through deep valleys. What are considered lowlands may include "hills" rising to four thousand feet.

Annual rainfall at higher elevations can reach 200 inches; below, on the western slopes, it is normally 140 inches. Such abundant moisture in a temperate climate produced one of the few northern conifer rain forests in the world, with seemingly inexhaustible stands of western red cedar, yellow cedar, Sitka spruce, silver fir, western hemlock, and Douglas fir. Rich in trees, the peninsula was also rich in fish and wild animals: salmon, razor and butter clams, crab, rock oysters, mussels, bald eagle, marmot, otter, bobcat, cougar, wolf, black bear, mink, deer, cormorant, kingfisher, pelican, loon, sandpiper, heron, steelhead trout, chinook and coho, halibut, cod, and smelt. Sea mammals included

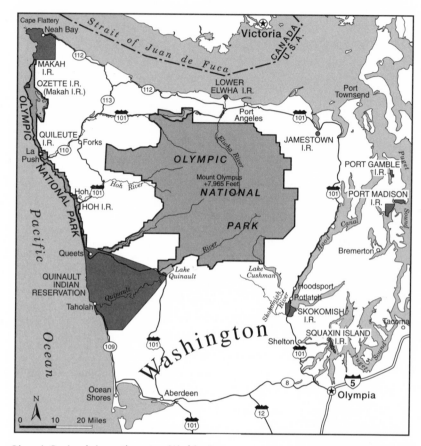

Olympic Peninsula in northwestern Washington.

porpoise, orcas, harbor seals and sea lions, and gray, humpback, and sperm whales. On land, the dominant creature in the Olympics and a prime motive for federal protection of the area was the Roosevelt elk, a beautiful, fast, and powerful large deer that can weigh up to half a ton.[1]

Such an environment seemed bountiful to the native people who lived on the coast, the strait, or Hood Canal before 1850, usually along rivers or at their outlets. Moving around the peninsula clockwise, beginning at Grays Harbor in the southwest corner, were tribal or band groups now consolidated on reservations: the Quinault, Queets, Hoh, Makah, Klallam, Chimacum, Twana, Skokomish, Chehalis, and Cowlitz. Although speaking three different languages, they all shared cedar and salmon as the material basis for society. A technological achievement, the canoe, provided primary transportation on salt water, but, contrary to what whites believed, Indians also lived inland, miles from the sea, and traveled through the interior mountains. Prior to European contact, bands gathered in small villages scattered along the rivers or on ocean beaches. Speakers of the Wakashan, Coast Salish, and Chimacum languages lived at winter and summer sites that lacked any common tribal government to unify the different groups. They engaged in warfare, practiced the potlatch and spirit dance, and held slaves as property. According to ethnologists, their social order, ceremonies, and technical ability reveal a "highly imaginative and skillful people."[2]

The Spanish arrived on the Northwest Coast in the 1770s, followed by British and American traders during the next fifty years. Permanent white settlement inland on Puget Sound and as far west as Gray's Harbor started in the 1840s and 1850s, well in advance of official conveyance of Indian title. Territorial governor Isaac I. Stevens successfully negotiated federal treaties in 1855, treaties that ceded most of the peninsula, established reservations, and set a pattern of tribal-land holding that persists to the present day. Once opened, the Olympic Peninsula's "green gold" of trees soon created a logging frenzy among whites that still continues. As elsewhere, traditional native culture changed rapidly because of loss of land, population, and resources, and through the influence of new towns at Hoquium, Aberdeen, Port Angeles, and Shelton.

Less than forty years following the first white settlement, it became apparent to conservationists that logging and hunting could destroy the entire peninsula as it had existed prior to 1850. Learning from woodland disasters in New England and the upper Midwest, Congress passed the Forest Reserve Act of 1891. This provided the initial basis for a long, complicated, and bitter controversy over protecting Olympic timber. The effort resulted in a national park by 1938, a development that did not please everyone or end disputes over how to use rain forests.

The first proponent of a national park in the Olympics was Judge James Wickersham of Tacoma. During the summer of 1890, Wickersham and his family hiked up the Skokomish River for twenty days, exploring a southeastern corner of the peninsula. His account of the trip is so skewed and inaccurate that one doubts he ever visited the places claimed. But whatever the source of his knowledge, Wickersham reported that "we climbed mountains, waded torrents, slept above clouds, and, for the last seven days, lived on water and flour cakes." He knew that no national park existed west of the Missouri River or north of California, and here was the perfect place for one:

The forests are being felled, and destroyed, the game slaughtered, the very mountains washed away, and the beauties of nature destroyed or fenced for private gain. The beauty of Switzerland's glaciers is celebrated, yet the Olympics contain dozens of them, easy of approach. . . . A national park should be established on the public domain at the headwaters of the rivers, centering in these mountains. . . . It would include . . . the headwaters of all its rivers, the glaciers, Olympus, Constance, the snowfields, mountain meadows, grand canyons, and the homes of the last remaining elk, deer, and bear. It should include Lakes Cushman, Quinault, and Crescent.[3]

Sharing the sentiments of his contemporary John Muir and of modern preservationists, Wickersham feared that wanton killing of Roosevelt elk would cause their extinction; unlike early park officials elsewhere, he valued cougars and wildcats as well as bear, elk, and beaver. Above all, he believed that the ancient stands of fir, spruce, and cedar must be preserved:

The heaviest forest growth in North America lies within the limits of this region, untouched by fire or ax, and far enough from tidewater that its reservation by the government could not possibly cripple private enterprise in the new state, and by all means it should be reserved for future use. The reservation of this area as a national park will thus serve the twofold purpose of a great pleasure ground for the Nation and be a means of securing and protecting the finest forests in America.[4]

Like George Bird Grinnell, James Wickersham was a collector of native artifacts, an amateur ethnologist, and a self-proclaimed "friend of the Indian." On the other hand, at the time of his Olympic expedition he was striving as a Tacoma lawyer and booster to open the Puyallup reservation to white settlement. He sought to discredit an honest BIA agent, Edwin Eells; he lobbied Congress on behalf of land speculators; and he manipulated leases of Indian land for the benefit of his white clients. As for the Olympics, Wickersham felt that native removal would be unnecessary because Indians were frightened by legends of spirits back in the mountains and of cannibalism by savage gods—thus they stayed near the water and never penetrated the interior.[5]

Wickersham would live to see the mountains preserved, but the actual park status he favored remained fifty years in the future. The amount of federally protected land between 1891 and 1938 would fluctuate between the 2.1 million acres set aside by Grover Cleveland in 1897 to less than a fifth that amount. William McKinley eliminated 700,000 acres in the lowlands, the timber destined for private speculators who cut 20,000-acre tracts at a time. Such logging practices, along with the reduction of the elk population from many thousands to about 500 by 1903, led to proposals in 1904 for a 400,000-acre "Elk National Park." After that effort failed, Theodore Roosevelt used the Antiquities Act to create Olympic National Monument in 1909. Its 600,000 acres were reduced in 1915 when Woodrow Wilson excluded most timber lands.

Subsequent battles over elevating the monument into a park involved lowland virgin timber and acquisition of ocean beaches. After 1897 the dominating concerns over a national park that 85 percent of the local population would oppose by 1934 were timber jobs and profits, tourism, park boundaries, game protection, federal spending, mining, drilling, and relations with white inholders. Manganese, elk, and oil gained more attention than did native rights.[6]

In September of 1937, Franklin D. Roosevelt visited the Olympic Peninsula and proposed that Congress create a park twice the size of the existing monument. The personal visit of a popular president failed to convert most park opponents. The *Daily Olympian* called his legislation the "Nation's Biggest Lockup," a sentiment echoed by the *Port Angeles Evening News* in "Ickes's Big Grab." Pickets at the state capitol carried signs comparing Secretary of the Interior Harold Ickes to Hitler and Stalin: "This Isn't Russia!"

Even though Indian treaty rights would be explicitly protected in the park's enabling legislation, at no point in these protests or the political process were tribes consulted or their interests openly discussed, except for one comment by Roosevelt during his tour around the peninsula. Roosevelt disliked clear-cuts on Quinault land and recommended that the remaining uncut tribal timber be included in the park. The Park Service, in response to pressure from Ickes to add tribal forests, feared that a possible controversy over "unjust discrimination" against Indians would jeopardize passage of the Olympic bill. The service recommended putting the matter on hold. Two months after passage of the legislation, the NPS reported that tribal timberland would be impossible to acquire.[7]

Olympic National Park as it exists today contains over 900,000 acres (1,500 square miles), close to the size that Wickersham proposed in 1890. Most of the park consists of mountains in the peninsula's northern and central interior. Three narrow western extensions run through Bogachiel, Queets, and Quinault valleys but do not reach the ocean. Over 600,000 acres on the immediate perimeter of the park, including five wilderness areas, remain under the Forest Service. Olympic also boasts a special jewel, the 52-mile stretch of primitive ocean beach and headlands extending from the Quinault reservation on the south to Makah Indian land on the north. If one considers tribal beaches safe from roads and development, virtually the entire Olympic coast is now protected. Designation as a World Park is well deserved.

Through the BIA, Indian tribes around Olympic control 350 square miles, which is about 10 percent of all federal land and less than one-third the amount of land held by timber companies. Of tribal lands, 90 percent belong to the Quinaults. Each reservation has its own problems and history of relations with the Park Service, making it easier to understand the entire picture if we visit particular tribes.

Although the Park Service in the past did very little to inform visitors—or itself—about Olympic's Indian history, anyone traveling "the Loop" of Highway 101 will observe a ubiquitous native heritage in names of rivers and places: Wynoochee, Satsop, Wishkah, Skokomish, Twana, Sequim, Pysht, Ozette, Oyhut, Calawah, Kalaloch, Moclips, Tshletshy, Copalis, Humptulips, Hoquium, Cloquallium. Our travel begins in the southeast corner at Skokomish, moving north, west, and then south along the ocean coast.

Skokomish

Hood Canal, natural and not man-made, veers southwest for fifty miles off the Strait of Juan de Fuca before it abruptly hooks back to the northeast for another twenty miles. The Skokomish Indian Reservation occupies the south shore of the sharp bend in the canal, with the Skokomish River swinging in a semicircle around the five-thousand-acre reserve before emptying into the bay. Much of the land is tideflat. The small town of Hoodsport straddles Highway 101 just north of the reservation.

Indians here descend from the Twana and Skokomish bands who once occupied the entire length of Hood Canal.[8] The Skokomish, like the small bands at Squaxin Island, Port Gamble, Port Madison, and Jamestown, possess no common border with the national park. Their grievances in the past have been with Tacoma City Light, which appropriated part of their land to build Cushman Dam in 1926, flooding traditional grounds and crippling fish runs. Today the tribe is mainly concerned with reacquiring land and with their right to gather shellfish on private beaches, a potentially explosive issue that will not affect the park. Occasionally rangers have suspected Indians of poaching elk, but no more so than other local residents.

A recent point of contention, however, is a proposed land exchange between Tacoma City Light and the NPS to accommodate flooding thirty-five acres within the park. Nearly twenty miles distant from the reservation, the proposed land exchange contains a Skokomish ritual bathing site, a fact liable to change under City Light or private ownership.

The Skokomish believe that, prior to redrawing boundaries, City Light, the NPS, and the tribe need to discuss fish runs, archaeological sites, stream beds, and water release from the dam. Feeling ignored and fearful that the Park Service will capitulate to City Light and local landowners, the tribe claims the issues are linked. According to council member Joseph Pavel, powerful interests have "put heat on the park" by convincing Congressman Norm Dicks to support their side. City Light and the recreationalists are like cowboys who have "culled a steer out of the herd" on national park lands and now seek to "pick it off." The tribe, Pavel says, is simply "not as loud" when it comes to manipulating the Park Service. His tribal attorney agrees, viewing the service as reluctant to support a Skokomish role in negotiating the land trade.

The legal status of Cushman Dam further complicates matters. Like the Elwha River dams, Cushman falls under the licensing authority of the Federal Energy Regulatory Commission (FERC). Since 1978, FERC has granted City Light only annual renewals, pending a decision about the dam's environmental and social impact. The tribe intervened in this process; the park did not. The Skokomish argue for tying the license renewal to the land exchange, a position the Park Service initially resisted. Under pressure, park officials finally have agreed that "the issue of connectiveness is valid."[9]

Such a response from the Park Service would not have happened a decade ago. At Skokomish, as elsewhere, Olympic National Park is slowly beginning to establish relations and forge alliances with Indian communities that share its interests.

Port Angeles

Zigzagging north from Hoodsport to Port Angeles, Highway 101 follows Hood Canal. Every five or ten miles one crosses a stream draining the Olympic Mountains' eastern flank: the Lilliwaup, Hamma Hamma, Duckabush, Dosewallips, Quilcene. After reaching Discovery Bay the road rises before turning west to drop toward Sequim Bay, where traffic becomes heavy in a booming urban area that was isolated and quiet thirty years ago.

The Jamestown Klallam's new tribal facility at the head of Sequim Bay sits just off the highway. Highly independent beneficiaries of a federal experiment in self-determination, this band of two hundred members has few relations with Olympic Park. In 1991 they joined the Port Gamble S'Klallam (thirty miles east), the Skokomish, and the Lower Elwha Klallam to protest against logging practices that they thought threatened the Dosewallips elk herd.

Having canceled their own hunting season and feeling betrayed by the Forest Service, the Washington Wildlife Commission, a timber corporation, and the state's Department of Natural Resources, the small bands sought support from the Park Service. The service agreed with the Klallam that only a cooperative management program could save the elk in question, a small herd that annually migrated from the park's higher elevations down the Dosewallips River to winter forage where clear-cuts now exposed the elk to hunters and severe weather. The Klallam enlisted Olympic's superintendent, Maureen Finnerty, in their behalf, and in Port Angeles park officials now use the Dosewallips elk management problem as an example of new, more positive relations with Indians. The tribes, they believe, have approached the NPS because the service and Indians share similar attitudes toward wildlife habitat. "They've been very agreeable," one ranger commented. "We've been meeting them more than halfway. . . . It's a good sign."[10]

Twenty miles west of Jamestown the park's Port Angeles headquarters sits on a hillside overlooking the city, with the Canadian city of Victoria directly across the Strait of Juan de Fuca. In 1944 Thomas Aldwell, a successful businessman who had settled in Port Angeles in the 1890s, gave the NPS thirty-eight acres within the city limits. A secluded trail through a stand of second-growth timber connects offices and shops with the park visitor center, the setting and structures being one of the service's nicer administrative complexes. A highway leads directly from the center into the hills, passing a campground and rising to sixty-four hundred feet on the edge of Hurricane Ridge, the only panoramic view of the Olympics reachable by auto.

In 1994 the visitor center contained a dugout canoe donated by the Makahs, with a brief description of its construction and use. An attractive display provided directions to the Makah Tribal Museum at Neah Bay. No other tribes were mentioned. The only gift shop book on native culture was Hillary Stewart's *Looking at Indian Art of the Northwest Coast*—the clerk had not heard of books about Quinault and Quileute tribal history. A brochure mentioned the Quinault, Quileute, and Hoh reservations, but the Makah, Skokomish, Lower Elwha, and Jamestown were missing. The brochure's text, after referring to ocean village sites, observed that "by any standard the Indians of the Olympic Peninsula lived a sophisticated, well-ordered life" before Europeans arrived.

At the Olympic visitor center, Indians and their park history no longer remain completely invisible, but the amount of cultural information, in keeping with the park's philosophy of minimal interpretation, is scant. After completing our circuit of Olympic's reservations, we shall return to Port Angeles to discuss that policy.

Elwha

The route to Lower Elwha leaves Highway 101 five miles west of Port Angeles at the Neah Bay junction, jogs north around farmland section lines, then breaks over a forested hilltop to curve sharply downward onto the Elwha River floodplain. The reservation occupies 450 acres between Freshwater Bay to the west and Ediz Hook to the east. A tribal center faces north toward the strait and Vancouver Island. South of the reserve, the Elwha River valley cuts through Olympic foothills, the peninsula's only view from the seashore into remote interior ranges. During early morning or dusk, alpine peaks framed by valley walls resemble a Bierstadt painting. In this spectacular setting the reservation appears isolated, peaceful, and quiet despite its proximity to the seventeen thousand people in Port Angeles.

The several hundred Klallam Indians of Lower Elwha have had a variety of experiences with the Park Service. Convinced that the park occupies their homeland, some would like entrance fees waived. An Olympic anthropologist has worked with elders; a few members unofficially hunt elk on park land, and still others would like to see the forests logged to provide local jobs. Jerry Charles, former tribal chairman and lifelong resident of the reserve, considers himself an Indian first and a U.S. citizen second—"The United States made me a citizen; I was born an Indian"—but he shares an outlook held by many local whites toward the park and its regulations: "They have so many laws. You can't take a dog out in the park anymore. You can't horseback ride anymore. You can't do this, you can't do that. The taxpayers get very upset about that. Something's going to happen, one of these times."

Jerry Charles, who claims that Indians make no distinction between the park

and any other land, expresses views that would not endear him to preservationists: "Another thing is the timber. I logged a lot, you know, and the timber
resource is just rotting away, the bugs are eating it up. They should selectively
log *some* of that stuff, because it's just going to waste, it really is."[11]

Charles concedes the tribe was partly to blame for "a real bad lack of communication" with the Park Service during his tenure as chairman, but he adds
that the agency showed little interest in the Klallam. Attitudes seemed to
change with a new tribal government and the new park superintendent, Maureen Finnerty, as both parties sought common ground on employment, wildlife
habitat, and removal of the Elwha River dams.

In his late fifties, Jerry Charles could recall only a few Klallam ever working
for the Park Service, and those mostly as seasonals and firefighters, with perhaps a permanent employee at Quilcene. During 1991 the tribe and Olympic
met specifically to discuss the problem. In August the Park Service signed a five-
year job training contract similar in philosophy to one at Pukaskwa National
Park in Canada. The program aimed at attracting and preparing Klallam, Hoh,
and Quileutes for careers with the service.[12] By the end of the year the tribe was
also calling on Olympic to sponsor a 1993 "Paddle to Bella Bella." Details
included possible carving demonstrations at the visitor center, use of NPS heavy
equipment, and the salvage of cedar trees to make dugout canoes. Even more
important than these details was the attitude of a new tribal government:

> The intrinsic value of the park and the tribe working together on the
> [canoe] project is unique. The tribe is indigenous to this area. The park is
> entrusted with preserving the park in its natural state for the enjoyment
> of future generations. The tribe is in the process of preserving its unique
> culture for future generations. . . . This can be a "win-win" project. There
> will be national and international publicity for the project. The USFS
> gained excellent PR for its assistance with the Quileute tribe for the
> "Paddle to Seattle." The [Klallam] would benefit with any assistance from
> the park. . . . That both the tribe and the park are a part of the Depart-
> ment of the Interior makes this a natural. . . . All involved will have the
> satisfaction of working together. . . . We eagerly await to hear from you.[13]

New jobs and the trip to Bella Bella notwithstanding, the crucial matter at
Lower Elwha has always been fish. The Klallam belong to the Point No Point
treaty group. Along with other Washington tribes, under the 1974 "Boldt Decision" they are entitled to one-half of all the salmon entering the Strait of Juan de

Fuca. An abundance of fish had once supported precontact cultures and, in the case of Indians along the strait, continued to do so for sixty years after white settlement. Key to accessible and ample fish for the Klallam was the Elwha River, which flowed straight, flat, and due north from deep inside the mountains, dropping twenty-one hundred feet without a major waterfall for seventy-five miles. The river ranked as one of the world's ideal anadromous fish runs until 1913, when a hydro-electric dam was built five miles from the mouth. Fourteen years later a dam eight miles upstream at Glines Canyon on Forest Service land blocked the river a second time.

The dams represented another kind of dream. Thomas T. Aldwell had settled at Port Angeles in 1890 and by 1910 had become a successful booster of the northern peninsula. He foresaw that attracting a paper mill could permanently buttress the local economy, but this required cheap power to complement the supply of water and trees needed for producing pulp. Aligning eastern capital and working in secret to acquire the dam site by purchasing individual land claims, Aldwell's diligence paid off with the Elwha dam in 1913. By 1950 Crown Zellerbach, the corporation that used the dam, had a payroll of over $3 million for 620 mill workers and another 190 men in the woods.

Aldwell seemed oblivious to Indians who lived on the river and totally unconcerned about the salmon, whose existence depended upon the stream. He had also ignored an 1890 Washington law that required fish escapement at dams such as his.[14] The free-flowing Elwha had supported annual runs of 250,000 to 500,000 fish: cutthroat trout, Dolly Varden, coho, sturgeon, steelhead, sockeye, pink salmon. Some chinook reached one hundred pounds or more. In the years after 1913, Indians and whites watched the migrating fish die in great masses at the base of Aldwell's dam.

A local cannery protested to no avail against the Elwha dam. For a state that would celebrate the Grand Coulee dam even though that structure made no provision for salmon or for the Colville Indians who depended upon them, for a state that joined with the federal government to flood a huge Indian fishery at Celilo Falls, and a state that by 1980 had virtually destroyed one of the world's greatest fish habitats, the Columbia River—in such a jurisdiction breaking a law to block the small, remote Elwha River and cripple the Klallam seemed a small price for progress.

After Olympic Park was created in 1938, its managers found that they had inherited Glines Canyon dam and a 415-acre reservoir called Lake Mills. They discovered a similar situation a few miles outside the park at Elwha dam and

Lake Aldwell. Even if it had so wished, an unpopular Park Service in the 1940s would not have risked public wrath by questioning dams. In 1952, Washington Department of Fisheries researchers reported that the Elwha dam had ignored state law and harmed a magnificent migratory run.[15] By the 1970s it had become clear that the great fishery was nearly extinguished. "Time Is Running Out for Beautiful Chinook of the Elwha," a *Seattle Times* headline announced, and the *Daily Olympian* in the state capitol reported "Much Wampum to Make Elwha Great Again." A Chinook-rearing channel and a tribal hatchery on the reservation had not solved the problem. Furthermore, by the seventies informed public opinion knew that removing fish from a river affected much else, from eagles and bears to aquatic microorganisms.

Matters came to a head in 1976. The fifty-year license for the Glines Canyon Dam expired, and two years later a judge ruled that Elwha Dam, too, required federal permission to exist. By this time the Crown Zellerbach Corporation owned both sites, giving the dams powerful legal advocacy in government and the courts. A compromise process began, with FERC issuing annual licenses pending adequate mitigation of environmental damage. Crown Zellerbach eventually sold its Port Angeles holdings to James River Corporation, which in turn sold the paper mill to Daishowa America while retaining the dams.[16]

As had occurred elsewhere with Indian tribes, the 1960s and 1970s saw the Lower Elwha Klallam begin to organize politically. For decades after 1913 they had watched the fish runs dwindle, knowing why but feeling resigned and powerless. Then in 1976 the Army Corps of Engineers refused to build a dike to protect a housing project being constructed on the reservation by the Department of Housing and Urban Development. The Corps considered the fifty- and sixty-five-year-old earth-fill/concrete dams upriver to be unsafe. As the tribe investigated, it learned that the structures had affected far more than fish and wildlife. Changes in the natural tidal flows of the river, groundwater salinity, shellfish and beach conditions, river sedimentation, and land accretion on Ediz Hook—all could be traced to the dams. And if a dam should collapse, that would bring death and destruction to the reservation. The tribe also claimed that Klallam ancestors had run fish camps far up the river, a river that had played "an essential role in the subsistence, economic, and cultural life of [our] tribe."[17]

In the late 1970s the tribe addressed these problems by negotiating with Crown Zellerbach for fish ladders and spillage control. Jerry Charles remembers meeting with Crown Z to figure out some program on the flooding: "It was very hard to work with them at first because they were in the paper business and we talked fisheries. We met and met and met trying to get a fish ladder. We asked them if they'd build a fish ladder, but it never went anywhere because they said 'We're in the paper business, not the fish business.' One year we got very close, then I stepped down and nothing came of it." Sometimes, according to Charles, Crown Zellerbach opened all seven gates at once, killing fish runs below the dam and destroying Indian nets. "My feelings were that Crown Z didn't care, at that time. They do now, but I don't know if they will ever do anything. We learned to live with it. We fought tooth and nail. My job was to work with these people and try to work out the best [deal]. . . . Energy versus fish, or energy versus whatever [laughs]—that's a tough battle to fight."

The paper company did agree to inform the tribe in advance about spills. An early warning system was installed, giving the Klallam seven minutes to evacuate if the Elwha dam burst. Jerry Charles, who does not live on the flood plain, doubts that the dam will fail—"I don't think that sucker will ever go." His meetings with the Park Service on the dams proved even more fruitless than those with Crown Zellerbach: "Nothing really came of it. We just talked."[18]

Charles's son Rodney is more militant than his father. He fears the lower dam will break but knows his people will not move whatever the danger. Rod Charles believes that, without the dams, large native fish stock would return in place of the small hatchery "paper fish." To him, the Park Service resembles the BIA: "Big words, then we never see them again."

Leaders in recent Lower Elwha governments seem to agree with Rodney Charles that "we should knock the dams out and take our chances with the river." By the mid-1980s the tribe requested license denial and removal of the dams. Having previously formed alliances with environmental groups in opposition to an oil port in Port Angeles, the Indians now joined forces with the Sierra Club, Friends of the Earth, Friends of the Elwha, Seattle Audubon Society, the National Parks and Conservation Association, the Olympic Rivers Council, and the Northwest Rivers Council in a campaign to "free the Elwha." Dam mitigation or removal likewise gave the tribe common ground with Trout Unlimited and local sportsmen's organizations. Olympic Park Associates, which in its 1968 Wilderness Plan for the park had ignored the dams, now supported the crusade.[19]

In 1989 the Klallam passed a resolution stating their case against the dams and calling for a study of river restoration:

WHEREAS, the Elwha River is the principle economic and cultural resource of the Elwha Reservation; and . . .

WHEREAS, the two dams comprising that hydropower project have virtually destroyed the anadromous fishery which the Tribe had reserved by treaty and which constitutes the reservation's most valuable economic resource; and

WHEREAS, the lower dam . . . has been considered unsafe with the result that the Tribe . . . lost on-reservation housing, a flood control project, and economic development . . . and

WHEREAS, both dams block downstream passage of sediments needed to maintain the beaches of the reservation with the result that the Tribe's land base is eroded away; and

WHEREAS, the Tribe has been subsidizing the "cheap" power generated by the dams . . . and . . .

WHEREAS, phased dam removal . . . is a reasonable alternative . . .

BE IT RESOLVED, the Lower Elwha Klallam Tribe considers dam removal to be the alternative most likely to serve the best interests of both the Tribe and the larger community in the Port Angeles area, but recognizes the need for a thorough and impartial study evaluating both the risks and benefits of removal . . . and

BE IT FINALLY RESOLVED, the Tribe directs its officers [and] staff attorneys . . . to take appropriate actions without delay.[20]

In a struggle that could become a precedent for two hundred older power dams facing license renewal,[21] the Lower Elwha Indians see the park as their greatest asset and the Park Service as an important ally. Unlike other fish runs harmed by dams, the river above Glines Canyon flows in pristine condition for over sixty miles from its headwaters. Tribal leaders recognize that the park is crucial in this, and they also say that the Park Service shares their values about nature and protecting habitat.

As with other controversial issues, such as timber protection or the removal of exotic mountain goats, Olympic National Park reacted cautiously to dam complaints. "The driving management imperative in Olympic National Park," writes critic Carsten Lien, "is avoidance of conflict." The service backed away from supporting possible legislation proposed by U.S. Senator Daniel Evans. Although he wanted the dams taken out, Evans dropped his proposal.[22]

By 1986, the park, now buttressed with more scientific reports that spoke of "decimated" and "destroyed" anadromous fish runs, admitted that the dams had done severe damage to the river system. It also recognized Lower Elwha treaty rights and opposition to relicensing. The service called for more research and monitoring but halted short of endorsing dam removal. Although restoration of Elwha salmon constituted "a critical issue and priority for Olympic National Park," Superintendent Robert Chandler asked Congress to authorize FERC to license the dams for another ten years. Fish habitat renewal, he claimed, "can be accomplished with modifications to the existing dams":

> We are concerned that dam removal at this time could jeopardize the remnant wild stocks of salmon and steelhead in the Lower Elwha River which are essential as broodstock. Although the Glines Canyon Dam is an intrusion in Olympic National Park, it has stabilized and Lake Mills has provided . . . recreational opportunities since the park was established. If we are successful in establishing anadromy in the upper watershed with the dams in place, it may be more desirable to retain the projects. . . . A ten-year period would provide more frequent opportunities to evaluate the fish restoration programs.[23]

Internally, the Park Service seemed confused. Assistant regional director William Briggle acknowledged that the dams affected the fish and caused flooding but insisted they were important in supplying power and water to Port Angeles. He pointed out that both dams had been built prior to the park, that they did not conflict with any Park Service mandate, and that to remove them for environmental reasons would alarm industry: "They're there and that's it." Olympic headquarters in Port Angeles took essentially the same position. Conceding that the dams blocked fish runs, it agreed with the tribe on the goal of restoring native salmon stock but found the idea of removal impractical and disruptive to an ecology that had evolved since 1913. Pressed on whether Glines Canyon dam inside the park might ever be dismantled, Assistant Superintendent Don Jackson replied in 1987 that "if Crown Z wants a dam there, the dams will stay there."[24]

Three years later Olympic changed its position to favor removal and intervened in the FERC process to oppose relicensing. Pressure from environmentalists and the Lower Elwha tribe, a change of superintendent, the park's own studies showing the difficulty of artificial enhancement, and support from the

USFWS, the BIA, the General Accounting Office (GAO), the National Marine Fisheries Service, and Congressman Bruce Vento of the House Interior Committee convinced the park to recommend "termination and removal" of both dams "as the only alternative which will accomplish full fish restoration."

In taking this position, Olympic had bolted ahead of Interior. Secretary Manual Lujan's office rebuked the Park Service for going "way outside of channels. . . . Everybody's running around doing their own thing." A year later, however, when it appeared FERC would license the dams, Interior itself contested the agency's jurisdiction over dams located in national parks.[25] Even with Olympic and the Lower Elwha Klallam lined up on the same side, dam removal crept slowly ahead but remained uncertain. As local Congressman Al Swift once pointed out, extreme demands causing years of litigation will probably doom the fish and cost millions. Swift, whose support was a key element, refused to endorse demolition until funds are available to address the consequences.

The problems are complex: Who will buy James River's title? What will replace the power to Daishowa America? Who will provide Elwha water to ITT-Rayonier, Daishowa, and local communities? Pending removal, who will operate the dams? How many persons will lose jobs? Who will own a drained Lake Aldwell? Who will restore the lake beds, and how? How will natural flooding affect Indians on the flood plain? Should "paper fish" be planted in the river? Which agencies will manage the fishery? Can the national park and the Klallam cooperate if their goals and needs differ? At present, neither the tribe nor the Park Service will speculate on the answers to these questions.

Given America's resource history, the prospect of removing two hydroelectric dams for the benefit of Indians and fish seemed remote indeed, yet Congress passed a 1992 Elwha Restoration Act for which the Clinton administration supported full funding at over $110 million. Al Swift's resignation in 1994 and the advent of a conservative Congress made the appropriation doubtful. In 1997, however, Senator Slade Gorton cautiously began to favor removal. If someday a remarkable precedent is set at Lower Elwha, the accidental juxtaposition of Olympic National Park and the Klallam tribe will be largely responsible.

Neah Bay

Over a century ago it required three days for James Swan to paddle from the Elwha River to Neah Bay. Today by auto, whether one follows the twisting route along the strait or leaves 101 at Sappho to cross a low pass to Clallam Bay, the trip requires less than three hours. Swan's sea journey risked storms but the scenery was splendid, whether in sunshine or through clouds and mist common to this northwestern tip of the United States, where annual rainfall averages 105 inches.

We continue west from Clallam Bay through clear-cuts, a condition that does not end when one enters the Makah Indian Reservation and its only town, Neah Bay. In the 1920s the tribe signed a long-term timber contract with Crown Zellerbach; more recently, 60 percent of the twenty-seven-thousand-acre reservation has been cut again through a bidding process. Even Cape Flattery and its two humps, Archawat and Bahokus, are presently barren.[26] Even so, the tribe occupies ancestral land on a cape that ranks high among the prime pieces of real estate in North America.

Most of the twelve hundred tribal members live in Neah Bay, a small port town that has had Air Force and Coast Guard stations, a few stores and cafes, a motel, commercial fish wholesalers, a log dump, and marinas and sport fishing outfitters. For centuries the Makah were expert seafarers who relied on halibut more than salmon and who hunted whales by canoe in the open sea. Besides having a different native language and being related to the Nootkas of Vancouver Island, Makahs are distinct from other peninsula Indians in various ways. Living on their actual homeland, the people are almost all Makah in background, not members of various consolidated tribes and bands lumped together by the government during the nineteenth century. This history, and relative isolation in the twentieth century, have sustained an intense attachment to land and sea—the Strait, Cape Flattery, Neah Bay, Ozette, and Makah Bay.[27]

For thirty years after Theodore Roosevelt created Olympic National Monument, the Makah had no common border with the park. After NPS acquisition of the ocean strip in 1940, the service and tribe found themselves in close proximity. The new addition extended north to the Point of Arches, separated from the reservation by Shi Shi Beach, and it encircled but did not include the Ozette Indian Reservation located at Cape Alava six miles below the Makah southern border.

Since 1940, the Makah Indians and the Park Service have enjoyed generally amicable relations, with almost all of their interaction centering around Ozette. Both sought to acquire the deserted reservation, a contest that the tribe won by defeating environmentalists in 1970. The Makah and Olympic cooperated extensively and positively on the Ozette archaeological excavation, one of the more significant discoveries of the twentieth century. Park and tribe worked closely together to combat a major oil spill in 1990. The next year, when a possible conflict arose over acquiring Shi Shi Beach, desired by both parties, the history of good relations permitted the service to add this final northern seashore to its fifty-mile ocean strip without Indian resistance or litigation.

"The Makah? I love 'em," said a park administrator in the Seattle regional office. The feeling is shared in Port Angeles, where Olympic officials respect Neah Bay leaders. Park staff describe current relations as excellent, a model of how the NPS and a tribe should relate. No one recalls any harsh reactions against Olympic's 1976 and 1986 expansion, which took one hundred coastal islands in Makah traditional territory. Sometimes administrators feel the tribe considers the service to be "an old milk cow" to be squeezed for money, but they understand why.

Attitudes at Neah Bay reciprocate. Tribal attorney Alvin Ziontz described the service over the years as accommodating and understanding. He admitted that the agency has its own mandate: Indians and rangers "live in two different worlds." Makah leaders praise the Park Service, claiming that if they had to choose between dealing with the park, county, state, Forest Service, or private developers, they would always choose the NPS because it has been more open-minded and shares many of their goals, especially protection of old growth forests. They recognize that since 1980 the NPS, like the tribe, has suffered severe budget cuts, making it impossible to fund joint projects such as Ozette archaeology and the tribal museum. Nonetheless, "we still try to help each other."

A museum curator praised the park for sending tourists to Neah Bay, not just out of Port Angeles but from around the peninsula. Tribal council members recall no disputes and report no complaints over hunting or other matters. The council appreciated a visit by Superintendent Maureen Finnerty, but said that most Makahs "don't even think about the Park Service." Like other Indians on the Olympic Peninsula, the Makah make a sharp distinction between the Park Service and "the environmentalists."

This may paint too rosy a picture. In August 1963, a dispute did arise when a ranger confiscated a rifle and then burned down an Indian smokehouse and canning structure on parkland at the mouth of Ozette River. The equipment belonged to Makah vice-chairman David Parker. Parker's tribal council responded by protesting the action as a violation of the 1855 treaty.[28] In June of 1964, after Indians had erected another smokehouse, the Park Service acknowledged the treaty rights, then drafted regulations that allowed for seasonal structures, prohibited cutting of trees, banned firearms, and required prompt disposal of litter. A year later the structure still stood and the tribal council, ignoring the NPS, had referred the proposed policy to Alvin Ziontz.[29]

This conflict between the Makah and Olympic originated in two unresolved questions. The first concerned the terms of the 1855 treaty, in particular whether the words "open and unclaimed land" meant national park lands, the major issue in the Quinault hunting case. The other question was whether the Makahs owned the Ozette Reservation.

Before white contact, the Makah lived in five principal villages near Cape Flattery, one of which was Hosett (Ozette). They also had seasonal fishing, hunting, and sealing sites along the coast as far south as Cape Johnson. Out of ignorance and haste, in 1855 Isaac Stevens included none of the five main villages in the reservation. In 1873 Ulysses S. Grant enlarged the reserve, but Ozette once more was excluded, even though Makahs continued to live there. President Grover Cleveland corrected that oversight on April 12, 1893, through an order establishing an "Ozette Reservation" at Cape Alava.[30] From that action, the belief developed among whites that an "Ozette Tribe" existed.

When the government forced "Ozettes" to send their children to school in Neah Bay, most of the families moved north. Eventually only one "Ozette," Elliot Anderson, retained title to the southern tract. Because Anderson had no heirs, it became apparent that Ozette would someday become an Indian reservation without Indians. Preston Macy, future superintendent of Olympic, foresaw this in 1937 and urged the Park Service to acquire Cape Alava before Queets Indians claimed allotments there. "The greater part of the area embraces the Ozette Indian Reservation," he informed his superior, "which at this time has but one living indian [sic] with allotment rights. The one indian does not live on the reservation. His name is Elliott Anderson, and he is getting well along in years so will perhaps not last a great many years." Macy described petroglyphs and a marriage ceremonial site, as well as many artifacts:

Just to the right of Ozette Island is another small island which may be reached on foot at low tide. The island was a favorite burial ground. . . . I walked across to this old burial ground and found that every visible grave had been robbed of its treasure, which was the indians only guarantee of happiness in his Happy Hunting Ground. Not only were the trinkets gone, but also the bones. I understand there are some burial grounds which have been unmolested, and I truly hope so. Above the beach out of reach of any high tide is the remains of an old tribal community house. . . .

The Indian Reservation would make a very valuable Monument if the Department of Interior could arrange for its preservation through purchase of the only [allotment] rights now established. Every effort should be made to prevent establishment of other rights on the Reservation.[31]

The next year, following Olympic's designation as a national park, one of Seattle's leading conservationists, Irving Clark, warned that "it would be sheer folly to permit the destruction of [Ozette's] virgin forest," and he urged Harold Ickes to add the Indian lands as well as Lake Ozette to the park before loggers removed the Sitka spruce.[32]

The tribal council in Neah Bay was well aware that others had eyes on Ozette. In a resolution passed on February 24, 1941, calling for transfer of title to the Makah, the tribe claimed that they needed the land for homes, that they had fishing rights to the Ozette River, and that they recognized the commercial value of the timber. The Park Service responded by asking Ickes to take "some speedy action" to add the reservation to Olympic. A BIA attorney then advised Interior that Ozette belonged to the Makah, which led John Collier to inform Arthur Demaray that the legal status did not "necessarily rule [out] the acquisition of this reservation by the Park, but I suggest that if handled cooperatively by your service and ours, [placing] the Ozettes back on the reservation might create an attraction and interest from the Park's standpoint." Two days after Pearl Harbor, faced with the legal opinion, the Makah claims, and treaty rights to the river, the service dropped the Ozette addition and instead offered to assist the BIA "in its efforts to improve the economy of the Indians concerned."[33]

World War II postponed development of the Olympic Strip. By 1946 Elliott Anderson was in Tacoma's Cushman Indian Hospital. Celestine Hopkins, a BIA forester, visited Anderson and tried to buy the 719 acres at Ozette for the Makahs. He found that "Elliott's sentimental attachment to this land of his is very great and it is difficult for him to look upon its sale with clear realism." Realism for Hopkins meant five dollars per acre plus $16,000 for the timber, whereas Anderson wanted $100 an acre. Hopkins pointed out that when Anderson died the land might go to the Park Service instead of his own people, but the elderly Indian did not acquiesce.[34]

In 1953, following transfer of the ocean beaches to Olympic, the NPS considered acquiring Hoh, Quileute, and Ozette lands, "reservations no longer needed as such." The plan evoked a bitter attack from a local justice of the peace and foe of park expansion, Lena Fletcher of Forks. The BIA and Park Service, she wrote to Secretary of the Interior Douglas McKay, "have now embarked in a plan of still further extending the Olympic Park by a plan where the Indian Service proposed to sell at least two and possibly three of the smaller reservations."

> This is being done over the protests of the Indians involved who would thereby lose *all* the cultivatable lands, most of their fishing rights and be restricted to a few lots. This land is being logged since the Park Service did not have money to pay for the timber. The rich river bottom will probably be sold for only a few dollars per acre. This will leave the next generation of Indians without homes or a chance on the reservations that were kept for their fathers. . . . I have been informed that these older Indians were swindled into signing away their treaty rights. Since they were illiterate that must have been easy.

The NPS dropped its proposal.[35]

When Elliott Anderson died in the late 1940s, the Makah realized they would need to prove the land was theirs by heritage. They hired an attorney and marshalled anthropologists Herbert Taylor and Erna Gunther to argue that "Ozette Indians" never existed, and that only Makah Indians had lived at Ozette village. Gunther pointed out that village members had signed the 1855 Neah Bay Treaty and that Stevens in fact had designated an Indian from Ozette as the Makah head chief. "Furthermore," she asserted, "the myth that Elliott Anderson was the last of the Ozettes is ridiculous."[36]

Ozette nevertheless remained in limbo for another decade. With the beginning of the archaeological project in the mid-1960s, ownership took on even more importance for both tribe and park. By 1968 the Makah had hired Alvin Ziontz, one of the state's most skilled lawyers. Clallam County and Congressman Lloyd Meeds joined their cause. Ziontz wrote a persuasive brief and Meeds introduced a bill in the House. The Park Service and Interior now conceded Makah title but still sought control over the land to protect the coastal strip. In the House hearings, Meeds, a former county prosecutor, demolished Assistant Secretary of the Interior Harrison Loesch under cross-examination. Meeds then made an argument that Congress found difficult to dismiss:

I feel very deeply that the property in question is in fact, in justice, and in equity the property of the Makahs. . . . There is no question of its great beauty. There is no question but that valuable artifacts have been uncovered. . . . Nor should its location in relation to the Olympic National Park be minimized. . . . But above this I am concerned with people's rights. . . . We have far too few chances to correct the mistakes and inequities which mark the history of our dealings with the American Indian. Let us not detract from this opportunity to do full justice.

Congress passed the bill on October 22, 1970, and Richard Nixon signed Public Law 91-489. The Makah had regained Ozette.[37]

Years later Lloyd Meeds recalled Ozette as his first serious "big fight" with environmentalists, the strongest opposition to H.R.9311 having come from a private organization committed to wilderness preservation, the Olympic Park Associates (OPA). A brief analysis of this organization's tactics and its reaction to defeat illustrates how tension and bitterness over park issues can develop between Indian tribes and doctrinaire environmentalists.

In 1968 the OPA, knowing of the Makah demands, urged transferring Ozette to Olympic National Park. The group thought that an on-site cultural exhibit might be permitted, but opposed auto access because "an indian cultural center surrounded by car parking" would be "most inappropriate."[38] The associates believed that Meeds and Ziontz were railroading the Ozette bill through Congress without full debate and thereby ignoring legal opinions in 1956 and 1969 that the Makahs and Ozettes were separate peoples—and hence the former possessed no interest in the land. The OPA pointed to a provision in the 1893 executive order that provided for reversion of vacant Indian land to the government.

Noting that the Quinault and Lummi tribes had closed their beaches to non-Indians, the environmental group grew alarmed about public access to Cape Alava. They worried even more that Indians might log the land, establish a settlement at Ozette, and pursue other uses "inconsistent with the natural beauty of the region and its surroundings." OPA wanted ironclad guarantees against residential and commercial development. "If you could see the town of Neah Bay," wrote the group's vice president, "you would understand what I mean."[39]

At a meeting with Ziontz, the OPA obtained a statement of limitations on use but found unacceptable the loopholes that the attorney built into it. The Associate board of directors, anticipating defeat in Congress yet in no mood to compromise, drafted a rider to the Meeds bill. This provided for "permanent and perpetual" public access to the beach and along the Ozette River; it banned roads, airstrips, commercial leasing, logging, buildings, and any structures "inconsistent with a national park."[40] The proposal irked the tribe, which in 1955 had already set aside part of the reservation as a roadless area.[41] A meeting between the OPA and the Makahs grew acrimonious after conservationists expressed fear that Ozette might become another Neah Bay. Associate leader Polly Dyer tried to win Indian support by saying how much she loved and cherished Ozette, but Alvin Ziontz later recalled that "she really chilled the Makahs—it was like telling a man you love his wife."[42]

The OPA's power rested in its having the ear of Senator Henry Jackson, which prompted the tribe to draft its own rider to the bill. This resolution declared their intent to preserve the area while allowing for hunting and for Makah residence. All visitors would be welcome, but no commercial uses inconsistent with native use or "the natural beauty of the area" were permitted.[43] Even though the OPA rider was not attached to Meeds's bill, over twenty years later Makahs still recall environmentalist opposition to the return of Ozette.

So does Carsten Lien of the Olympic Park Associates. Although he concedes that the Makah have honored their pledge thus far, Lien claims that three years after the legislation passed they denied having made any such commitment. For Lien, Ozette was "a major oversight" in the 1938 bill that created Olympic, and it remains a potential trouble spot in the park. Two decades after the fight, he maintains that Elliott Anderson was the sole rightful owner of the reservation, and he is still angry with Lloyd Meeds, "whose part-Indian heritage proved stronger than his ties to preservation."

Even more, Lien blames Park Service waffling. The NPS could have taken Ozette "many times . . . but lacked determination and any internal push." When the park supported Ozette exclusion from wilderness classification in 1988, environmentalists, according to Lien, reacted with dismay and fear: "The future of the Ocean Strip remains perilously in doubt." Just as a president of the Seattle Mountaineers had referred to the Makah in 1958 as "a tiny special interest group" who threatened Olympic National Park, in 1991 Carsten Lien continued to express the same negative view of the tribe.[44]

Lloyd Meeds, on the other hand, remains proud of having secured the land for the Makahs. He believed at the time that the tribe would protect the environment without the government's imposing restrictions that "smack of the worst kind of paternalism." In 1969 he told his colleagues that they had an "opportunity to do full justice." Twenty-two years later Meeds used these exact same words to justify his legislation.

Two other events demonstrate the friendly relations between the Makah and Olympic: cooperation on a major archaeological excavation at Ozette, and the park's acquisition of Shi Shi Beach.

Makah oral tradition indicated the earlier existence of a large village at Ozette. Soon after 1938 the park began receiving letters from Charlie Keller, a white resident in the area who told of Ozette's archaeological wealth. Although the abandoned reservation had become thick with undergrowth after the elimination of the elk and the emigration of the Indians, Keller could see that, around the lake, along the river, and above the beach between Sandy Point and Cape Alava, the area once had supported a considerable native population. He also realized that artifacts needed protection. Years before the NPS added "cultural resource management" to its vocabulary, Charlie Keller had realized that it was essential:

> One of the chief attractions of this bit of country is the chance of seeing the Indians in their Native habitat, and in seeing them at their primitive occupations—principally fishing. And it occurs to me that a very complete collection of articles used in the ancient trades, arts and amusements would be a very valuable and essential part of your planned development here. . . .
>
> These articles of ancient manufacture and those that link the present with the past, are disappearing at an alarming rate. Many thru the lack of proper care, some destroyed by accident, some being purchased and removed to far places by private collectors.[45]

Following World War II, archaeologists at Ozette discovered a site buried beneath a mudslide centuries earlier, a calamity that had resulted in the near-perfect preservation of more relics than Charlie Keller could have imagined. Although the site was first tested in 1955, excavation by Professor Richard Daugherty of Washington State University did not begin until 1966, just as the Makahs began to press hard for ownership of Ozette. Daugherty calculated that the site had been continuously occupied for two thousand years; the mudslide happened 550 years ago, encasing tools and wooden implements while in actual use. Over the next eleven years Daugherty and his crews uncovered fifty-five thousand artifacts, forty thousand building pieces, and over a million animal remains. In addition to the university, the BIA, the Makah tribe, and the National Science Foundation, the Park Service also supported the dig, contributing $2.3 million to this project in a decade.

Because the site was on the land of Indians—Indians with an attorney—the tribe's right to the artifacts could not be glossed over. Part of the Ozette land settlement in 1970 was an understanding that the National Park Service and the Makahs would cooperate in creating an Ozette Cultural Park. In 1978, a year after Daugherty closed the excavation, the tribe received funding that allowed it to build a museum and research center at Neah Bay. Plans for a public facility at Ozette continued, the tribe and Park Service reaching a joint management agreement in October 1979. Ziontz, however, was raising jurisdictional questions based on the 1970 Makah resolution, and the tribe also worried that cultural displays at Ozette would compete for Neah Bay tourists. The council then voided a joint agreement signed only a few months earlier. In Port Angeles, Superintendent Roger Contor graciously and wisely did not contest the default.[46]

Contor had good reason not to protest the abrupt, unilateral cancellation of a joint program that Olympic had funded for ten years. The park was in the process of acquiring Shi Shi, a pristine sand beach north of Point of Arches and adjacent to the Neah Bay Reservation. Not only could the Makah make a case for owning the land, they controlled the best access to the beach as well as the best parking areas.

The NPS obtained the beach and, in retrospect, tribal members seem content with the decision. They would like the beach as tribal land yet are pleased that the Park Service finally took control to prevent possible development by the state.[47] The service, with the aid of tribal police, evicted "squatters" and "potheads" in a "hippy colony" that had made Shi Shi a nudist beach the Makah considered unsafe for their children. Tribal members remain grateful to the NPS for "cleaning it up."[48]

Olympic Park had gained the beach, but, except for a difficult ten-mile hike from Ozette, the only access was through Neah Bay and across Makah land. After 1983 the park considered but did not pursue options for better southern access. By 1990 over seven thousand hikers visited the beach annually. Thus when the tribe closed the road and trail in 1991, the press interpreted the action as an economic and political tactic comparable to the Quinault beach closure twenty years earlier. Actually it was the BIA, not the Makah, that officially closed access because no right-of-way existed across nine allotments en route, creating potential liability for landowners. Although the Park Service wanted the trail reopened as soon as possible, a sentiment shared by the Makahs, Olympic's superintendent supported the tribe's reasons for the closure.[49]

La Push

Park contacts with the Quileute Indians of La Push, thirty miles south of Ozette, have been less cordial than those with the Makah. Quileutes still resent the Stevens treaty that reserved only 640 acres out of their aboriginal 900-square-mile homeland. In the 1930s tribal leaders such as William Penn worked through the Queets Olympic Club to oppose creation of a national park.[50] As the park expanded after 1938, according to tribal historian Deanna Penn, Quileutes lost traditional lands, campsites, and homesteads along the beaches and in the mountains. She sees the Park Service as rigid, aggressive, and unapproachable.

Penn seems mild compared with the late David Forlines, a non-Indian raised in a native foster home and a resident of La Push, where he led a revival of traditional culture. Forlines, an expert craftsman, organized the Quileute "Paddle to Seattle" and worked as a counselor at the village school. Shortly before his death, we talked with David on a bright, windy April morning as he carved a thirty-two-foot dugout racing canoe. Behind him grey whales blew and breeched in the bay, the ocean blue with white breakers. At one point a siren wailed and men rushed along the beach to their nets—the smelt had arrived.

Forlines, who often referred to himself as being Indian and as "working for [his] people," hit his chisel for emphasis as he spoke of park administrators being mean, arrogant, negative, and ignorant. Park land as such is valuable, he said, but the Park Service is a "Gestapo" and collection of "penal colonizers" plotting to control the entire Olympic Peninsula, including every town and reservation. The NPS is a huge hand, fingers extended and spreading over the peninsula; from time to time the hand closes, grabbing land, then re-extending its fingers to grasp more. The NPS, in Forlines's opinion, had enforced absurd rules and restrictions on Indians, regulations having nothing to do with human survival or nature. It did so because the government plans to develop Olympic into a World Park for foreigners at the expense of local people, including the tribes.

Federal bureaucrats, Forlines said, wanted to destroy the village of La Push, which it had trapped against the ocean like the Quileutes themselves, who were barely hanging onto an edge of the continent. The native way of life—"freedom and self-sufficiency"—contrasted with NPS control, oppression, and "enforced dependency." In his opinion, the Quileute once owned the entire Olympic Peninsula. Even other tribes do not belong here, with the Quinaults being very late arrivals and the Makahs not coming until the 1840s. Like Deanna Penn, he claimed that the Quileute had always been opposed to the park.[51]

Compared with the Makah, the Quileutes have been especially difficult for park staff. Tribal elections often negated progress made with a previous council. During the mid-1980s, officials in Port Angeles especially resented an outside consultant named Sherwin Broadhead. With Broadhead present, meetings became emotional as the tribe used impossible demands as a negotiating tactic. "He's not an Indian and not a lawyer, despite his posturing," was the Port Angeles view of Broadhead. More recently, park officials have been pleased with the leadership of Chris Morganroth, a Quileute whose grandfather was chief ranger at Olympic National Monument. Morganroth, they feel, is a reasonable person who shares the service's values. For his part, Morganroth describes recent superintendents as cooperative and willing to listen. The tribe, he says, has no animosity toward the NPS, although the park "needs to do a lot more" in educating visitors about Quileute laws on privacy, beach use, clam digging, and trespass.[52]

La Push takes its name from a corruption of the French for "the mouth" of the Quillayute River. A confluence of the Solduc ("sparkling water"), Calawah ("middle"), and Bogachiel ("muddy") Rivers near the logging town of Forks creates the Quillayute River, which, as it enters the ocean, separates the village from the park. On the north bank, the NPS operates Mora campground, where sixty thousand people a year visit Rialto Beach. On the south side, four hundred Quileutes live in a reservation fishing village encircled by the park. Before contact, the Quileutes had traveled inland as well as seaward. They had thirty-two place names for Bogachiel River sites and one for the Blue Glacier, fifty miles east on Mt. Olympus. Of all Olympic peoples, they were the furthest from white settlement; culture change through logging and tourism came late.[53]

For years the NPS and the tribe have had disputes over hunting, law enforcement, firearms, power transmission lines, net fishing in the river, tribal closure of the Quillayute to sportsmen, vandalism, and, once, the confiscation of a bow and arrow. In 1980, when the Quileute sponsored an urban Indian youth camp on Toleak Point inside the park, rangers angered David Forlines by enforcing NPS rules. It did not help matters when a teenager killed a deer, then reported his feat with bow and arrow in an Indian newsletter. On the positive side, the park was "really cooperative" when La Push faced a serious water shortage.

Olympic also helped transport cedar logs for building the "Paddle to Seattle" canoes in 1988. Chris Morganroth credits the park with promoting tourism at La Push. He contends that the tribe retains treaty hunting rights inside the park but elects not to exercise them. Today the Quileute encounter no problems when they notify the service that they plan to use Toleak Point for spiritual training and for teaching children.[54]

An unresolved dispute between the Quileute and Park Service involves their boundary. In 1968 Indians argued that park boundaries had been misdrawn; eight years later the tribe finally recovered 220 acres. Following another study, the Quileute in 1980 claimed that the natural mouth of the river originally had been further north before it shifted south in 1910 as a result of a wrecked ship in the channel. If true, this meant that 10 acres on the park side belonged to the tribe. The NPS, accused of being "without shame on this issue," reacted negatively. The Quileute also claimed 200 acres on the opposite (south) side of the river, as well as 1,400 acres that included more than a mile of ocean beach from Quateata Point to the Jefferson County line. The debate fizzled off and on during the 1980s, the park saying that Congress must decide.[55] In December 1989, a Quileute delegation met in Washington, D.C., with park director Ridenour, who promised to investigate.

The park faced three problems with the new Quileute claims: (1) the service did not want to lose Mora campground and Rialto Beach; (2) they wanted a continuous Olympic strip; and (3) they opposed total Quileute control of the river. Chris Morganroth says he realizes the boundary error was an honest mistake in 1953 and that the tribe supported the ocean strip expansion to avoid a state highway through their land. He will compromise by surrendering Rialto and the northern ten acres if the Quileute can acquire southern land adjacent to the reservation.

As at Ozette, the Olympic Park Associates spoke out against Indian claims. "We would oppose anybody, I don't care who it is," an OPA member told the press. Carsten Lien in a radio interview described the Quileute desire for more parkland as an "outrageous move fueled by greed." In 1993 the tribe kept a low profile as it continued to negotiate with Olympic.[56]

Hoh River

The 120 Indians living at the mouth of the next major drainage south of La Push, the Hoh River, are a Quileute subgroup. Part of their one-square-mile reservation on the south bank of the Hoh lies in the ocean, and part has been eroded by current and surf. The band considers Olympic Park as a friendly neighbor for which it now has positive feelings. Mary Leitka, however, remembers as a girl hearing angry complaints about loss of land to the park in 1953. From the tribe's viewpoint, the Park Service "just took the land" without negotiations. Indians living north of the river were assigned new homes to the south and told to move. The Hoh Indians also claim traditional land upstream inside the park.

Like other peninsula Indians, the Hoh believe they have a right to hunt inside Olympic, but even though game near the reservation is declining, they do not exercise that privilege. With tribe and park on opposite sides of the river, as at La Push, jurisdictional tussels over fish and clams arise. The Hoh also want the NPS to protect a cemetery north of the river. Offering to cooperate with rangers in the apprehension and prosecution of grave-robbers, they acknowledge that protection of burial sites is difficult. In the early 1980s the service relocated a road at Indian request to avoid the burial grounds.[57]

For over a decade the main issue between Olympic and the Hoh reserve has not been hunting or graves, but a narrow strip of parkland that runs the entire length of the reservation's east border. Because the reserve is landlocked on the Hoh floodplain, creation of federal housing as well as a new cemetery, a fire district, and possible tourist development have been blocked. Negotiations for cession of the eight-hundred-foot right-of-way, originally intended for a beach highway, began in 1978. Although a cession would fragment its ocean strip, the Park Service seemed open to the proposal. In 1982 the tribe thought it would secure the land, but by 1984 Interior had stalled, and the plan fell through after Mary Leitka resigned as tribal chair to attend college.[58]

Leitka, a no-nonsense, articulate leader, eventually returned to help the tribe. Her first goals were to breech the park strip, enlarge the land base, and then develop social services for the Hoh and their non-Indian neighbors. Olympic National Park in 1992 seemed open to a transfer but doubted that Congress would authorize it.[59]

Taholah

After leaving Hoh tribal headquarters, the road back to state highway 101 crosses three jurisdictions: the BIA, the NPS for eight hundred feet, and Jefferson County. Going south, 101 skirts the ocean beaches for a dozen miles until it passes Kalaloch Ranger Station to enter the Quinault Indian Reservation at the small village of Queets. Quinault forms a triangle, the base running twenty-five miles along the ocean and the eastern apex inland at Lake Quinault. The route from Queets to tribal offices in Taholah goes around the apex, southwest to the ocean, and then back north through Moclips. It is not a pretty drive. The 200,000-acre reservation has suffered from some of the worst logging practices in the West. For mile after mile of clear-cut, undecayed cedar slash lies tangled on the ground, smothering regrowth.[60]

Joseph DeLaCruz of Taholah has spent his career as a Quinault leader trying to rectify abuses of tribal land. In September of 1971, the young tribal business manager barricaded Chow Chow logging bridge over the Quinault River to protest BIA timber contracts. When the tactic and subsequent lawsuits succeeded, DeLaCruz became tribal president and appointed a group of social activists determined to restore Quinault fisheries, reforest the land, and receive fair market prices for tribal resources. In the process, Joe DeLaCruz became the most influential and respected Indian politician in western Washington.

Outspoken, direct, and well connected, DeLaCruz has never considered the NPS a threat. "I'm really not concerned about the Park Service," he claimed in 1987. "It's the entire federal government I'm after. For the bicentennial of this state we're going to make them realize they've still got these treaties and it's time they did something about them." When necessary, DeLaCruz used federal contacts in Washington, D.C., to bypass Port Angeles: "I can get on the phone and make a call to the right place, and the Park gets very interested in our views."[61]

DeLaCruz did not encourage battles with Olympic because he saw the NPS as being on the tribe's side. The service might disagree over introduction of hatchery stock into the Queets and Quinault Rivers, but they agree about the importance of fish. Like the Lower Elwha, Quinaults believe that the park, in contrast to the Forest Service, will protect rivers as pristine fish habitat. In 1987 the tribe did blow a whistle to embarrass Olympic when road crews drove a bulldozer into the upper Quinault River, killing thousands of coho and steelhead fry. Superintendent Chandler admitted the error, and today the park downplays the incident as "small potatoes" resolved in "good faith" by Olympic.[62] Joe DeLaCruz claims that Olympic and Taholah have always been reasonable in such matters, the two best examples being a dispute over the reservation's northern boundary and the 1982 arrest of Gregory Hicks and Steven Shale for hunting in the park.

Before 1938 some conservationists had hoped that the remaining virgin cedar forests on tribal land and around Lake Quinault would be included in Olympic National Park. Indians protested and were supported by the BIA. When Franklin Roosevelt visited Quinault in 1937, he, too, wanted the forest preserved. This led Acting Superintendent Fred Overly to propose acquiring three reservation areas for the park: a corridor from Lake Quinault to Taholah, an ocean strip from the Raft River to the Queets, and a buffer zone to hide logging along Highway 101. Overly noted that Indians did not use this land except when they guided fishermen and canoeists down the Quinault, a business they could continue if the river were added to the park. The three scenic strips would interfere very little with timber harvests, he assured his superiors. Like Glacier's attitude toward its Blackfeet border, one of Overly's main concerns was that "numerous unsightly shacks" erected by Indians along the beach and highway not offend tourists.

Secretary Harold Ickes sent Overly's recommendation to John Collier, who found it unacceptable. The Quinault depended on the timber for income, and they strongly favored clear-cutting rather than Overly's selective logging. Collier advocated outright purchase of all Quinault forest lands "as first proposed by the President," except that the unit would remain under BIA supervision, not that of the Park Service. The Overly and Collier plans came to nothing, in part because of a bewildering maze of allotments on the reservation.[63]

Another issue between tribe and park involved the location of the reservation's northern boundary. In 1873 Ulysses S. Grant enlarged Quinault land by executive order, redefining the northern border as extending from "the northwest point [of Lake Quinault] thence in a direct line to a point a half mile north of the Queetshee River and three miles above its mouth."[64] Unknown to Grant, the lake does not lie on a north/south axis, which makes it difficult to determine a "northwest point." In 1892 the BIA surveyed from a point more to the west and further south. This excluded the lake's northwest shore from the reservation, a shoreline that white settlers, including relatives of bureau officials, had already settled. Using the southern survey point cost the Quinault 16,000 acres.

When Olympic National Park was created in 1938, it included the north shore of the lake with 3,000 acres inside the true reservation boundary, 542 acres of which belonged to inholders. In 1976, H.R. 14934 adjusted park lines to exclude the 542 acres, an area of much contention and ill will for nearly forty years. Liberated from the NPS, inholders now found themselves faced with owning property on an Indian reservation—if Joe DeLaCruz succeeded in the Quinault claim for a correct northern border.[65]

The dispute lasted another decade before Congress in 1988 restored the 1873 border intended by Grant. The Quinault, however, lost the park and inholder lands within their original 16,000 acres, being compensated instead with 45 percent of the cash income from 5,000 acres of Forest Service timber south of the lake. DeLaCruz was disappointed but did not blame the NPS. The tribe plans to cut the old growth, leaving four acres for traditional harvesting; they expect protests from environmentalists, whom most Quinaults distrust.[66]

The other confrontation between Olympic and Quinault involved individual Indians more than the tribe. It also challenged a sacrosanct principle of national park policy: the ban on hunting.

Parks as game refuges originated with the earliest proposals by George Catlin, Frederick Law Olmsted, John Muir, and George Bird Grinnell. Only a few years after the creation of Yellowstone, Secretary of the Interior Carl Schurz outlawed all hunting. Schurz's regulation remains the general rule in all parks, although some exceptions exist. Subsistence hunting by whites and natives is legal in Alaska, as is sports hunting in Grand Teton. Canadian parks have been much more liberal than the United States in allowing hunters to take game. The early NPS policy of predator extermination often resulted in over-population of deer and elk, which in turn brought pressure from private hunters and Indians to thin the herds. But beginning with Mather and Albright, the Park Service has usually enforced the mandate set down by Secretary of the Interior Frederick Lane in 1918—"Hunting will not be permitted in any national park."[67]

Olympic, some claim, became an exception to this rule through Section 5 of the 1938 enabling legislation, H.R.10024, which provided that "nothing herein shall affect any valid existing claim . . . nor the rights reserved by treaty to the Indians of any tribes." If the "existing claims" did include hunting, Congress precluded that possibility in 1942 when it decreed that in Olympic "all hunting or the killing, wounding, or capturing at any time of any wild bird or animal . . . is prohibited within the limits of the park."[68]

When Hicks and Shale broke this law in March of 1987 near Salmon Creek in the Queets valley, they also violated regulations of their own tribe, as well as a long tradition of discretion when poaching in the park. Many Indians around the peninsula concede that through the 1960s their people, like many whites, had hunted in Olympic. It was done prudently and with apparent tacit consent from the Park Service. Only when the American Indian Movement (AIM) sought to force the issue during the 1970s did the park clamp down.

Joe DeLaCruz, who contends that traditional Quinault hunting territory extended far into the mountains, recalled that for years Indians had "an understanding" with the park and that rangers "looked the other way" in instances of ceremonial and subsistence hunting. Clay Butler, a Quinault and the ranger responsible for the arrest of Hicks and Shale, thinks the young men were "just stupid." In the past, Butler says, the park probably ignored some Indian hunting as long as no one "walked out on the Queets road with a deer carcass in front of a busload of tourists." He believes that the Religious Freedom Act may now become a factor, a law about which the park is poorly informed. Butler also insists that tales of Indian poaching are exaggerated. In 1987 he knew of only two such arrests—he had made both of them.

Such feelings are widespread. At Lower Elwha, Jerry Charles contends that a few Klallam have hunted for food in the park since 1938 and that as long as no one wasted meat or abused the right, rangers did not bother them. "Now you can't just go up on Hurricane Ridge and knock a couple of tame deer on the head and walk out with the carcasses. The park won't stand for that, and we don't want to do that. We're not that dumb. We keep a low profile and don't make a fuss." Charles is emphatic that he has a treaty right to hunt Olympic, but prefers the tolerance policy because it is such a "hot issue" with the public and the state.[69]

The Hicks/Shale arrest broke any tradition of tolerance with a loud bang. Instead of going to the Quinault tribal court, where the teenagers probably would have been convicted (the tribe never defended the two in the federal system), Olympic took the case to a federal magistrate, where the two Indians won. In January of 1984, Hicks and Shale won again in the U.S. District Court of Judge Walter McGovern.[70]

Indians now had a legal right to hunt in Olympic, causing a public uproar by environmentalists and hunters that threatened to turn ugly. A national sporting magazine called on Congress to abrogate all Indian treaty rights in order to stop the "rampant excesses" of "super Americans." The NPS became alarmed that native hunting would spread to other parks; it predicted that non-Indians could follow suit in Olympic, placing hikers and tourists at risk. Peninsula sporting groups, anticipating "violence and bloodshed," began to organize within days after McGovern's decision. "We have nothing against Indians," proclaimed Margaret Mitchell of Port Angeles, "but the judge's ruling is going to make war between the whites and the Indians."

If these rules are allowed to stand, it's going to make friction among us, and the Indians will become our enemies instead of our brothers. It's destroying the "peace treaty," and when that's destroyed, that's when there's going to be trouble. . . . The court ruling is racial discrimination against whites. It should be the same for everybody, all equal, and nobody should be allowed to hunt in the park. We need the park to protect the animals. We're losing the largest share of our fish to the Indians, now the animals. Next they'll let them take the trees from the park and then there'll be nothing left.

On February 8, Congressman Swift introduced a bill to ban all Indian hunting in Olympic. A week earlier the government had filed a motion asking McGovern to reconsider his ruling. He agreed and on April 9 reversed the decision.[71]

Most Indian leaders on the peninsula—DeLaCruz, Chris Morganroth, Jerry Charles, Ed Claphanhoo of the Makah—realized even before McGovern changed his mind that they faced a serious public relations problem. The Quinault had banned taking park game before the Hicks incident; less than a month after McGovern had initially dismissed the charges, the Quileute, Hoh, Makah, and Lower Elwha councils passed resolutions making Olympic off limits for hunting. On March 20, representatives from the peninsula tribes met with the NPS at the Hoh Tribal Center to discuss future game management policy, a meeting remarkable for bringing eight tribes and the Park Service together at one table.

After Judge McGovern ruled against them, the peninsula Indians continued to assert their right to hunt in the park, but no tribe promoted the practice and most officially opposed it. Today, fifteen years after Greg Hicks and Steve Shale killed three elk along the Queets River, the Park Service considers the controversy settled and is cooperating with tribes to protect the Dosewallips elk.[72]

Kalaloch

The Kalaloch subdistrict of Olympic National Park is immediately north of the Quinault Reservation, its terrain running east from ocean beaches through rain forest to the mountains. The ranger station faces Highway 101 a few miles above Queets. Clay Butler has been in charge here since 1980. He is a Quinault

Indian and former tribal police officer. When Hicks and Shale killed the elk in his district, he investigated and assembled evidence that led to their conviction.

Born on the peninsula in Port Townsend, Butler was raised in a foster home east of the Cascades before moving to the reservation in the early 1970s. Besides police jobs, he worked in construction and for the BIA before finding a vocation with the Park Service. Butler resembles old-time rangers of the Albright era: He admits spending "probably too much time" outdoors, he dislikes paperwork, he prefers patrolling the backcountry to supervising campgrounds, and he believes that being a ranger is better than jobs with higher salaries. Proud of his Quinault heritage, Butler places the welfare of Indians high on his personal agenda; nevertheless, his ethic requires that he enforce the rules, earn respect, play no favorites, and make no distinctions between people. He believes that the NPS and Olympic tribes would all benefit if more Indians worked in the park.

Pressed on his loyalty to the system, Clay Butler asked us to "just look at what you have outside the park." The entire Olympic Peninsula would be "a barren wasteland and devastated area" without the national park, a park that has saved wildlife and preserved what little remains of the original forests. As evidence of how it happened, he points to the Quinault Reservation, remembering the day his father sold the family's timber holdings.

One evening a logging company official came to the door and invited the elder Butler to dinner. When they returned, his father had a check for $28,000. "We got a new car, electricity, which meant a stove . . . and a television set. If you've been poor, it's almost impossible to resist those goodies. But even at that time the price was peanuts, a theft. You can only rob people so long before they wake up. The Quinaults have caught on and they aren't taking it anymore. Joe DeLaCruz is smart, so they're doing really well now with their resources." In the past, Butler says, all other agencies, from the state of Washington to the BIA, had a dismal record protecting resources because, unlike the park, their prime motive was money.

But why preserve the land? For two reasons. First, Butler believes that wild places have an inherent value. He likes to fish and hunt, and he guides river tours during his free time. Yet, "even if I never set a foot in there, or they banned fishing, I'd want to know it's there." Second, the land once was an important part of his Indian heritage. He, and the tribes, need the forests, the cedar, and the game in order to know who they were, who they are today.

For Clay Butler, being a Park Service ranger and an American Indian involves no contradiction. His job is a second side to the same coin of protecting land and wildlife:

We have the best salmon streams on the coast, and because of that we have bear activity, eagle, osprey. We have the rain forest. We have visitation but not so heavy that you have to spend all your time with people. You can go out and look at the timber, look at the trees, look at the elk population and the fish population, then you can come back to the office to get involved in the management of those things. . . . I like the resources, the people, and this area. My duties are to protect the park and the people. So a lot of the work is law enforcement and management policy, but a lot is also understanding the resources, the elk, the timber, the fish. They're not only important to me, they're important to the tribe and they're important to everyone.

That's the way the Quinault live, that's the way I've lived all my life, always having fish, always having elk, being in the forest to gather cedar bark. Everything's there you need. Outside the park it's not going to last, but I think it will in the park, and even if you can't use it, you can at least visit it. You can still be a part of it. . . .

The whole idea of the Park Service doesn't fit as just a job. . . . A national park is a protective system. At least what is left will be protected, hopefully forever. I'll be here to protect the part I can.[73]

Port Angeles

"We're very aware we are surrounded by Indian tribes," reflected an official at Olympic National Park in 1991, "and we try to be sensitive to that, not only when we are talking with them, but when the staff talk with each other." Such sensitivity is recent when placed in the context of Olympic's creation and history. From 1909 to 1938, and then until the mid-1980s, the park looked upon tribal relations as unofficial business. Even as late as 1986, Olympic's expert on fish management responded to an inquiry about treaty rights by writing that "I truly have little to discuss. My work is of a technical nature, usually [with] non-Indian biologists. . . . I confess to having little personal interest in cultural studies."[74]

David Forlines's harsh accusation that for the Park Service Indians "are just little brown people running around, getting in the way, who don't count," contained more than a grain of truth, yet Forlines did not recognize changes taking place even as he spoke. Olympic had slowly and laboriously moved from ignoring Indians, or avoiding and delaying decisions about them, to awareness and to actively seeking positive interaction.

Several factors explain the park's earlier haphazard approach to native relations. Throughout the entire Park Service during its first fifty years it was common for Indians to be invisible, other than as tourist attractions. Olympic followed that pattern, not even bothering with tourist appeal. Port Angeles was also one of the most distracted headquarters in the system, few other parks having faced such bitter public opposition to their creation. Even within the Park Service itself opposition had arisen. In 1929 Horace Albright thought the area too large, a needless duplication of Mt. Rainier. Three years later Conrad Wirth argued that although the Olympic mountains impressed him, they did "not quite come up to the standards set for a national park." Skepticism within the NPS and an outside attitude that the peninsula was "over-conserved" may partially account for the park's timidity and fear of controversy, or, as Carsten Lien charges, clarify why it has been easily "cowed" and ready to "curl up and die" when faced with opposition.[75]

Not all blame resides in Port Angeles. The heterogeneity and political disunity of the tribes themselves made development and practice of a consistent Indian policy difficult. Despite many similarities, the peninsula's native people are culturally diverse. They originally spoke three different languages; their social organization involved bands and villages, not "tribes." The Makah mastered ocean fishing, while the Klallam followed rivers back into the mountains. Fourteen inches of rain fell annually on the Klallam at Sequim Bay; 140 inches fell at Queets and La Push. Nor did the groups live in harmony with each other. As late as 1860 Suquamish warriors led by Chief Seattle exterminated a people called the Chimacum. Earlier, Makah and Klallam had invaded the strait, forcing the Quinaults south. This warfare produced an abundant oral tradition relating to blood feuds, slave raids, vendettas, mass beheadings, and fear of attack:

A young [Klallam] girl was picking crab apples on the east side of the mouth of the Elwah River. . . . She could see the Quinault all painted black and ready to make war. . . . The Quinault gathered all the children together and killed them by cutting them in half. One boy hid under a bluff and escaped. He ran back and told his people. One woman of the

Eenis spit near Port Angeles dressed like a man when the Quinault came for the children. She tried to make her voice sound like a man's. When they came she said she was a certain woman's husband. The Quinault were frightened and let the children go.[76]

When Theodore Roosevelt created the monument in 1909, the violence had ended, but tribal relations still festered. The issues today range from dam removal and boundary adjustments to timber, fish, tidelands, and social services. At the Port Madison Reservation, tribal members are 3 percent of the total population on a reserve of 12 square miles where Indians own 41 acres; 140 Klallam live on two-thirds of a square mile at Lower Elwha. Neah Bay's 1,200 Makah occupy 43 square miles; at La Push only 10 out of 600 acres are private property. There are no private allotments at Hoh, yet the Quinault Reservation of 200,000 acres is half private. At Skokomish, tribal property covers 16 of 5,000 acres. Such extreme differences obviously affect what Indians need from the park and how they view themselves. Non-tribal Indians from Puget Sound to the east, claiming certain rights on peninsula reservations, further complicate matters.

Such diversity would bewilder anyone. The Park Service for decades kept a safe distance or simply ignored the small, disparate native communities encircling it. Then, despite the difficulties, Superintendents Chandler and Finnerty instituted a shift toward involvement.

Olympic administrators had traditionally taken the position that cultural interpretation was none of their business, but rather a matter for the tribes themselves. Despite being out of step with general NPS policy, such an approach can be justified. Keeping hands off cultural programs avoided the risk of paternalism, and therefore had the support of tribal leaders like Jerry Charles, who insisted that public education about Indians was none of the Park Service's business. On the other hand, Clay Butler and Joe DeLaCruz believe that the NPS has refused to rank human resources and cultural history equally with natural resources. The park needs to do much more, they feel, especially building a long-promised coastal interpretative center at Kalaloch. An NPS shift toward cultural awareness is also evident with its displays and in its sponsorship of a 1991 program to "celebrate" Indian history. Employment of an anthropologist in Port Angeles and of an ethnologist in the Northwest Regional Office (1991) meant that cultural studies were now someone's explicit responsibility.[77]

In the past, Olympic has refused to appoint any staff as a tribal liaison. Once again a sound reason, avoiding more bureaucracy, can be advanced: "We don't have one person responsible for all tribal issues, and I hope we never get one," argues Hank Warren.

It has to do with the way we run the park. We want to keep our relationships at a grassroots level. In other words, it's up to the district ranger at each district to build a cooperative relationship with the local people. They know the issues firsthand. We don't need a separate, formalized program out of [Port Angeles]. We need people working together with people. . . . There's a tendency in government to say if you don't have an official position [on top], you are neglecting something. I just don't think that's the case.[78]

On the other hand, this approach can create confusion and inconsistency while underscoring the disunity between peninsula tribes. Placing a full-time anthropologist on the staff helped change the policy, as it did at the Grand Canyon, and in the 90s the NPS worked with Hoh leader Mary Leitka to develop an employment training program.

Olympic's distance from the tribes also shrank under the pressure of events. Boundary disputes at Skokomish, Quileute and Quinault, the Ozette dig culminating in the Makah Museum, controversy over the Elwha dams, and a proposed oil port on the Strait, all forced park and tribes closer together. In the summer of 1990 when a large oil spill threatened northern ocean beaches, the Park Service and other federal agencies worked out of Neah Bay to contain the damage. The crisis turned into a positive experience of cooperation with Indians instead of confrontation. "There was a terrific feeling of working together out there," recalls Olympic resource manager Paul Crawford, "it was a real coming together. They had three big salmon bakes for everyone in appreciation and recognition of working together."[79]

Other reasons lie behind Olympic's change. Park officials now realize that they need support and alliances from the outside if they are to be more than a "helpless giant" in protecting land and that Indians can be a powerful ally on environmental issues. Most park administrators also understand that tribes are "not just another township or county government" but a people who view themselves as "nations," who have a different relationship to the land, and who have treaties with the federal government. Furthermore, seasonal employees in the park tend to be idealistic and romantic in their attitudes toward Indians, bringing internal pressure for change and tolerance. In Seattle, park officials will concede that "it's easy to be a horse's ass" by overzealous enforcement of regulations instead of allowing leeway for cultural differences. When Olympic "got tough" with Indians at Ruby Beach, two outhouses were blown up. The Service decided to "back off."

Port Angeles has its best relations with Neah Bay where mutual respect is no accident. The Makah are the most cohesive of peninsula tribes, and also a people who early retained aggressive, highly skilled private legal counsel. At Neah Bay after 1960 the park not only faced the BIA and tribal leaders, but a Seattle law firm destined to become one of the most successful in the region at Indian advocacy. Some in the tribe today question whether retaining expensive lawyers has been worth the price—one need only compare high-rise legal suites in Seattle with the tribal headquarters to comprehend the justice of this complaint—but it is doubtful that the Makah could have prevailed at Ozette had they not hired the best attorneys available. The Makah argued from strength; strength earned respect.

The most difficult issue in the future for Olympic will be river and fisheries management. If the two dams come out, it will raise fishery issues at Lower Elwha. Potential conflicts also exist on all rivers that flow from the park through reservations, or indeed, on any salmon stream to which Indians have treaty rights, which means virtually all rivers. If Olympic National Park follows its historic pattern, it will ignore and sidestep these problems until confronted with a crisis over fish. Should recent changes in Port Angeles prove firm, if Indians are no longer seen as just another interest group, and if the tribes can overcome their traditional divisions to achieve a consistency and cohesion in dealing with the Park Service, then perhaps the park and native people can plan the future together.

"A NATURAL WONDER ABSOLUTELY UNPARALLELED"

The bearer of this is a very intelligent Su-pai Chief. His name is
Navaho. His home is on the lower part of Cataract Creek where
he and his people live. They will always be found hospitable
and by this paper I request any whites who may pass their way
to treat them kindly and respect their lands and property.

—Governor John C. Fremont
Arizona Territory, November 23, 1878

If Glacier, Yellowstone, Yosemite, and Mesa Verde are the crown jewels of the
national park system, then the Grand Canyon is a diadem. All parks have
tourists who visit in season, and most parks have passionate local defenders
who, year after year, guard against desecration and loss. But the Grand Canyon
is viewed by many as the foremost national treasure, and although the Canyon
has its local associations, trusts, chapters, and clubs, more than any other park it
is watched over and defended by powerful national organizations.

Try to reduce, limit, pollute, alter, or transform the Grand Canyon, and
environmentalists from California to Maine react as the nation did after Pearl
Harbor. President Theodore Roosevelt visited the canyon in 1903 and told
Americans that in Arizona they had "a natural wonder which . . . is absolutely unparalleled throughout the rest of the world." It should never be blem-
ished by the hand of humans, Roosevelt admonished his listeners. "Leave it as
it is. You cannot improve on it. The ages have been at work on it, and man
can only mar it." Impossible advice to follow, yet preservationists ever since
have read and quoted Roosevelt's words like fundamentalists reading and quot-

ing scripture. Not surprisingly, when Indians, the NPS, and environmentalists met in public battle over the Grand Canyon, it evoked intensity unequaled elsewhere.

Grand Canyon National Park encompasses 1,216,000 acres, nearly 2,000 square miles. The canyon severs the earth's surface, a gash up to a mile deep and from 600 feet to 18 miles wide. The Colorado River, released from Glen Canyon dam, flows into Marble Canyon at Lees Ferry; after 277 miles and a drop of 2,000 feet, it leaves the park at Pierce Ferry on the Grand Wash. By comparison, it requires 1,900 miles for the Danube and 1,200 miles for the Columbia to lose the same elevation. Uplift, wind, rain, snow, and heat combine to create not simply a single river course, but an endless series of side canyons, many of which could qualify as national parks on their own. Taken together, the array of rocks, plants, colors, mountains, caves, chasms, waterfalls, and hidden valleys creates one of the earth's most stunning landscapes.

Three Indian reservations border this park: the Navajo, Havasupai, and Hualapai. Five more tribes, the Hopi, Zuni, Kaibab Paiute, Shivwits Paiute, and San Juan Paiute, live nearby and consider parts of the canyon traditional land. To the east, 200,000 Navajos occupy a 14,000,000-acre reservation with a sixty-one-mile park border. Until 1975, the Havasupai tribe, with 400 members, owned 3,000 acres west of Grand Canyon Village, 518 of those acres being an original reserve surrounded by the park.

In 1975 the Havasupai regained 180,000 acres of plateau land, plus 95,000 "traditional use" acres inside Grand Canyon National Park, creating a common border of approximately sixty miles. Still farther west, the Hualapai tribe's twelve hundred members live on a million acres that include a 108-mile-long park border along the Colorado River. Thus 85 percent, or 230 miles, of the Grand Canyon's southern and eastern borders face Indian tribes whose landholdings are nearly twelve times the size of the park.

Before Don Garcia Lopez de Cardenas of the Coronado expedition became the first European to see the Grand Canyon in 1540, Yuman-speaking ancestors of the Hualapai and Havasupai had occupied the plateau south of the Colorado River for a thousand years. During the same time, Pueblo Indians lived inside and then vacated the gorges north of the river. When Cardenas arrived, Athabaskan ancestors of modern Apache and Navajo Indians were migrating onto lands northeast of the Colorado; they would eventually surround the Hopi, whose myths and heritage included the Grand Canyon. Paiutes lived on the plateaus north of the river, used side canyons for shelter and hunting, and retreated from the Navajo incursion.

Two centuries after Cardenas came, saw, and did not conquer—did not even reach the river after a week of effort—priests in the Escalante expedition of 1776 descended to and crossed the Colorado. White trappers entered the land in the 1830s, a generation before John Wesley Powell first navigated the entire canyon in 1869.

Powell ventured into terra incognita as he approached Glen, Marble, and Grand Canyons. Within a decade, miners, railroad surveyors, and tourists began to enter Indian homelands that Powell and others had considered desolate enough to repel white civilization. In 1882 Senator Benjamin Harrison, probably acting on Powell's behalf, introduced a bill in Congress to set aside a national park. Had his legislation passed, Harrison would have created the third national park in the world, following Yellowstone and Mackinack Island.

A decade later, President Benjamin Harrison used his office to establish the Grand Canyon Forest Reserve, which Theodore Roosevelt reclassified as a game preserve in 1906. Two years later, Roosevelt used the Antiquities Act to elevate USFS land to a national monument. The century of tourism began in earnest when a railroad reached the south rim in 1901. In 1919, nearly forty years after Harrison's first proposal and three years after the birth of the NPS, Grand Canyon became a national park.[1]

As with Yellowstone, Yosemite, Mt. Rainier, Glacier, and later Olympic, this process ignored Indian rights and prior occupation, including sites inside the canyon. Modern place-names indicate how quickly Europeans asserted ownership and put an imprint on the canyon. Of today's 230 place-names, 8 are Havasupai, 13 Paiute, and 4 Hopi. Except for the Paiute, more Grand Canyon names originate with Asian and Egyptian mythology than from native words.[2]

As happened at Glacier and Mesa Verde, local Indian lore and the people themselves served as tourist attractions and labor crews. Employment of Indians in park management was rare, and personal interaction with guests was infrequent, resulting in stereotypes held by rangers, tourists, Indians, and environmentalists alike. Reality eclipses stereotype, as white and Indian firefighters learn when they join in one of the few cross-cultural activities within the park.[3] We will place NPS/Indian relations in historical context, then examine four areas of controversy between the park and the tribes: dam building, the selling of beads, cultural interpretation, and, in chapter 8, the Havasupai land transfer.

Indian Relations: 1919–1969

For years after the creation of Grand Canyon National Park, NPS reports seldom mentioned Indians. While unpublished park documents indicated frequent and at times intense interactions with native people, one might conclude from the park superintendent's annual reports between 1920 and 1932 that the nearest tribe lived along the Mississippi. A 1932 report gave the Havasupai one page out of seven volumes, listing structures at the village. Thirty years later a Mission 66 proposal did not mention Indians at all.[4]

Indians, if invisible in official reports, were present in symbol and reality. Fred Harvey Corporation, the canyon's premier concessionaire, hired native workers and built Hopi House near lavish El Tovar Lodge, while promoting Indian motifs and Indian entertainers at other tourist facilities. Native dancers occasionally developed friendships with rangers and seasonal workers. Above Tanner Canyon, Fred Harvey replicated a puebloan tower. Havasupai worked for wages in Grand Canyon Village, on trails, on constructing a sewage plant, and on a suspension bridge across the Colorado. The jobs resulted in a residential area called Supai Camp, an ongoing NPS headache for years to come. In another instance, seventy Navajos joined a futile 1924 attempt to drive deer from the Kaibab Plateau down Nankoweap Canyon, across the Colorado, and up the Tanner. On an interagency level, Superintendent Miner Tillotson "made it a practice to cooperate in every way possible with the Indian Service" by repairing reservation trails, loaning equipment, and providing supplies to the BIA.

Indians guided pack horses for tourists. Unauthorized natives who panhandled or wandered through Grand Canyon Village faced expulsion if they violated NPS standards of decorum. So did packers who left dead horses to decompose on the trail below Hualapai Hilltop. In fact, they risked arrest. On a more personal level, the service found itself negotiating disputes and paternity claims within Indian families.[5]

Attitudes, those slippery but powerful nonentities of history, are crucial to understanding both official and personal relations among tribes, tourists, and the NPS. In northern Arizona of the 1920s and 1930s, most Indians looked upon tourists and rangers with a mixture of confusion, incredulity, and resentment, while the average visitor saw Indians as quaint people who sold crafts and danced; a few visitors did know and respect trail guides. In trying to understand the NPS, it is helpful to search for the individuals behind the official language. Some Grand Canyon employees, such as Michael Harrison, made special efforts to study the Navajo and Hopi, but few rangers between 1920 and 1950 understood the rudiments of ethnology. If Grand Canyon staff had read George Wharton James's *What the White Man May Learn from the Indians* (1908), *Indians of the Painted Desert* (1911), or *In and around the Grand Canyon* (1911), they might have avoided certain errors and begun to look beyond the confines of their own culture. James, who with Charles Lummis and John C. Van Dyke began Arizona's environmental tradition, respected the tribes, grasped their diversity, praised the skills and habits he considered superior to those of white culture, and never doubted or belittled Indian humanity. He knew that the Havasupai once occupied the entire Coconino Plateau and had followed trails into the canyon.

A former Methodist minister, James disliked Havasupai smoking, gambling, lack of hygiene, and the mistreatment of pets, yet he found that native children did well in school and their parents merited trust and respect. "Of no tribe of Indians in the United States," James wrote of the Havasupai in 1911, "has more wild nonsense and foolish exaggeration been written."[6]

George Wharton James died in 1923, not having stopped the exaggeration and nonsense. Dama Margaret Smith had worked for the Park Service less than two years before publishing "The Home of a *Doomed* Race" in a 1923 issue of *Good Housekeeping*. Visiting Supai village, she found "the Noble Red Man" a vanishing race of superstitious and fear-ridden people, "savages" and weaklings who succumbed to disease. The "bucks," Smith reported, howled and chanted, the children ran around naked, and "fat, greasy squaws gibbered" at visitors. In another article, Smith described a Hopi snake dance in which, quoting a park ranger, "the crazy redskins bounce around with rattlesnakes in their mouths so it will rain." She decided to "peep into" a kiva and saw enough to convince her that the government must suppress pagan worship.[7]

Seven years later Dama Margaret Smith gathered her observations into an autobiography, *I Married a Ranger*. She patronized most Indians. "Indians! Navajos!" she exclaimed in one chapter, were people who made gaudy rugs that "appealed to the gypsy streak" in her, rugs that "Navajo bucks" peddled door to door at Grand Canyon Village. She fed one "buck," who wore a red headband and was called "Navvy . . . a vile, smelly, old creature with bleary eyes and coarse uncombed gray hair tied in a club." At Navajo ceremonies people spoke in grunts or bellowed "a blood-chilling war whoop." Watching "giggling native belles" and nude young men dance, "I fell to dreaming of what it would have meant to be captured by such demons only a few years ago."[8]

If Dama Smith in 1930 tolerated or fantasized about the Navajo, she saved her contempt and invective for the Havasupai, a people whom she described as drinking quarts of castor oil and burying their dead with an arm exposed. When she spent a night at "that accursed place," Supai, a "fat old squaw" begged for a gown, and the chief, Watahomigie, "came strutting into our house." She ridiculed two men named Big Jim and Captain Burro for their speech. Other Indians rightly despised the Havasupai as savages: "Half-clad, half-fed, half-wild . . . they hide away in their poverty, ignorance, and superstition." Even the babies seemed hopeless and helpless. "It is a people looking backward down the years with no thought of the morrow. . . . Not many more morrows for that doomed tribe."[9]

Dama Margaret Smith worked for the NPS during Grand Canyon National Park's first decade. *I Married a Ranger* was endorsed by Associate Director Arno B. Cammerer, who found the book humorous and "most delightful." A few years later he would recommend removal of the Havasupai from their reservation.[10]

Horace Albright's *Oh Ranger!* (1928) avoided Smith's racial language, yet even Albright described Indians as a quaint curiosity. It required a generation for the service to reform its language. "Please make a point," a superior reprimanded the Grand Canyon superintendent in 1949, "of referring to Indians, living or archeological, as men, women, and children—not as bucks or braves, squaws or papooses."[11]

Proper ethnic language and attitudes were not a major concern for Grand Canyon administrators during the park's first fifty years. Expansion of boundaries to include sufficient land and wildlife ranked much higher among NPS goals. In 1919 most of the new park's 645,000 acres were below the rim. Besides dealing with a morass of mines, power sites, and trail claims, on the south rim the service found itself surrounded by Indian reservations, traditional use areas occupied by cattlemen and Indians, railroad lands, Forest Service holdings, and private tracts. Typical of Mather's era, the NPS searched for ways to consolidate, develop, and enlarge the park without alienating Arizona's white population.

Efforts to expand north or south from a narrow strip along canyon rims encountered Forest Service land used by stock growers and hunters. The park did acquire 45,000 acres in 1927, but when it tried to add 125,000 more in 1930 opposition arose from the state as well as private sportsmen, who did not want Kaibab forests turned into "a zoo" or a "sociological laboratory." Arizona outdoor clubs called upon members to "don [your] war bonnets. There's a battle to be fought."[12]

The other direction for park expansion was east-west. The service had earlier considered Navajo land between the park's eastern boundary and the Little Colorado as desirable, but in 1925 Mather had ruled this out.[13] He preferred moving west, where the NPS could connect Havasu Canyon and Great Thumb Mesa by building a road from El Tovar Lodge to Mannakaja Point. In 1919 Mather had received a report urging construction "with the utmost of promptness" of a route from El Tovar to Cataract Canyon. From there, it was pointed out, tourists on horseback could visit Supai Village, where the Park Service should build a campground, making this "one of the finest three-day trips in the world—and absolutely unique."[14] Plans for the road soon expanded: From Mannakaja Point it was a short, direct trip to Supai Village and Navajo Falls. After inspecting Havasu Canyon in 1927, Albright reported that "there is no question but what a road to this section of the Park should be built. First, to give old people, the sick and the crippled an opportunity to see the Canyon from below, and second to make available the extraordinary scenery of Havasu Canyon."

Although Albright found peach, pear, apple, apricot, and fig trees on the canyon floor, he concluded that the "picturesque" Havasupai would offer no impediment: "Most of them do not live in the valley, but have their hogans in the Park upon the rim." More difficult were mining claims near the waterfalls. Here Albright hoped that accurate surveys would place the falls inside the reservation, compromising any claims. Several months later he received news "too good to be true"—that Navajo and Havasu and perhaps Mooney Falls were on Indian land. With the mining claims invalid, the NPS could have moved ahead, except that in 1927 engineers projected Havasu road costs at $2 million. The Great Crash of 1929 saved the Great Thumb.[15]

After 1930, the NPS began to meet opposition when it sought native land. In 1948 conservationist Frederick Law Olmsted II recommended that Grand Canyon expand past Havasupai, but a 1954 boundary study concentrated on Forest Service land to the south, ignoring native lands. A 1971 Master Plan would return to improving conditions at Hualapai Hilltop and Havasu Canyon, much to the eventual regret of the NPS.

At Grand Canyon, the NPS initially related to tribal governments through the Bureau of Indian Affairs. Interagency correspondence covers not only such major ongoing problems as Supai Camp but also everyday details. For example, when the Park Service paid Havasupai workers twice the BIA wage scale, it damaged morale of BIA labor in Havasu Canyon as well as causing an exodus of young men. The BIA asked the Park Service to help it punish one Jess Chick-apanyja for forging a check, requested that the NPS not install a free water line to an Indian camp, and, when the Havasupai were "playing foxsy" about send-ing their children to school, urged the park superintendent not to employ par-ents who violated BIA school policy. When ill Indians needed rides to Flagstaff, park vehicles were used. The NPS even found itself mediating the paternity claims of a Navajo laundress, Stella Begay, against a married Havasupai truck driver, Lorenzo Sinyella, both employed by Fred Harvey.[16]

One long-standing controversy with Indians took place at Grand Canyon Village, almost on the front steps of park headquarters. The dispute involved 160 acres of parkland used as living quarters for Havasupai laborers, a site called Supai Camp (distinct from Supai Village on the reservation). Today the camp is a cluster of small cottages in a loop off the Rowe Well Road, located less than a mile from Bright Angel Lodge on the south rim. The NPS has an uneven record when dealing with small communities and individuals dwelling inside or next to parks, whether white mountaineers in Shenandoah or Indian villages at Yosem-ite and Death Valley.[17] At Grand Canyon, response to the Supai community has varied from upgrading facilities to seeking removal.

Exactly when modern Havasupai began living in Supai Camp is uncertain. Although NPS documents do not mention native occupation near Grand Can-yon Village, the present Bright Angel and Hermit trails are old Pueblo routes established well before the Havasupai began to use side canyons for farming and collecting resources. Later the tribe occupied sites between Indian Garden Creek and Hermit Basin, with seasonal camps on the rim as far east as Desert View. Havasupai oral tradition tells of Theodore Roosevelt in 1905 ordering Swedva ("Big Jim") to "get your people out" of Indian Garden. Forest Ser-vice records show that Swedva was moved from the rim and granted an occu-pancy permit at Rowe's Well on the plateau in 1913. Captain Burro and his children continued to use Indian Garden until evicted in 1928, by which time the Park Service had surveyed and set aside Supai Camp just south of the main tourist area.[18]

From the NPS viewpoint, the large number of Havasupai employed by the service, the Santa Fe Railroad, and Fred Harvey in the 1920s justified a separate Indian community. Miner Tillotson, a superintendent sympathetic toward the Havasupai, told Horace Albright in 1930 that he hired local Indians whenever possible: "The policy has developed to the point where the local Supai Indians are employed in preference to outside white labor. . . . We have found that the

Supai Indians are good workmen." Indians worked on seasonal road crews and carried mail, helped construct the first sewage treatment plant, and held full-time jobs as truck drivers, powdermen, and compressor operators.[19]

Whatever the origin of the camp—and Havasupai claim its use predated the arrival of whites—numerous people lived there in the late 1920s and early 1930s. After 1933, the NPS drafted a plan to enlarge and improve the site. Twenty-two "shacks" would be demolished and replaced by thirty-two three-room cabins neatly arranged in four semicircles, each building with running water and electricity. Four six-car garages, two restrooms, two ramadas, and a schoolhouse completed a plan approved by four NPS officials, including Director Arno Cammerer.[20]

Nothing happened, and Cammerer would rebuke Tillotson who, "without proper authority," had allowed various Havasupai to live inside the park. The director ordered that habitation in native villages inside Yosemite, Death Valley, and Grand Canyon be limited to Indians employed by the government. At the same time, James Brooks, the chief ranger, became alarmed by sanitary conditions that he felt were "below the standards of the White People and may be questioned by them." Someone sent a photographer to the camp who, unannounced and uninvited, entered homes and took photos later captioned "unsightly, dilapidated shacks," "ramshackle quarters," "a need for constant supervision," "untidy," and "family food supply mixed with a collection of dirty clothes, old shoes, and accumulated filth."[21]

Ranger Brooks persisted with his campaign. In May 1936 he warned Tillotson that "uplifters" seeking "bally-ho" about the park had been at Supai Camp meeting with Indians. The superintendent, Brooks warned, needed to act:

The Indians living in these hovels of dirt and filth are bound to breed diseases that may spread to other parts of the community. . . . The village grounds would give one the creeps and goose-flesh. . . . The pit toilets are filthy, pit holes are flowing over and open to house flys [sic]. Food particles and excrement litter the grounds and swarms of flies are everywhere.

I am firmly convinced that the housing standards are far below standards of these people when they [lived] their own primitive way. . . . However, this is a white man's community and it has no place for a hottentot village. Whenever I discuss this with our people, the response invariably is, "They would not be clean if they had the opportunity." From personal experience with these people I know the theory is untrue.

It is just one way of passing the buck. . . . [The Indians] have no place where they can bathe, the only water is hauled there for culinary uses. I doubt very much if the average run of Whites would be any cleaner than these Indians if they had to live under like conditions.[22]

In 1939, with Tillotson no longer superintendent, the Park Service dismantled the Indian dwellings, delivered the scrap lumber to Hualapai Hilltop, and built six new cabins on the site. The camp remained and so did the Havasupai.

By the 1950s, national policy toward Indians tribes had shifted toward ending federal support and dispersing native communities. At Grand Canyon, the NPS followed the trend and decided to eliminate Supai Camp. Ample justification existed. The six cabins intended solely for NPS employees were filled with families, children, and visitors—the population at times reaching forty or fifty persons, two or three of whom worked in the park. Buildings in disrepair were augmented with tar paper shanties. Cats, dogs, and horses wandered into Grand Canyon Village; in 1953 rangers arrested a resident for killing deer. And by the 1950s the Havasupai themselves had changed. A tribe once known for friendliness, hard work, and resistance to white culture, now experienced frustration, despair, and violence exacerbated by alcoholism. By the mid-1960s arrests for drinking, disturbing the peace, and fighting became common at the camp and in Supai Village. Years later, retired rangers would consider dealing with the Havasupai a thankless task at Grand Canyon.[23]

To complicate matters for the NPS, some Havasupai began to assert themselves. After residents at Supai Camp hired a lawyer to establish title to that site and Indian Gardens, as well as a right to hunt in the park, a ranger who had known the tribe for a quarter century complained that he had never seen camp members "so aggressive in their thinking toward the National Park Service."[24] The park responded with yet another campaign to close the camp. In November 1955, the superintendent recommended that the cabins be razed, the area "cleaned up," and Indians who were "just plain squatters" evicted. By spring, the service had accomplished its goals. With shacks and trash removed, Supai Camp met NPS standards for tidiness. Native squatters had been moved to Seligman, Peach Springs, and Hualapai Hilltop, leaving only residents employed at Grand Canyon Village.[25]

Or so the Park Service believed. Some Havasupai hid friends in their cabins, while others, like Flynn Watahomigie, had secret shelters in the woods. During the next decade Indians filtered back into the camp, and conditions returned to normal.

If Supai Camp had not changed, attitudes had. In the early years the park had considered its Indian neighbors quaint, colorful, and, to some, socially inferior. In the 1920s and 1930s a relatively large number had been employed by the service and by Fred Harvey. Under the sympathetic Miner Tillotson, plans were drawn for tribal living quarters, and there was even talk of developing "a model Indian colony" integral to the park. When that plan faltered, the NPS, viewing Indian homes as "littering the park," moved against unauthorized structures.

By 1960, the Park Service had not only cleaned up Supai Camp but it had also waged a campaign to remove Indian hogans and log cabins along the rim— at Grandview, Pasture Wash, and Drift Fence. The rangers who in 1967 confiscated the possessions of William Little Jim and burned his plateau cabin fed a growing Havasupai resentment toward the NPS and toward outsiders. It reached a climax in the 1970s, the subject of chapter 8.

Flooding the Sistine Chapel

"Shall We Let Them Ruin Our National Parks?" asked conservationist Bernard DeVoto in the July 22, 1950, *Saturday Evening Post.* He was referring to the Army Corps of Engineers and the Bureau of Reclamation, and by "ruin" he meant erecting dams at Glacier, Dinosaur, Yellowstone, and the Grand Canyon. Dinosaur and the Grand Canyon fell within the Colorado River Storage Project, a visionary scheme dating back thirty years. By turning one of North America's most remarkable rivers into a series of reservoirs, storage would permit Utah and Arizona to develop on a scale rivaling that of southern California. The Colorado River would supply rural irrigation systems and urban faucets, as well as generating power for farms and cities.[26]

When the *Reader's Digest* reprinted DeVoto's article in November, the alarm bell began a contest of rivers versus dams, environmentalists versus engineers. The struggle reached its climax in the 1960s at Marble and Bridge Canyons, dam sites within the Grand Canyon on the Navajo and Hualapai Reservations where the federal government had reserved development rights. Conservationists, having defeated the Bureau of Reclamation at Echo Park in Dinosaur and paid the price at Glen Canyon, would achieve a landmark victory in the Grand

Canyon. As at Dinosaur, environmentalist victory came with a price—the anger
of Hualapai Indians.

Like their Havasupai neighbors to the east, the Hualapai Indians had once
occupied the Coconino Plateau south of the Grand Canyon. They lived between the Little Colorado, the San Francisco Peaks, and the Colorado River,
gathering native plants and hunting antelope, bighorn sheep, elk, bear, turkey,
and quail. Hostility toward prospectors, railroads, cattlemen, and other American settlers led to war in 1866. The U.S. Army defeated the Hualapai and
interned them at La Paz on the Lower Colorado. After a desperate captivity,
seven hundred survivors were given a million-acre, U-shaped reservation extending west from Havasupai lands to the Grand Wash, the point at which the
Colorado River emerges from the Grand Canyon. Their population reduced
further by smallpox and measles, the Hualapai survived by working for railroads, on ranches, and in mines. During the twentieth century, a few families
successfully marketed cattle, yet on the reservation poverty often approached
starvation.[27]

Having lost much of their land, the Hualapai retained one resource of value
to white civilization. At a gorge called Bridge Canyon, the cliffs above the Colorado River narrowed sufficiently to permit a dam. During the 1930s Arizona
designated Bridge Canyon as a potential power site. Although the area now fell
within Grand Canyon National Monument, created by Herbert Hoover on
December 22, 1932, NPS director Horace Albright assured the Bureau of Reclamation that the new classification would not affect construction plans.

The monument, Albright wrote, "could not possibly have the effect of inter-
fering with, delaying or rendering impractical the Bridge Canyon Project. . . .
We have had [it] in mind all the time."[28] The Park Service still had it in mind as
World War II ended. Miner Tillotson, now regional director for the Southwest,
did not believe damming Bridge Canyon would damage the park. "This is a
case," he wrote to Arthur Demaray, "where the danger is more apparent than
real. Certainly we could get little or no popular support for any objection we
might raise to so remote an intrusion."[29]

Even though a study by Frederick Law Olmsted also recommended a dam,
by 1950 the NPS had second thoughts. When Arizona congressmen proposed a
Bridge Canyon dam as part of the Central Arizona Project, the NPS objected.[30]
Later in the decade, as Los Angeles maneuvered to build a dam in the canyon,
the Arizona Power Authority (APA) signed an agreement with the Hualapai
promising the tribe $150,000 outright and $2,000 a month, with additional

benefits to follow. After suspension of that agreement, the APA in 1966 offered the tribe a million-dollar annual payment, construction jobs, a share of the power, and a royalty on every kilowatt sold. Without doubt, Bridge Canyon Dam would have meant an instant jolt for the tribal economy.[31]

The Bridge Canyon and Marble Canyon projects were defeated by a fierce campaign led by the Sierra Club's David Brower. Even though John Muir's defeat in the battle over flooding Yosemite's Hetch Hetchy Valley stood as the unforgivable crime in Sierra Club history, prior to the 1950s the organization had not opposed dams in national parks. Indeed, in 1947 the club's board of directors, including Brower, had endorsed a high dam at Bridge Canyon. Now, spearheading the first effective national environmental campaign, Brower ran full-page ads in the New York Times between June 9, 1965, and April 16, 1967. He accused Secretary of the Interior Stewart Udall of being ready to sell the Grand Tetons, the redwoods, Yellowstone, and all other wilderness areas "if the Grand Canyon is dammed for profit." Would Americans flood the Sistine Chapel, Brower asked, "so tourists can get nearer the ceiling?"

The struggle placed Arizona's need for water, power, and jobs against demands to keep national parks, especially the Grand Canyon, inviolate: "Leave it as it is. You cannot improve on it. Man can only mar it." Would Americans heed Roosevelt's advice when faced with warnings of "the greatest water crisis in the nation's history?"

Almost totally absent from both sides of the debate was discussion of Hualapai interests.[32] A thoughtful and persuasive statement from Stewart Udall to President Lyndon Johnson cited the potential revenues, the national park, recreational development, and the Southwest's water crisis in support of the dam, but did not mention the tribe. The private papers of Morris and Stewart Udall for 1965–67 contain thousands of letters about Grand Canyon dams. Although a vast majority of writers (including many in Arizona) opposed the project, almost no one mentioned the Hualapai Indians.[33] Nor did the Bureau of Reclamation speak of Indian needs. Likewise, strategy sessions at the Sierra Club ignored benefits to the Hualapai.[34]

Indians, however, knew of the stakes on the Colorado. The Navajo dissented over Marble Canyon, but eight other tribes supported the Colorado River Basin Act because of Bridge Canyon Dam. George Rocha, Hualapai chairman, accused environmentalists of "denying us, the first Americans, our right to help ourselves and condemning our families to lifelong poverty by forcing us to keep our homeland a wilderness." In the 1960s tribal chairmen

simply were not heard, Indian needs and rights not weighed, and Indian publications not read by the congressmen, developers, or environmentalists who
debated and decided uses for the Grand Canyon.[35]

When Congress approved the Central Arizona Project in 1968, it banned
further power development between Glen Canyon and Hoover Dams. Three
months later Lyndon Johnson designated Marble Canyon a national monument. David Brower and the Sierra Club had won this fight against the dams,
but, as Brower was first to admit, environmental defenders could not rest. Both
the Hualapai and Havasupai protested a 1969 bill to enlarge Grand Canyon
National Park, with the Hualapai especially upset over losing Bridge Canyon.

A few years later, when the Enlargement Act began moving toward passage,
S.1296 alarmed environmentalists by including a transfer of park land to the
Havasupai. While the Sierra Club and others accused the Havasupai of planning to develop parkland commercially, the Hualapai and their attorneys reopened the Bridge Canyon issue. With tribal unemployment at 50 percent,
they proposed a joint venture with the Arizona Power Commission that would
create construction and powerhouse jobs, pave reservation roads, allow recreational development similar to that at Lake Mead and Lake Powell, and bring
the tribe millions of dollars in royalties.

Knowing that they faced strong opposition, the Hualapai sought support
from Rotary and Kiwanis Clubs, local editors, politicians, and professional
groups that favored economic development. The project, now renamed Hualapai Dam, was endorsed by the Arizona Senate, the Arizona Water Commission,
utility and irrigation districts, the state's Inter-Tribal Council, the NCAI, the
Arizona Municipal Power Association, the *Arizona Republic*, and many county
supervisors. Speaking for the Mojave County Republicans, a mine owner in
Oatman declared that "an energy crisis, a mineral crisis, a monetary crisis, plus a
water crisis" had been created by federal "bureaucratic monsters" that blocked
the Indian dam and sought to kill the Central Arizona Project.[36]

Despite support from local businessmen and the Republican Party, tribal
chairman Sterling Mahone knew he must refute environmental arguments. He
testified before the House National Parks Subcommittee that American Indians, and Hualapai in particular, for centuries had demonstrated "utmost concern" for land and for protecting natural beauty. Whites had begun to share
such values, "but the catchwords of the conservation movement can become a
mask for arbitrary destruction of the rights and opportunities of others. We
cannot and will not stand idly by while the interests of a few people are served

in the name of conservation at the expense of the few economic development resources still available to Indian tribes."[37] The dam offered a last hope for Hualapai prosperity and full employment. Speaking to the Kingman Rotary Club, Mahone pressed the attack against environmentalists:

> The extremely remote territory of the Hualapai Dam site is currently available to only a few hardy adventurers who can afford the costly boat-ride through the canyon. Construction of the dam will create a ribbon of blue in the narrow inner gorge, making the Hualapai section of the Colorado readily available to all. Fifty miles of azure lake would enhance the rugged beauty of the steel-gray canyon, still leaving 190 miles of open, running, wrenching river for the dedicated river runners . . . .
>
> The Colorado River earmarked for the Hualapai Dam is now available to thrill-seekers who once in their lifetime join a small party in a costly boat-ride through the canyon. . . . The body of water behind Hualapai Dam could be used for the entire gamut of recreation, including fishing, swimming, and water skiing. . . . One million people enjoyed Lake Powell in 1972 while only 16,000 floated down the Colorado River.[38]

Sterling Mahone could count on Rotarians, water skiers, realtors, fishermen, developers, and most of Arizona's congressional delegation, but he had lost Congressman Mo Udall and Senator Barry Goldwater. By 1973 Udall considered any dam in the Grand Canyon "a monstrosity," and Goldwater knew that attaching hydro power to his bill would kill the legislation. In March 1974, at the urging of tribal attorney Royal Marks, Mahone accused Goldwater and Udall of playing politics and being in league with "persons who want to keep the country for just a few. . . . Are you now for the dam? We are entitled to a direct answer, either yes or no."

Mahone received a blunt answer, an unequivocal "no" from Goldwater. "You and your people are certainly entitled to my feelings," the senator replied, "so I am going to give it to you straight: Sterling, I want to level with you because I don't think people have been doing this. There is no way in God's green world that I can see a dam being built at Bridge Canyon at this time or anytime in the foreseeable future. It is not a case of what I want, or what you want, or what Mr. Marks wants, or the Arizona Power Authority wants. It is squarely up to the Congress and the Congress has shown no inclination to allow this dam."[39]

The Hualapai did not quit, but continued to plead for the dam until the Enlargement Act passed, then lobbied for it afterward. Royal Marks introduced

new legislation through Arizona congressman Sam Steiger and urged the tribe
to organize a Hualapai Dam Association to pressure Congress. Defeating the
Sierra Club, Marks cautioned, would be difficult.[40]

After losing the dam, the Hualapai position was more complex. Today, with
tribal unemployment running at 66 percent, some leaders still believe that a
dam would bring jobs, recreation, royalties, and a dependable supply of power
and water. Edgar Walema, a councilman, recalls a meeting in Kingman when
the tribe had convinced the Sierra Club to support Bridge Canyon Dam. He
still wonders why they turned against it: "I don't think there was anything
negative about building the dam. But it's a dead issue. It probably isn't possible
anymore because the opposition was so very strong. It's not going to happen."[41]
Goldwater's message had finally hit home.

By 1990 younger Hualapai leaders began to doubt if the dam had ever been a
good idea. Working closely with the Park Service's Jan Balsom in studying the
downstream impact of Glen Canyon Dam, the tribe shifted toward thinking
that the entire Grand Canyon should remain an intact ecosystem. Balsom
describes her Hualapai work in terms that should impress the most skeptical
Sierra Club member:

> All of the tribes trace ancestry to the Canyon and the river. It's the
> maintenance of that system, for their ancestral sites, for their spiritual
> sites, for their traditional cultural areas, in total, without degradation,
> which is the common bond. . . . That is totally in synch with what the
> Park Service feels is important. There is no debate. What is most impor-
> tant is saving the integrity of the ecosystem. So it has been very, very
> easy. Someone at the D.C. meeting told me that when the Hopi and
> Hualapai talked about the sacredness of the river, it gave one goose
> bumps, it just gave you the heebie jeebies. It was a real powerful message
> that the Secretary heard loud and clear.[42]

It has been thirty years since the first dam struggle, twenty years since the
second. Bridge Canyon Dam is dead. Edgar Walema, an older Hualapai councilman, regretfully concedes that reality. Clay Bravo, a younger Hualapai wildlife manager, says the same thing with a pride and eloquence that, according to
one observer, "gives you goose bumps."

Reconciled to losing the dam, the Hualapai have sought other ways to turn
their 108 river miles into cash. Tourists, sportsmen, and river rafters provide an
obvious answer. The tribe hopes to learn from the NPS, which they feel had

condescendingly ignored the reservation for years. A change of superintendents in 1987, Walema says, transformed NPS attitudes. The Hualapai have now
joined the Park Service and other tribes in studying the effects of Glen Canyon
Dam; this, along with a more respectful NPS attitude toward sacred sites, seems
a positive sign for future cooperation. Clay Bravo and Don Bay of the tribe's
wildlife management program assert that the service could learn something
from them as well: "Very few Indian tribes have an outright depletion of any
wildlife species because it has always been our culture to make sure the different
species were looked after. We had a good relationship with them, in tune with
everything around us, and we still have that today."[43] They do not consider
guided trophy hunts for elk, lion, bighorn sheep, or deer to be in conflict with
that relationship.

In addition to sponsoring hunting expeditions, the tribe in 1987 opened a
tourist enterprise called Grand Canyon West. At the end of fifty-seven miles of
dirt road north of Peach Springs—a four-hour trip by Jeep—Grand Canyon
West features Hualapai interpretations of land and history, a five-mile bus tour
along the rim of the Colorado, traditional wickiups, a barbecue lunch on a
promontory, and, added in 1994, a casino. Tourists from Las Vegas visit the site,
arriving by Adventure Airlines or bus. It costs $15 if one drives, $100 by bus,
and $150 by plane. Walema claims that the tribe has netted a million dollars in
three years, and he hopes to siphon off overflow from Grand Canyon Village
through promotion in Japan, China, Germany, and England:

> We're looking at what we can do with our portion of the Grand Canyon.
> It's going to be similar to the park on the South Rim. We've got a place on
> the reservation where we are bringing tourists in by plane and bus, and
> that's been very, very profitable. We are looking at paving the airstrip.
> There'll be a terminal, a gift shop, a restaurant, even a hotel out there. It's
> going to be an out-of-sight, what do you call it, resort.[44]

A dozen years before opening Grand Canyon West, the Hualapai began a
river rafting enterprise that still continues, although not without problems. The
reservation's Diamond Creek is the only place below Lees Ferry, 225 miles
upstream, where the Colorado River can be reached by vehicles. In 1973 the
tribe applied for and received a five-year commercial permit from the NPS that
allowed Hualapai rafts to run the river between Diamond Creek and Lake
Mead. Requesting a permit conceded that the park boundary included all of the
river and that the NPS controlled its use and access. For years prior to that, the

Hualapai had insisted that their 108-mile border extended to the middle of the river. In 1979, while continuing to conduct tours, the tribe refused to apply for a renewal. Edgar Walema explained: "When we first started our river running, the Park came to us and they said that we had to have a concession permit because they controlled the river. Then we went back and said, 'No,' the river is on Indian land, therefore we have jurisdiction over it. We want to do what we want with the river as far as river running is concerned."[45]

The Park Service, not wishing to contest the boundary issue or create conflict over a seemingly minor matter, set policy aside and allowed Indian rafters to operate without a permit. Tribal guides continued to receive NPS training for motorized rafts. The tribe advertised the "Hualapai River Runners" as the only Indian-owned rafting company in the nation, adding that they provided services "under the authority of the Grand Canyon National Park."

Tolerance of Hualapai rafting worked well until August 13, 1988, at 5:20 P.M., at mile 234 below Bridge Canyon Rapid. As a poorly equipped raft abruptly turned to rerun white water, French filmmaker Daniel Lesoeur fell overboard. As the raft churned above him, a propeller hit Lesoeur in the head and shoulder. Badly mangled, the Frenchman eventually was evacuated by an NPS rescue unit and rushed to Las Vegas. His head fractured and his face badly disfigured by injuries to the ear and right eye, Lesoeur also lost a thumb and suffered permanent facial paralysis. He later sued the United States for $3.8 million, claiming that Grand Canyon National Park had been negligent in not regulating and supervising the Hualapai as it did other rafting companies. In October 1992, a federal judge in Phoenix ruled that the Park Service had acted within its discretionary power—that it could overlook the Hualapai operation because of special political considerations. At their Grand Canyon headquarters, however, park officials nevertheless would have second thoughts about "looking the other way" when confronted with boundary disputes and claims of tribal sovereignty.[46]

Bead Sellers and Fred Harvey

The NPS did not look the other way when Navajos began marketing jewelry inside the park. Vigorous suppression of Navajo roadside vendors, seen by Indians as an NPS defense of Fred Harvey's corporate monopoly on the South Rim, began when park concession policy collided with Navajo free enterprise.

For nearly fifty years after the founding of Yellowstone, the government liberally granted permits and leases to business firms that provided food, lodg-

tower, "intended to bring about a better understanding of the American Indian." The tower contained a kiva, altar, sandpainting, Hopi myths, and relics of the Snake Dance. A Hopi artist named Kabotie decorated one room. Today tens of thousands of tourists visit the tower each year to glimpse Hopi culture, an introduction that exceeds any similar information available about the Navajo, Havasupai, or Paiutes. A few miles west of Desert View, the Tusayan Museum provides compact anthropological displays on five tribes, including the Hopi, and offers several dozen books on native culture. No Hopi have been arrested for selling beads or silver. The NPS recognizes the special status of the Hopi religion by banning hikers from the Colorado salt mines and discouraging visits to Sipapu, the location where the Hopi believe they entered the world.

Modern Hopi fulfill Park Service and environmentalist expectations. Relations improved steadily after the tribal council in 1989 appointed Leigh Jenkins director of a new cultural preservation program. Jenkins grew up at Third Mesa, received a degree in business administration from Northern Arizona University, and helped manage the tribe's health programs for fourteen years prior to the new assignment. When asked about the tribe's distance from the Grand Canyon and lack of common border, Jenkins found both factors irrelevant. The Hopi, he pointed out, had no voice in the location of their reservation, in being encircled by the Navajo, or in the division of land into counties, state parks, national forests, and national parks. Lines on maps are arbitrary.

What matters is that Sipapu and the ritual site Blue Springs lie on land forever "owned" by the Hopi, whose word for boundary, qulalni, carries a subtle overtone of spiritual stewardship. A cairn, marker, or fence may indicate where a people's particular stewardship begins and ends, but it does not reduce anyone else's spiritual ties with the area. Stewardship, according to Jenkins, means that "we are placed here to care for the land." The goal of life in the Hopi religious world is to understand and fulfill those obligations.

Leigh Jenkins praises the Park Service for its cultural stewardship. He conferred daily with the regional NPS office in Santa Fe, where Ed Natay kept him informed on matters affecting the Hopi. The superintendent at Wupatki has sought his advice on tribal history and culture, and has invited Hopi elders to offer presentations and examine artifact collections. At Grand Canyon, the NPS frequently seeks Hopi advice; the service has protected sacred sites and unofficially allowed traditional gathering activities that include taking ritual birds as well as piñon nuts and medicinal herbs.

Jenkins hopes to change limited Hopi employment in the park by securing seasonal jobs for interpreters and by organizing a student intern program with the NPS. He wants a more accurate program at Tusayan Museum, and Jenkins's conciliatory approach becomes apparent when he discusses the tower at Desert View. "They designed it in isolation," he says. "Maybe they talked to a few individuals, but they didn't consult the tribe or the elders. We think some of the material may be sensitive, but we haven't studied it closely. When we get the umbrella agreement with the park, we'll need to discuss it among ourselves." He promises that the tribe will commit money as well as advice to cultural interpretation.[53]

Leigh Jenkins becomes most enthusiastic about the Park Service when he turns to Jan Balsom and the Glen Canyon Dam assessment project. The Hopi have much at stake in controlling damage caused by fluctuations in river flow due to power demands. The tribe claims 180 archaeological sites along the river from Marble Canyon to Hualapai. They consider golden and bald eagle nests to be in danger, and they worry about ritual willows and reeds. Due to high flows, the beach has advanced within twenty yards of salt caves below the Beamer Trail. Park cooperation has been invaluable, Jenkins says, in studying these problems and lobbying Interior.[54]

Jan Balsom, the NPS Grand Canyon archaeologist since 1984, shares Jenkins's enthusiasm. She admires the Hopi for hiring scholars to study Glen Canyon Dam while offering to act in concert with NPS impact studies. As far as educating park visitors, Balsom admits that Grand Canyon has much to learn and that the Hopi can help:

> The Hopi interpretation is that first there were the Hopi, then the Spanish, then the Navajo, and then there were the white people. The Paiute interpretation is first Paiutes, then Hopi, then Spanish, Navajo, and the white people. The Park Service must be more sensitive to the whole continuum. As the Hualapai told me last week, this place was not discovered in 1540 by Cardenas, or the Spaniards, or anybody else. "We have been here." And the Hopi say they too have been here, and it's not like us saying "Where did these people go?" They didn't go anywhere, they're still here. And we need to look at how they choose to interpret their history.
>
> We can begin by hiring Indian interpreters. We used to, but park management backed down from the hassle. Now we sanitize history and present one view, a view that's written in Harper's Ferry, West Virginia,

with no input from local tribes. The Hopi want us hiring native people to work here, not in the low-paying housekeeper jobs, which is where we hire most Indians at Grand Canyon, but actually working for the Park Service as a uniformed ranger.

As NPS liaison with seven tribes, Balsom frequently faces Indian anger over past neglect, land grabs, and inconsistent policy, an anger often expressed in personal terms against whoever represents government. In Leigh Jenkins and the Hopi, however, she finds a different spirit: "The Hopi are pretty philosophical about their history and they say, 'Well, we've all made a lot of mistakes in the past, and there is no reason why we need to make them any more. We'll start from here and go forward. We're not going to dwell on the problems because in the last couple of years the Park Service has come a long way.'"[55]

One does not encounter that attitude among Havasupai leaders. The Hopi name for Havasupai is Coconino, and the Hopi consider them the stewards or "Keepers" of the Grand Canyon. Unlike the Hopi, the Coconino have lived directly under park administration since 1919. Errors of the past, such as the opinions of Dama Margaret Smith or the burning of Havasupai cabins and camps, cut deeper than interpretive errors at Desert View and Tusayan Museum. For years the issue that most estranged the Havasupai was park control of traditional plateau land. That conflict culminated in 1973–74 with the Grand Canyon Enlargement Act, legislation promising hope to the Keepers of the Grand Canyon, the Coconino.

8

"THE JUST AND NECESSARY PROTECTION OF THE GRAND CANYON"

Besides, how can you have a reservation in the middle of a
national park?

—Aaron J. Elkins, *The Dark Place*, 1983

More than anything else that I have attempted to do in [my]
years in Congress is get the Grand Canyon bill passed. . . . This
bill is long, long overdue. It will give the Grand Canyon the
protection it is going to need. It will not affect the cattlemen, it
will not affect the Indian, it will only affect those people who
want to abuse the Canyon, and, believe me, as one who has
practically spent his life in it, the numbers are growing.

—Barry Goldwater to Morris Udall, April 26, 1973

On January 3, 1975, President Gerald Ford signed PL 93–620, the Grand
Canyon Enlargement Act. In doing so, the president also transferred 185,000
acres from Park and Forest Service lands to the Havasupai Indian Reservation.
Furthermore, the legislation created an additional 95,000-acre traditional use
area inside Grand Canyon National Park. PL 93-620 was a victory for the
Havasupai in their century-long struggle to regain plateau land. It signaled
defeat for the NPS and park defenders. When Ford signed the law, he ended the
most bitter clash between Indians and environmentalists in U.S. history.

Havasupai means "people of blue water," a people idealized as original inhabitants in a canyon Shangri-la of trees and waterfalls that had been their
home for centuries. Environmental groups in the 1970s did not realize, al-

though George Wharton James had in 1900, that the Havasupai were a plateau people who "at one time owned the whole of the Kohonino Forest region and also the trails into Hack-a-tai-a (the Grand Canyon). From time immemorial they have hunted from Cataract Canyon to the Little Colorado."[1] Using modern landmarks, the 2.3-million-acre aboriginal Supai homeland of at least seven hundred years ran south from Tuba City to the San Francisco Peaks, west along I-40 to thirty miles northwest of Ash Fork, and then north to the Canyon rim.

In the summers people tended gardens in Cataract and other side canyons of the Colorado. After fall harvest, they occupied the plateau to hunt. Flora Gregg Iliff, BIA teacher at Supai Village in 1901, caught the rhythm of this annual cycle: "As jealously as the Havasupai guarded their canyon and as passionately as they loved it, the tang of autumn in the air turned their thoughts to a winter home on the mesa, and started them packing their possessions with a happy abandon. All summer they had planned for this . . . to get outside, where they could look about with the full sweep of the vaulted sky above, with endless miles in which to wander."[2]

The Havasupai, a tribe that claims its members have never killed a white person, lost the plateau when they did not resist early incursions by Americans. They avoided warfare against the United States in the 1860s and also escaped forced eviction from their ancestral lands. Nevertheless, growing pressure from miners, cattlemen, sheep herders, and railroads reduced their range and eliminated their water sources, pressures that led President Rutherford B. Hayes in 1880 to set aside a twelve-by-five-mile reservation that included Cataract Canyon. In 1882, the same year that Benjamin Harrison introduced the first Grand Canyon bill, another executive order cut the reservation from 38,400 to 518.6 acres inside a tight canyon above Havasu Falls.

On paper, the government had confined the Havasupai to a single garden site. In reality, annual migrations between canyon and rim continued. After 1890, as the government defined the plateau as a forest and game preserve, pressure arose to move the tribe. Forcefully defended in 1896 by BIA agent Henry Ewing as "the most industrious Indians I have ever known," the Havasupai kept their reservation but faced increasing harassment from outside.[3] Ewing warned his superiors against attempts at removal. The Havasupai loved their land "as no white man ever loved his native country, and so sure as the sun shines they will never be peaceably removed from it. . . . Should force be used, then every man and boy, who could carry a rifle must first be killed."

Ewing described the Havasupai Indians as progressive farmers, expert horse-men, and skilled hunters who only wished to be left alone. W. P. Hermann, a forest manager for the Department of the Interior, came to different conclu-sions. Hermann knew that Indians killing deer and antelope on the plateau alarmed tourists. His 1898 letter to the Indian Office was the first salvo in a contest between conservationists and the area's native people: "The Grand Canyon of the Colorado River is becoming so renowned for its wonderful natural gorge scenery . . . that it should be preserved for the everlasting pleasure and instruction of our intelligent citizens as well as those of foreign countries. Henceforth, I deem it just and necessary to keep the wild and unappreciable Indian from off the Reserve."[4]

In the years that followed, the Forest Service, Park Service, and environmen-tal organizations sought to regulate Havasupai use of traditional land, but the tribe did not forget. "A long time ago," one Havasupai wrote to the commis-sioner of Indian affairs, "the Indians all go out on the plateau and hunt deer for two or three months. . . . Now the Indians are all afraid about the hunting and never go far away. I want you to send me a hunting license and tell me good and straight that I may hunt deer. Long time ago these Indians do not fight white man. The white man should now help the Indians by giving him permission to hunt deer."[5]

The BIA, Indian reformers, lawyers, and the tribe strove to recover portions of the Supai legacy. Nearly 100,000 acres could be leased at no charge from the federal government, yet this left the tribe feeling insecure.[6] As the Grand Canyon shifted in status, from forest reserve to game preserve to monument to park, the BIA and tribal supporters tried in 1908, 1920, 1931, 1943, 1952, 1957, 1968, and 1973 to expand the tiny reserve by adding up to 300,000 acres of plateau land. Thrown on the defensive in 1919 by Carl Hayden's national park legislation, which headed toward passage without recognition of existing In-dian permit and use practices, tribal supporters successfully lobbied Section 7 into the bill: "That nothing herein contained shall affect the rights of the Havasupai Tribe of Indians to the use and occupancy of the bottom lands of the Canyon of Cataract Creek . . . and the Secretary of the Interior is hereby authorized, in his discretion, to permit individual members of said tribe to use and occupy other tracts of land within said park for agricultural purposes."[7]

As evident in the story of Supai Camp, NPS relations with the Havasupai after 1919 depended largely on the attitude of individual superintendents. In administering the plateau and Havasu Canyon, the service has been described as arrogant, oppressive, and racist. For the Havasupai who hold this view, creation of a park meant the coming of rangers who insisted on no hunting, no travel, no harvesting of wild plants, no littering, no gardens except on the reserve, and no cremation of the dead.[8]

More positively, the NPS consistently issued use permits to Indians needing plateau land. It hired Havasupai at fair wages, helping the tribe make the transition from a gathering to a cash economy. Conflicts with the tribe resulted in part from different goals. The Park Service had a mandate to protect the canyon and promote recreation; it certainly did not see itself as a social agency adept at serving Indians. To the extent that the NPS did recognize the tribe, most messages could only have confused matters: rumors of land exchanges between the park, Forest Service, BIA, and Biological Survey; complaints about overgrazing by Indian horses; paperwork to renew annual grazing permits; proposals for a direct road from Grand Canyon Village to Manakacha Point; promises to build water tanks; NPS plans for a tramway and hydro plant; plans for a "modest tourist enterprise" with lodge, cabins, and cafeteria at Supai Village; and repeated rumors about moving to the Hualapai Reserve. The Hava- supai, for their part, asked to be left alone in their village and on the plateau— and they wanted title to their land.[9]

Despite assurances from the NPS that it would continue to lease plateau lands and would consider a binding agreement to that effect, the Havasupai and BIA believed that only permanent enlargement of the reservation would provide se- curity.[10] Two events, one a local incident in 1939 and the other a U.S. Supreme Court decision in 1941, inspired Havasupai attempts to acquire park property.

In the summer of 1939 a white man named Rudolph Kirby built a fence around a spring at the head of Cataract Canyon, land that he had leased from the state. Blocked from the watering hole, twenty-eight head of Havasupai cattle died. Three Indians, including an elder named Sinyella, complained to the park superintendent. The tribal council also wrote to Commissioner of Indian Affairs John Collier. The affair inspired the NPS to suggest once again that the tribe be placed on the Hualapai reserve, with the 518 acres in Havasu Canyon transferred to the NPS. The Havasupai had a very different response to the incident.[11]

When the government informed the tribe that Kirby's actions were legal, it increased determination to regain control of the plateau. An opportunity ap- peared on December 8, 1942, when Justice William O. Douglas announced the 9-0 Supreme Court decision upholding native title to Santa Fe Railroad land grants south of the Grand Canyon.[12] Shortly afterward, a legal team from Interior reported that the Havasupai retained "exclusive right of use and occupancy" to odd-numbered sections of traditional land on the plateau. With this legal foundation, the tribe and BIA pressed for NPS cessions. Collier insisted that Indians had valid claims to even-numbered sections as well as the Santa Fe lands in an area needed not only for water and grazing but also for tribal self-confidence and a sense of security. Collier might have added a sense of justice, the central argument made by the Havasupai Tribal Council:

> This land was used by our tribe long before the coming of the white people. When white people first came we did not understand that they were to finally deprive us of the use of it. We permitted them to use our springs and water holes and never tried to make trouble. We see now how this land was taken from us, but did not realize it at the time. If a rancher wanted to use some of our land he would come to us and make an agreement to put up a fence or build a tank and would tell us that he was not trying to take our land but we all could use it together. In a few years this fellow would leave and another fellow would come along and tell us that he had bought the land from the fellow who built the fence and tank and that we would have to get off. Within the last few years we have learned that this land was not a part of our reservation. We have been gradually pushed back until we are now on a reservation of 518 acres.

By the spring of 1943, the tribe, Indian agent John O. Crow, and Collier had gained the support of the Forest Service, the Department of Agriculture, and the state and county governments. Only the NPS opposed the transfer.[13]

Faced with legal and ethical arguments, Director Newton Drury appointed a committee to study land transfer. Within two weeks it had published a report "entirely sympathetic" to the Indians but finding any legal claims invalid and their moral argument outweighed by larger considerations: "The greatest objection to the proposal is one of principle and precedent. . . . It eliminated from a great National Park approximately one-fifth of the entire area [and transferred] that fifth . . . for industrial, commercial or other economic objectives. . . . On the strength of this general objection alone it [is] the clear duty of the National Park Service to oppose that part of the proposal."

In addition, the committee argued that transfer would remove forty miles of the Colorado River from the park, destroy potential studies of "perfectly natural conditions" on the Great Thumb, and cut off access to views of Havasu Canyon

that would "remain uniquely interesting and beautiful for centuries to come—
perhaps long after the last of the Havasupais shall have passed away." The
committee did allow for ceding certain park as well as USFS land of no value.
The grazing and water supply needs of the tribe could be solved by interagency
cooperation. Otherwise, NPS ownership remained "the best available guarantee
of preserving inspirational qualities unimpaired for the enjoyment of future
generations, as provided by law."[14] In a hectic battle of reports, telegrams, and
legal briefs, the NPS prevailed. From this 1943 controversy the Havasupai
gained twenty-five hundred acres at the head of Cataract Canyon, thirty miles
south of their village.

A few years later, the NPS considered elimination of other parklands north
and south of the river, lands "valuable for grazing purposes" where white ranchers had water rights. "I know of nothing," advised Regional Director Miner
Tillotson, "that we could do better to improve our public relations throughout
Arizona and other western states than to release for [grazing] lands such as
these which are not really needed for park and monument purposes."[15]

Havasu Canyon and the Great Society

Following World War II the Havasupai persisted in claiming plateau land, as
changes in their culture made that goal more important and difficult. The BIA,
trying to quickly assimilate Indians into American society, reduced and eliminated programs at Supai, including the school. Among the Havasupai themselves, with economic depression, a sense of confinement, a rise in alcohol and
drug abuse, family quarrels and sexual promiscuity, suicide, violence, and weak
law enforcement, nature's Shangri-la turned into a social nightmare. Gossip,
slander, beatings, and "vicious jokes and slashing comments" became a way of
life in the narrow canyon. At the heart of the problems, according to anthropologist John Martin, were destructive BIA policies and an unworkable system
of land tenure. By the mid-1960s, with Havasupai population rising, "every
square inch of reservation land below the talus slopes" was claimed by one or
more persons, with no effective system of inheritance or for settling ownership
disputes.[16]

At the nadir of Havasupai history, the NPS renewed its plans for their canyon. In 1957, without consulting the tribe, the service purchased the 62-acre
Johnson mining claim below Supai Village. This land, which the tribe had long
sought to acquire, contained cremation and burial sites. The NPS removed

fences and razed cabins before building a campground along the main stream between Havasu and Mooney Falls, the only access being through Supai Village. In response, the tribal council passed frequent resolutions demanding return of the plateau and removal of the campground. The protests were futile until the mid-1960s, when three conditions changed: tourism boomed, the war on poverty began, and the tribe won a judgment from the ICC.

By the end of the 1950s, several hundred visitors a year would use the eight-mile trail from Hualapai Hilltop to the village.[17] In 1964 that number jumped to over four thousand; on Easter weekend alone, twelve hundred persons arrived at the NPS campground. For the tribe this meant new business, cash flow, and a shortage of plateau forage pack horses.[18] To capitalize on this influx, the BIA built a new campground on the talus slope above Havasu Falls, complete with tables, grills, and water taps. Exposed, rocky, hot, and windy, the tribal campground had no trees, although it did have ample scorpions and rattlesnakes. The project failed, yet pack trains and backpackers kept moving down Havasu Canyon.

A second major change at Supai in the 1960s involved the federal war on poverty. Here as elsewhere, the program brought dollars and idealistic volunteers who transformed reservation life. With new resources beyond BIA control, the Havasupai moved from despair onto the long road to social recovery, as well as onto a shorter road that would lead to their victory in 1974 over the NPS. In concrete terms, the Great Society meant construction projects, reopening of the Supai school, a sixfold increase in tribal per capita income between 1964 and 1975, and the arrival of two energetic schoolteachers, Lois and Stephen Hirst. When the Hirsts joined forces with outside attorneys and with an assertive tribal council that now controlled a few economic resources, the fifty-year Havasupai campaign for parkland acquired much needed political acumen and historical-research skills.

The decade's third critical event was a 1968 ICC award of $1,240,000, to compensate for 2.2 million acres lost a century earlier. After debating whether to accept money for land, the tribe voted 52-10 in favor of the cash. The NPS read the settlement as extinguishing Havasupai claims to the plateau; so did environmentalists, who, five years later, used the ICC payment to argue that the tribe had no claim to the plateau.

In 1968, after a Havasupai land transfer failed in Congress, the Sierra Club and the Park Service drafted a master plan consolidating all federal Grand Canyon lands as park. The canyon, instead of being administered as a single ecological unit, had fragmented into a park, two monuments, two recreation areas, and a national forest. Other areas, the 1968 planners noted, were on Indian reservations and beyond control. The master plan recommended giving the park Long Mesa, the precontact Moqui trading trail, upper Hualapai Canyon, Cataract Canyon, and portions of the Havasupai trail "to insure appropriate management and development above the reservation and Havasu Canyon." Placing Cataract Canyon under NPS jurisdiction was crucial: "It will give park protection to this scenic and scientific area rim to rim." The plan also gave an indication of NPS ideas about the growing Havasu tourist traffic, protecting the "charm and beauty" of the reservation, and developing new facilities to meet park standards. The Master Plan neglected to state that a Havasupai Reservation existed.[19]

The tribe, led by council members Juan Sinyella and Lee Marshall, protested at public hearings, then developed a proposal demanding return of 200,000 acres on the plateau, plus permanent title to Supai Camp and the NPS campground at Havasu Falls. When the NPS found this unacceptable, matters stalemated.

In November 1972, the Indians learned that Barry Goldwater would sponsor a park enlargement bill during the next Congress. Knowing that Goldwater had been instrumental in the 1970 restoration of Blue Lake to Taos Pueblo, and that six months earlier President Nixon had returned twenty-one thousand acres of Gifford Pinchot National Forest near Mt. Adams to the Yakamas, the tribe invited the senator to Supai Village. Goldwater, who considered himself an authority on the Grand Canyon and a lifelong friend of Arizona Indians, immediately accepted.

When Goldwater arrived, on January 27, Chairman Oscar Paya presented Tribal Resolution 1-73. The document cited reduction of aboriginal territory from 3,000,000 to 518 acres, then succinctly traced failed efforts to restore grazing areas and sacred sites. It concluded: "NOW, THEREFORE, BE IT RESOLVED that the Havasupai Tribal Council and people request the return of all Havasupai allotments and permit areas presently under U.S. Park Service and U.S. Forest Service control, including the 160-acre Havasupai residency area at Grand Canyon [Village] and the return of Havasu campground to the Havasupai Tribe as part of the Havasupai Reservation."

Following intense discussion, Goldwater promised to add the tribe's request to his enlargement bill. As he began referring to "we," the Havasupai realized they had won their most important political ally since agent Henry Ewing.

Recalling the dramatic day, Steve Hirst described how Goldwater "finally looked at the gathered Councilmen and said, 'We are in better shape to get land than we have been in many years. . . . I have no hesitancy offering the whole ball of wax. I hope we will have no trouble getting your wants met. I promise to put in everything you ask for, but I can't promise you'll get it.' The crowd broke into unaccustomed applause."[20]

A Noisy Crisis

The ensuing two-year struggle over the Havasupai land transfer is too complex to recount step by step, the details being readily available in Stephen Hirst's *Life in a Narrow Place*. In short, Barry Goldwater and Morris Udall introduced S.1296 and H.R.5900 with a provision (section 12) restoring 169,000 acres of land to the tribe. The Sierra Club and Friends of the Earth, supported by other environmental groups, led the opposition. The NPS also opposed section 12. After opponents forced deletion of the Havasupai land transfer, replacing it with a "study," Udall introduced a compromise that still evoked opposition but gained support from Richard Nixon, a dubious victory for the tribe as the president sank under Watergate. After effective lobbying by Bill Byler of the New York–based American Association for Indian Affairs and Phoenix attorney Joe Sparks, Udall, a Democrat, and Republican House minority leader John Rhodes of Arizona brought H.R.5900 to a vote on October 10, 1972. It passed 180–147, was amended in the Senate, and signed by Gerald Ford as PL 93-620 on January 3, 1975.

Goldwater's original legislation had contained strong protection of Indian land and provided for cooperative management agreements between tribes and the NPS. A radical concept, "Grand Canyon Zones of Influence," had given the NPS authority to protect the canyon from activities outside its borders, excluding Indian reservations. Development of reservation tourism was strongly encouraged, except that the law prohibited the Hualapai from building any structure within a mile of the Colorado River. Havasu Creek was protected from diversion, and 169,000 acres on the plateau shifted from the USFS and NPS to the Havasupai. A large segment of the remaining park would become wilderness.

When President Ford signed the bill, zones of influence and wilderness designations had been replaced by a section allowing dam construction at Bridge Canyon. The Havasupai had 185,000 additional acres, including the area from Havasu Creek to Beaver Falls, which meant that the tribe now owned the NPS campground. They also secured exclusive right to 95,000 acres of "traditional use lands" inside the park. At no point did the legislation refer to Supai Camp. Political compromise produced strict controls over the 185,000 acres: All nontraditional uses had to be approved by Interior, and any non-agricultural uses required prior study, public hearings, and submission to Congress. Logging, mining, and manufacturing were banned. The Havasupai had regained acres, not sovereignty.

These changes had occurred over two years as the bill wound through Congress. Without a bipartisan effort by the Arizona delegation, especially Goldwater and Udall, Havasupai land claims would have brought only more "study." When the Senate removed the land transfer, Mo Udall devised compromises that led to passage in the House and eventually the Senate. The bill's most effective support came from the Association for American Indian Affairs and the Havasupai themselves; the opposition consisted of environmentalists, especially the Sierra Club. The NPS kept a low profile.

The land transfer was opposed by the Audubon Society, the Wilderness Society, the Izaak Walton League, the National Parks and Conservation Association, forty-two organizations in the Federation of Western Outdoor Clubs, the Western River Guides Association, and the National Wildlife Federation, all led by the Sierra Club and Friends of the Earth.[21] Environmental arguments ran from relevant to trivial to derogatory, falling into biased language and false accusations that would cripple Indian/conservationist relations. The NPCA, for instance, condemned a "Havasupai land grab." The *Sierra Club Bulletin* reported a Grand Canyon "giveaway," and the *New York Times* accused the Havasupai of a "raid" on public land.

Opponents often took absolute stands: Indians could continue with grazing permits, "but beyond that, nothing. . . . Not a single acre." "It is time," wrote a woman from Prescott, "that we stopped feeling sorry for people and giving them whatever they want." One letter to Mo Udall protested that the Havasupai lacked education, that "great gobs of horses," not cattle, roamed the permit lands, that the tribe no longer lived as it had in 1880, and, quite correctly, that the park stood to lose Mooney and Beaver Falls. Yet, of the hundreds of letters that Udall received from constituents against the land transfer, none contained overt racial prejudice.[22]

To protect the park, David Brower revived tactics from the 1960s dam struggle. His July 1974 advertisement in the *New York Times* played on fear by accusing Indians of being dupes of developers and the tourist industry:

> *They're after the Grand Canyon Again? The Grand Canyon!*
>
> This time the would-be despoilers are exceedingly clever. . . . They are using Indians as a ploy: oppose their scheme and you are "unkind to Indians" . . . This time the Havasu are involved, some 425 of them, living in the Shangri-la of Havasu Canyon (which brings them substantial revenue from tourists . . .). They would like some more land—180,000 acres from the heart of Grand Canyon National Park! (If you know the River, they want Elves' Chasm and forty-four downstream miles.)
>
> What *do* we have here? Is it a cigar-store Indian of the proportions of a Trojan Horse, being wheeled in kindness within the walls? Are dam builders and never-tiring developers hidden inside, ready for a windfall at everyone else's expense? Tramway, road, and marina builders, too, ready to demean one of the world's last great experiences?
>
> We think so, with reason. The pattern is an old one: Disarm the defenders, deceive a tribal council, and move in. Remember Black Mesa and the Four Corners? . . . How often have Indians been finessed into playing such an unhappy role?[23]

Brower's tactics had succeeded ten years earlier against large utilities and the Bureau of Reclamation, but they seemed crude overkill against a tiny band of Indians. Other environmentalists, fortunately, employed more honest arguments against land transfer: (1) it would set a precedent for future loss of parklands; (2) Indian title to the plateau had been extinguished when the tribe accepted $1.2 million from the ICC; (3) the Havasupai, being poor, would place economic development ahead of preservation; (4) the land of the arid, overgrazed plateau offered meager benefits; and (5) regardless of past injustice (whenever they spoke, opponents always expressed "sympathy" for Indians), the Grand Canyon now belonged to all Americans.

The five arguments had merit. Future use of precedents was impossible to prove or disprove, but environmentalists knew that Blue Lake and Mt. Adams had been used as precedents for Grand Canyon, and they could point to instances in which tribes had made even larger claims to public land. The Hopi might want San Francisco Peaks. The Navajo could claim Oak Creek Canyon, Sunset Crater, Mt. Taylor, and the eastern half of the Canyon. The Blackfeet wanted Lewis and Clark National Forest and parts of Glacier, as did the Kootenai. The Umpqua sought the Oregon Dunes, and Pit River Indians insisted on having Mount Lassen National Park.[24] On the other side, one could cite a much longer list of parklands released to non-Indians in the past. The argument cut both ways.

The second point, the ICC settlement, made the Havasupai appear hypocritical—they had accepted payment and then wanted the land too. Havasupai defenses against this charge were weak and contrived, including an offer to return the money. Anyone who remembered the 1969 tribal debate, when those willing to accept cash won by 80 percent, knew that the Havasupai understood the implications of their vote.

On item three, the pressure to escape poverty through environmental sacrifice, opponents of transfer used concrete examples. "Southwestern Indians have a poor record as conservationists," contended Toby Cooper of the NPCA. He pointed to Navajo coal leases at Black Mesa and the Hualapai agreement with the Arizona Power Authority to build Bridge Canyon Dam.[25] He could have mentioned tourism at Taos, Miccosukee alligator wrestling in the Everglades, Makah clear-cuts at Neah Bay, or the Kaibab Paiute tourist site fifty miles due north of Supai Village.

Fourth, when environmentalists questioned the economic benefits from the transfer, they calculated that the plateau land's grazing capacity for cattle and horses would produce slight gains in tribal income. That prediction has proven correct, especially under the congressional restrictions placed on land use.[26] By using such arguments, environmentalists had to discard romantic stereotypes and face the poverty of reservations. Poverty did not sway many; one environmentalist victory involved the economic restrictions added to Udall's bill.[27]

The final point—who owns this part of the Grand Canyon—was an ethical principle. Here, as discussed below, acting solely on theory and ideology, environmental leaders failed in their homework.

The Havasupai, on the other hand, drew upon the research and writing of Steve Hirst and the political organizing of Joe Sparks to wage a campaign that outflanked even the veteran David Brower. Throughout 1973 the tribe distributed leaflets and mass mailings. In June they testified at a Senate hearing and in November tribal spokesmen appeared before the House subcommittee on national parks to masterfully combine legal arguments, historical facts, and emotional appeal. Lee Marshall began by claiming that the NPS had betrayed his people: "We know liars and bureaucratic land robbers when we see them: The time has come for us to talk straight out. We are mad, and now we see we are fighting for our lives. . . . Your people's ignorance about our people has been making us poor. Well, we're going to make sure you have no excuse for being ignorant any longer."

Marshall traced Havasupai dispossession from 1880 to the present. Quoting Arizona congressmen, General Nelson Miles, Felix Cohen, Henry Ewing, John Crow, and endless BIA reports, he cited promise after promise, concluding after each one, "Nothing was done." Marshall next read a 1914 report from Indian agent J.J. Taylor, who advised Commissioner of Indian Affairs Cato Sells that "it would be a greater 'Monument' to our government to dedicate [the land] to the use of these Indians. It is absolutely certain that they cannot carry it away nor tear it down. In a thousand years they could neither fill up these canyons . . . if they kept busy all the time." Even the 1943 NPS report rejecting any land cession provided evidence for returning the plateau. "The morale of the Tribe," the NPS conceded, "would be greatly improved by . . . their getting back their ancestral country as reservation of their very own, to which they could admit outsiders on sufferance instead of themselves being admitted to it only on sufferance."

Marshall then described how rangers drove Indians from the land, burned homes, destroyed sacred places, and desecrated burial grounds. He closed by turning the argument for preservation against the NPS:

> Ask the Park Service what they did to our old homes in 1934. Ask them what they did to Big Jim's place in 1953. Ask them what they did to our burial ground below Havasu Falls. That's how they protect things. We have no faith in the Park Service. . . . Who was it who paid people to kill all the mountain lions around the Grand Canyon? We could have told them the foolishness of that, but no one listens to Indians.
>
> For years the Park Service has neglected and mismanaged Havasu Campground, where we once cremated our people. Dead people's things have long since walked off with hikers. They let people use the campground with no limit. We have seen 2,000 people in that campground. . . . The place was a disaster: toilets full, the stream polluted, the wood cut, trash all over . . . nudity, marijuana, smoking and trash everywhere. . . .
>
> They make us laugh when they talk about protecting the environment which they just noticed. Have you seen Grand Canyon Village? . . . We do not believe the South Rim can support another Disneyland, whether it has so-called environmentalist approval or not. You should replace every Park Service employee on the South Rim, including the superintendent,

with a Havasupai before they destroy our homeland forever. We suggest this as the best way to manage all our National Parks.[28]

Havasupai testimony, despite its eloquence, failed to persuade the committee. By March, section 12 on the land transfer had been stricken from H.R.5900. Stunned, the tribe wired Mo Udall to correct "a terrible mistake." The tribal council pleaded that he come immediately to Supai for a conference. Udall declined, saying that political opposition made reservation enlargement impossible: "We just cannot win on this point." The Havasupai responded that they had always trusted him, but by failing to support Sam Steiger and Lloyd Meeds in their behalf, Udall had betrayed that trust. Worse, he had condemned them to extinction. "We are endangered. . . . The Grand Canyon will always be here. Without your help we won't be."[29]

Meanwhile, Bill Byler in New York had organized a national campaign to counter the environmentalists. Support came from dozens of tribes and native federations, including the National Congress of American Indians, the Indian Historical Society, Alaska Federation of Natives, and the Arizona Intertribal Council. Two native journals, *Wassaja* and *Akawesasne Notes*, published extensive reports throughout 1973 and 1974, and La Donna Harris, one of the most influential Indian leaders in the nation, personally asked Udall to change his position.

Among non-Indians, the Havasupai had many prominent allies: Ted Kennedy, Roger Baldwin, Alvin M. Josephy, the League of Women Voters, the United Mine Workers, United Steel Workers, Harry Bridge's Longshoreman's Union, the Indian Rights Association, the National Education Association, the Protestant Episcopal Church, and the United Church of Christ. Eighty-seven newspapers backed the tribe, from the *Christian Science Monitor, Los Angeles Times,* and *Wall Street Journal* to the *Barstow Desert Dispatch, Statesboro-Herald,* and *Coos Bay World.* Probably the most powerful help was a *60 Minutes* program, "Canyon Shadows," broadcast on February 3, 1974.

Byler and Sparks also enlisted scholars, including the anthropologists Robert Euler, Alfonso Ortiz, and John Martin. Many of the Southwest's leading ethnologists lived in Udall's district: Edward H. Spicer, Bernard Fontana, Henry Dobyns, and Keith Basso. Dobyns savagely attacked the NPS:

The National Park Service mounted its bureaucratic war over half a century ago. . . . Urged on by racist "environmentalists," the rangers [will] terminate permits and . . . finally imprison the Havasupai on a 518-acre concentration camp without adequate food, without safe water to drink, thus forcing them to either die or abandon their homeland forever. . . .

Uniformed rangers of the National Park Service instead of Army troops fight the current war against the Havasupai people. These bureaucrats employ trucks instead of horses, lobbyists instead of guns. . . . Lily-white rangers . . . zealous rangers . . . righteous rangers. . . . Warriors in the federal war on the Havasupais know that poverty and economic necessity are [their] powerful allies.[30]

Bernard Fontana, taking a calmer approach, mailed well-reasoned letters to the Udalls and to newspaper editors. Fontana explained Havasupai history and, without using hyperbole, pointed out that the National Park Service was not the BIA—that its mandate did not include solving social problems.[31] Grand Canyon anthropologist Robert Euler also spoke out, persuading local environmental groups to break with national leaders on the issue.

The most important contribution came from Edward Spicer, a highly respected anthropologist at the University of Arizona. After tracing Havasupai history and deploring blind opposition to the land transfer, Spicer informed Morris Udall that the tribe had drafted land-use restrictions that they would accept as binding in a transfer bill. Udall jumped at the idea. Within a few weeks he had shifted his position, gained Goldwater's support, and predicted "clear sailing" in Congress. After Udall's amendment, the tribe passed a resolution renouncing "any dams, tramlines or railroads which would flood, harm, or otherwise damage the environment." They revoked support for the Hualapai Dam, and accepted external regulation of their land.[32]

When the revised bill reached the House floor on October 10, 1972, debate brought the usual arguments about precedent, tramways, roads, motels, and the ICC settlement, but Udall's limits on Havasupai sovereignty had cut the ground from under those who predicted the tribe would defile the Grand Canyon or be a stalking horse for developers. The bill passed the House by thirty-three votes and survived the Senate conference intact.[33]

The not-so-quiet crisis had ended.

Aftermath: 1975–1990

At Supai Village, January 3rd is an official holiday commemorating passage of PL 93-620, the largest Indian land restoration act in U.S. history. For the

Havasupai, according to their advocate Stephen Hirst in 1976, the bill's passage ended centuries of injustice: "Their beloved winter homeland is again reunited with them. Their long nightmare is over."

If the nightmare ended, pleasant dreams did not follow. Tribal land, in Hirst's words, may have "shed the fiction" of being a national forest or park, yet the NPS remained a powerful neighbor of the enlarged reservation. Provisions in the legislation mollifying environmentalists and park officials meant that the Havasupai had land but no sovereignty. Return of the plateau, as opponents of transfer had predicted, brought little financial benefit. Nor did the tribe's internal social and political problems disappear on January 3, 1975: Economic dependence on the federal government actually increased, while poverty, diabetes, and alcohol abuse continued. Nor did Havasupai attitudes toward environmentalists and the NPS change. Hirst's belief that the tribe would "forgive all" proved too optimistic.[34]

The Grand Canyon Enlargement Act, while allowing certain uses that included traditional hunting and gathering, mandated that transferred land "shall remain forever wild." In lobbying for the bill, the Havasupai, much like the Makah at Neah Bay, had pledged themselves to preservation. No logging, mining, resorts, or industrial development would be allowed. Any tribal enterprises and uses needed approval by the secretary of the interior, who required a general land-use plan. No development could "detract from the existing scenic and natural values" of the land. Non-Indians had limited access rights for recreation in and across the reservation. On the ninety-five thousand acres designated for traditional use inside the park, most notably the Great Thumb Mesa, Indian control was even more limited. Oversight of these conditions and approval of the mandatory land-use plan lay with the secretary of the interior, who, in turn, was instructed by Congress to protect scenery and wildlife. Furthermore, the Enlargement Act extinguished all Havasupai claims to any land outside the new reservation, presumably including Supai Camp.

Idealistic goals, mixed jurisdictions, and unclear responsibilities ensured continued friction between the tribe and the park. Whatever the law's language, the Havasupai insisted that they had not surrendered Supai Camp. When NPS anthropologist Robert Euler began to study traditional use areas, the tribal council arbitrarily halted the inquiry, even though Euler had long been an outspoken advocate of their cause. The council quickly drafted a land-use plan, but Interior approval meant NPS acceptance and environmentalist surveillance, a process that would stall progress for seven years.[35]

The tribal plan appeared for public review nine months after passage of the Enlargement Act. It affirmed "traditional concepts of harmony with all life" and a Havasupai desire to protect the beauty of their homeland, then turned to practical matters. Wells, the diversion of Havasu Creek, solar panels, wind generators, and power lines across the Hualapai Reservation were required for water and power to support families who moved from Supai Village to Pasture Wash, Moqui Tank, and Hualapai Hilltop on the plateau. The tribe proposed a school for Pasture Wash. Transportation included airstrips, graded dirt roads, and paved roads east to Grand Canyon Village and south to Peach Springs. Off-road vehicles were banned, with public access to Manakaja Point and Great Thumb Mesa restricted to foot or horse travel using Havasupai guides. Indian hunters had first claim on deer, antelope, and rabbits; bighorn sheep were protected and all trophy hunting banned. With eight thousand persons visiting Havasu Canyon annually, the problems of sewage and solid waste disposal confronted the tribe.

These were the easier issues. Other matters posed dilemmas that the tribal plan did not resolve: Was incineration, land fill, or chemical treatment the best answer to waste disposal? Could the plateau support grazing by horses and cattle, and, if not, which had priority? Should juniper trees be removed to enhance the range and restore native food plants? Should mountain lions be restored to the plateau? Were there limits to tourism and camping in Havasu Canyon? And should the tribe build a cafe, gas station, lodge, and store at Topocoba and Hualapai Hilltops? In pursuing these goals, the Havasupai anticipated federal funding.[36]

The NPS reacted to the proposal by surveying its Grand Canyon personnel; the Sierra Club demanded an environmental impact statement. In April 1976, Secretary of the Interior Thomas Kleppe rejected the plan. It took until 1982 to reach an agreement, by which time nerves on both sides had frazzled over debates on the carrying capacity of land, grazing horses, fee collection from visitors, hunting, and boundary fencing. Land transfer had not revolutionized life at Havasupai; rather, the added responsibility and planning had made Indians even more dependent on federal dollars.

Native management of the ninety-five thousand acres of traditional lands inside the park also proved vexing. Robert Euler's ethnological survey of Havasupai uses on the Esplanade was soon halted by the tribe for no apparent reason. Next, the NPS allowed horses in the area, then banned them; the Havasupai agreed to remove their ponies, only to ignore the agreement. As rangers prepared to shoot several dozen wild horses, the standoff ended when a new superintendent retreated on stock reduction and elected to ignore the few remaining horses at large on park lands. To one federal manager, in this instance and others, it seemed like the Havasupai always got their way, either through legal threats or by Park Service tolerance: "Even though it's called the Grand Canyon Enlargement Act, sometimes I think of it as the Havasupai Enlargement Act."[37]

Questions of livestock management, employment preference, park entry, roads, cultural interpretation, and NPS lassitude in promoting tribal enterprises further contributed to poor relations after 1975, but the main irritant continued to be Supai Camp. With the extinguishing of Havasupai title to all except reservation lands, the NPS no doubt believed it had finally achieved control over this bothersome settlement on the fringe of Grand Canyon Village.

Supai Camp

On the Rowe's Well road, less than a mile southwest of Bright Angel Lodge on the South Rim, there is a circle of five run-down houses surrounded by discarded household goods and protected by free-ranging dogs. The seventy-year-old, 160-acre camp is an officially sanctioned residence of Havasupai Indians working in Grand Canyon Village. The park's two anthropologists, Jan Balsom and Robert Euler, have described the site as "sort of a sticking point . . . a bone of contention" for the NPS, and as the last stronghold on the rim for the Havasupai. Despite repeated and nearly successful efforts by the Park Service to dislodge Supai Camp, it has survived.

Long before Europeans arrived, Indians had occupied sites along the canyon's rim as far east as Desert View. When Grand Canyon Village began to provide seasonal employment early in the twentieth century, local Indians built dwellings nearby. Some accounts relate that the NPS itself created the camp in the 1920s, while others, Indian and white, remember hogans in the area at least a decade before 1919. Michael Harrison, among the first NPS staff at Grand Canyon, insists that Havasupai had used the site years earlier and "sure as hell were there in 1922."[38]

One oral tradition among the Havasupai traces the camp to Theodore Roosevelt's 1903 visit: "We knew Theodore was coming. They told us about it. He was riding a big white horse, from what they tell me. Theodore gave a medal to Big Jim . . . and said we could live here as long as we like." Whatever the origins,

Indian huts constructed from dump waste became a growing annoyance to the Park Service.[39]

By 1930 at least three dozen people lived at the camp, inspiring Superintendent Miner Tillotson's plan to make the site into a modern Indian village that included four horseshoe clusters of nine cabins each. The new village, like the old, would straddle the sewer line from Grand Canyon Village.[40] As we have seen, Tillotson's plan for a "model Havasupai colony" hit snags, and within a few years the NPS, with its penchant for tidiness, called for removal of "unsightly ramshackle quarters [with] dirty clothes and accumulated filth."[41]

In 1936, when Chief Ranger James Brooks reported on a "Hottentot village" that made his flesh crawl, he concluded that for the good of everyone, especially Indian children, the camp's intolerable conditions must be remedied. Brooks acknowledged that precontact Havasupai would have lived much better.[42] After an internal debate and BIA conference in 1939, park officials decided that only Indian employees could live at Supai Camp. Rangers then dismantled four buildings and delivered the scrap to a reservation trailhead, an action that Havasupai have not forgotten two generations later.

This debate, replete with legal opinions on original title, takings, and rights of occupancy and eviction, continued until the Enlargement Act. Antagonism increased as horses, dogs, and cats ran loose; some Havasupai poached deer and collected firewood, and others, now "just plain squatters" in the superintendent's eyes, were arrested for petty crimes, fights, and drunken driving. During the 1950s, Fred Harvey layoffs aggravated matters by undercutting the rationale for an Indian employee residence. In 1966 the service demolished several more buildings and removed all jobless Havasupai. Supai Camp, anthropologist Robert Euler recalled years later, had a history of "just terrible relations":

> The Park Service said, "Well, we have these nice homes for you, small cabins, but you can't move in because you don't know how to take care of them, you won't keep them clean," that sort of attitude. There was one communal toilet and bathhouse, but no hot water. The sewer line from Grand Canyon Village ran right through Supai Camp and leaked tremendously. You would see these kids in the winter eating yellow icicles, it was just terrible. On the other hand, the Supai who lived there for the most part were drunk most of the time. They would come into the Village and accost tourists on the steps of El Tovar. "What are you doing here, white man, this is my country, you don't belong here." That sort of thing.[43]

Incidents and insults continued into the 1970s. On one occasion a ranger entered the camp with a drawn gun, claiming fear of vicious dogs; once several Indian residents invited Euler, the superintendent, and his wife to Thanksgiving dinner, only for the hosts to spend the evening in a drunken stupor.

In 1971 the NPS assigned specialist Gary Howe to investigate the camp. As Howe interviewed native tenants, he found few relationships with reservation Havasupai. The camp was more appealing than moving to Grand Canyon Village or back to Supai—partly because of the $18.50 monthly rent. A lack of electricity, potable water, and private toilets did not bother tenants, but the negative racial attitudes of NPS maintenance workers made Indians reluctant to request services. Howe reported that buildings needed new roofs, glass windows, and safe wood stoves. He recommended $3,000 worth of repairs, painting, and new equipment, including a bath house. While making the camp safer and more livable, Howe urged that the NPS should "respect the wishes of the residents and not impose our living standards on them unnecessarily."[44]

These problems seemed resolved by the 1975 Enlargement Act, which extinguished Havasupai title to all nonreservation land. The NPS, interpreting this to include Supai Camp and forgetting that throughout the enlargement struggle the Havasupai had insisted on acquiring ownership of the site, again set out to raze the settlement. Eviction notices in 1976 elicited protests from tribal attorney Joseph Babbitt of Flagstaff. Babbitt expressed "shock and heartbreak" upon hearing reports of forced removal, another chapter in the Park Service's history of burning Indian homes, job discrimination, and dislike of natives—"a microcosm . . . of the red man's whole experience in this country. What needs to be questioned is the long-standing assumption that the Grand Canyon National Park should be Havasupai free. The whole idea smacks of Hitlerlike thinking. What would be the harm in recognizing that the Havasupai have a unique and historical place in the Grand Canyon—that their culture and way of life, including their traditional separateness, have value?"

Tribal chairman Clark Jack requested reconsideration and delay, claiming that his people had lived near Supai Camp for centuries and that their occupation had been specifically recognized in the 1919 park legislation. Past NPS officials, Jack said, had respected this tradition, but the new superintendent, Merle Stitt, "did not seem impressed by former promises." Copies of Jack's letter to NPS chief Gary Everhardt reached the BIA, Senators Goldwater and Fannin, and lobbyist Bill Byler.[45]

Despite having the law on its side, the NPS balked. With the arrival of

Superintendent Richard Marks in 1980, policy changed to allow continued Havasupai occupation of the camp through special-use permits, a compromise that dismayed older park rangers. The first five-year permit of 1982 set terms followed to the present. The NPS, on paper, retained tight control over the 160 acres; the permit required the tribe to install sewage and water systems, survey the land, protect the environment, and "maintain the premises in an orderly manner" subject to park inspection. The expense of adding public toilets, a sweat lodge, and cabin repairs remained unresolved, although the Havasupai did gain permission to replace existing houses with duplexes, thereby potentially doubling the number of camp residents. The tribe retained free access through the park, with a right to renew the permit subject to NPS regulations. Both sides made disclaimers: The Park Service recognized no Indian title; the Havasupai retained their sovereign immunity.[46]

Even following this agreement, the NPS hoped to remove Supai Camp, the key being water and sewage requirements. The tribe solved the drinking water problem, but in 1985 the park closed its old sewage treatment plant and required the Indians to connect with a new system at a cost of $134,000. This became, in the words of a staff member, "the government's way of saying, 'Good-bye, Supai Camp.'" But after several uncertain years, a special congressional appropriation allowed the camp to build its own septic system and connect with the park's water main. Eviction plans had backfired again.[47]

By 1990, much like a Shoshone camp in Death Valley, the Havasupai settlement on the South Rim remained a bone stuck in the Park Service's throat. An NPS anthropologist says it is time for the NPS to "start being landlords instead of slumlords." Others see the site as a privately occupied eyesore that the tribe cannot afford to maintain and the park will not. Law enforcement at the camp, according to the chief ranger in 1991, differed little from that in other Grand Canyon residential areas, yet dogs, drinking, fights, and illegal guests created enforcement problems that the Park Service often ignored or avoided. Overt pressure against Supai Camp had ceased. "We're good to them now," a ranger declared. "Nothing changes a bureaucrat's mind faster than passing a law."[48]

During the 1980s, Grand Canyon officials, recognizing the historical antagonism, had committed themselves to more positive relations with the Indians. But, as in the case of Supai Camp, old habits of thought persisted. A 1984 management plan of 240 pages devoted 55 of them to prehistory or cultural resources and only 4 pages to current relations with the tribes. Park planners thus allocated contemporary Indians as much space as feral burros, dead trees, air flights, or the humpback chub. As late as 1993, guests could learn much about the Hopi, Navajo, and Anasazi, but virtually nothing about the Hualapai or Havasupai.[49] For some Supai leaders, little had changed. The Park Service made promises but mainly rotated administrators who promoted their own careers. As superintendents came and went, Havasupai Wayne Sinyella remembered the loss of land, relocation, evictions, and the burning of Indian homes by rangers. For him, attending the park's seventy-fifth anniversary gala was akin to honoring Columbus.[50]

Environmentalists and Indians

During the 1950s a religious organization announced its plan to build a chapel that would extend from the edge of the South Rim out into space. Those who opposed the structure repeatedly used language evoking awe and mystery, pointing to the canyon as a sublime cathedral, a sanctuary, a sacred place, an inspiration. Churches, they insisted, reflected human ideals, human history, human architecture. The Grand Canyon, on the other hand, transcends humanity. Such a conviction lies at the heart of radical protection. No one stated the belief better than Teddy Roosevelt had in 1903, when he uttered words now repeated for almost a century: "Leave it as it is. You cannot improve on it; not a bit."[51] Men and women who took Roosevelt's mandate literally found themselves fighting against dams, hotels, mines, air flights, traffic congestion, noise, imported animals, exotic plants, smoke, and sewage. Caught between defenders and boosters, the NPS usually accepted compromises such as allowing the Shrine of the Ages to be built a half-mile back from the rim.

To conservationists, native people, unlike a church cantilevered into space, usually remained invisible, prehistoric, or part of the scenery. Not until the mid-twentieth century did Indians gradually emerge as lovers of the earth or, as in the Hualapai dam project, a threat. These perceptions grew more complex in the 1960s and 1970s with the growing popularity of "the Indian" as an environmental model.[52]

In this stereotype, Indians had always lived in harmony with nature, revered Mother Earth as sacred, and offered a special wisdom to non-Indians. The myth embraces Chief Seattle's speech, an apocryphal document in various versions composed and refined by white men. Now accepted as authentic by many Indians, the speech is cited throughout the world in sermons, on calendars, in government documents and environmental newsletters, on television, and in scholarly research. Its message: The earth is sacred; all things are connected; humans must respect other species; and, unless people heed the Indian, Western civilization may destroy the planet.

When projected by Euro-Americans onto native people through texts such as the Seattle speech, the "Indian as Environmentalist" evokes powerful reactions. Like most stereotypes, its shard of truth can cause more harm than good. Indians who ride motorcycles instead of ponies, who fish with nylon gillnets instead of wooden weirs, who clear-cut tribal forests rather than seek visions, or who live in Supai Camp instead of Hopi House find that non-Indians, including environmentalists, can react with dismay, anger, and disbelief. The ecological mandate freezes Indians as an idea and artifact, a static and quaint people who have few economic needs. Natives by definition should favor protecting the Grand Canyon, which, to environmentalists, means keeping the national parks intact; if Indians oppose Park Service control, they betray their own tradition and become tools of exploiters. The false dilemma seems obvious, yet many environmentalists failed to detect it during the Grand Canyon enlargement debate. Flawed thinking turned a misunderstanding into an ugly, bitter struggle over land.[53]

In 1973, as we have recounted, the Havasupai owned 518 acres inside a narrow canyon, supplemented with thousands of plateau acres leased through special grazing permits. Under the Enlargement Act the tribe hoped to gain 250,000 acres of parkland. Protests from environmental groups compelled Udall and Goldwater to compromise, the eventual 185,000-acre transfers pleasing no one. With the Sierra Club in the vanguard, many environmental groups, racked with internal strife, officially opposed any land restoration. It became, Mo Udall later lamented, "a very tough issue for all of us."

Environmentalists set forth a series of arguments that ran from personal experience to precedence. The Sierra Club's regional director, John McComb, claimed that 180 days of Canyon hiking provided special insights. An Arizona voter wrote to Udall that "our forefathers shed blood to get land from the Indians and you're giving it right back. That's not very nice." Letters contained language such as "boondoggle," "theft," "land grab," "giveaway," and "raid" to fan emotions against Indians who, at the worst, were described as being greedy, paternalized, romanticized, invaders themselves, and the dupes of developers. Rumors circulated about paved highways, trams, plush lodges, and trophy hunters shooting bighorn sheep, but environmentalists also posed legitimate questions about the 1969 ICC settlement and about the park's losing Mooney

Falls. Would Indians, not professionally trained in land management, be any better than the NPS? Navajo coal mining, native oil and timber leases in Alaska, tourism at Taos, overstocked ranges, and Yakama cattle grazing on the meadows of Mt. Adams raised doubts.

The most frequent and effective argument of environmentalists warned that transferring 250,000 acres of USFS and NPS land would open a Pandora's box. The view that wilderness boundaries are fixed made any adjustment of park borders seem a violation of protected areas. The precedent argument also portrayed the Havasupai as a stalking-horse for other Indian claims to fifty-seven million acres of federal land: To accept native claims that land itself is sacred, one writer predicted, would place the entire public domain at risk.[54]

The Havasupai and their supporters used convincing counterarguments that, coupled with superior political organizing and a willingness to compromise, enabled them to prevail. They attacked the "slippery slope precedent" argument by pointing out that national park boundaries across the country had changed hundreds of times and that, in fact, entire parks had been abolished without compromising the system.[55] When Stephen Hirst reconstructed Havasupai history, the tribe obtained a knowledge of their past and NPS flaws that the opposition lacked. As for commercial development, the Indians justly complained that preservationists tolerated Grand Canyon Village's growing into a small congested city, ignored sprawl near the park at Tusayan, and overlooked a travesty called Flintstone Village further south.

In Havasupai eyes, the Sierra Club, Friends of the Earth, and other groups appeared to be wealthy, selfish, outside busybodies who knew little about the Grand Canyon and even less about Indians. When hiking experiences were pointed to, Lee Marshall asked how a few treks compared with having centuries of ancestors:

> These people can't even know what they are talking about. They haven't even seen most of the land they want to steal. . . . These people are really ignorant of nature, as most of them know only what they read in books. We live on the land, and these people from the cities think they know something about it. We'd like to put some of them out there with nothing and see if they could stay alive.
>
> We heard this McComb bragging about how he has spent all of 180 days in the Grand Canyon, but he's just a city man like all the rest thinking about taking these lands so he can come up once or twice a year and

have some recreation. Recreation! We are talking about survival while they talk about recreation. Where does the greed of these people stop?[56]

Like Marshall, members of Congress denounced environmentalists who placed animals, insects, and plants above human welfare. Sam Steiger of Arizona scorned Sierra Club protests as "just baloney," and "crocodile tears." When another congressman called the club a group of "green bigots," Steiger disagreed: "They are not bigoted just about things green, they are bigoted about everything." Representative Craig Hosmer of California matched Steiger's rhetoric in rebuking the "rabid environmentalist campaign" against the Havasupai:

The Sierra Club is an organized lobby consisting of a bunch of people who go out throughout the country and get people to contribute money, and who make fat salaries as they run around fighting so-called environmental issues that they probably dredged up themselves to begin with. . . . In this instance, they come in and jump on some poor Indians . . . in total disregard of other values besides environmental values. But that does not count. The Sierra Club lobbyists have another victory so they can keep themselves in their lush jobs. . . . I am a voice crying from downtown America which the environmentalists are trying to lock up and turn into a park for birds and bees and animals first and people last.

Even Morris Udall considered Sierra Club tactics unworthy of the organization. He distinguished between an inflexible national leadership and its grassroots members who, he reminded Congress, supported the bill.[57]

By the spring of 1974, despite strong support for the Havasupai, Congressmen John Dellenback (Oregon), Tom Foley (Washington), and John Seiberling (Ohio) had managed to cast the outcome in doubt. The Havasupai then did what the Makah tribe would do to secure Ozette: The council passed a resolution renouncing all plans for economic development and promising to accept any regulation "reasonably necessary" to protect the environment. This allowed Udall to guarantee that sixty-five thousand acres passing from NPS to tribal control would remain "forever wild."[58]

In supporting the expansion and protection of Grand Canyon National Park while blocking restoration of tribal lands, environmental spokesmen became the archenemy in Havasu minds.[59] They also faced revolts from their own members. Leadership of the moderate National Parks and Conservation Association opposed land transfer in principle and believed that large corporations exploited southwestern Indians. Instead of having the government surrender parkland, the NPCA lobbied for permanent nontransferable leases to allow tribal grazing, river access, and use of sacred sites. Privately, NPCA staff spoke of a Havasu "land grab" and worried about "keeping Udall's backbone stiff," but their public posture remained conciliatory. Relatively few members resigned or castigated the leaders.[60]

Compared to the NPCA, David Brower's Friends of the Earth waged a slashing campaign against restoration. Convinced that tactics he had used against government dams in the 1960s would succeed against Indians a decade later, Brower blundered. Facing defeat, he indulged in racial name-calling, exhibited poor taste, then slid into hypocrisy and deception. Friends of the Earth insisted that returning plateau land to the Havasupai disguised a conspiracy by developers to build motels, dams, and marinas. Morris Udall's patient explanations did not assuage Brower's fear that "something extremely damaging is afoot . . . [a] threat posed to the Grand Canyon—all too cleverly posed."

Friends of the Earth predicted that Arizona precedents would enable other Indians to acquire federal lands: "This *is* happening," one writer announced. "The American Indian Movement has called for the giving to Indians of 110 million more acres."[61] Yet if Friends of the Earth did not trust AIM, Brower could still embrace environmental Indians. In 1974, as his newsletter warned of an avalanche of Indian land claims, the publication also praised Navajo help in protecting Rainbow Bridge, used native imagery to support an environmental cause in Alaska, and carried a full-page advertisement featuring a Navajo in traditional garb to promote Brower's new book, *Song of the Earth Spirit*.[62]

As upsetting as dealing with real Indians may have been for Friends of the Earth and NPCA, they avoided the agony of the Sierra Club between 1973 and 1975. The club managed to offend influential environmentalists such as Wallace Stegner, alienate powerful politicians like Goldwater and the Udalls, become the "whipping boy" for angry Indians, and be stigmatized in Congress as a group of country club elitists unconcerned with human poverty. The organization embarrassed itself when grassroots chapters rejected official policy and the San Francisco headquarters abolished its Indian Issues Committee.

Since its founding in 1892, the Sierra Club had paid scant attention to Native Americans. In the 1960s it adopted several motions on Indian affairs, including a resolution to expand Grand Canyon National Park by securing 410,000 acres of Hualapai and Navajo land. John McComb, Martin Litton, and Jeff Ingram worked closely with the NPS to draft a master plan that became the blueprint for Barry Goldwater's original enlargement bill. Their plan ignored decades of Havasupai effort to regain plateau land, and after Goldwater introduced his bill the club so vigorously and persistently opposed any land transfer that Goldwater eventually resigned from the organization.[63]

While denouncing crimes against Indians of the past and supporting justice in the future, the Sierra Club stressed that national parks belonged to all Americans and that Indians must accept the modern world. The land transfer seemed gratuitous, a thinly disguised theft from a crown jewel.[64] Local chapters in Arizona and Colorado, however, came to see matters differently, mainly because they met native people who explained Havasupai history and culture.

After an angry screaming match with Indians at Goldwater's home in January 1973, members of the Flagstaff branch of the club traveled to Supai Village eleven months later, listened with open minds, and changed their opinions. Members from Phoenix then met with the Havasupai, and, following an acrimonious debate, the club's state board voted to support land restoration. Further backlash emerged as the national Indian Issues Committee of Alvin Josephy, Tom Mudd, and Susanne Anderson supported land transfer. "The Sierra Club has an opportunity," the committee urged, "unique in the Club's recent history of conflict with proposals to develop Indian land, to reach out in a cooperative spirit to help a people survive." The San Francisco headquarters did not budge. Instead, the *Sierra Club Bulletin* urged members to write Congress in opposition to the bill.[65]

Outflanked and outfought by attorney Joe Sparks and lobbyist Bill Byler, misinformed and oblivious of history, misreading the public appeal of Indian demands, and disappointed that the Havasupai did not act like model ecologists, the Sierra Club pursued a policy out of touch with native people and its own membership. Distracted by this, the club fumbled two important innovations in the original enlargement draft: creation of "zones of influence" outside park boundaries, and designation of new wilderness areas around Grand Canyon. It lost perspective on legislation which, while transferring 65,000 acres of NPS land to a tribe, expanded the park from 675,000 to nearly 1.2 million acres.

In addition, the Sierra Club missed an opportunity to educate its membership. One might expect the average conservationist to react negatively when Congress shifted 185,000 acres of park and USFS land to only 465 people— nearly four hundred acres for each man, woman, and child. That "giveaway" might appear different if one learned about actual Indians instead of mythical ones, and about the Coconino Plateau. Grassroots members and the Indian committee examined specifics. As Edward Spicer observed about the local Grand Canyon chapter: "Here are deeply convinced conservationists who, through taking a little time for study, have come to understand the situation from the Havasupai point of view. The failure of the more active lobbyists of the Sierra Club and others to pay attention . . . indicates a peculiar blindness."[66]

After the Enlargement Act passed and the Sierra Club abolished its Indian committee, some members responded "in a mood of considerable bitterness and disappointment." The national organization seemed incapable of understanding Indians and was "reluctant to admit that people are part of the environment, many of them being minority groups and other impoverished people." The committee's Alvin Josephy, a distinguished historian, made his point in public. Friends of the Earth and the Sierra Club, he wrote to the *New York Times*, had they studied history, could have avoided humiliating defeat at the hands of a tiny tribe. Ignorance, distrust, and "an outworn, pristine brand of preservationism [that] seems contemptuous of people and oblivious to their needs," Josephy concluded, had resulted in confrontation and anger instead of cooperation.[67]

Twenty years later the Havasu battle still rankled a few environmentalists; some had learned from it, and others had repressed the events. Jeff Ingram acknowledged his ignorance of Indian and park history, confirming Robert Euler's belief that most whites in 1974 knew little about Indians; if one could inform them, as Euler did the Sierra Club's Durango chapter, minds could change. Euler's successor at Grand Canyon, Jan Balsom, agreed:

> Environmental organizations need to be educated. We've got an awful lot of "wannabe" Indian sorts, but they don't truly understand tribal views. They have this magical, mystical view of what should be, not the real world. They need to be humbled a bit, to realize that the tribes have much more of an interest in the well-being of the system than they do. . . . Some groups need to get off their high horse of environmental elitism and deal with the people who are part of the land to begin with, not some yuppified version of what it should be. They need to consider local tribes of the area, a factor they never think about."[68]

Today the Sierra Club has another Indian committee. The club's hiking guidebook to the Grand Canyon contains a chapter by Balsom, an accurate and unromanticized description of the canyon's native people, past and present. The Sierra Club and other national groups now consistently report on tribal issues; twenty years ago they published virtually nothing.[69] Brock Evans, a

Sierra lobbyist in 1974, still maintains that he was right to oppose land transfer. Evans warns that we "should not fall prey to the notion that just because a person is a Native American, that means they automatically care about the land." And he still believes that, when conflicts arise, protecting rare and unique places holds priority over tribal economic needs. Yet Evans now speaks in terms that emphasize shared concerns. Addressing a conference of Indians and environmentalists in 1991, he told an audience that included Vine Deloria, Jr., LaDonna Harris, John Echohawk, and Jewel Praying Wolf James that "we environmentalists love the land as you do. Our culture and religion do not permit us to call them 'holy places'—but they are. We call them national parks, wilderness areas, wild rivers. . . . We and you Indians are the only two groups in our society who will stand up to fight for nature on a daily basis. Perhaps the time has come to walk together down this path we both love."[70]

Whatever the progress in attitudes, after twenty years the 1975 legislation has had little effect on the land. Supai Camp remains part of Grand Canyon Village, Indian horses graze at large on the Great Thumb, and a paved instead of dirt road now takes one to Hualapai Hilltop, but no motel, resort, or tramway awaits at the end. Tourists still must hike or ride horseback for eight miles to Supai Village, where they find a modern lodge. Along the way they pass bread wrappers, pop containers, horse feed bags, and beer cans. At Supai, polite but guarded hosts still speak their native tongue as well as English. Between the village and the falls, a thick, acrid smoke from the garbage dump settles over lower Havasu Creek, which flows past a campground that does not meet NPS standards. Even so, to stay one night a party of four must pay eighty dollars. Like most places in Arizona, this is no Shangri-la and never was. Without a doubt, the National Park Service could have turned Havasu Canyon into a cleaner, safer, and better "interpreted" place. And, without a doubt, if that had happened, it would no longer be an Indian community or homeland for its people.

NAVAJOLAND

Sharing the Gift of Changing Woman

Asdzą́ą́ nádleehé [Changing Woman] danced on the eastern
mountain to create clouds. She danced on the mountain to the
south to obtain adornments such as jewels and clothing. She
danced on the mountain to the west to bring forth all varieties
of plants. And she danced on the northern mountain to
summon corn and animals. . . . But even with her dancing
Asdzą́ą́ nádleehé had begun to feel lonely, for she had no
companions.

—Paul Zolbrod, *Diné bahané: The Navajo Creation Story,* 1984

. . . especially the Apaches de Nabajo . . . with the condition of
not dispossessing them nor expelling them from what they
have occupied previously, but to treat them with love and
Christian sincerity.

—Governor Pedro Fermin de Mendinueta, January 20, 1768

National Park Service rules and regulations no doubt at times bewilder the
average Indian. In 1994 at the Grand Canyon a young Hualapai NPS employee
was dismissed but not arrested for removing hematite to sell to the Hopi at
forty dollars a pound. In the same park the NPS arrested, jailed, and prosecuted
Navajo vendors for selling beads to tourists. At nearby Glen Canyon National
Recreation Area a park ranger stopped a Navajo medicine man from collecting

native plants, but Navajo and Hopi could collect plants, berries, and seeds in the Grand Canyon without interference.[1]

Park Service supervision of commerce in rocks, piñon nuts, sage, and beads contrasts with its promotion of a huge Navajo destination resort on Antelope Point near Glen Canyon dam. Should it come to pass, the project on Lake Powell, involving moorage for hundreds of power boats and modern facilities for hundreds of thousands of tourists a year, will be the largest joint venture in the history of NPS/tribal relations. That it might happen in Navajoland is no accident; few tribes have had such an involved and contentious relationship with the Park Service.

Dispossessed and exiled by the United States in 1864, the Navajo, or Diné, returned to their homeland to become a population of nearly 200,000 today. Their reservation covers twenty-five thousand square miles, a land base larger than Massachusetts, Rhode Island, New Hampshire, and Connecticut combined. Once considered marginal terrain, Navajo land contains coal, oil, and gas, plus 500,000 acres of timber. The most important water source in the Southwest, the Colorado River, marks the tribe's northwest border. A nationalistic yet adaptive people, the Diné migrated into the Four Corners area five centuries ago. They assimilated elements of Pueblo, Spanish, and American cultures: weaving, horses, sheep, horticulture, representative government, liquor, pickup trucks. In 1923 they became one of the first tribes to organize a government capable of expanding its land base and economy while resisting pressures from the United States. Initiative and assertiveness account for the term that smaller tribes apply to the Navajo: "the Second Coming of the White Man."

The continued vitality of the Navajo language, survival of traditional culture, and rich legends combine with a sense of place to produce a tribal sovereignty beyond rhetoric. Navajos own and control their homeland. "These treasures which you see will be yours," Changing Woman had told the Diné. "This home will be yours. The mountains that you see around you will be yours. The sky overhead will be yours. . . . Soon [the clans] were participating fully in the life of their kinsmen as though they had all been of one single tribe from the very beginning of life in this world."[2] To protect special places, the Navajo became the first American Indian tribe to authorize their own park system. After the establishment of Monument Valley Tribal Park in 1958, the council added seven more units in less than a decade.[3] While appreciation for the beauty of their land was one motive, the tribe also felt under siege—not by the U.S. Army, but by the National Park Service. Whereas Olympic and the Grand

Canyon National Parks are surrounded by tribes, the Navajo, if they turned in any direction, saw the NPS.

Occupying parts of Colorado, Utah, New Mexico, and Arizona, the Navajo have relations with three NPS regional offices (Southwest, Rocky Mountain, and Western) and sixteen park units: El Morro, Chaco Canyon, Aztec Ruins, Mesa Verde, Hovenweep, Natural Bridges, Navajo National Monument, Rainbow Bridge, Glen Canyon, Grand Canyon, Wupatki, Sunset Crater, Walnut Canyon, Petrified Forest, Hubbell Trading Post, and Canyon de Chelly. Not surprisingly, the complex relationships have been uneasy, emotional, and, at times, volatile. Navajo relations with the Grand Canyon have been described in chapter six. Here we shall examine Wupatki, Chaco Canyon, Navajo National Monument, Rainbow Bridge, the Escalante proposal, and Canyon de Chelly, concluding with the tribe's own park at Monument Valley.

Wupatki

The Wupatki ruins thirty miles north of Flagstaff were occupied Navajo territory but not reservation land when Congress proclaimed the area a national monument in 1924. That shift in U.S. jurisdiction made little sense to men like Clyde Peshlakai who continued to think of the land and ruins as his property.

For the next three decades the Peshlakais and three other Navajo families peacefully coexisted with the NPS. Indeed, with ranger Davy Jones and his wife, Courtney, they more than coexisted. As neighbors, relations between the Peshlakais and Joneses grew from being polite and helpful into a close friendship. Park staff helped Navajos with irrigation projects, vehicle repair, and firefighting. On one occasion Jones insisted that Sally Peshlakai be served in a Flagstaff restaurant, and during World War II he wrote letters for illiterate Navajo parents to their sons overseas. Jones and his wife exchanged gifts with local families; they frequently attended the all-night sings, dances, and ceremonials of "our Navajos." In many ways, the attitudes and relations at Wupakti in the 1930s and 1940s could be considered ideal, a model for any parkland carved out of Indian country.[4]

Expansion of the monument from twenty-two hundred to thirty-five thousand acres in 1937 did not affect these cordial relations, but the appointment of a new superintendent in 1949 did. Navajo presence at Wupatki now seemed an inconvenience or intrusion that the government decided to eliminate through asserting its legal rights to the land regardless of native claims to traditional use and occupancy. Relations became bitter, a situation that even the appointment of a Navajo as superintendent could not resolve. Through a complex series of permit agreements, one Peshlakai family was allowed to remain and graze sheep. After their death, the Navajo of Wupatki would exist only in memory.[5] And at Chaco Canyon, the NPS would ignore the positive model set by Davy and Courtney Jones as it pursued removal as the best solution to Indian claims on parkland.

Pueblo Bonito

Anglo-Americans once considered the Southwest the most inhospitable and uninhabitable quadrant of the United States, a perception that perhaps explains the large size of the Navajo Reservation. Yet no area of North America contains so rich a prehistoric human record. Archaeologists estimate that the Grand Canyon alone has over sixty thousand sites, two or three thousand of which have been officially identified. Of the dozens of ruins now under NPS protection, Mesa Verde and Chaco Canyon are the "crown jewels," with Chaco by far the most dramatic and inexplicable. Within Navajoland but outside the reservation, Chaco is a thirty-four-thousand-acre NPS unit from which all Indians have been removed.

Chaco Culture National Historic Site lies in New Mexico's San Juan Basin one hundred miles west of the Rio Grande and fifteen miles east of the Navajo Reservation in what the tribe and federal government call the Checkerboard Area.[6] The town of Farmington is fifty air miles north, Crownpoint thirty miles south. Throughout the basin are tiny, isolated communities with such names as Nageezi, Becenti, Bisti, and Nahodishgish; many, like Chaco, are reached only by dirt road. What especially distinguishes Chaco Wash is its extensive network of pre-Columbian trails, kivas, plazas, and Anasazi dwellings. The ruins (A.D. 900–1150) stand on open ground or at the base of sheer cliffs. Traces of Anasazi roads, some up to sixty miles long and serving purposes not yet understood, reach the wash from a variety of directions. Ruins at Chetro Ketl, Pueblo Bonito (the local name for the entire area), Pueblo del Arroyo, and Casa Rinconada reveal architectural, masonry, and craft skills superior to those seen at other southwestern sites.[7]

The Anasazi replaced Basketmaker peoples who had replaced earlier hunting societies. When the Navajo arrived in 1720, the Anasazi had disappeared five centuries earlier. Evidence of continuous if sparse Navajo occupation dates from 1774.[8] During their Long Walk and traumatic captivity at Bosque Redondo (Fort Sumner, 1864–1868), some Navajo probably found refuge at Chaco; others settled there after 1868. In the 1880s and 1890s they became one of four groups vying for control of Pueblo Bonito, the other three being white and Hispanic ranchers seeking open range, professional and amateur archaeologists seeking artifacts, and the federal government seeking parks and monuments.

The Chaco Navajo asked to be left alone on what they considered part of their homeland, a homeland not included in the 1868 treaty, which stipulated conditions of their release from Bosque Redondo and set tribal boundaries that included Canyon de Chelly but not Chaco. Under the treaty, Navajos could claim 160-acre homesteads on the reservation but relinquished all claims and settlement rights elsewhere. The document had been signed under duress, a condition justified by the government because Navajos had a history of violating agreements.[9] The treaty notwithstanding, within a few years Diné stockmen seeking forage had moved off the reservation toward the Rio Grande. An executive order in 1880 added eastern land that included Window Rock, the present tribal capital. At the urging of the BIA, a 1907 order by Theodore Roosevelt extended the reservation further east past Chaco Wash. Subsequent executive orders in 1908 and 1911 restored the Checkerboard to the public domain, yet during the interim opportunistic Diné had occupied the eastern lands and established allotments on water sources.[10]

Navajo expansion met ranchers moving west from the Rio Grande and south from Colorado, among them a Quaker cattleman from the Mancos Valley named Richard Wetherill. Discoverer of the ruins at Mesa Verde and a guide for eastern archaeologists, Wetherill became infatuated with the Anasazi ruins in Chaco Wash. In 1897 he filed for a homestead and then opened a trading post at the Pueblo Bonito site; soon he and his wife, Marietta, had moved there permanently. Relic-hunters and professional archaeologists, invited and hosted by the Wetherills, worked in the remains while competing for control of Chaco. On March 11, 1907, a year after passage of the Antiquities Act and eight months before he would add this land to the Navajo Reservation, Theodore Roosevelt proclaimed Chaco Canyon a national monument.[11]

A desire to protect Chaco had been voiced in 1901 when General Land Office agent J. S. Holsinger reported that "no interest would be injured by . . . the establishment of a National Park, unless such reservation would exclude the

Indians. [It] is ample for the Indians and to deprive them of the land would be robbing them of that which in all its humbleness and poverty is very dear. As a National Park, the presence of the Navajo would not be detrimental to public interests and they would not only add picturesqueness but protection to the objects of scientific interest."[12]

Holsinger's assessment proved overly optimistic. The monument would experience the same confused mix of NPS relations with Indians that occurred at Glacier, Olympic, and Grand Canyon. On the positive side, some Navajo, despite cultural taboos against visiting ruins and burial sites, were trained in restoration, stabilization, and preservation techniques, a skilled craft that continues today among southwestern Indians.

On a personal level, NPS custodians and rangers assisted injured residents, delivered babies, repaired cars, and pulled vehicles from winter mud. The BIA played a constructive role as Navajo agent Samuel Stacher defended and promoted Indian interests for twenty-six years (from 1909 to 1935). Stacher and his successors had their hands full, as life at Chaco involved liquor, claim jumping, battles over title, leases to powerful ranchers, racial tensions, water rights, grazing, erosion, trade debts, lynchings, oil exploration, and the 1911 murder of Richard Wetherill by Chis-chilling-begay, a Navajo.[13]

The monument itself remained Indian country for fifty years. Navajos traversed the trails, ran livestock, conducted sings, and occupied scattered hogans along the wash. Indians owned 160-acre sites at the Peñasco Blanco and Kin-yai ruins.[14] The shift in NPS policy from accepting Indians to removing them evolved largely because of sheep in the ruins. Frank Pinkley had assured Stacher in 1927 that he did not want removal of Indians from contested land: "Willie [George] needs no permit from us. We are not going to bother him as long as he remains a good Indian." Yet the NPS used Stacher and archaeologist Neil Judd to acquire land and "improvements such as they are" from Navajos. The Indian agent helped obtain forty acres of Hosteen Tah be-kins land at Peñasco Bonito. "I have signed the blanks and completed same for heirs," Stacher wrote to the NPS, because "it would probably require considerable work to hold hearings."[15]

By 1933 the Park Service had decided to exclude Navajos, permitting custodian Hurst Julian to wage a "war" against Indian sheep, goats, horses, and dogs. "I have been given complete charge of grazing," Julian informed the NPS office, "a miniature Mussolini, as it were, of the grazing of this region."[16] The next year NPS fences brought protests from Tomacito, one of the few Navajos still living inside the monument:

Tomacito, a Navajo, with his wife and three grandchildren at Chaco Canyon in 1934, when the NPS initiated a policy to remove Indians from the monument. (Photograph by George Grant, courtesy of Harpers Ferry Center, Charles Town, W. Va.)

My wife and I are old. Our children are all born here at Chaco Canyon. We have lived here for 52 years. Up to two years ago, we lost our land here when the National Park people took away our allotted land. Now the land is all fenced in. We have our hogans on all our land. . . . Our Indians used to dig wells down in the washes anywhere to get water for their stock, but now they cannot do it anymore. White men won't let us do it. We are very poor now, hungry most of the time and thirsty all the time.[17]

The NPS became identified with John Collier's stock reduction program of the 1930s, to Navajo minds an atrocity ranking with the Long Walk. Even though the BIA opposed fencing Chaco, the Park Service finished its project in 1947; two years later Tomacito, the last Navajo, departed.

Removal did not end NPS relations with Indians of the San Juan Basin. Anasazi ruins spread for miles in all directions, creating the problem of how to protect valuable archaeological sites beyond Chaco Wash. In 1980 when legislation expanded the monument and identified ten Navajo-owned archaeological sites totaling over four thousand acres, Congress provided for cooperative management of what NPS official Charles Voll calls "the great Chaco outlier mess and monstrosity." Preservationists agreed with Voll, describing the joint effort as "a complete failure" and recommending that the government buy out tribal holdings or else arrange a massive land exchange for all Navajo-owned ruins. In 1986, after an NPCA survey identified eighteen major Anasazi sites owned by the Navajos, the organization sponsored a bill to transfer the land from BIA to Park Service jurisdiction.[18]

Dislodging the Diné outside Chaco will be much more difficult now than it was in the 1930s; inside the monument the tribe has cooperated by not renewing grazing permits on NPS land.[19] As far as Chaco guests are concerned, living Indians have disappeared. The Chaco visitor's center in 1989 had an excellent exhibit on the Anasazi; for the modern era, it offered Tony Hillerman's *Thief of Time* and a book on general Native American history. Indians belonged to Chaco cultures of the distant past.[20]

Keet Seel and Betatakin

Navajo National Monument lies 160 miles northwest of Chaco Canyon and directly below Black Mesa. Clarence Gorman, the superintendent in 1991, had been with the NPS for nearly thirty years. Fluent in his native Navajo, Gorman followed "a different way of doing things" than at Chaco, such as letting local Navajos guide horse trips to the ruins, run the gift shop, commute daily on the Park Service road through the headquarters parking lot, and, with several Hispanics, fill most of the permanent and seasonal jobs. Gorman solved the vending problem not through lawsuits, permits, or arrests, but by encouraging local craft sales at the gift shop and by limiting each outdoor vendor to an hour a day. "If you start a fuss," he told sellers, "I'll just close the whole thing."[21] Even before Gorman, the monument considered local people "partners in the park" who could interpret Navajo culture. When the new visitor's center opened in 1966, Navajo shamans blessed the building while native women wove rugs and baked bread next to a hogan exhibit.[22]

Geography in part dictates the positive approach. Created out of Navajo lands as a fourteen-hundred-square-mile park by President William H. Taft in 1909, the monument originally extended thirty miles north, from Black Mesa to the Utah border; on the east it included Monument Valley and modern Kayenta. Three years later Taft changed his mind and turned the site into three

Clarence Gorman, a Navajo, began his NPS career as a maintenance worker at Canyon de Chelly. He worked as a ranger at Pipestone and Wupatki National Monuments before becoming superintendent at Sunset Crater, Aztec Ruins, and Navajo National Monuments. After retirement he became director of the Navajo tribal park system. (Photograph by Fred Mang, Jr., courtesy of Harpers Ferry Center, Charles Town, W. Va.)

postage stamps: 160 acres at Betatakin ruins, 160 acres at Keet Seel, and 40 acres at Inscription House, all "subject to any valid existing rights." Keet Seel is eight miles north of Betatakin, with Inscription House twenty miles west. The NPS visitor center is at none of these places; under a 1962 arrangement with the tribe, it occupies 240 acres of reservation land.

This small, scattered monument is surrounded by traditional Indians whose ancestors had avoided or escaped the Long Walk. As a foreign inholder encircled by Indians, arrogant superintendents could not survive. Frank Pinkley, in charge of the Southwest in 1934, described the monument as "a very special type of job" that required "a man of the country, who knows his country, knows his ruins, and knows his Indians."[23] Flexible, sensitive administrators such as Arthur White (1956–1965), Stephen Miller (1980–1986), and Gorman (1986–1993) first of all built sound relationships with their neighbors.[24]

Keet Seel, Betatakin, and Inscription House have had their share of problems. In 1897 Navajos kidnapped two wealthy members of a Wetherill pothunting expedition and successfully held the hostages for ransom. The monument has seen tension over grazing in the ruins, cut fences, public drunkenness, an encounter with the American Indian Movement, and disputes about concessions, including a feud between two local Indians, Pipeline Begishie and E. K. Austin, over guided pack trips to the ruins. Safety and liability on uninsured horse trips also worry park officials. Water rights, vandalism, rights-of-way, sewage disposal, police jurisdiction, fee collection, landfills, and requests for electricity add up to headaches for superintendents who must respond to three chapter houses, tribal politicians in Window Rock, and the regional NPS office in Santa Fe.[25]

Sixty years ago a keen-eyed visitor noticed problems at Keet Seel. Frederick K. Vreeland, a New York inventor and businessman who knew Horace Albright and Arno Cammerer, had hiked and camped in the Far West thirty years earlier. When he returned in 1934, "like Rip Van Winkle to my old stamping grounds of thirty years ago," the proliferation of roads and automobiles shocked him. So did grazing in ruins, botched trail construction by the CCC, and efforts by white entrepreneurs at Betatakin and Keet Seel:

What right have we to exploit what we cannot preserve? . . . The influx of tourists bound to come could be made a source of revenue for the Navajos. Why not make this a *Navajo* National Monument in fact as well as in name? Is it not time for the National Park Service to have some *living* habitat groups?

Why not get the Dinne interested in preserving, rather than destroying, the Cañons? In other words, put a gate across the trail, get a Navajo to guard it. Second, use Navajos as guides to the ruins. Third, let the Navajos furnish horses to parties going down the trail. Fourth, let the Navajos have a store—their own store, not a white man's—beside the trail.[26]

Frank Pinkley thanked Vreeland for the "sound ideas" but raised objections to most of them: Insufficient traffic existed to support a gatekeeper; Indians were not capable packers; native businesses would harm local white traders and drive up the price of goods. However, Pinkley added, "the thing that jumped into my mind at once was, 'This would work at Oraibi.' Some of us have had our eye on that [Hopi] village for several years as a possible National Monument."[27]

Vreeland's ideas stretched the limits of NPS imagination in the 1930s, but by the early 1960s the monument desperately needed Navajo land for expansion under Mission 66. In exchange for leasing 240 acres near Betatakin, the Park Service agreed to a Navajo-owned crafts outlet in the visitor's center. The NPS also promised to support "in every manner possible" the tribe's desire to acquire Bureau of Reclamation land at Antelope Point on Lake Powell east of the Grand Canyon.[28] By 1970 the Navajo had regained Antelope Point, along with NPS help in developing it, but plans at Lake Powell then stalled. The proposed resort might have pleased Frederick Vreeland for the level of Diné participation, but its impact on a southwestern landscape would have horrified him: a three-hundred-slip marina plus space for sixty rental boats and sixty houseboats, a store and restaurant, a 225-unit motel, dry storage on land, 150 RV sites, a gas station, employee housing, a cultural center, and, very likely, alcohol—"a quality destination resort . . . a distinctive and unique visitor experience" for several hundred thousand people a year, unlike anything they might experience at Navajo National Monument.[29]

Rainbow Bridge

A major attraction for Antelope Point would be Rainbow Bridge National Monument. The highest rock arch in the world and claimed as a sacred site by some Navajos, Rainbow Bridge was under Navajo National Monument jurisdiction prior to the flooding of Glen Canyon. Fewer than fifty people a year saw it before 1970, either by hiking a rugged thirteen-mile trail from the south or by running the Colorado River. In 1992, seventy-four thousand people visited the monument by motorboat, another sensitive development in NPS/Navajo relations.

The first white expedition to Rainbow Bridge, led by a Diné guide named Nashja-Begay, left the Oljeto trading post and rode north past Navajo Mountain to reach the arch on August 14, 1909. Nine months later the group convinced President Taft to create a new monument in Navajo territory. Taft apparently did not consult the tribe.[30]

For years the 160-acre site remained a splendid but distant stepchild of Navajo National Monument. When Congress passed the Colorado River Storage Act of 1956, authorizing Glen Canyon Dam, the Sierra Club's David Brower and other environmentalists gained an exemption to prevent flooding in national parks. That protected Rainbow Bridge, six miles up a side canyon from the Colorado. Although Congress explicitly requested the Bureau of Reclamation to "preclude impairment" of the site, the word "impairment" bristles with ambiguity. Less ambiguous was the projected $25-million structure needed to prevent flooding. Another unacceptable alternative would have left Lake Powell half full.[31]

Stewart Udall inherited this dilemma upon becoming John Kennedy's secretary of the interior on January 20, 1961. With dam construction already underway, Utah's powerful senators wanted the water, Congress did not want to spend $25 million to protect a remote rock hardly anyone ever saw, and environmentalists such as Brower, Howard Zahniser, Newton Drury, Olaus Murie, Horace Albright, and Sigurd Olson now proclaimed Rainbow Bridge "one of the wonders of the world." Failure to protect it, they warned, "will place the entire national park system in jeopardy."[32]

As a congressman, Stewart Udall had hiked into and climbed the arch. He pronounced the site "unquestionably the most awe-inspiring work of natural sculpture anywhere in the United States [with] a rugged beauty comparable only to that of the Grand Canyon itself." Dismissing the cost argument, he claimed that congressional honor and resource conservation came before dollars. He nevertheless concluded that diversion dams to appease Brower and others would do extensive damage; backwater was less harmful than massive construction, which, among other things, would mean roads to the bridge that would destroy the site's "wild scenic beauty" and solitude. "Rainbow Bridge is not a park for sedentary America," Udall insisted with remarkable lack of foresight. "In the long run it will be 'conserved' only if it remains secluded in this fantastic area of canyons and cliffs—a prize to be really won only by hardy Americans willing to undertake a long hike or horseback trip." For true protection, Udall urged greatly enlarging the boundaries of the monument, making it a huge primitive park. The land in question was Navajo, but he felt the tribe would trade this "uninhabitable and unproductive" terrain for a superior area.[33]

Congressman Stewart Udall could propose; Secretary of the Interior Udall could act. Ten days after taking office he met one evening with NPS director Conrad Wirth and Bureau of Reclamation's Floyd Dominey. Faced with "not a very nice choice," Udall said that he needed a creative way around Congress to protect Rainbow Bridge while avoiding a pitched battle between dam supporters and conservationists. He proposed a land trade with the Navajos in which the tribe would cede approximately 640 square miles, an area running from Navajo Creek just east of Antelope Point to either Chu Canyon or Dashu Creek north of Navajo Mountain. Wirth remained silent, but Dominey responded enthusiastically about a boat dock and easy trail to Rainbow Bridge as boons to the public.

The Navajo, Udall cautioned, had "become pretty shrewd traders" who would want some valuable sites along the lake for their own park system. "This is another factor which I wish our conservation friends would take into account," he grumbled. "Congress does not attempt any longer to deal willy-nilly with Indian lands. We do not say 'we are just taking some of your land and giving it to the Park Service.'" Language in a Paiute Strip transfer of 1934, Udall noted, called for the NPS to develop Navajo land, an item that could now be useful in negotiating with the tribe. Tribal monopoly of concessions and retention of mineral rights could sweeten the package.[34]

When Udall announced plans for a new 400,000-acre national park on the Navajo Reservation, he met opposition from all sides. Senator Clinton Anderson denounced transfer of so-called "trading stock" lands in New Mexico, while the NPCA feared logging, mining, hunting, and grazing under Navajo jurisdiction. Tribal chairman Paul Jones, "deeply incensed" and "profoundly shocked," took offense at Udall's public announcement before consulting the tribe. Jones wanted water and hydro projects for municipal and industrial uses, not more tourists, as already promised at Glen Canyon, and he did not want submarginal land in lieu of 180 miles of lakefront.

Paul Jones may have recalled that five years earlier the tribal council, when it ceded land for dam construction at Page, had prohibited the federal government from taking shoreline areas for "park, recreational, scenic or waterfront protective purposes." The idyllic environmentalist Indian that Udall would describe in his book *The Quiet Crisis* no longer existed on the Navajo Reservation. Faced with protests, Udall dropped the plan, in part shifting blame to Conrad Wirth. "It was painfully obvious to me again," he lamented, "that the Navajo leaders have a very inadequate appreciation of the significance of the National Park System. . . . There seems to be residual hostility toward the Park Service as a result of the manner in which Park Service lands . . . have been administered in the past." Udall also blamed tribal attorney Norman Littell for sabotaging Rainbow Bridge negotiations.[35]

The Navajo land trade failed, but construction of the dam moved toward completion in 1967, Rainbow Bridge having been transferred from Navajo National Monument to the new Glen Canyon Recreation Area three years earlier. When backwater entered the monument in 1970, David Brower successfully

Paiute Mike James, who discovered Rainbow Bridge six decades earlier, sits near the flooded site in 1974. An NPS representative gives him cash and a Pendleton blanket. (Bureau of Reclamation photograph, courtesy of Harpers Ferry Center, Charles Town, W. Va.)

sued in federal court. The U.S. Supreme Court would eventually overturn Judge Willis Ritter's lower court decision as the lake continued to rise, reaching half its maximum depth directly under Rainbow Bridge by 1977. This led the Park Service to build a dock and pontoon marina near the arch, causing three chapter houses and six individual Navajos, including three medicine men, to sue the NPS for violation of their religious freedom.

Stewart Udall's earlier suspicion that some Navajo had opposed the monument in 1910 for religious reasons proved prophetic. The Shonto, Inscription House, and Navajo Mountain chapters now contended that Lake Powell had drowned their gods, that shamans could not pray or conduct ceremonies at the cave and spring, and that tourists desecrated a holy place.[36] The Navajo lost in federal district court and lost again on appeal to the Tenth Circuit. Applying no historical or ethnographic analysis, the court ruled that medicine men had access to the site just like anyone else and that to provide special rights by policing the disruptive conduct of tourists, restricting access, and lowering the lake would promote religion and violate the Establishment Clause. Moreover, storage of Colorado River water and generation of power involved public interests that outweighed religious claims. Quoting Judge Learned Hand, the court admonished Lamarr Badoni, Jessie Yazzie, Begay Bitsinnie and others that they "must accommodate their idiosyncrasies, religious as well as secular, to the compromises necessary in communal life."[37]

Stewart Udall still believes that the Navajo should have traded the Rainbow Bridge region for land rich in coal and uranium. According to Clarence Gorman, the huge rock arch remains a sacred place for his people, but another former superintendent of Navajo National Monument rejects that idea. Art White, whom the Shonto Navajo respect, scoffs that "a lot of this religious significance that the Indians claim is for the birds":

> For instance, "Rainbow Bridge is a sacred place to the Navajo." Well, hell, the Navajo didn't even know about it until the last sixty years. Well, phooey! You know, you can find somebody to say, "Yeah, it's sacred." Buy them a pint of wine and to hell with it. I just bite my tongue every time somebody comes out with this religious significance for the American Indian. It's a real good crutch, one you can't argue with, used by the environmentalists, do-gooders and nature lovers and all that. I just find it hard to swallow.[38]

Religious or not, Rainbow Bridge meant a lot to a few people, Indian and white, who knew it before the flood. Horace Albright's daughter remembers how she felt after her first hike up from the river. Years later she came back with her son and grandchildren: "I had tears in my eyes when we came up in the boat, what a magnificent, wild thing that place had been. Now here was this big old wharf and hot dog stand or whatever it was, and I just shuddered."[39] Marian Albright also remembers her father's grand design for a Navajoland national park much larger than Stewart Udall's plan, even larger than the original Navajo National Monument, a scheme that, had it succeeded, could have saved not only Rainbow Bridge from flooding but also all of Glen Canyon.

Escalante

At the Park Service's origin in 1916, Stephen Mather believed that the agency needed to expand, not only to protect areas at risk but also for its own survival in the federal bureaucracy. Under Mather and Albright the NPS continually looked for ways to enlarge Grand Canyon National Park to the north and south, Yosemite and Glacier to the east, and Crater Lake in all directions, often at Forest Service expense. Less well known than the NPS's ongoing conflict with the USFS is the service's drive to acquire ruins, historic sites, and desert lands. These goals placed the service in competition with private corporations as well as other agencies in Interior scrambling to develop the Far West's oil, coal, and water. Regarding valuable Indian land, only the methods and rhetoric had changed since the 1800s. Everyone still wanted the resources.[40]

Unlike the previous century, now exploitation was not the only motive at work, especially among rich men such as Mather or among middle-class professionals such as Albright. Frederick Vreeland, a friend of both men, taking seven months to traverse the United States by auto, became deeply troubled by what he saw:

> I must admit that the changes and destructive development that I have observed have struck me with dismay. . . . With motor roads penetrating the most remote corners of our land and carrying throngs of thoughtless and heedless people, with the American zeal for exploiting and developing everything with more energy than forethought, with the present day obsession for building roads everywhere on any pretext—how *can* anything natural survive except in rigidly protected areas?

New Deal programs worsened the problem. The one hope, Vreeland believed, was for the federal government to turn the entire Four Corners area into a gigantic national park, much of it carved out of the Navajo Reservation.[41] The idea was not new. In 1934 the Park Service was pursuing just such a goal as it sought to realize a dream that Horace Albright called Escalante.

The attempt to make a national park out of spectacular northern Navajoland actually began in 1909 with plans for the 900,000-acre Navajo National Monument. In the 1920s the NPS began negotiations to obtain Canyon de Chelly while the agency's supporters lobbied for another parcel called the Paiute Strip. Making the strip into a national park, Louisa Wetherill explained to the Navajo tribal council, would bring development, roads, and "the right kind of people into the country."[42] A year after Wetherill's plea, Yellowstone superintendent Roger Toll examined the area and sent Albright an enthusiastic report on the Glen Canyon region. Toll proposed creating a Navajo National Park that would include Monument Valley (four hundred square miles), Navajo Mountain (nine hundred square miles) and Tsegi Canyon (seventy square miles); if possible, Blue Canyon, Coal Canyon, and the Goosenecks of the San Juan should be added. All land except for the Paiute Strip, which the Indians wanted returned, was on the reservation. Toll recommended "a mutually satisfactory agreement" with the BIA to create a new park "for the advantage of the Navajo Indians."[43]

Horace Albright, after spending most of the following spring in the area, agreed with Toll in proposing "Escalante National Park." After lukewarm responses from Hoover's BIA, Albright fared better with the New Deal and John Collier. The NPS proposed a Paiute Strip transfer to the Navajo in exchange for tribal cooperation in creating a park. If necessary, the NPS could begin with a monument "as a starter." As at Canyon de Chelly in 1931, the Navajo would retain ownership of the land.[44]

On March 1, 1933, the Navajo regained the Paiute Strip. Except for some internal boundary differences with the BIA, by April the Escalante project seemed in place. The Park Service drafted a bill authorizing "Navajo National Park within the Navajo Indian Reservation"—1.3 million acres that began just east of Antelope Point and contained Glen Canyon, Rainbow Bridge, Navajo Mountain, Inscription House, Betatakin, Keet Seel, Tsegi Canyon, Monument Valley, and the Goosenecks of the San Juan River. The NPS would provide tourist facilities, restore and preserve ruins, and build roads and trails. "Nothing herein," the bill stated, "shall be construed as in any way impairing the right, title and interest of the Navajo Tribe of Indians which they now have and hold to all lands and minerals, including oil and gas, and the surface use of such lands for agricultural, grazing and other purposes." Passage required consent of the Navajo Tribe.[45]

Albright, about to resign as director, believed he had succeeded in capturing another crown jewel as his final contribution to the service. John Collier agreed to the plan. Chee Dodge, the powerful leader of the Navajo, agreed. The states of Arizona and Utah concurred. Albright had support in Congress and from the president. Confident of success, he organized a seventy-five man reconnaissance party of archaeologists, cartographers, geologists, biologists, three Wetherills, and an ethnographer to visit the area in the summer of 1933. All was poised. As for approval by the tribe, Albright anticipated no difficulty, although he considered it wise to "give the Indians a little time to consider the proposition before the July council meeting."[46]

In July of 1933 John Collier presented his Escalante legislation to Chairman Thomas Dodge and the tribal council, which referred the matter to committee. When the council next met in Tuba City the committee had no report, prompting James Stewart of the BIA's land office in Washington, D.C., to speak out in favor of the bill. Stewart observed that, as at Canyon de Chelly, the Navajo had nothing to lose and much to gain from cooperating with the Park Service. He then proposed amendments retaining BIA control of water and range management and also recommended that the council require preferential employment of Navajos, that the tribe receive half of all entrance and concession fees, and that the NPS train young Indians as rangers.

The divided council took no action. Boyd Peshlakai favored the prospect of jobs that the Navajo had enjoyed at Mesa Verde, while Albert Sandoval felt obligated to the Park Service for helping the tribe secure the Paiute Strip and San Juan River. Other delegates, however, worried about NPS fencing and other possible "evils." Chairman Tom Dodge warned that the NPS coveted Navajo Mountain and Monument Valley, that tourists would want sheep and goats removed, and that without an explicit contract, one could not trust the NPS— "one of the most powerful organizations in Government."[47]

If Escalante had had a chance at Tuba City, later events doomed it, beginning with Albright's resignation in July. Pothunting at Betatakin and Keet Seel had become serious, prompting the NPS to build fences as it had at Chaco Canyon to protect ruins from grazing, even though Arthur Demaray warned that any fence across the trail to Betatakin "will be cut every night." Opposition to BIA livestock reduction programs would soon become so bitter as to overshadow all other government relations with the Navajo, including those of the Park Service. Frank Kittredge in the NPS San Francisco office warned that restrictions on grazing at ruins had antagonized Indians and that the service needed to value living Indians at least as highly as dead ones. Demaray agreed that "we should go slow before antagonizing the Indians." Faced with delay, the NPS considered having Congress pass the bill but not forward it to Franklin Roosevelt until the tribe had approved, but others pointed out that this tactic would place the NPS at the mercy of the tribal council, which in turn might interpret the ploy as circumventing them. The service decided to wait.[48]

Waiting proved in vain. When the tribal council next met at Keams Canyon in July 1934, it voted to develop its own park system rather than allow the NPS to supervise an estimated two thousand square miles of reservation land. Tom Dodge introduced a resolution that passed unanimously, one of the earliest acts of American Indian resistance to the National Park Service. The Navajo proclaimed that their homeland contained areas of scenic value that needed protection from outsiders:

> WHEREAS, the Navajos have a greater love for their country and its beauty than any other people can possibly have . . .
>
> WHEREAS, the Navajos know more about their country and always will have greater interest in its welfare than any other people or organizations,
>
> THEREFORE, it is hereby resolved that all areas of scenic beauty and scientific interest . . . be hereby reserved as Navajo Parks, Monuments, or Ruins, to be managed by the Navajos themselves, and be it further resolved that [the BIA] take immediate steps to have the National Park Service relinquish any rights that they may have acquired to any of our areas.[49]

Although Escalante was dead, the NPS retained hope. Director Arno Cammerer reprimanded two superintendents, Miner Tillotson and Frank Pinkley, for failing to promote friendly relations with the Navajo. Frank Kittredge continued to insist that unless the NPS cultivated the confidence of the tribe, it would encounter constant trouble at all levels. When Emil Gammeter, a member of the Utah state legislature, repeatedly asked when the NPS would begin building roads through Escalante, he was told that the service faced problems on Indian land with no solution in sight. Finally in 1939 Conrad Wirth informed Gammeter that Escalante had been dropped because of protests from the Navajos. Privately, the Park Service blamed the BIA for stopping "a most worthy project," a view perhaps confirmed when John Collier set aside 2.4 million acres of the northern Navajo reservation as a tribal wilderness area.[50] The Navajo eventually would revoke that classification. By 1991 their tourism director, Fred White, could look upon the Four Corners with a vision as grand as Horace Albright's. Once a paved road connected Chaco Canyon with Crownpoint, forming the eastern link in a tourist circuit, White believed the area would boom, bringing the tribe billions of dollars annually.[51]

Although most environmentalists today do not realize it, the defeat of Escalante delivered a crippling blow to their cause. In the opinion of Stewart Udall, had Albright gained his park, "there would be no Glen Canyon dam." Horace Albright himself agreed with that assessment.[52] Yet Albright never understood why Chee Dodge, the powerful Navajo elder statesman whom he considered a friend, had turned against him.

Horace Albright's daughter, Marian Schenck, considers Escalante the most fascinating story and unsolved riddle in her father's career. One day he remarked, "I'm going to tell you something, girlie, I never told anybody, nobody."

He said, "You know, I've only had three losses in my whole life. One was your mother, my worst loss, and the death of your brother. And then it was my defeat. I only had one real defeat in my time with the Park Service, and that was Escalante. I wasn't used to defeat. I always won. I always got what I wanted. It has hung on me, it has hung on me all my life." He said it would have saved so much. That Glen Canyon thing always hurt him and he felt so badly about it. He loved the Southwest. Once somebody sent him a big book about Glen Canyon and he said, "I don't want to look at that, take that out of here."

It would have been, of course, by far the largest national park, double the size of Yellowstone. Daddy just drew me a sketch map. He had the whole thing destroyed, the whole file. He said all the big maps and the plans and the geological surveys, every single one of them were burned or destroyed. He called it Escalante, the biggest national park. You see, way back even then they were already talking about these dams. He was so worried about the dams. He could see the population growing by leaps and bounds in the early 30s, and he was so afraid that the dams would just take over entirely, that they would ruin the various canyons, all the canyons that are now under water. He wanted them saved.

It was all drawn up and approved by the senators from Utah and Arizona, and everything was all set. He had known Chee Dodge for a long time, many, many years back to the beginning, Canyon de Chelly, Daddy had done that personally just one on one with Chee Dodge. So he went to Chee Dodge and outlined this whole thing. Chee looked at the maps and said he thought that it looked very fine. Then suddenly Daddy got word that Chee Dodge wanted to see him, and Dodge said, "I wanted you to know, Horace, I've been thinking about this and I'm not going to present it to [the] council. I'm not approving it, I don't want it." And Daddy could never get a reason, he never could get one single reason out of Chee. Nothing. He tried for years after he was director, and Chee would say, "No, I don't want it." And that was that.[53]

Michael Harrison knew what Albright never learned. After mustering out of the army in 1922, Harrison had joined the Park Service at Grand Canyon, where he acted as a secretary for Mather and Albright when they visited Arizona, leading to a lifelong friendship with Albright. After ten years in the NPS, Harrison moved to the BIA in Santa Fe. Having known Tom Dodge well from contact with Navajos at the Grand Canyon, Harrison was told by his superiors, "Anytime you can help Tom, drop whatever you're doing and help him." Harrison and Dodge subsequently would meet for several days before council meetings to review the agenda and draft resolutions.

Prior to the 1934 Keams Canyon session, Harrison cautioned Dodge about Escalante. If the area became a national park, Harrison warned, complaints from tourists and concessionaires would drive out Navajo sheep and horses: "I could see a conflict between the Navajo and the other people, the concessionaires. That was my sole purpose. So I drew up a resolution to not accept the Park Service proposal. Now that's a confession for which I hope the great spirits will forgive me."[54]

As much as it once desired Monument Valley, Glen Canyon, and Navajo Mountain, the National Park Service may owe Michael Harrison a vote of thanks. In the light of Chaco Canyon, Wupatki, and Rainbow Bridge, it is difficult to see how Escalante could have worked. The test of Horace Albright's dream, in fact, was Canyon de Chelly, where the NPS had eighty-four thousand acres to do exactly what he hoped to accomplish with two thousand square miles.

Canyon de Chelly

When the Navajo tribal council at Keams Canyon rejected the Escalante proposal, it also voted to repeal a three-year-old agreement allowing the Park Service to establish and administer Canyon de Chelly National Monument. Demands for return of the monument to the tribe have been repeated consistently for sixty years, and while not all Diné agree about removing the NPS, most concur that the canyon, the "soul" of Navajoland, is crucial to their culture.

The monument is actually four canyons. None are as awesome as the Grand Canyon, but they are perhaps more beautiful: Canyon del Muerto, Canyon de Chelly, Bat Canyon, and Monument Canyon. Diné have lived in the thirty-mile-long bottoms since the early 1700s, raising corn, beans, squash, peaches, melons, and alfalfa as well as livestock. Kit Carson interrupted their occupation in 1863 by destroying the farms and removing families, but the Navajo returned after Bosque Redondo.

Another attraction besides hogans brought Americans to Canyon de Chelly: Anasazi pits, kivas, rock art, and cliff houses at Junction Ruin, Antelope House, White House, Mummy Cave, and Sliding House testify to an extensive civilization a thousand years before the Navajo. Frederick Vreeland described it well in 1934:

> . . . a combination that is perfect as a vision of unalloyed delight. The dramatic scenery different from anything else on the Continent; the ancient dwellings, perched like swallows' nests on the cliffs; the kindly and gentle spirited Navajos living on the canon floor as they have done for generations—it all makes a picture and human document that is unsurpassed, and unspeakably refreshing in the hurly-burly of our "modern" life. To allow this to be spoiled by the exploitation that has marred our National Parks would be a crime against civilization.[55]

Others shared Vreeland's sentiments, inspiring proposals to protect de Chelly from pothunting and vandalism. In 1923, when Hunter Clarkson of the Fred Harvey Co. urged that the canyon become a national monument, the initial Park Service reaction was cool. Arno Cammerer told Clarkson that the 1868 Fort Sumner Treaty explicitly set aside the entire canyon system for exclusive Navajo use. A change in status, Cammerer cautioned, would require the consent of 75 percent of the tribe's adult males. The NPS nonetheless asked the BIA to investigate, resulting in a report by special commissioner Herbert J. Hagerman, who learned that both the Navajo and local traders opposed any change in jurisdiction.[56] When the NPS decided to pursue the matter in 1925, Hagerman brought the request to a council meeting at Fort Wingate, the second such gathering in the history of the tribe.

Hagerman secured unanimous approval at Fort Wingate for making de Chelly a federal monument. He promised that the tribe would retain title, grazing rights, and full treaty rights. The Chinle delegate requested that local Indians replace the trader in providing horses for tourists. Deshna Clahzhesehillige from Shiprock insisted that no tribal dollars be spent on roads.[57] The BIA and the Park Service then began negotiating jurisdictional procedures.

Other issues interfered and the government did not return to the tribe until 1930. Meeting again at Fort Wingate, the NPS and BIA sought approval of

readjusted boundaries and new language protecting tribal rights on the eighty-
four thousand acres: "Nothing herein shall be construed as in any way impairing
the right, title, and interest of the Navajo Tribe of Indians . . . to all lands and
minerals, including oil and gas, and the surface use of such lands for agricultural, grazing, and other purposes."

The tribe secured the right to lease saddle horses, while the Park Service had
authority over ruins, roads, and tourists.[58] Cheschille Todechenie from Fort
Defiance responded to the plan by reminding everyone that the Diné and
Anasazi "have lived in that canyon for ages" and that Indians must be assured
that they can stay "for as long as the sun goes down and comes up," adding that
an arrogant trader at Chinle had monopolized the guide service. Albert Sandoval requested a recess to discuss the proposal, but councilman J. C. Morgan
moved immediate approval and the measure passed 16-1.[59] After a flurry of
petitions pro and con by local Navajo, Congress passed a Canyon de Chelly
bill on February 10, 1931, and Herbert Hoover signed it four days later. The
National Park Service had acquired responsibility for a monument on land that
it did not own.

How this joint occupancy worked out is a long, complex story told in detail
by David Brugge and Raymond Wilson in their *Administrative History of Canyon de
Chelly*. Within three years the tribal council had grown angry over fences and
stock controls and sought to rescind its action, the first of numerous such
efforts. Brugge and Wilson show that almost every possible relationship, both
positive and negative, between the Navajo, the BIA, the NPS, and the American
public has occurred at Canyon de Chelly. Conflicts there stimulated men such
as Meredith Guillet, John Cook, and Art White to think carefully and creatively
about tribal relations. They saw the importance of hiring local people, of close
relations with Window Rock, and of learning to speak the Navajo language.
Their concerns also led to an innovation called the Navajo Lands Group
(1968–1982), formed to coordinate relations between the tribe and a dozen or
more NPS units.[60]

In the beginning, however, the NPS showed little awareness that it had
moved onto an Indian reservation. Regulations for de Chelly prohibited littering, collecting firewood, loud radios, firearms, curing of fish, digging worms,
gambling, hitchhiking, hunting, and washing clothes. Bans on nude bathing
and "scanty" clothing along with limits on public speeches hardly posed a problem for Navajos, but requiring burning permits and a warning that stray dogs
would be shot did. More serious disputes arose over control of Thunderbird

Navajo dwelling on reservation land inside Canyon de Chelly National Monument, 1934.
(Photograph by George Grant, courtesy of Harpers Ferry Center, Charles Town, W. Va.)

Ranch at the mouth of the canyon, boundary lines, sewage and garbage disposal, grazing, vandalism, excavation in the ruins, panhandling, and theft.
Archaeologists disturbing human remains, water rights, and access to utilities,
especially electricity, also caused tension. On one occasion a superintendent
required a Navajo drilling a well on his own land to apply for a permit.

Tourists disturbing the Diné living inside the canyon has remained a constant irritation for sixty years. The NPS's inability to keep climbers off Spider
Rock, a sacred site for some Navajo, was seen as bureaucratic indifference to
native religion. Some Park Service employees, most notably Superintendent
Paul Berger (1958–1962), seemed to be unaware, unconcerned, and ethno-
centric. Art White recalls "a little Navajo cemetery, and Berger started going in
there with a bulldozer one time, and that's a no-no, needless to say. I'm sure he
knew that cemetery was there, but he just didn't give a damn." The NPS often
forgot the terms of the original agreement—forgot that Canyon de Chelly was
Diné land, that the service and not the Navajo were guests.[61]

NPS relations with the BIA at Canyon de Chelly, perhaps more extensive than
in any other park, became strained when the BIA supported Navajo demands for
return of the canyon. The BIA considered NPS opposition to exotic plants for

erosion control to be "petty bickering." In 1936, as the Indian Office realized that de Chelly served as the hub for a Park Service wheel encircling the reservation, a condition that it felt would inspire constant pressure for more NPS controls, James Stewart and other officials in Washington, D.C., called for repeal of the 1931 legislation. The service responded that its loss of authority would result in uncontrolled commercialization by traders, destruction of the ruins, and "pauperization" of the Navajo. Secretary of the Interior Harold Ickes ultimately supported the NPS.[62]

Over the years, as at Chaco, Betatakin, and Antelope Point, the Park Service at Canyon de Chelly has not only assisted the tribe through training programs and tourism development; it has also helped individual Navajos. Rangers drove critically ill people to the hospital and helped to bury others. "The old style ranger," Charles Voll recalls, "never wrote a ticket out on anybody. If you caught someone breaking a rule, you would explain what was wrong and, if need be, chase someone." Art White concurs: "If we could bend the rule, we would bend it. If somebody had to be buried at Canyon de Chelly, well, OK, send the backhoe up there and dig a hole for them, you know, what the heck. That's just being a good neighbor. It's illegal, maybe, but, you know." The NPS assisted tribal police while superintendents worked with the BIA to smooth out frequently ruffled relations between local people and Cozy McSparron, owner of the Thunderbird Ranch for over four decades. For a number of years NPS staff held Easter egg hunts for hundreds of Navajo children.

Rangers also killed rogue bears and rescued dozens of domestic goats from canyon walls, but not as many goats as the number of Indians they extracted from the sands of de Chelly wash—177 in March 1964, alone. Meredith Guillet (1945–1960, 1963–1966), more than most superintendents, understood that "feeding Grandma Benally's goat and chickens when she is away, helping sick people get care at the PHS Clinic, rescuing goats and sheep . . . establishing good 'grass roots' relationships with the individual Navajos" was essential for cordial relations. Guillet recognized that most Diné did not distinguish between official NPS duties and the acts of a good neighbor.[63]

World War II put Canyon de Chelly management issues on hold. With the return of veterans needing jobs, increased vandalism at overlooks, and more thefts in the campground, relations grew strained. Exacerbated by official comments that the Park Service owned the canyon and that the site "belonged to the people of the United States," matters came to a head. The Navajo demanded that the Park Service leave.

In 1958 the NPS responded by appointing Paul Berger, Art White, and Meredith Guillet to investigate the crisis at de Chelly. Their analysis of the problems was astute, their solutions a step toward change. They recognized that Navajos distrust anything and anyone from "Washington." For Indians, land especially was "a hot and burning issue," and the tribe resented any government effort to weaken their hold on any treaty area. Marching into this situation, the committee noted, have been tourists, BIA agents, technicians, archaeologists, Park Service rangers, congressmen, analysts, "and general crackpots." Frequent turnover of NPS personnel further disrupted relations. The Navajo, while appearing docile, had always resented outsiders. Now, with oil, gas, uranium, and timber income, they "can thumb their nose at the world and they are doing so." The tribe would do what it pleased at Canyon de Chelly in its own good time: "Navajo cannot be hurried."[64]

Finding no easy solutions, the committee recommended the appointment of Tom Dodge as NPS liaison to the tribe, the employment and training of young Navajos, turning visitor fees over to the tribe, and education in native culture for all superintendents in Arizona and New Mexico. Although the NPS acted on a number of these recommendations and also created the Navajo Lands Group, problems continued. Theft, begging, and drunkenness bothered guests in the campground. The reappointment of Guillet in 1963 improved conditions at de Chelly, yet hostile relations with Window Rock continued. The tribe passed more resolutions opposing the NPS and called for return of the canyon, actions which, according to Art White, "rattled brains all the way back to Washington."[65]

By the 1980s some issues at de Chelly had been resolved, many old problems persisted, and some new ones had emerged. Navajo employees had moved from maintenance jobs into administration, including the superintendent's office, with sixty-five out of seventy NPS employees in the park being Indian in 1991. With the tribe in charge of interpretation, the visitor's center sold excellent books on ethnohistory yet still had a limited exhibit on the modern Navajo. The Long Walk is glossed over, viewers being told that "before 1864 the Navajos frequently raided Pueblo and Spanish settlements for livestock, supplies and women" but nothing about Kit Carson's invasion. A model hogan stands outside the center, a silversmith works by the front door, and the bulletin board tells guests, an increasing number of whom are Navajo, about the Indian community college, the tribal museum, a Hopi museum, and Navajo tribal parks. In the parking lot an assistant superintendent drives off sheep, while in a nearby campground visitors from Denver look with dismay at the stray, sick, and starving dogs. One camper remarked that "this is the worst managed national park I've ever seen."[66]

Many visitors, unaware of de Chelly's tribal status, would also be upset to learn that hunting, trapping, and logging take place inside the monument. After sixty years park borders are not defined, with even the headquarters boundary in dispute. Paradoxes abound. A few years ago this became the only national park in which a white ranger had shot and killed a local Indian, yet no public outcry erupted. Here a Navajo superintendent, Herb Yahze, took a Navajo vendor to court for selling goods near her own property. The campground, in the words of Charles Voll, remains "a great sea of conspicuous consumption in an ocean of poverty."[67]

At the chapter house in Chinle, a small town in the process of becoming a reservation metropolis, Theodore Evans serves as president. Born twenty miles west at Black Mountain in 1922, he spent nine years in the military and various other jobs, including employment at Los Alamos while the atomic bomb was being built, before returning to help his people grapple with the future. Evans considers the national monument a place apart—"We don't have much to do with them." Local people, he says, do not understand the Park Service or protecting ruins. The NPS provides jobs but remains distant, although no more distant than Window Rock, which, Evans complains, has no idea of what is going on in Chinle or Canyon de Chelly. Evans, a quiet, serious man, is more concerned about Navajo youth "with nowhere to go" who are exchanging the old ways for drugs and violence than about the NPS. Chapter member Deswood Bitsoi, who worked as a park mechanic for twenty-three years, claims that things were much better when Anglos ran de Chelly. Bitsoi too worries about children ingesting mouthwash, booze, and hairspray, about Navajo teenagers having wild keggers in the canyon.[68]

Urban growth at Chinle poses problems for the chapter and monument alike. Power lines threaten to crisscross the canyons to serve arc-lighted subdivisions and trailer courts on the rim. As population increases at the fastest rate in North America, feelings become strained over the park boundary and housing development on the peninsula separating del Muerto and de Chelly. Disputes become acute over the canyon floor, where every acre is claimed. Tribal clear-cutting and grazing threaten to invade Monument Canyon, a pristine place with abundant wildlife. Growth means random trash dumps, degraded air and water, and a maze of off-road vehicle tracks; development affects runoff, which causes severe erosion on canyon bottomland, threatening ruins and rendering farms useless.

Thus local Indian leaders like Evans see themselves "caught in a trap" between modern development, destruction of traditions, and Window Rock's indifference. The number of cars, tour companies, and campers at the monument increases every year; so do the number of trips that twenty-four-passenger trucks take up and down the canyons daily, the young Navajo guides at times insulting native residents along the way. As the population grows in Chinle and the tribe promotes tourism, pressure builds to allow dune buggies, hang-gliding, hot-air balloons, and helicopter flights at de Chelly. In the midst of all this, a Navajo park ranger, Lupita Johnson, patiently explains why she lives "in the most beautiful sacred place in the world."[69]

During the 1930s the NPS claimed that Canyon de Chelly demonstrated how well parks could operate inside Indian reservations. What the place actually revealed was how complex and difficult such a relationship could become.[70] Conditions shifted as tribal government increased its power, the native population grew, the culture changed, tourism boomed, and federal funding dwindled. Errors, mistakes, confusion, and misperceptions multiplied.

For its part, despite the good-will and competence of various rangers and superintendents, the NPS largely ignored the terms of the 1931 agreement until the 1970s, assuming that technical "know how" could resolve differences in attitudes and culture. The Navajo, on the other hand, distrusted government, resented past injustice, and made painful cultural transitions. Tribal government lacked coherent programs, and Navajo leaders, despite their election-year threats, balked at taking over responsibility for the NPS payroll at de Chelly. In Window Rock, tribal council leadership changed as frequently as NPS staff. Oil and coal leases, World War II, struggles over the Checkerboard Area, poverty, alcoholism, and population growth loomed larger than acquiring Thunderbird Lodge or recapturing a sacred canyon. Moreover, Window Rock could barely run its own parks.

Monument Valley

When Michael Harrison wrote the resolution for Tom Dodge that scuttled Escalante, he in effect launched the Navajo tribal park system. It required twenty-four years for the first park to emerge and for the council to develop a program, but by 1966 a system of eight parks was in operation, although they occupied a low place on the tribe's agenda.[71] Thirty years later Navajo parks remain at a standstill. Rangers are reassigned to manage livestock, leaving most sites without supervision. The 109 chapter houses can veto new parks in their locales; if some could undo the past, there would be no parks of any kind.

Staff morale is low, planning confused, and training weak, despite opportunities to work with the NPS. Most Navajos in the system, given a choice, prefer NPS employment. The National Park Service puts more dollars into Canyon de Chelly than the tribe does into its entire system, a situation that precludes expansion or improvements. In 1991, parks received $673,000 out of an overall tribal budget of $300 million. NPS-trained Fred White left the program after a dozen years because he saw no future. One of White's superiors in the president's office understood, remarking that no one could take pride in Navajo parks and recreation.[72]

If Navajos can be proud of any park, it is Monument Valley. One of the most spectacular landscapes in North America, the location for John Ford's *Stage-coach*, its buttes and mesas awash in brilliant oranges, maroons, and purples, Monument Valley epitomizes "the West" of the American imagination. Tribal and NPS officials acknowledge that Monument Valley is the jewel of Navajo-land—Escalante's having been but one of many attempts to seize it.

In 1958, responding to persistent NPS efforts to acquire the valley, the Navajo council proclaimed it the first tribal park. Local Navajos objected to that classification, then objected even more strenuously in 1974 when the council proposed ceding the valley to the Park Service. A bitter meeting in December at the Oljeto chapter house, whose members split over promoting tourism but united against NPS fencing and Window Rock's broken promises, stopped talk of transfer.[73]

All superintendents at Monument Valley have found it difficult to manage. Fred White was trained at the NPS Albright Center but could not speak Navajo, a crippling handicap. Wilson Davis speaks Navajo, but locals consider him an "outsider" from elsewhere on the reservation. Lee Cly, in charge of the valley for seventeen years (1976–1993), had been born there, was fluent in the language, and would live nowhere else, yet like Davis he had trouble controlling vendors, film crews, herders, and inholders. When Cly tried to remove vendors from the park to "section 52" on Utah state highway land, enforcing the ban— "chasing your own people"—proved difficult. Davis, Cly's successor, describes the resulting section 52 shantytown as "just out there," beyond his control and causing safety hazards at the highway junction.[74]

Wilson Davis spent twenty-one years in law enforcement with the NPS, until he resigned at Canyon de Chelly, frustrated at finding himself between the NPS and local people. A burly, serious man with a good sense of humor about himself, Davis deplores the tribe's failure to update its 1983 master plan for the park, forcing him to manage "from day to day." He believes that Window Rock has little long-range vision. Among the Navajo, whether in tribal government or at nearby Oljeto and Kayenta chapters, "people just don't understand parks." Davis, who finds his job challenging and discouraging, contemplates returning to the NPS.

The 1983 master plan identified many of the immediate problems at Monument Valley: visitation increasing from 55,000 in 1979 to over 100,000 in 1982 (it reached 260,000 in 1991 and, despite a health scare, 340,000 in 1994), no gift shop (one opened in 1991), traffic congestion, vendors (still working the improved campground and the tour routes in 1994), the water supply (piped from seven miles outside the park), and the lack of interpretation of Navajo history or culture at the visitors' center.[75]

As serious as these problems were, the master plan neglected more sensitive issues. Park entry and camping fees are sent to Window Rock. All special-use permits for film crews, arriving every week (unannounced and often out of control), are processed in Window Rock, as are permits for the Goulding Trading Post just outside the park and for tour buses from Goulding and elsewhere. Monument Valley produced about a million dollars a year in revenue, a quarter of which comes back from Window Rock to the park—the same system the U.S. Congress has applied to its Park Service.[76] Furthermore, land in Monument Valley has not been withdrawn. Of the ten inholding families, five have grazing permits, the others do not; none have homesite leases, creating a difficult situation much like that in the Hopi freeze lands. Wilson Davis believes that once the park relaxes a ban on grazing and settlement, a human tide will flood Monument Valley.

Parks of the Navajo Nation, and Monument Valley in particular, replicate NPS problems: private vending, lack of money, inadequate cultural interpretation, external threats, mistrust and resentment by local communities and inholders, visitor numbers soaring beyond capacity, commercialization, livestock management, law enforcement. Clearly, disputes that arise between native peoples and American parks are more a result of public land dilemmas than of race.

Having Navajo rangers and superintendents at Canyon de Chelly and Monument Valley may improve public relations, but ethnicity alone neither avoids nor resolves conflict.

When the Diné agreed to stay with Changing Woman, the people discovered that each clan "has a different story to tell." That is true of the more than twenty parks, tribal and federal, on or near the Navajo Reservation. The Chaco Navajo were evicted, their land bought or taken. At Wupatki, families held on for generations, while at Navajo National Monument the Park Service became the supplicant. At Antelope Point the tribe and NPS cooperate in promoting a $10 million resort at the same time they struggle to develop policy to allow shamans to collect herbs along Lake Powell. For years the Navajo demanded the return of Canyon de Chelly yet declined responsibility whenever opportunities arose. They lost Rainbow Bridge, but the tribe and BIA defeated William H. Taft, Horace Albright, and Stewart Udall, powerful men who sought to create magnificent monuments out of the Navajo lands where Asdzáá nádleehé once "danced on the northern mountain to summon corn and animals."

The Navajo Tribe has vast lands, many members, and small parks. Another people, the Miccosukee and Seminole Indians of Florida, small in number and owning little land, who live next to the third largest NPS complex outside of Alaska, also have "a different story to tell."

EVERGLADES NATIONAL PARK AND THE
SEMINOLE PROBLEM

It seems we can't do anything but harm to those people even
when we try to help them.

—Old Man Temple, *Key Largo*, 1948

Swollen by tropical rains and overflowing every summer for millennia, Lake Okeechobee releases a sheet of water that drains south over grass-covered marl prairie, seeping through Florida's wetlands into the Gulf of Mexico. Fifty miles wide and a hundred miles long, this shallow river of grass that the Seminoles called Pa-hay-okee is the heart of today's 1.4-million-acre Everglades National Park. An International Biosphere Preserve and World Heritage Site best known for roseate spoonbills, bald eagles, osprey, peregrine falcons, snowy and great egrets, herons, white ibis, anhinga, and flamingos, the park is also home to manatees, green sea and loggerhead turtles, bear, deer, alligators, crocodiles, and the Florida panther.

For more than two hundred years this subtropical wilderness of pines, palms, and palmettos also sheltered Florida's Seminole and Miccosukee Indians, a people who have hunted, trapped, and fished in Pa-hay-okee since the eighteenth century. Today the Miccosukee's 333-acre Forty Mile Bend Reservation lies within Everglades National Park on the Tamiami Trail. More traditional than the Seminoles who live on the Brighton and Dania reserves, the Miccosukees finally gained federal recognition in 1972—fifteen years after the Everglades became a national park. Florida's Miccosukees and Seminoles participated in the creation of the park and Big Cypress National Preserve. Our story concerns only the Everglades, leaving events in Big Cypress for future study.[1]

Invaders and Swamps

Large numbers of Americans began migrating into south Florida during the late nineteenth century after railroads had cut through the forests and wetlands below Lake Okeechobee. By the 1880s engineers and land developers began promoting drainage projects, convinced that technology could transform this water-sogged country into land suitable for agriculture. At the turn of the century, steam shovels and dredges hissed and wheezed their way into the Everglades, bent on draining the Southeast's last wilderness. They were the latest of many intruders.

Although Spanish explorers had arrived on the Florida coast early in the sixteenth century, Spain's imperial toehold never grew beyond a few fragile outposts. Inland remained mysterious, a cartographic void, El Laguno del Espirito Santo. Following Spain, the British too had little success colonizing the interior. After several centuries, all that Europeans had established were a few scattered coastal forts. Nonetheless, Europe's hand fell heavily through disease and warfare upon the aboriginal Timucuan, Apalachee, and Calusa people. By 1700 the peninsula's interior and both coasts were almost devoid of Indians. The vacuum did not last long. Creeks from Georgia and Alabama soon filtered into Florida's panhandle and beyond, occupying native hunting grounds.

The Creek (Muskogee) Confederacy to the north comprised sixty allied towns with a total population of nearly twenty thousand people speaking two languages, Muskogee and Hitchiti. Sharing many cultural traditions, the towns joined together for war, trade, and celebrations. Georgia's "Lower Creeks" had raided Spanish and Apalachee villages in northern Florida since the early 1700s. Besides booty, they acquired valuable knowledge of Florida's terrain and wildlife. By the mid-1700s, several Muskogee-speaking "Upper Creek" towns had taken hold in northern Florida. When Americans crushed their confederacy in the Creek War of 1813–14, Indians fled southward into Florida seeking safety and sustenance. Eventually they reached the peninsula's end at Cape Sable. Rigging canoes with sails, the Creeks visited Cuba and other Caribbean islands, where they reestablished a Spanish trade. By 1830, Florida Creeks had adapted to a new homeland and become "Seminoles," a Muskogee word more properly pronounced *simano-li* and perhaps evolved from *cimarrón*, Spanish for "wild" or "runaway."

In north Florida, Creeks maintained traditional large towns with an agricultural economy, but to the south their way of life changed. The Everglades

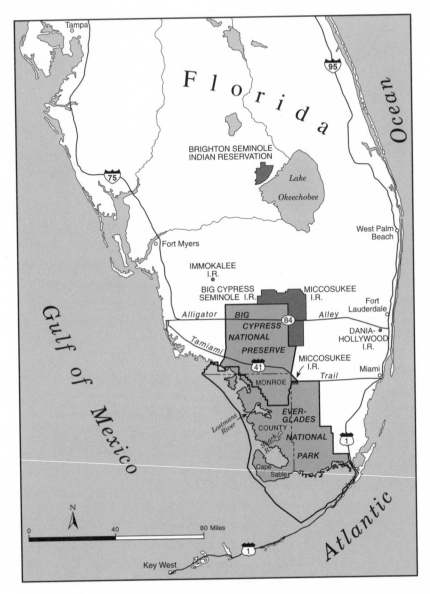

Everglades National Park in southern Florida.

afforded no place for towns or extensive gardens: Creek villages became Seminole camps; traditional Creek log homes became open-sided, thatch-roofed Seminole *chickees*. On hummocks—mounds of fertile soil higher than seasonal floodwaters—the Seminoles cultivated corn, melons, squash, and pumpkins. Cattle made no sense in cypress forests, so Indians kept semiwild boars, creatures well adapted to rooting out a living in bogs and swamps. Where horses fared poorly, canoes did well; thus Seminoles became expert at building, paddling, and sailing watercraft as they harvested Florida's abundant fish and wildlife.

The former Creeks continued expanding their range during the early nineteenth century, becoming well adapted to life on the river of grass. Their dominion remained unchallenged until the United States defeated Great Britain in 1814; three years later the Seminoles were at war with Americans.[2]

Seeking retribution for Indian aid to the British, Andrew Jackson advanced into Florida after defeating the Creeks in Alabama and Georgia. Jackson wanted the Seminoles removed; colonial planters coveting north Florida land also sought to prevent fugitive slaves from joining Seminole villages. Between 1818 and 1850, Americans and Seminoles clashed in Florida's tangled swamps and forests. The Indians, using hit-and-run guerrilla tactics, held off the U.S. Army at great cost in dollars and human life until the Americans eventually overwhelmed most of the bands and forced their relocation to Oklahoma. Not all Seminoles moved, however, as several hundred diehards retreated into the Everglades and Big Cypress Swamp. The government, confronted by a wilderness maze of water and tangled vegetation, decided to ignore them.[3]

Easily evading the sparse white population of south Florida, the tiny bands stayed isolated for several decades. As long as the Everglades and Big Cypress were wild, the Indians controlled interior forests and marshes, where they felt at home in what appeared to most Americans as an insect-infested swamp teeming with crocodiles, a wasteland requiring drastic reclamation to be fit for human occupation. Most early settlers in south Florida kept to the coasts, yet by 1870 a few "crackers" living at remote outposts began an Everglades trade with Indians who exchanged exotic feathers, pelts, plumes, and gator hides for beads, bolts of cloth, guns, ammunition, and liquor. Within a generation this trade pattern and the Seminole way of life had begun to unravel as the next invasion began.

At the turn of the century, draining, damming, and dredging Florida's wetlands opened another wilderness to American enterprise. A frenzied construction of rails, canals, and roads brought a new breed of farmers, developers, and sportsmen. The Seminoles, once self-sufficient hunters, faced a shrinking territory. Suddenly losing their food supply and source of trade goods, families slid rapidly into poverty. Roads and canals brought white hunters deep into the wilderness, where newcomers soon surpassed the Indians in the wild animal and bird trade. Adding to native woes were changes in fashion coupled with state and federal legislation to protect plumed birds: Growing concern for wildlife conservation now threatened the Seminole way of life in the wetlands.[4]

In 1912 the BIA's Lucien A. Spencer, after finding a significant decrease in Seminole trade goods, recommended that a wildlife preserve and Indian reservation be established in "the vast area of overflowed land" in southwest Florida. Others supported his sentiments.[5] Responding to conservationists, the Florida legislature in 1917 created a 100,000-acre Seminole Indian Reservation and game preserve. Located on the Monroe County coast northwest of Cape Sable, the reserve's Shark and Lostman's Rivers and its mangrove swamps, with streams and creeks flowing into the maze of Ten Thousand Islands, left virtually no dry land. Most Seminole camps and villages lay northeast in the Everglades and Big Cypress, but as a hunting ground, the new reservation met tribal needs.

The 1920s witnessed yet another Florida land boom. Completion of the Tamiami Canal Highway 41 connecting east and west turned a sleepy little village on the Miami River into the bustling city that ended south Florida's isolation. A free-for-all soon took place in Pa-hay-okee. Timber companies seeking cypress, pine, and mahogany moved into the Big Cypress, new canneries scoured clam beds in the Ten Thousand Islands, and south Florida's tiny commercial fishing fleet exploded into an industry. Sport and commercial hunters decimated alligator and waterfowl in the recently opened Everglades, while professionals joined tourists to collect rare plants and animals, with newborn alligators becoming the item of choice. Rumors of oil strikes resulted in exploration, roads, and the arrival of drilling crews.

Alarmed, conservationists organized to protect the wetlands. Robert T. Morris, a New York physician, and Ernest F. Coe, a landscape architect from Rhode Island, spearheaded the crusade. By the mid-1920s, after they had founded the Tropic Everglades Park Association, Coe launched a letter-writing campaign that would last for two decades. He organized public meetings, gave magic lantern shows, and enlisted his wife to lobby garden clubs. When the Everglades emerged as a national issue, public opinion appeared to favor a park, but local politicians and sport hunters remained skeptical. Coe and Morris, originally committed to Everglades plant and animal life, also became concerned about the welfare of Seminole Indians.

The Park Problem

By 1930 the federal government had little to show for trying to improve the Seminoles' condition in Florida. After setting aside two small reserves and an even smaller amount of money, the BIA failed to coax Seminoles out of their interior camps onto reservations. Both the BIA and Florida ignored or failed to understand political factions within the bands, divisions that eventually resulted in formation of the Miccosukee Tribe. With little federal or unclaimed state land available, the option of creating a single large reservation, even if Seminoles could have agreed on one, no longer existed. Wherever the bands occupied state or private land, government officials classified them as squatters. Adding to the quandary, areas that Indians depended on for food might now become a national park.

Ernest Coe claimed that a new park in Florida would benefit Indians. Knowing little about native cultures in general and less about the Seminole in particular, Coe assured fellow conservationists that Indians could find park jobs as canoe guides. Restrictions on hunting and trapping would lead to increased wildlife, which, he predicted, would overflow beyond park boundaries to help Indians who resettled to the north.

Coe had a jump on the NPS. After Congress requested a study in 1929, the service reluctantly became involved with the Everglades. NPS hesitation came from a bias in favor of spectacular western peaks, canyons, and geologic curiosities. A decade earlier, the Everglades ecosystem would have flatly failed NPS scenic criteria, but by 1929 priorities had begun to change. After Horace Albright took a personal interest in the region, the Everglades would become the first national park created for biological reasons.[6] Albright shrewdly realized that a Florida park could provide the NPS a large East Coast site near a growing urban center and a major tourist destination. When he joined Coe's campaign, Albright knew that victory would not come easily: The problems of private land acquisition and sport hunting required solutions, as did the Seminole question. But Albright had been dealing with Indians throughout his career, and, as of 1929, they had not proven a stumbling block.

Active NPS involvement in the Everglades started with a series of field trips.

Albright, Arno Cammerer, and a team of Interior specialists visited Florida in 1930, taking with them a group of prominent conservationists that included Dr. T. Gilbert Pearson, president of the National Audubon Society. Once back in Washington, Albright requested a BIA report on the Monroe County Seminole reservation. When Commissioner Charles Rhoads informed the NPS of federal lands held in trust, plus the nearly 100,000-acre state reserve, the director assigned Cammerer to study possible land acquisitions. Probably to his surprise, Cammerer discovered state enabling legislation providing that the Monroe County reserve would "terminate if the Indians cease to reside on the reservation for a period of 18 months, and that, as the Indians have never lived continuously on the reservation, the reservation may be cancelled." Cammerer had found a lever with which to pry loose the Seminole reservation.[7]

Horace Albright was not the only federal official working in south Florida. BIA special commissioner Roy Nash's research led him to conclude that an Everglades park would have a negative effect on Indians, especially if the NPS prohibited hunting. Although Nash did not trust Florida to protect native land, suspecting that the state would reclaim any ground once it became valuable, he hesitated to recommend transfer to the NPS. In his view, the Seminoles had to retain hunting rights in any acceptable trade. Nash's final report included a precise map of permanent Seminole camps, illustrating what he called "the intimate connection between the Indians and the Park."[8]

Further NPS assessment of the Everglades was conducted by conservationist Augustus Houghton in February 1932. Houghton, too, did not relish a Seminole removal; nevertheless he recommended that the state lands be exchanged for a new reservation north of the cross-Florida highway (Tamiami Trail). By now, Ernest Coe also vigorously recommended land exchange to solve the Seminole problem and secure the 100,000-acre reservation for a park.[9] Coe and others realized that a major NPS problem in Florida was the lack of vast unclaimed federal lands that had existed when western parks were carved out of USFS, Land Office, and BIA holdings. Thus when Congress did authorize a future Everglades National Park in 1934, it restricted property acquisition to land donated by the state or by private owners, which meant that the Florida legislature had to be convinced to hand over, not sell, the Monroe County reserve.[10] As unlikely as that might seem, matters soon got worse.

Although park sponsors dreaded the prospect of Seminole removal, sympathy for the Indians waned after plans for oil exploration on the reserve alarmed everyone. Knowing that a boom would halt their plans, park advocates decided to secure the reservation immediately. Ernest Coe now called for a Seminole removal that would void their hunting and fishing rights in the Everglades. Others pressed for a national park that would give displaced Seminoles an outlet for handcrafts and a new role in the growing tourist economy.[11]

Tourism posed a dilemma. By 1934 the Seminoles had been involved for several decades in what might be called the curiosity trade. Between 1914 and 1918 Henry Coppinger opened Miami's first Indian attraction, "Coppinger's Tropical Garden, Alligator Farm, and Seminole Indian Village." Located in a grove of palm and cypress trees along the Miami River, this exotic menagerie featured alligators, crocodiles, monkeys, and Indians. The village contained several native chickees complete with live families. A rival enterprise, Musa Isle Village, soon opened, and by the 1920s Seminoles had become popular. Guests could wander among Indians in an exotic tropical setting, see native women make clothing on Singer sewing machines, and watch a traditional food called *kunti* being cooked over open fires. Seminole weddings at Coppinger's and Musa Isle drew hundreds of onlookers. But the most popular attraction, one which still draws tourists to similar villages now operated by the Indians themselves, were the spectacles in which Indian men wrestled with live alligators.[12]

Coppinger's and Musa Isle set the standard for the Seminole tourist village heyday between 1920 and 1940. The attraction provided many Seminoles with seasonal employment and a place to live. Although most Indians had positive memories of Coppinger's and Musa Isle, the BIA, civic leaders, and clergy concluded that such places contributed to native alcoholism, prostitution, and venereal disease. Some reformers campaigned for total elimination of the camps; others preferred sites relocated near the Everglades, where, it was argued, tourists could purchase genuine native arts and crafts, take canoe trips with Seminole guides, and see natives undefiled by Miami vulgarity.[13]

Secretary of the Interior Harold L. Ickes and his Indian commissioner, John Collier, believed that an Everglades park would offer an ideal setting for Seminole gift shops and guides. Ickes and Collier, who had supported protection of the Everglades since the early 1930s, worried about the cultural impact of a park; yet, after visiting two remote Seminole camps, Ickes announced that a park "would contribute . . . to [their] economic and social rehabilitation." Accepting Coe's wildlife overflow theory and considering Indians inherent conservationists, Ickes and Collier concluded that a new reservation north of the park would serve as a game refuge. Unlike others, they also recognized that Indians enjoyed special status: "For a considerable time to come," Ickes declared in

Seminole Bobby Tiger prepares to wrestle with an alligator. Indians were tourist attractions in Miami before Everglades National Park was established. (Courtesy of the Fort Lauderdale Historical Society)

1935, "the Seminoles ought to have the right of subsistence hunting and fishing within the proposed park, and they should always have the labor preference."

Ickes's comment on native rights was part of a remarkable NBC radio address on national parks that he delivered on March 30, 1935. Never before had a secretary of the interior spoken directly to the entire nation on principles of Indian-white relations, on Indian ties to the land, or on the thorny question of national parks and historic injustice. During a recent visit to Florida, Ickes explained, he had learned that the Everglades "provided a refuge to the Seminole Indians, to whom it once belonged exclusively." He also discussed the national monument at Fort Marion, including its darker side:

> Under American rule Fort Marion was often used as a prison, and one of the most famous of its occupants was valiant Osceola, patriot Chief of the Seminoles, who was treacherously seized, to our everlasting shame, while negotiating a treaty of peace at the time of the Seminole War. Perhaps preservation of the Everglades as a national park, and the establishment of the Seminole reservation adjacent to it on the north, will, in some degree, make up for the sufferings of Osceola and his fellow tribesmen at our hands.[14]

Harold Ickes, the "righteous pilgrim," had made creation of Everglades National Park a moral issue.

Section 3

The day after his radio address, Ickes and John Collier flew to Florida, where they toured the proposed park, attended a Sun Dance "powwow," visited a remote Seminole village, and accepted a petition from Sam Tommie, Charlie Cypress, Charlie Billie, and other Seminoles. The experience deeply affected both government officials. Ickes promised land, employment preference, and protection of hunting rights.

Collier saw the park as a means to preserve a noble and endangered way of life while protecting wildlife being slaughtered by sport hunters. The Seminole camp existed in "the true wilds [as] an incarnation and victory of the wilderness itself," because Florida Indians had an emotional bond with nature unknown by whites: "They are not cruel hunters or trappers; they even make pets of such creatures as raccoons and otters." Collier recognized that creating a national park, along with the intrusions of his own BIA, could destroy a culture that had survived several centuries of onslaught: "It is by the spirit that they live. Hence, beyond restoring those equilibriums of the natural environment which the white man has destroyed, and thus making possible a better life [through] their own social structure and their own unhesitant and powerful and sane instinct— beyond that point, we should go with extreme caution in Seminole matters, and perhaps we had better not go at all."[15]

In his determination to protect the Seminoles, John Collier inserted Section 3 into the Everglades National Park Act of 1934: "[Nothing] in this Act shall be construed to lessen any existing rights of the Seminole Indians which are not in conflict with the purposes [of] Everglades National Park." Others in the BIA found Section 3 too vague and anticipated problems. Gene Stirling of the bureau's anthropology division warned Collier that the NPS would never allow hunting and trapping, nor would the Park Service permit Indians "to run cattle, raise hogs and practice agriculture." Stirling doubted that any economic net gain for the Seminoles would occur if they had to depend upon NPS good will.[16]

Stirling, Ickes, and Collier needed to be concerned about more than the NPS. Section 3, even with its ambiguous language, infuriated Ernest Coe. Expressing shock, anger, and dismay, Coe demanded repeal. The provision, he maintained, was unnecessary because "liberal and most favorable provisions have [already] been made in favor of the Seminoles." Not only did Coe attack the clause, he called for immediate removal of all Indian camps and villages from Pa-hay-okee. Seminoles had no right to special privileges not granted to other citizens, and, if they continued to live inside the park, Coe warned, they would compromise "one of the most precious of the national park standards"—namely, the prohibition against hunting. That restriction made national parks a place "where all forms of life cease to fear man," a condition Coe did not want suspended to mollify Indians.[17]

Faced with Ernest Coe's flurry of letters, Arno Cammerer at the NPS waffled. Indian occupancy of the Everglades, he told Coe, was "incidental to the main land acquisition problem, and can be taken up at the proper time." A month later Arthur Demaray summarized NPS policy: "We have no intention of moving the Indians bodily from the areas which they find profitable; we are not ready to say that their hunting privileges would be abrogated."[18] Yet by 1936, a year after Ickes and Collier had spoken with the Seminoles, federal policy shifted. Ickes softened his defense of subsistence hunting, and the BIA assured Coe that Indians had "no special rights or privileges within national parks." Even though the BIA's Florida agent, Francis J. Scott, warned Collier that the park created a severe disadvantage for the Seminoles and that Indians would protest bitterly against restrictions on hunting, the Washington office informed Ernest Coe that Indians could claim only specific treaty rights in parks.[19]

At this point the Seminoles themselves spoke out. In 1937 Corey Osceola, Josie Billie, and Ingraham Billie informed the press that they refused to leave the Everglades and would continue hunting, the federal government notwithstanding. Ingraham Billie's camp on Lostman's River lay well within park boundaries, as did several other sites.[20] Press coverage of the protest produced a Park Service report, "The Seminole Problem," in which J. J. Cameron blamed the BIA for initiating Seminole removal. The bureau, according to Cameron, in 1931 had suggested that Indians be relocated. He found the original BIA plan "eminently satisfactory" to the Park Service and Congress. Moving the Seminoles from Monroe County to a new reserve north of the proposed park, he advised, enjoyed "the whole-hearted support of the State of Florida."

J. J. Cameron conceded that removal had been pursued quietly to avoid bad publicity. Despite Section 3 of the 1934 legislation, the NPS and BIA had worked together to solve "the Seminole problem." Cameron recommended further cooperation, but he cautioned that "moving of the Indian is apt to be a long-drawn out and controversial matter, and . . . may not be successful."[21]

Rangers and Rules

Acquiring land for the Everglades National Park proved to be a long, drawn-out affair as well. State and private donations came slowly. After Florida finally relinquished the Monroe County reservation in 1944, Seminoles continued to fish, trap, and hunt there. Despite alarms from Coe, the NPS proceeded with caution.[22]

Following World War II, efforts to establish the park gained momentum as threats to the Everglades mounted. The 1934 legislation had "authorized" a park but did not create one or protect a single blade of grass. In 1947 the Florida legislature, having already donated considerable state land to the federal government, appropriated $2 million for acquisition of inholdings. To guard the site until the Park Service took over, it was administered by the U.S. Fish and Wildlife Service as a national refuge. Manager Daniel Beard, who had authority to enforce state conservation laws, was instructed to work with BIA agent Kenneth Wilson on a census of Seminoles remaining in the old reserve.

After meetings with the Tamiami Trail bands in the spring of 1947, Beard reported that at least one permanent village under William McKinley Osceola remained within park boundaries. The Osceola band refused to move. Beard found John Jumper's and Chief Charlie's hunting camps at the headwaters of the Shark River, and a dwelling belonging to Jimmie Temmy deep in the Everglades. Beard described Temmy's and Jumper's places as "the real McCoy," meaning that they were not suitable for tourists. Both families agreed to vacate.[23]

Although Beard opposed bawdy Miami-style attractions in the park, he hoped to protect the Jumper and Temmy camps and especially the hummock gardens that grew a rare species of pumpkin. After the NPS rejected the idea of indigenous guides, Beard suggested training Indians as ranger/interpreters, allowing families to maintain their hummocks while informing park visitors about traditional life in Pa-hay-okee. Archaeology and native history, too, could be included. "Complete avoidance of the Seminole in [our] program," Beard counseled, "seems unwise to me."[24]

Daniel Beard, the future superintendent of Everglades National Park, formed further opinions while drafting his refuge management plan. After World War II, when Seminoles began using airboats and swamp buggies, the day of cypress canoes had ended. Indian camps were changing: Washing machines had arrived, along with the "white man's buildings," where Fords and Chevies sat next to traditional chickees. Seminoles still caught frogs and "fire hunted" alligators in the glades, but acculturation proceeded apace.

From his observations and from discussions with tribal members, Beard developed guidelines for Indian activity in the future park. He decided that all temporary camps a mile or more south of the Tamiami Trail must be abandoned; those within a mile could remain, with no hunting allowed. Swamp buggies, air boats, and other motorized vehicles were confined to immediate camp areas, with no new "white man's buildings" or improvements; such sites must not be sold or exchanged. Fires south of the highway, except for cooking and warmth, would result in fines or jail. Seminoles could fish under state laws, but no frogging would be permitted. Beard's requirements made NPS rules at Canyon de Chelly appear mild.

Although BIA agent Kenneth Marmon had not examined Beard's regulations, he agreed in principle. Marmon anticipated no enforcement problems, nor did he believe that reasonable rules would face opposition.[25] Marmon then explained the future to the Seminoles. He asked Ingraham Billie, Jimmie Billie, and Cory Osceola to inform their councils about the new system. Later, Osceola assured him that the councils agreed "to go ahead and establish the park, and not to worry about the Seminoles."[26]

Pleased that the tribe agreed to its management plan, the NPS remained nervous about Indians residing inside a park. Throughout 1947 the Fish and Wildlife Service and NPS gently urged Seminoles to depart. After William Osceola, John Jumper, and Jim Tiger expressed concern about future hunting and fishing, the service said that taking frogs and garfish could continue. The three Indians promised to move but repeatedly found reasons to delay, keeping a low profile. Thus when President Harry S Truman officially dedicated Everglades National Park on December 6, 1947, he saw no Seminoles. Unlike similar ceremonies at Glacier, Grand Canyon, Navajo National Monument, Canyon de Chelly, and Apostle Islands, Indians had not been invited and none were present. Truman did not mention Indians, yet some still lived in the new park and all expected to use it—in their own way.[27]

"The Land I Stand on Is My Body"

By 1950 the BIA had established three small Seminole reservations in Florida: Brighton, Big Cypress, and Dania (Hollywood). Some families, mostly Christian, moved to the reserves; others, retaining their native religion, stayed in the traditional camps and villages that dotted the Tamiami Trail. Prior to World War II, state, federal, and private landowners had shown little concern over such Indian occupation. Attitudes quickly changed in the early 1950s as land values skyrocketed after rumors of another oil boom, and when Florida's rising population began seeking new recreational retreats.

Private landowners now called for ousting the few Indians who impeded oil exploration, leisure activity, and agriculture. Events outside Florida further contributed to arousing political activism by the state's Indians. When the Eisenhower administration announced plans to end federal responsibility for certain tribes, the Seminoles were on the list. Meanwhile, a rift widened between the three reservations and the traditional Miccosukee faction, creating a complex situation that affected the national park.

The BIA during the 1950s assisted reservation Seminoles while ignoring Miccosukee demands for official recognition, hoping that the latter would move to a reserve. Traditionalists living along the Tamiami Trail and in the park had no such intention. The NPS, while tolerating its Miccosukee residents, tried to control their hunting and fishing. By 1954 roughly four hundred "Trail" people led by Ingraham Billie, Buffalo Tiger, George Osceola, and Jimmie Billie had organized a council called the "Mikasuki Tribe of Seminole Indians," seeking recognition as a distinct group. This in turn would separate them from an Indian Claims Commission case involving the 100,000-acre reserve in Monroe County. The Miccosukee rejected the ICC process and government money— they wanted land, lots of it, and the land they wanted included most of southwest Florida.[28]

All this seemed improbable two decades before the Passamyquoddy land claim in Maine alarmed Americans. Nevertheless, even after a reduction to 1,500,000 acres, the Miccosukee still claimed a conservation district, the old Monroe County reservation, and a twelve mile strip along the Tamiami highway. The conservation area lay submerged for most of the year but the Miccosukees wanted more wildlife habitat along with exclusive hunting and fishing rights in the national park, a park that, in their view, had been created as "a homeland for animals" to the exclusion of humans.

With expert legal help and their own persistence, the Miccosukees eventually prevailed. After the federal government granted official recognition in 1962, the band acquired a fifty-year lease from the NPS for a strip five and half miles long and 600 feet deep along Highway 41. The new Forty-Mile Bend Reservation provided space for Miccosukee offices, a school, housing and the Green Corn Dance ceremonies. Most of all, it answered a plea that elderly shaman Sam Jones had made to Ingraham Billie, George Osceola, and Buffalo Tiger a decade earlier: "This land I stand on is my body. I want you to help me keep it."[29]

"The Park Is Our Home"

By 1990 the Miccosukees and Park Service were again at odds over the Everglades. A Highway 41 special use permit, much like NPS agreements with the Havasupai and the Makah, placed restrictions on tribal development and made new projects subject to NPS review. As the growing band faced a housing shortage, its council platted a forty-five unit subdivision without NPS permission. After the Park Service ordered construction halted, tribal chairman Billy Cypress met with superintendent Robert Chandler to explain that for Miccosukees "the park is our home." They did not lease the land, Cypress said, but rather had given the government over 2,000 square miles in exchange for the 333-acre strip.[30]

The Park Service did not see matters that way. It contended that the bands enjoyed special access to a large area in Big Cypress where they could hunt, log, and operate air-boat tours, an area outside the park to which the NPS hoped the Miccosukee would eventually migrate. The negotiations, especially after the NPS accused the tribe of dumping meliluca-contaminated fill into park wetlands to create mobile home pads, became "a painful, contentious process." Pain and contention also marked futile federal efforts to convict James Billie after the Seminole chief killed an endangered Florida panther in 1983.[31]

The claim that "this land is my body" can be difficult for non-native rangers to accept when Indians build casinos, kill rare panthers, press for oil and gas exploration in nature preserves, introduce exotic species, or zoom through cypress swamps in boats powered by aircraft engines. To park staff, remarked a former Everglades superintendent, "tribes are often seen as problems, as difficulties":

> There's the negative perception, and in some cases it's more than a perception, that the tribes really want to get as much as they can from the park. They push an issue to its limits. Our staff see the Miccosukees with a huge bingo parlor, see them working with Shell Oil to slant drill under the Everglades to enhance their financial base. They act on economic imperatives. On the other hand, they talk about traditional ways and sacred land. It creates a lot of resentment, and it's painful for the park manager because you recognize the validity of their claims and history and human needs, yet you have a responsibility to protect the park. It's sometimes very difficult. It's sometimes impossible.[32]

For Miccosukee and Seminoles the park relationship has also been uneasy. Miccosukees feel unwelcome and seldom use the park except for traditional burials; they and the Seminoles prefer Big Cypress where they can hunt, fish, trap and practice traditional ceremonies. Communication with the NPS has been poor—neither the Everglades or Big Cypress has had a tribal liaison. Few Indians have been hired, and as at Olympic, Glacier, Grand Canyon and elsewhere, frequent NPS staff turnover poses a problem. Few attempts to work with the tribes on park interpretation have been made.[33]

In Florida, unlike the Navajo in Arizona or Blackfeet in Montana, small bands living on tiny reserves have filed vast land claims against the nation's third largest park outside of Alaska. The Seminole problem reveals that, set apart though they may be, national parks are not exempt from the anomalies of history.

PARKS AND INDIANS IN AMERICA

All our landscapes, from the city park to the mountain hike, are
imprinted with our tenacious, inescapable obsessions.
—Simon Schama, *Landscape and Memory*, 1995

When Horace Albright wrote *Oh, Ranger!* in 1928 he echoed George Catlin's
original idea that national parks should be closely associated with America's
native people. In 1832 Catlin described the Plains Indian in "classic attire,
galloping his wild horse, with sinewy bow, and shield and lance, amid the
fleeting herds of elks and buffaloes." A century later Albright described "picturesque and colorful tepees of the Blackfeet . . . mighty hunters and valiant
warriors, tall, proud, dignified, the very personification of the redskin," and he
praised Indians for providing local color. "Indians!" he wrote in 1928, "There!
See them? Real, live Indians!"

Albright then conducted his readers on a circuit of Grand Canyon, Frijoles
Canyon, Mesa Verde, Glacier, Yellowstone, Rocky Mountain, Zion, Yosemite,
Crater Lake, and Mt. Rainier, pointing out that in parks one could still find "real
Indians, the kind that wear feathers, don war paint, make their clothes and
moccasins of skins. . . . The best place for the Dude to see the Indian in his
natural state is in some of the national parks." Here "redskins" still herded sheep,
wove blankets, and remembered buffalo kills. For Albright and George Catlin
alike, Indians were a curiosity, remnants of the land's ancient past, a people
without distinct personalities and without political power.[1]

The nineteenth-century romanticism of Catlin, Thoreau, and Bierstadt inspired a vision of wilderness as beautiful and sacred, which in turn instilled a
desire for parks as remnants of Eden and Acadia. National parks also arose in
America after its citizens realized that the frontier had closed; landforms served

as nostalgic monuments to the individualism, moral courage, and authentic lives of the pioneers. But twentieth-century parks had to be safe, free from violence, and devoid of human conflicts. If Eden did have inhabitants, they should be innocent. Instead of being noble savages, actual Indian residents and neighbors seemed distant and uncooperative, a vague, sullen, invisible threat. "In the debates about pristine natural areas primitive peoples [are] idealized, even sentimentalized," William Cronon observes, "until the moment they do something unprimitive, modern, and unnatural, and thereby fall from environmental grace."[2] At times Indians in national parks were not sublime but repulsive and jarring to affluent tourists, and thus they had to be removed by the Park Service or ignored by the public: Blackfeet living along a highway, Havasupai in a camp, Yakamas killing deer in a mountain meadow, Paiutes needing water.

In this book we have looked at changes in park relations with Indians since Catlin's initial idea, beginning with the creation of Yosemite and Yellowstone, and, after the birth of the Park Service, continuing under Mather and Albright. Much remains unexamined—Big Bend, the Badlands, Grand Teton, Nez Percé, Great Smoky, Death Valley, Alaska, Hawaii, and more. Many of our discoveries, such as finding the Bureau of Indian Affairs a consistent and surprisingly effective advocate for native interests against the Park Service, certainly deserve more investigation. While conceding the risk in generalizing about dozens of park units and hundreds of tribes more noteworthy for their diversity than their similarity, a few conclusions can serve as starting points for further inquiry.

To begin, park/Indian relations seem to fall into four phases: (1) unilateral appropriation of recreational land by the government; (2) an end to land-taking but a continued federal neglect of tribal needs, cultures, and treaties; (3) Indian resistance, leading to aggressive pursuit of tribal interests; and (4) a new NPS commitment to cross-cultural integrity and cooperation.

Creation of Mesa Verde and Glacier represented the first phase, between 1864 and 1916. Here the government used strong-arm treaty-making techniques of the nineteenth century to acquire parklands, showing little regard for tribal rights. This period ended with creation of the National Park Service in 1916. During the service's first half-century, Mather, Albright, and other directors either chose not to use such heavy-handed tactics or hit snags when they tried, as with Escalante. Fixed on growth as necessary for agency survival, the NPS "grabbed every possible remain in the nation—shrine, site, cemetery," but it demonstrated little genuine concern for native rights, as seen at Pipe Spring and Olympic.[3]

Apostle Islands and Grand Canyon serve as examples of a new era, between 1965 and 1987, when such tribes as the Chippewa and Havasupai not only protested against government and conservationist expansion but actually won major political battles with the Park Service. The NPS response included creating the Navajo Lands Group (1968–1982) in the Southwest and Director Russell Dickenson's appointment of Bill Fields (a Cherokee) as a servicewide tribal liaison in the early 1980s.

Finally, in 1987, the NPS made an official commitment, in its Native American Relationships Management Policy, that, more than merely tolerating native presence in or around parks, it would respect and actively promote tribal cultures as a component of the parks themselves.[4] Verne E. Chatelain, the Park Service's first chief historian, had proposed the same policy considerations fifty years earlier, an indication of how sluggishly the NPS could move on Indian matters. The process of drafting an Indian relations policy began in 1978 and required a decade for official adoption.[5] The new approach after 1987 has been most fully realized in the Southwest region's Santa Fe office and by such Washington, D.C., officials as Muriel Crespi and Jerry Rogers.

As Charley John of the Navajo and Doug Brown of the NPS both told us, nothing gets a bureaucrat's attention faster than changing a law or formal policy. Or as Frank Kittredge, one of the service's early leaders, put it, "A bureaucrat is held upright by pressure from all sides."[6] A need for pressure and change within the NPS can be measured by looking at Freeman Tilden's *National Parks*, first published in 1951 and revised seventeen years later. Tilden's index entry for Indians reads: "see pre-historic peoples." Aside from his short section on "Americans before Columbus," Tilden mentions the Navajo and Sioux three times each, the Hopi and Seminole twice, and the Blackfeet, Makah, Chippewa, and Havasupai not at all. Most references are passing allusions, such as noting that the Cayuse in their "primitive passion" killed Marcus Whitman. Nor did benign neglect end with Tilden. As late as 1989, NPS personnel, including a park historian and three of the service's directors, continued to publish books that treated Indians more as artifacts and scenery than as people.[7]

The NPS has improved in awareness and sensitivity during the past several decades, and one hopes it no longer embraces such limited history. Slowly, more native presence has found its way into park gift shops and interpretative programs. The mile-long Cottonwood Springs Trail at Joshua Tree, for example, has twelve signs describing Cohilla Indian use of the desert. Yosemite, joined by a local Indian council, broke new ground in 1982 with a program that interpreted Miwok and Paiute life during the park's early years.[8]

As with all social progress, old attitudes, habits, and wounds persist on all sides. Indians living near parks, like George Kicking Woman and Vicky Santana at Glacier, remember with passion that the land once belonged to their grandparents. "We lost everything up there," Kicking Woman laments, "and someday we will get it back." Loss of territory for Indians will remain a sore point no matter how enlightened NPS policies may become. The essential issue between Indians and whites has usually been land. "All the cultural understanding in the world," as Patricia Limerick points out, "would not have changed the crucial fact that Indians possessed the land and that Euro-Americans wanted it."[9]

Even in 1987 many NPS staff still saw themselves as the best custodians of Indian land and culture because, as Northwest regional director William Briggle said with some justification, "We do a better job of it than anyone else can." He promised that the Service would surrender control whenever tribes had the training, money, and desire necessary for change.[10]

As for cultural sensitivity, by 1990 no other region came close to the Southwest in awareness of native needs, and none had yet gained the level of confidence and cooperation from tribes that the Santa Fe office enjoyed.[11] The NPS strove to promote tribal enterprises and management at Pipe Spring, Montezuma's Castle, Nez Percé, Canyon de Chelly, Zuni-Cibola, and elsewhere, yet problems persisted. The service still had difficulty viewing small human communities as a part of its mission, places worthy of its limited time and resources.[12]

A passion for neatness and order, or, as Germans say of themselves, wanting "every blade of grass to point in the same direction," often produced friction between rangers and local people. Even next to the Ute and Navajo Reservations at Mesa Verde, or at Olympic, with ten tribes on its perimeter, the NPS had limited success hiring Indians. And while achieving fair treatment of native arts and crafts has been on the federal agenda since the Indian Reorganization Act of 1934, NPS policy and practice still do not satisfy Indians such as the Navajo bead-sellers, who see the service as protecting Fred Harvey tourist shops against small family businesses. At Canyon de Chelly, where 90 percent of the staff are Navajo, numerous antagonisms linger on, bead-selling being one, and cultural interpretation lags. Canyon de Chelly, once a favorite model for tribal/ NPS cooperation, differs little from other parks in that respect. De Chelly resembles Olympic, Glacier, Mt. Rainier, Yosemite, and Yellowstone in ignoring tribal history. While it is no longer totally accurate to say that for the NPS the only important Indian is a dead Indian, that aphorism retains some truth even at the progressive Grand Canyon. On the positive side, the service has discarded the once-widespread misconception promoted by Albright, Wickersham, and others that Indians feared spirits, geysers, and mountains and thus would never use or occupy parklands.

In the United States one seldom finds native training or comanagement programs like those across the border in Canada. The conclusions reached by West and Brechin in *Resident Peoples and National Parks* are not yet NPS policy: Tourism, even "ecotourism," can be detrimental to small communities; prohibitions on the use of renewable resources by native people can harm parks; local people must have a voice in planning; it is necessary to explore comanagement innovations; and "hire the natives where appropriate."[13]

While ideals are important, many conflicts in park/tribal relations involve inherent conditions or dilemmas not easily resolved. The National Park Service, first of all, is a large bureaucracy located inside the super-bureaucracy of Interior, making it inevitable, as Horace Albright warned when he resigned as director in 1933, that the service could eventually act like any bureaucracy.[14] Furthermore, for Indians and the NPS alike, except in rare cases such as the Havasupai land restoration, their relationship is seldom a primary concern for either party. Rangers at the Grand Canyon first and foremost must worry about 5 million people a year, part of a total park system that manages over 340 million visitors annually; tribal councils every month must deal with poverty, U.S. senators, and state governments. As a result, tribes and parks often see each other as slow, inattentive, unresponsive bodies.

Problems of park administration, while at times cultural and racial, are common to Indians and non-Indians alike. If one compares Monument Valley or Ute Mountain Tribal Parks to NPS units, many of the same problems appear: law enforcement, inholder and neighbor relations, weak support from the central government, personnel issues, commercial exploitation of parklands, environmental degradation. At Montezuma's Castle, to cite another example, the Camp Verde Apache painfully discovered the daily headaches of operating a tourist facility next to a national monument.

Employment policy illustrates how complex park management can become, one instance being the irony of Navajos managing and interpreting the ruins of their traditional Pueblo enemies at Keet Seel, Inscription House and Betatakin.

Overall, the NPS in 1992 had 309 permanent native employees out of a total full-time staff of over 14,000.[15] Hiring and promotion of Indians progresses slowly because entry-level jobs are poorly paid. In addition, many natives prefer to remain near reservations and relatives, whereas administrators advance in the NPS through long-distance career moves.

Indians also may identify the Park Service as simply more government, federal or otherwise, a negative association for many. "The 'government' is the 'government' to the Indians," Frank Pinkley observed in 1935, "and it is going to be difficult to make them understand that the Park Service is not responsible for . . . the Soil Conservation Service. Even if they understood, they might still be hostile, as many intelligent white people are hostile to the whole government."[16] It is not easy for some Indians to work for the United States, and doubly hard if it means wearing a federal uniform among their people. Finally, in the opinion of former NPS director Russell Dickenson, resistance to Indian employment exists within the service itself.[17]

A promotion-by-frequent-transfer system compromises NPS Indian employment policy. If Russell Dickenson is correct in claiming that prior consultation and mutual trust provide the keys to successfully negotiating with native people, then constant personnel changes can only harm the process. A superintendent making a determined effort to understand an unfamiliar culture requires at least two years to meet local tribal leaders and begin gaining their confidence. Many park superintendents transfer after three or four years and, compounding the problem, tribal leadership can change even more frequently. Navajo Bob Martin complained to his tribal council in 1930 about transient school teachers, but his stricture applies to park staff as well: "How are these employees going to advance our race when they come here and only stay two or three months and then they ask for a transfer? Then they get a transfer and go some place else, and then over there they only stay one or two months and they ask for a transfer, and they keep on shifting around. We don't want that kind of employees, we want employees that stay here for a long time and study the Indians and find out how to teach the Indians [Applause]."[18]

Another inherent limitation is that tribes have immediate interests and explicit rights, whereas the Park Service has a sweeping mandate to serve everyone. "The rights of all American citizens," Arthur Demaray said of Canyon de Chelly, "transcend those of any individual or group of individuals," a mission further complicated by ambiguous definitions. "National parks must be maintained in absolutely unimpaired form for the use of future generations,"

Secretary of the Interior Franklin Lane wrote to Stephen Mather in 1918, and they are "set aside for the use . . . and pleasure of the people."[19] It is therefore no surprise that park administrators must weigh the general public interest against exclusive Indian use of sacred sites, water rights, hunting-gathering, bead-selling, occupation of parklands, religious freedom, and claims of sovereignty. The dilemma of tolerance policies toward hunting in parks or the Hualapai river-rafting enterprise illustrates the hard choices confronting the Park Service.

Indian tribes and environmentalists should not expect perfection when Park Service leaders face such dilemmas, any more than we can expect Indians or the Sierra Club to be perfect in all their decisions. As Dwight Rettie, a strong advocate of the NPS professional staff, concedes: "Sometimes they forget. Sometimes they resist even the best of changes. Sometimes they simply do not know. Sometimes a policy or practice, believed right at the time, turns out to have been a mistake. Sometimes the hardest thing of all is to admit being wrong."[20]

The service, with most of its staff displaying positive attitudes toward Indians and often going out of their way to help tribes and individuals, is not alone in its confusion over native demands at places like Bridge Canyon, Rainbow Bridge, Yosemite, and Chief Mountain. The NPS can cite the U.S. Supreme Court as equally befuddled.[21] Yet whatever the confusion over large policy issues, a tally of the small daily, monthly, and yearly ways in which the Park Service has concretely aided Indian tribes reveals a positive side for which the NPS receives too little credit—for pulling vehicles out of the sand at Canyon de Chelly, for providing technical assistance in tribal construction and tourist programs, for its role in establishing the native organization Keepers of the Treasures, for helping with a Ute Mountain Ute economic feasibility study at Mesa Verde, for training Indian rangers at the Albright Center, for restoring an ancient Nez Percé canoe, for funding the Makah Museum, and hundreds of other cultural programs.[22]

Today, Indian and Park Service relations remain in flux, leaving the future unpredictable. Native rangers who organized the Council for American Indian Interpretation will perhaps strengthen their role within the service. In February 1995 the NPS created a new American Indian liaison office in Washington, D.C. A few months later, in July 1996, director Roger Kennedy proclaimed "a new era" by accepting twelve Indian tribes as full partners in the NPS historic preservation program, placing them on equal footing with state governments. Yet such positive efforts have not diminished attacks against the service: In 1966 five tribes supported by NARF launched an Alliance to Protect Native Rights in

National Parks; in 1997 one alliance member, the Timbisha Shoshone, hired legal counsel and held a public forum in Los Angeles to demand restoration of their land in Death Valley.[23]

These recent disputes notwithstanding, the NPS over time has obviously improved its relations with Native Americans. Environmentalists likewise have slowly learned from the relationship between parks and tribes. For the Sierra Club and Friends of the Earth, a hard lesson came home when they erred at the Grand Canyon by acting ideologically instead of seeking information and conversing directly with the Havasupai. Awareness of history and a commitment to discussion will not necessarily change policy in a national advocacy organization, but honest dialogue can help idealists realize that protecting land is no simple matter. Moving beyond "us versus them" raises dilemmas, especially when the land saved is for recreation at the expense of people living in poverty. When environmentalists do achieve valid trade-offs and make promises to Indians, they need to keep their word.[24]

Better knowledge of history also can bring a necessary if painful awareness that conservationists such as George Bird Grinnell, Theodore Roosevelt, and Horace Albright, when they created parks out of Indian land, took yet another significant step in the conquest of North America. This irony, as Alston Chase discerned at Yellowstone, arose from

> the underlying conflict between Indians and well-intentioned preservationists. Congress, in creating the park "for the benefit and enjoyment of the people," destroyed the livelihood of another people. From the beginning this sad fact was a skeleton in the closet of our park system, a past too embarrassing to contemplate, for it demonstrated that the heritage of our national park system and environmental movement rested not only on the lofty ideal of preservation, but also on exploitation.[25]

Finally, park defenders need to dispense with stereotypes of the Indian-as-ecologist/Indian-as-victim, and cease seeing tribal members as colorful, nostalgic versions of environmentalists themselves. Indians, like national parks, have changed since George Catlin had his vision along the Platte in 1832. Indian tribes do not fit myths that have them dancing with wolves, uttering Chief Seattle's speech, living "in harmony with Nature" in preindustrial cultures without impact on the land, or dwelling in some pristine paradise that existed "before the white man came." Alfred Runte has commented that we often see national parks as places suspended in time. To seek an "enforced primitivism" in natives and treat them as museum pieces serves to suspend people in time. It leads to an unjust demand that Indians who adapt to modern culture should forfeit all rights.[26] Expecting any people to remain unchanged, to never alter the land, is to ask too much—just as it asks too much to expect national parks and their keepers to preserve the earth in "absolutely unimpaired form."

To reject environmental myths about native people does not mean suppressing their historical associations with the land. These associations and memories are essential for Indian and non-Indian alike. Tribes in America today represent 0.5 percent of the total population, yet their centuries of occupation on the land and their many distinct cultures count for far more than numbers would indicate. Alfred Bierstadt's *Rocky Mountains* has native people settled below crags and waterfalls: Bierstadt's landscapes are awesome, sublime, and sacred, but people lived in this aboriginal North America—not in Shangri-la or Utopia, but mired in the everyday business of human existence.

The challenge is to accept the kaleidoscope of our past, to find diverse visions and at times conflicting memories embedded in our national parks, and to embrace this heritage as accurately and as fully as possible. Native people must take their rightful place in recapturing and telling the stories—Hopi and Havasupai at the Grand Canyon, Chippewas on Lake Superior, Paiutes at Pipe Spring, Blackfeet in Glacier, Quinault and Klallam at Olympic, Pueblos at the Petroglyph National Monument in Albuquerque: "The wilderness, after all, does not locate itself, does not name itself . . . [and] though it may sometimes seem that our impatient appetite for produce has ground the earth to thin and shifting dust, we need only poke below the subsoil of its surface to discover an obstinately rich loam of memory. . . . The sum of our pasts, generation after generation, like the slow mold of the seasons, forms the compost of our future. We live off it."[27]

ABOUT THE SOURCES

Preparation for this book involved exploring in parks, listening on Indian reservations, taking notes at museums and archives, and reading extensively. Like all writers, we gained insight and inspiration from sources beyond those cited in the notes. Our thinking was especially influenced by the ideas of Joseph Sax, Francis Paul Prucha, Alvin M. Josephy, Jr., Angie Debo, Charles Wilkinson, Patricia Limerick, Wendell Berry, Roderick Nash, Susan Schrepfer, Vine Deloria, Jr., Barry Lopez, and Wallace Stegner.

The best introduction to park history is Alfred Runte's *National Parks: The American Experience* (Lincoln: University of Nebraska Press, 1979). Joseph Sax's *Mountains without Handrails: Reflections on the National Parks* (Ann Arbor: University of Michigan Press, 1980) expresses our own hopes for the system. Two excellent references on early NPS history are Horace Albright's *The Birth of the National Park Service: The Founding Years, 1913–1933* (Salt Lake City: Howe Brothers, 1985) and John Ise's *Our National Park Policy: A Critical History* (Baltimore: Johns Hopkins University Press, 1961). John Miles's *Guardians of the Parks* (Washington, D.C.: Taylor and Francis, 1995) critically appraises the NPS and examines the internal problems of an environmental organization.

NPS official reports and glossy brochures are significant for both their information and their omissions. Readers can quickly access basic sources through Lary Dilsaver's 450-page *America's National Park System: The Critical Documents* (Lanham, Md.: Rowman & Littlefield, 1994). The NPS can be proud of its dedicated scholars, such as Robert Utley and David Brugge, who provide a model for public history research.

We consider Aldo Leopold's *A Sand County Almanac, and Sketches Here and There* (New York: Oxford University Press, 1949) the starting and perhaps the ending point for discussions on environmental ethics. In our book, we have tried to provide Indian perspectives on land, parks, and politics. Our interviews with nearly one hundred Native Americans and tribal histories by Pauline Capoeman, Harry Kersey, Stephen Hirst, Robert Euler, Harold Hickerson, John Ewers, and others were invaluable in advancing this goal.

A list of books, articles, government documents, interviews, and archival sources may be found at the University of Arizona Press website, www.uapress. arizona.edu/extras/keller/bib.htm. We regret that one interview is missing: Horace M. Albright died on March 28, 1987, nine days before our appointment with him.

NOTES

Preface

1. H. D. Guie and L. V. McWhorter, eds., *Adventures in Geyser Land* (Caldwell, Idaho: Caxton Printers, 1935); Mark Brown, "Yellowstone Tourists and the Nez Perce," *Montana, the Magazine of Western History*, 16:3 (July 1966), pp. 30–43; Bill Lang, "Making History: The Landscape of the Nez Perce Trail," *Northern Lights*, 3:4 (August 1987), pp. 14–17.

2. Alston Chase is the harshest critic of the park system: *Playing God in Yellowstone* (Boston: Atlantic Monthly Press, 1986); "How to Save Our National Parks," *Atlantic Monthly*, July 1987, pp. 35–44; "Unhappy Birthday," *Outside*, December 1991, pp. 33–40. Chase's polemics are nearly matched by Michael Frome in *Regreening the National Parks* (Tucson: University of Arizona Press, 1992). Thoughtful, sympathetic criticism comes from Joseph Sax, including "Helpless Giants: The National Parks and Regulation of Private Lands," *Michigan Law Review*, 75:2 (December 1976) and *Mountains without Handrails: Reflections on the National Parks* (Ann Arbor: University of Michigan Press, 1980), and from William R. Lowry, *A Capacity for Wonder: Preserving National Parks* (Washington: Brookings Institution, 1994). Europeans have an immense affection and concern for American parks, as seen in Siebo Heinken, "Zu Tode geliebt," *Die Zeit*, October 6, 1995, p. 79.

3. To push the parallels further: Most reform movements to save special lands and our Indian heritage originated in the eastern United States. An example that combined both was the Antiquities Act of 1906. Several historians have noticed the parallel between parks and reservations: Alfred Runte, *National Parks: The American Experience* (Lincoln: University of Nebraska Press, 1979), pp. viii, 6, 107; Frederick Turner, *Rediscovering America: John Muir in His Time and Ours* (San Francisco: Sierra Club Books, 1985), p. 282n. NPS founder and director Horace Albright recognized that both Indians and parks were consigned to lands considered unfit for settlement: *Oh Ranger!* (Palo Alto: Stanford University Press, 1928), p. 82.

244 NOTES TO PREFACE

4. Felix Cohen's *Handbook of Federal Indian Law* (Albuquerque: University of New Mexico Press, 1971), republished and updated in 1982 by Rennard Strickland and Charles F. Wilkinson, eds., (Charlottesville, Va.: Michie); Francis Paul Prucha, *The Great Father: The United States Government and the American Indians*, 2 vols. (Lincoln: University of Nebraska Press, 1984); Wilcomb E. Washburn, ed., *Handbook of North American Indians: History of Indian-White Relations*, vol. 4 (Washington: Smithsonian Institution, 1988); John Ise, *Our National Park Policy: A Critical History* (Baltimore: Johns Hopkins University Press, 1961). The best history of the parks, Alfred Runte's *National Parks: The American Experience* (Lincoln: University of Nebraska Press, 1987), touches briefly on a few Indian topics in the second edition, mainly Alaska, pp. 200, 205–6, 238–40. Other books that ignore native relations with parks are Robert Shankland, *Steve Mather of the National Parks* (New York: Alfred A. Knopf, 1951); Stewart L. Udall, *The National Parks of America* (Waukesha, Wisc.: Country Beautiful Foundation, 1966); Donald C. Swain, *Wilderness Defender: Horace M. Albright and Conservation* (Chicago: University of Chicago Press, 1970); Conrad L. Wirth, *Parks, Politics, and the People* (Norman: University of Oklahoma Press, 1980); Eugenia H. Connally, ed., *National Parks in Crisis* (Washington, D.C.: NPCA, 1982); William C. Everhart, *The National Park Service* (Boulder: Westview Press, 1983); John C. Miles, *Guardians of the Parks* (Washington, D.C.: Taylor and Francis, 1995). Nor does one find the subject covered by western historians: Donald L. Parman's excellent survey, *Indians and the American West in the Twentieth Century* (Bloomington: Indiana University Press, 1994), contains nothing about park/tribal relations. Even scholars of particular tribes, such as Lawrence Kelly, Richard White, Peter Iverson, and Parman on the Navajo neglect the topic.

5. John C. Freemuth, *Islands under Siege: National Parks and the Politics of External Threats* (Lawrence: University Press of Kansas, 1991); Frome, *Regreening the National Parks*; James M. Ridenour, *The National Parks Compromised* (Merrillville, Ind.: ICS Books, 1994); Lowry, *A Capacity for Wonder*. In Lary M. Dilsaver's useful *America's National Park System: The Critical Documents* (Lanham, Md.: Rowman & Littlefield, 1994), almost all entries on Indians concern archaeology and prehistory.

6. Russell Dickenson interview, March 22, 1996.

7. Patrick C. West and Steven R. Brechin, eds. *Resident Peoples and National Parks: Social Dilemmas and Strategies in International Conservation* (Tucson: University of Arizona Press, 1991), pp. 5, 17, 385. The works of Steven Pyne, Richard White, Alston Chase, Simon Schama, and William Cronon among others convincingly refute such concepts. For a forceful essay on how harmful romantic views of nature can be, see Rebecca Solnit, *Savage Dreams: A Journey into the Landscape Wars of the American West* (New York: Vintage Books, 1995), pp. 294–308.

8. See Theodore Catton's *Inhabited Wilderness: Indians, Eskimos, and National Parks* (Albuquerque: University of New Mexico Press, 1997).

9. West and Brechin, *Resident Peoples and National Parks*, pp. xv–28.

Chapter 1

1. Thomas Vennum, Jr., "Ojibwa Origin-Migration Songs of the Mitewiwin," *Journal of American Folklore*, 91 (July 1978), pp. 753–91. Also see Selwyn Dewdney, *The Sacred Scrolls of the Southern Ojibway* (Toronto: University of Toronto Press, 1975), for discussion of the Mitewiwin.

2. Vennum, "Ojibwa Origin-Migration Songs," pp. 753–91.

3. For general histories of the Chippewa or Ojibwa, see William Warren, *History of the Ojibway Nation* (1851; reprint, Minneapolis: Ross & Haines, 1957); Edmund J. Danizer, Jr., *The Chippewas of Lake Superior* (Norman: University of Oklahoma Press, 1978); Robert E. and Pat Ritzenthaler, *The Woodland Indians of the Western Great Lakes* (Garden City, N.Y.: Natural History Press, 1970); Harold Hickerson, "The Southwestern Chippewa: An Ethnohistorical Study," *American Anthropological Association Memoir No. 92*, vol. 64 (June 1962); and Robert H. Keller, "An Economic History of the Indian Treaties in the Great Lakes Region," *American Indian Journal*, 4:2 (February 1978), pp. 2–20. For the National Lakeshore region, see Hamilton N. Ross, *The Apostle Islands* (Batavia, Ill.: Batavia Herald Company, 1951) and *La Pointe—Village Outpost* (St. Paul: North Central Publishing Company, 1960); Reuben Gold Thawites, "The Story of Chequamegon Bay," *Collections of the State Historical Society of Wisconsin*, 13 (1895), pp. 397–425; Robert H. Keller, "The Chippewa Treaties of 1842 and 1854," *American Indian Journal*, 9:4 (Fall 1987), pp. 10–18.

4. Gaylord Nelson interview by Kathleen Lidfors, March 4, 1985, transcript, AINL Oral History file, Bayfield, Wisc.; "New Controversy over Apostles," *Ironwood Daily Globe*, Ironwood, Michigan, August 4, 1970, p. 5.

5. Bad River Tribal Resolution, May 10, 1962, AINL Cultural Resources file. The NPS realized in the 1950s that the Apostles area provided one of the few locations for public access to Lake Superior; it also foresaw how complicated the land title issues would be because of checkerboard ownership. Interview, Howard Chapman, May 8, 1992; Great Lakes Shoreline Survey, *Remaining Opportunities along the Wisconsin Lake Superior Shoreline* (Washington, D.C.: National Park Service, 1959).

6. "The Evolution of an Idea," Harold C. Jordahl, Jr., unpublished manuscript, AINL Cultural Resources file, hereafter cited as Jordahl MS.

7. Jordahl MS.

8. National Lakeshores as distinct National Park Service units were first proposed in 1963 when the Presidential Recreation Advisory Council concluded that federal shoreline areas were needed near major cities. Criteria suggested that the areas include at least twenty thousand acres, combine land and water access, and be within a day's drive of urban centers. A National Lakeshore, the council recommended, should be "well above the ordinary in quality and recreational appeal." Michigan's Pictured Rocks became the first National Lakeshore, in 1966, later that

year joined by the Indiana Dunes. Apostle Islands would be the third site in 1970. See Jeff Rennicke, "Wild Edges," *Backpacker*, May 1991; and Ronald J. Engel, *Sacred Sands: The Struggle for Community in the Indiana Dunes* (Middletown, Conn.: Wesleyan University Press, 1983).

9. House Committee on Interior and Insular Affairs, Apostle Islands National Lakeshore, Wisc.: Hearing on H.R.555 and S.621 before the Subcommittee on National Parks and Recreation, 91st Cong., 1st Sess., Ashland, Wisc., August 19, 1969.

10. Hearing on H.R.555 and S.621, statement of Gaylord Nelson.

11. Jordahl MS.

12. Jordahl MS.

13. A superb study of the role of wild rice in Chippewa culture is Thomas Vennum, Jr., *Wild Rice and the Ojibway People* (St. Paul: Minnesota Historical Society Press, 1988). Unlike rice that grows in the semitropics, wild rice thrives in the marshes and slow-moving waters of the upper Midwest, where the grain provided Chippewa with a staple food and valuable trade item. Harvested in the autumn, it could be stored and preserved for winter use or for trade. Wild rice also played an important role in Chippewa culture and religion. See Robert H. Keller, "America's Native Sweet: Chippewa Treaties and the Right to Harvest Maple Sugar," *American Indian Quarterly* 13:3 (Spring 1989), pp. 117–35.

14. Harold Jordahl to director, Resources Program, September 21, 1964, AINL Cultural Resources file. At this time Wisconsin did not recognize Indian rights to harvest wild rice.

15. Whitebird resolution of May 14, 1965, AINL Cultural Resources file.

16. *State of Wisconsin v. Mike Neveaux*, memorandum decision, Bayfield Co., September 15, 1965, AINL files.

17. *Congressional Record*, October 13, 1965, p. 25874. Tribal resolution of October 7, 1965, AINL files.

18. Martin Hanson to William Bechtel, October 27, 1965, AINL files.

19. Hanson to Bechtel, October 27, December 30, 1965. Hanson understood the importance of hunting and fishing to Bad River and hoped that the U.S. attorney general would submit a brief for the band. AINL files.

20. Red Cliff Tribe to Henry M. Jackson, March 11, 1969. AINL files.

21. Bechtel interview by Kathleen Lidfors, March 4, 1985, transcript in AINL Oral History file.

22. Senate Committee on Interior and Insular Affairs, Apostle Islands National Lakeshore, Hearings before the Subcommittee on Parks and Recreation, 91st Cong., 1st Sess., S.621, March 17, 1969. Statement of John Belindo.

23. Papp to Nelson, March 19, 1969. AINL Cultural Resource file. Years later, Stewart Udall observed that any attempt by Nelson to ignore Indian concerns

would have failed "because just taking Indian land couldn't be done in our time." Interview, January 18, 1991.

24. House Committee on Interior and Insular Affairs, Apostle Island National Lakeshore Hearings, 91st Cong., 2d Sess., H.R.555, H.R.9306, and S.621, March 23, 24, and June 3, 1970.

25. Morris K. Udall Papers: Legislative Correspondence, 91st Cong., Interior file, National Parks: Eric Westhagen to Udall, June 1, 1970. Local support for creating the Lakeshore was strong: The Ashland County Board supported the bill; Wisconsin attorney Arthur DeBardeleben predicted that the Apostle Islands would rank with Glacier and Yellowstone (June 12, 1970); and economist Walter W. Heller wrote from the University of Minnesota in support of wilderness protection: "What good is a trillion dollar GNP if we fail to protect the pure water, pure land, and pure air that enable us to enjoy it?" (September 9, 1969). Udall Papers.

26. Hearings, S.621, March 17, 1969. Belindo statement.

27. Nelson interview, March 4, 1985.

28. Aspinall told a Red Cliff and Bad River delegation that Indian treaties had been "written expeditiously" and were not relevant a century after their ratification. Jordahl notes, AINL file.

29. Halfmoon to House of Representatives, June 2, 1970. AINL Cultural Resources file.

30. *Washington Perspective: A Weekly Letter from Congressman Bob Kastenmeier,* 3:13 (March 27, 1970), AINL files. For George Hartzog's testimony on NPS acquisition of Indian land, see the March and June 1970 congressional hearings cited above.

31. Hartzog interview by Kathleen Lidfors, March 7, 1985, transcript in AINL Oral History files. *Washington Perspective,* March 27, 1970.

32. Bechtel interview, March 4, 1985; *Hearings,* March, June, 1970.

33. Besides government help in acquiring and developing land outside the lakeshore, the Chippewa would have had access to Park Service docks and freedom to cross NPS lands in order to hunt and fish; tribal members would have retained the right to fish, trap, and hunt on ceded lands. The proposed agreement allowed for Indian preference in timber cutting, Park Service employment, and visitor concessions. MKU: legislative correspondence, 91st Cong., confidential memo, Lee McElvain to Subcommittee on National Parks, May 1, 1970.

34. An Act to Provide for the Establishment of the Apostle Islands National Lakeshore in the State of Wisconsin, 84 Stat. 880, September 26, 1970. In a 1991 interview, Gaylord Nelson confirmed that Chippewa benefits had been tied to surrender of tribal land.

35. Vennum, *Wild Rice and the Ojibway People,* pp. 285–87.

36. General Management Plan, AINL, September 1989.

37. *Hearings,* March and June 1970.

38. Interviews with Ervin Soulier, June 7, 1991; Andrew Goakee, June 10, 13, 1991; Patricia DePerry, June 14, 1991.

39. Bechtel interview, March 4, 1985.

Chapter 2

1. Short and readable surveys of Indian history are William Hagan's *American Indians* (Chicago: University of Chicago Press, 1993); Angie Debo, *History of the Indians of the United States* (Norman: University of Oklahoma Press, 1970); and park historian Robert Utley's *Indian Frontier of the American West* (Albuquerque: University of New Mexico Press, 1984). More recent is Alvin M. Josephy's *Five Hundred Nations* (New York: Alfred A. Knopf, 1994); and Parman, *Indians and the American West.* These overviews can be supplemented with the Smithsonian *Handbook of North American Indians,* William C. Sturtevant, ed., especially vol. 4, *History of Indian-White Relations,* ed. Wilcomb E. Washburn. Francis Paul Prucha, S.J., has written over twenty books on the history of government policy, including *The Indians in American Society from the Revolutionary War to the Present* (Berkeley: University of California Press, 1985); for extensive detail see Prucha's *Great Father: The United States Government and the American Indians,* 2 vols. (Lincoln: University of Nebraska Press, 1984); *American Indian Treaties: The History of a Political Anomaly* (Berkeley: University of California Press, 1994); and *Atlas of American Indian Affairs* (Lincoln: University of Nebraska Press, 1990). Legal history is placed in perspective by Charles F. Wilkinson, *American Indians, Time, and the Law: Native Societies in a Modern Constitutional Democracy* (New Haven: Yale University Press, 1987). A view of how things really work can be gained from Vine Deloria, Jr., and Clifford M. Lytle, *American Indians, American Justice* (Austin: University of Texas Press, 1983); and Deloria, *American Indian Policy in the Twentieth Century* (Norman: University of Oklahoma Press, 1985). For the universal dispossession of hunter-gatherer cultures, see Jared Diamond, *Guns, Germs, and Steel: The Fates of Human Societies* (New York: W. W. Norton, 1997).

2. Simon Schama, *Landscape and Memory* (New York: Alfred A. Knopf, 1995), pp. 7, 18. Schama contends that all people carry eons of symbolic images and mythic cultural baggage that, even in highly industrial societies, compel people to seek the rural and the wild, pp. 78ff., 141. His extensive bibliography lists the major French, German, and English works on attitudes toward nature.

3. For California native history, see Theodora Kroeber and Robert F. Heizer, *Almost Ancestors: The First Californians* (San Francisco: Sierra Club, 1968); Julian H. Steward, *Indian Tribes of Sequoia National Park Region* (Berkeley: National Park Service, 1935); Robert F. Heizer and Alan Almquist, *The Other Californians* (Berkeley: University of California Press, 1971); Robert F. Heizer, *The Destruction of California Indians* (Lincoln: University of Nebraska Press, 1973); Alberto L. Hurtado, *Indian Survival on*

the California Frontier (New Haven: Yale University Press, 1988). For Yosemite, see: Elizabeth Godfrey, "Yosemite Indians: Yesterday and Today," *Yosemite Nature Notes,* (July 1941), pp. 49–72; Margaret Sanborn, *Yosemite: Its Discovery, Its Wonders, and Its People* (New York: Random House, 1991); Rebecca Solnit, "Up the River of Mercy," *Sierra* (November 1992), pp. 50–58, 78–84; and *Savage Dreams.* Lowell Bean and Sylvia Vane wrote a 1984 Yosemite ethnohistory for the Mariposa Indian Council; a manuscript copy is available in the NPS Regional Office, San Francisco. The tradition of ignoring native history continues in Milton Goldstein, *The Magnificent West: Yosemite* (New York: Arch Cape Press, 1988); and Alfred Runte, *Yosemite: The Embattled Wilderness* (Lincoln: University of Nebraska Press, 1990).

   4. LaFayette Houghton Bunnell, *Discovery of the Yosemite and the Indian War of 1851* (Chicago: Fleming H. Revell, 1880), pp. 28, 54, 76, 105, 237–38, 270–76, 285–87.

   5. Edward D. Castillo, ed., "Petition to Congress on Behalf of the Yosemite Indians," *Journal of California Anthropology,* 5:2 (1979), pp. 271–77.

   6. Solnit, *Savage Dreams,* p. 288.

   7. Solnit, *Savage Dreams,* pp. 276–79; Craig D. Bates and Martha J. Lee, *Tradition and Innovation: A Basket History of the Indians of the Yosemite-Mono Lake Area* (Yosemite National Park: Yosemite Association, 1990), pp. 193–94; Craig Bates, "Yosemite's Indians," *CRM Bulletin,* 6:2 (June 1983), pp. 8–9. Solnit has an excellent discussion of the meaning of "Yosemite" and the importance of native place names to Indians, pp. 309–27. Bates's and Lee's book is the single most important source for an appreciation of the persistent native presence in Yosemite; see pp. 203–16 for bibliography.

   8. Judith Basin Treaty with the Blackfeet, 1855; Fort Laramie Treaty with the Crow, 1868; Fort Bridger Treaty with the Shoshone and Bannock, 1868; Crow Agreement, 1880, in Charles Kappler, comp., *Indian Affairs, Laws, and Treaties* (Washington, D.C.: Government Printing Office, 1904–1941), vol. 2. Joel C. Janetski, *Indians of Yellowstone Park* (Salt Lake City: University of Utah Press, 1987), p. 54, claims that Philetus Norris negotiated "treaties" (ratified in 1882) in which Indians agreed to stay away from the park. Janetski provides no citation, and there are no such documents in Kappler, *Indian Affairs,* vol. 1.

   9. R. E. Trowbridge to Carl Schurz, May 14, 1880, and Hiram Price to S. J. Kirkwood, December 16, 1881, in *House Report No. 311,* 47th Cong., 1st Sess., pp. 1–3.

   10. Nathaniel Pitt Langford, *The Discovery of Yellowstone Park: Journal of the Washburn Expedition to the Yellowstone and Firehole Rivers in the Year 1870* (Lincoln: University of Nebraska Press, 1972), pp. 117–18.

   11. Alfred Runte in *Trains of Discovery: Western Railroads and the National Parks* (Niwot, Colo.: Roberts Rinehart, 1990) debunks much of the Langford story, giving major credit instead to Jay Cooke and the Northern Pacific, pp. 13–24.

   12. Janetski, *Indians of Yellowstone Park,* pp. 39–55; Richard A. Bartlett, *Yellowstone:*

A Wilderness Besieged (Tucson: University of Arizona Press, 1989), pp. 21–28. *Indians of Yellowstone: The Sheepeaters, Keepers of the Past* (1993), Earthtalk Video, P.O. Box 1540, Bozeman, Mont., 59771, is the first of a planned series on Indians and national parks.

13. Langford, *The Discovery of Yellowstone Park*, pp. 6, 9–12, 26, 92, 97; Superintendent of Yellowstone National Park, *Annual Reports*, 1879, p. 11; 1880, pp. 35–36; 1889, pp. 13–16.

14. The most passionate statements of this thesis are in Chase, *Playing God in Yellowstone*, p. 103ff.; Solnit, *Savage Dreams*, pp. 294–308.

15. NA: RG 75, CF 1907–1939, Crow Agency: J. Collier to Arno Cammerer, n.d.; W. V. Woehlke to Collier, December 2, 1935; Pfeiffer and Yellowtail internal memos, December 1935. Chase, *Playing God in Yellowstone*, p. 115.

16. NA: RG 79, E-7, Navajo Box 2301, J. W. Brewer to N. Drury, June 28, 1946, re Navajo National Monument. James Wickersham, "A National Park in the Olympics," [1890] *Living Wilderness*, 77 (Summer 1961), pp. 5–13; John H. Williams, *The Mountain that Was God* (Tacoma, Wash.: privately printed, 1910); Albright, *Oh, Ranger!*, pp. 95–96; Frank McNitt, *Richard Wetherill, Anasazi* (Albuquerque: University of New Mexico Press, 1966); Duane A. Smith, *Mesa Verde National Park: Shadows of the Centuries* (Lawrence: University Press of Kansas, 1988); Eivind T. Scoyen, *The Rainbow Canyons* (Palo Alto, Calif.: Stanford University Press, 1931).

17. Superintendent of Yellowstone, *Annual Reports*, 1880, p. 35; 1881, p. 38. Norris also claimed that "rushing cataracts" frightened the Indians.

18. Albright, *Oh, Ranger!*, p. 88; Udall, *The National Parks of America*, p. 190; Ake Hultkrantz, "The Fear of Geysers among Indians of the Yellowstone Park Area," in Leslie B. Davis, ed., *Lifeways of Intermontane and Plains Montana Indians* (Bozeman, Mont.: Museum of the Rockies, 1979), pp. 33–42. Not everyone believed the myth. As early as 1895, historian Hiram M. Chittenden rejected such a concept; see *The Yellowstone National Park* (Norman: University of Oklahoma Press, 1964), ch. 2. Park historian Merrill Beal had a low opinion of native culture but sought to demonstrate that geyser fear was a white misconception: *The Story of Man in Yellowstone* (Caldwell, Idaho: Caxton, 1949), ch. 5. A thoroughly documented and convincing analysis of the question, and especially of Hultkrantz's work, is Joseph Weixelman, "The Power to Evoke Wonder: Native Americans & the Geysers of Yellowstone National Park," Masters thesis, Montana State University, 1992. Weixelman concludes that native fear of the park was a white invention. For another critique of Hultkrantz's method, see Sam D. Gill, *Mother Earth: An American Story* (Chicago: University of Chicago Press, 1987), pp. 118–28.

19. Schama, *Landscape and Memory*, p. 7.

20. Michael F. Turek and Robert H. Keller, "Sluskin: Yakima Guide to Mount Rainier," *Columbia* (Spring 1991), pp. 2–7; Allan H. Smith, *Ethnographic Guide to the*

Archaeology of Mt. Rainier National Park (National Park Service report, 1964); Theodore Catton, "Indians and Mount Rainier," in a draft administrative history of the park loaned to the authors; NA: RG 79, CF Box 140: Ira D. Light to Franklin K. Lane, February 5, 1917; H. Albright to Cato Sells, October 18, 1917; E. B. Meritt to Albright, November 2, 23, 1917; T. A. Martin to O. A. Tomlinson, August 15, 1925. NA: RG 48, E-749, CCF Box 1991, file 12: Solicitor's opinion on "Mount Rainier Fish and Game" from Preston C. West, c. 1915.

21. Jeanne Nienaber Clarke and Daniel McCool, *Staking Out the Terrain: Power Differentials among Natural Resource Management Agencies* (Albany: State University of New York, 1985); Horace M. Albright, *The Birth of the National Park Service: The Founding Years, 1913–1933* (Salt Lake City: Howe Brothers, 1985); John C. Miles, *Guardians of the Parks;* Dwight F. Rettie, *Our National Park System: Caring for America's Greatest Natural and Historic Treasures* (Urbana: University of Illinois Press, 1995); Lowry, *A Capacity for Wonder.*

22. E. Louise Peffer, *The Closing of the Public Domain: Disposal and Reservation Policies, 1900–1950* (Palo Alto, Calif.: Stanford University Press, 1951); Janet A. McDonnell, *Dispossession of the American Indian: 1887–1934* (Bloomington: Indiana University Press, 1991); James McLaughlin, *My Friend the Indian* (Boston: Houghton Mifflin, 1910); Vernon R. Carstensen, ed., *The Public Lands: Studies in the History of the Public Domain* (Madison: University of Wisconsin Press, 1963); Roy M. Robbins, *Our Landed Heritage* (Lincoln: University of Nebraska Press, 1962).

23. Miles, *Guardians of the Parks* p. 1; Ise, *Our National Park Policy,* pp. 139–42. Originally called Sulphur Springs, Platt was established at the nadir of Chickasaw and Choctaw history and very likely involved removal of Indians. Early NPS racial obtuseness is revealed in matter-of-fact staff discussions of "Nigger Run Creek Bridge" at Platt. NA: RG 79: CCF:Platt, Charles A. Richey Report, July 13, 1934. The service finally reclassified Platt into a ten-thousand-acre recreation area in 1976 and renamed it to honor its previous Chickasaw owners instead of a U.S. senator from Connecticut.

24. Richard White, *"It's Your Misfortune and None of My Own": A New History of the American West* (Norman: University of Oklahoma Press, 1991), pp. 391–93, 409–415. White's theory regarding a sharp contrast between East and West land control can be quickly confirmed by glancing at an NPS acreage map.

25. Albright, *Oh, Ranger!,* pp. 81–96; M. R. Tillotson and Frank J. Taylor, *Grand Canyon Country* (Palo Alto, Calif.: Stanford University Press, 1929), ch. 3. Horace Albright died one week before our scheduled interview. According to his daughter, "he was deeply, deeply devoted to Indians. He had a great love, a very tremendous empathy with them, and admiration for their culture." Marian Albright Schenck interview, December 5, 1991. Only once, at his Flathead initiation, did Albright put on a headdress. His daughter cannot explain this exception.

26. See Ise, *Our National Park Policy*, pp. 296–97; Albright, *The Birth of the National Park Service*, pp. 128–35; Shankland, *Steve Mather of the National Parks*, pp. 221–24; Miles, *Guardians of the Parks*, pp. 48–52. The BIA opposed the Mescalero park project.

27. The first native woman superintendent was Ellen Hays at Sitka National Historic Park. Barbara Booher (Ute-Cherokee) managed Custer Battlefield during the controversy over its name change and is now tribal liaison for the Rocky Mountain Region.

28. Douglas H. Scovill, "Zuni Comprehensive Plan and After," *CRM Bulletin*, 3:3 (September 1980), pp. 10–13. Emil Haury and Edmund Ladd interviews, February 4, April 10, 1992; Virginia M. Robicheau, "Bandelier National Monument and Native American Concerns," *CRM Bulletin*, 3:4 (December 1980), p. 3. For the Nez Perce National Historic Park, see Alvin M. Josephy, Jr., *Nez Perce Country* (Washington, D.C.: National Park Service, 1983). The park includes the Spalding mission at Lapwai, and the Clearwater, White Bird Canyon, and Bear Paw Mountains battlefields; it does not include Big Hole Battlefield.

Chapter 3

1. For general works on the Utes of Colorado, see Joseph G. Jorgensen, *The Sun Dance Religion: Power for the Powerless* (Chicago: University of Chicago Press, 1972); Jan Pettit, *Utes: The Mountain People* (Colorado Springs, Colo.: Century One Press, 1982); Charles S. Marsh, *The Utes of Colorado: People of the Shining Mountains* (Boulder, Colo.: Pruett Publishing Company, 1982); William Sturtevant, ed., *Handbook*, vol. 11, *Great Basin*, pp. 336–67. Hal Borland's novel, *When the Legends Die* (New York: J. B. Lippincott Co., 1963), describes twentieth-century Ute culture in transition. Frank Gilbert Roe, *The Indian and the Horse* (Norman: University of Oklahoma Press, 1955), discusses the equestrian revolution in tribal history, pp. 73, 79.

2. Robert Emmitt, *The Last War Trail* (Norman: University of Oklahoma Press, 1954), p. 235. Also see Marshall Sprague, *Massacre: The Tragedy at White River* (Boston: Little, Brown & Co., 1957).

3. Jorgensen, *The Sun Dance Religion*, p. 59.

4. Smith, *Mesa Verde National Park*, pp. 10–15. Smith's book is exceptional for its attention to the Ute role in the park's history.

5. Smith, *Mesa Verde National Park*, pp. 16–19. For discussion of the Wetherills' role in southwestern archaeology, see Hal Rothman, *Preserving Different Pasts: The American National Monuments* (Urbana: University of Illinois Press, 1989); McNitt, *Richard Wetherill, Anasazi*; and David Roberts, "Reverse Archaeologists," *Smithsonian*, 24, (December 1993), pp. 28–38.

6. Smith, *Mesa Verde National Park*, p. 26. Frederick H. Chapin, *The Land of the Cliff-*

Dwellers (1892; reprint, Tucson: University of Arizona Press, 1988), pp. 117–19. Chapin quotes a Ute named Wap as saying of Richard Wetherill: "White man rich; Indian poor. White man dig up Moquis, make Ute sick; little Ute, big Ute, all heap sick."

7. Smith, *Mesa Verde National Park*, p. 43.

8. Smith, *Mesa Verde National Park*, pp. 44, 46, 53. Alice Bishop apparently had an agreement in 1903, but the Utes repudiated it within a year. When Patterson and McClurg visited in 1904, Utes claimed that the government had not kept Bishop's promise of rations and irrigation. The Indian Appropriation Act of March 3, 1903, provided "that the Secretary of the Interior be directed to negotiate with the Weeminuchi Ute Tribe of Indians for the relinquishment of their right of occupancy to the United States to the tract of land known as the Mesa Verde, a part of the reservation of said Tribe, situated in the county of Montezuma, in the State of Colorado, the said tract to include and cover the ruins and prehistoric remains situate therein. And the Secretary of the Interior shall report to the next session of Congress the terms and conditions upon which the said Tribe of Indians will relinquish to the United States the right of occupancy to said tract of land."

9. Smith, *Mesa Verde National Park*, p. 61. Ricardo Torres-Reyes, *Mesa Verde National Park: An Administrative History, 1906–1970* (Washington, D.C.: National Park Service, 1970), p. 9.

10. NA: RG 79, Mesa Verde, Box 100, Lands file: John F. Shafroth, Governor of Colorado, to Richard A. Ballinger, June 8, 1909; H. M. Randolph to Ballinger, July 1, 1909; John Spear to Robert Valentine, October 23, 1909; Valentine to Ballinger, July 1, 1909; U. L. Clardy to Francis Leupp, June 7, 1909.

11. NA: RG 79, Mesa Verde, Box 100, Lands file: F. H. Abbott to Clement S. Ucker, October 1, December 2, 1910.

12. McLaughlin, *My Friend the Indian*, pp. 272–87. McLaughlin disliked the Utes, whom he considered sullen and uncooperative; had they been "whipped" by the army, he felt, "they would not be the irresponsible, shiftless and defiant people they are today [1910]." He saw all Indians as children who must be made to recognize the superior intelligence and power of whites. For a critique of his role in implementing the Dawes Act, see McDonnell, *Dispossession of the American Indian*, pp. 94–98.

McLaughlin's 1911 mission to the Utes was not his first attempt to acquire Indian land for a national park. In 1899, he tried unsuccessfully to obtain a quarry from the Yankton Sioux in southern Minnesota. The government eventually acquired the site in 1929, with Franklin Roosevelt creating Pipestone National Monument in 1937. See William P. Corbett, "The Red Pipestone Quarry: The Yanktons Defend a Sacred Tradition, 1858–1929," *South Dakota History*, 8 (Spring 1978), pp. 99–106; and "Pipestone: The Origin and Development of a National Monument," *Minnesota*

History, 47 (Fall 1980), pp. 83–92. The Yanktons have demanded that the NPS return the quarry to the tribe. Sharon Metz, "NCAI Opposes Desecration of Red Pipestone Quarries," *Masinaigan* (Fall 1992), p. 6.

13. NA: RG 79: Mesa Verde, Box 100, Lands file: 1911 Ute Council Minutes, pp. 1–3. A copy of the minutes is also on file at the Ute Mountain Ute Tribal Office, Tawoac, Colorado.

14. Council Minutes, pp. 3–6.

15. Council Minutes, pp. 7–8, 12–13, 16–20.

16. Council Minutes, pp. 27–33.

17. Council Minutes, pp. 34–35.

18. *Mancos Times Tribune*, May 19, 1911.

19. Torres-Reyes, *Mesa Verde National Park*, p. 13.

20. Smith, *Mesa Verde National Park*, pp. 113, 178.

21. Torres-Reyes, *Mesa Verde National Park*, pp. 193–94; Smith, *Mesa Verde National Park*, pp. 113–122; Rothman, *Preserving Different Pasts*, p. 23. As early as 1900, Richard Wetherill hired Navajos to help excavate ruins. Besides the two Ute bands and the Navajo, the park also has relations with five Pueblo villages, including the Hopi.

22. NA: RG 79: E-7, Mesa Verde, Box 363: Cammerer to Finnan, August 14, 1931; Finnan to Cammerer, August 15, October 29, 1931; Box 1384: Thompson to Albright, October 24, 1933; Wright to Quaintance, March 5, 1935.

23. NA: RG 79: E-7, Mesa Verde, Box 1384: Watson to Collier, December 21, 1933.

24. NA: RG 79: E-7, Mesa Verde, Box 1384: Leavitt to Cammerer, May 9, 1935; A. R. Kelly to Cammerer, October 16, 1939.

25. NA: RG 79: E-7, Mesa Verde, Box 1384: Nusbaum to Cammerer, February 21, 1940.

26. NA: RG 79: E-7, Mesa Verde, Box 1384: Nusbaum to Regional Director, April 3, 1945; Torres-Reyes, *Mesa Verde National Park*, pp. 324–26; Smith, *Mesa Verde National Park*, p. 178.

27. Torres-Reyes, *Mesa Verde National Park*, pp. 326–27; Smith, *Mesa Verde National Park*, pp. 139, 179; interview, Meredith Guillet, September 19, 1991.

28. Jean Akens, *Ute Mountain Tribal Park: The Other Mesa Verde* (Moab, Utah: Four Corners Publications, 1987), pp. 8–17.

29. Ute guides who attend Mesa Verde's seasonal training find it worthwhile; tribal members would also like training in ruins stabilization. By 1994 the park had begun to move toward more contemporary interpretation. Interviews with Randolph Wing, September 20, 1991; Doug Bowman, September 16, 1991; Rhonda Lancaster, September 16, 1991; Brenda Tupek, October 12, 1994. Chief Ranger Art Hutchinson explained low native employment as the result of Ute dislike of being

stereotyped and of being made the object of religious evangelism by tourists. Interview, October 12, 1994.

30. NPS, Rocky Mountain Regional Office, Branch of Compliance, "Environmental Assessment: Realignment of Chapin Mesa Loop Road at Soda Point, Mesa Verde National Park," February 1987; "Finding of No Significance . . . Mesa Loop Road," 1987. "Heliocopters at Mesa Verde Cause Run-in with Utes," *National Parks*, November 1987, p. 8. Interviews with Robert Heyder, September 18, 1991; Doug Bowman, September 16, 1991; Ben Nighthorse Campbell, October 24, 1991; Bruce Craig, July 24, 1991.

31. Ute Mountain Ute Office files: Daniel Israel, attorney, "Statement of Facts," n.d.; Smith, *Mesa Verde National Park*, p. 80.

32. Craighead interview, October 12, 1994. Visitor centers and gift shops, run by local associations, not the NPS, vary widely in their displays of literature about Indians. In 1994 Mesa Verde had a selection of thirty-nine books on native people and prehistory, but only three items on Ute history. Large shops at Mammoth and Old Faithful carried eight or nine books on all the natives associated with Yellowstone, while the Grand Canyon had four dozen books plus several videos. Saguaro National Monument in 1992 had no information on its Indian neighbors.

33. Israel, "Statement of Facts"; Smith, *Mesa Verde National Park*, p. 80.

Chapter 4

1. Differing from most archaeologists, Brian Reeves puts the Blackfoot migration at five thousand years ago. "Ninaistakis: The Nitsitapii's Sacred Mountain," in *Sacred Sites, Sacred Places*, ed. David L. Carmichael, Jane Hubert, Brian Reeves, and Audhild Schanche (London: Routledge, 1994).

2. Jay Vest and C. Hansford, "Traditional Blackfeet Religion and the Sacred Badger–Two Medicine Wildlands," *Journal of Law and Religion*, 6:2 (1988), p. 469.

3. John C. Ewers, *The Blackfeet: Raiders of the Northwestern Plains* (Norman: University of Oklahoma Press, 1982); Walter McClintock, *The Old North Trail, or Life, Legends, and Religion of the Blackfeet Indians* (London: Macmillan, 1910); George Bird Grinnell, *Blackfoot Lodge Tales: The Story of a Prairie People* (New York: Charles Scribner's Sons, 1892); Percy Bullchild, *The Sun Came Down: The History of the World as My Blackfeet Elders Told It* (San Francisco: Harper and Row, 1985). James Welch, *Fools Crow* (New York: Viking Penguin, 1986); Hugh A. Dempsey and Lindsay Moir, *Bibliography of the Blackfoot* (Metuchen, N.J.: Scarecrow Press, 1989).

4. Warren L. Hanna, *The Life and Times of James Willard Schultz (Apikuni)* (Norman: University of Oklahoma Press, 1986).

Schultz (1859–1947) wrote more than thirty books, many based on his experiences with the Blackfeet. A 1926 book, *Signposts of Adventure* (Boston: Houghton Mifflin Co.), attempted to locate places in Glacier Park that Schultz claimed had had Indian names. A number of his sites are questionable, as Schultz seemed more interested in book sales than accuracy. For a more recent study, see Jack Holterman's *Place Names of Glacier/Waterton National Parks* (Helena, Mont.: Falcon Press, 1985).

5. James Muhn, *The Blackfeet Session of 1896: An Historical Evaluation of the Title Status and Petroleum Mineral Rights* (Denver, Colo.: U.S. Department of the Interior, Bureau of Land Management, June 1987), pp. 4–7.

6. Hana Samek, *The Blackfoot Confederacy, 1880–1920: A Comparative Study of Canadian and U.S. Indian Policy* (Albuquerque: University of New Mexico Press, 1987), p. 57.

7. Samek, *The Blackfoot Confederacy, 1880–1920*, p. 64.

8. Senate Document No. 118, 54th Cong. 1st Sess., 1896. "Letter . . . transmitting an agreement made and concluded September 26, 1895," pp. 7, 12.

9. Muhn, *The Blackfeet Session of 1896*, p. 7.

10. There is no definitive biography of Grinnell, but various historians have discussed his role in American conservation: John J. Reed, *American Sportsmen and the Origin of Conservation* (New York: Winchester Press, 1975); John G. Mitchell, "A Man Called Bird," in *The Man Who Would Dam the Amazon & Other Accounts from Afield* (Lincoln: University of Nebraska Press, 1990), pp. 223–65, originally published in *Audubon*, 89:2 (March 1987), pp. 81–104; Gerald A. Diettert, *Grinnell's Glacier: George Bird Grinnell and Glacier National Park* (Missoula, Mont.: Mountain Press, 1992); John F. Reiger, "George Bird Grinnell and the Development of American Conservation, 1870–1901," Ph.D. diss., Northwestern University, 1970.

No one has taken a close look at Grinnell's ideas about Indians. His complex and contradictory thinking is best studied in his own writings: *The Indian of Today* (New York: Duffield and Co., 1900), and "Tenure of Land among the Indians," *American Anthropologist*, 9:1 (January 1907), pp. 1–11. For example: "In its display of science and art, machinery and product, the Exposition [of 1898] stood for the bounding present . . . the welling tide of progress of an expanding people. . . . And over against all this, pathetic in contrast, was the Indian in his skin lodge, clad in primitive dress, and typical of a diminishing race. . . . The Indian has the mind of a child in the body of an adult. . . . By this I mean that it is a mind in many respects unused, and absolutely without training as regards all matters which have to do with civilized life. . . . No people are more easily handled; none give more frankly of their trust when it is shown to be deserved; none are more ready to follow the good advice of the trusted friend." Grinnell, *The Indian of Today*, pp. 5–6, 21–23, 408.

"The elder Indians often speak of the wrongs that their race has suffered, especially with respect to their land, regarding which they have a deep feeling—a feeling which we can hardly comprehend. Thus in the view of the Indians our treatment of them contains an element of outrage and extortion far beyond the worst that sympathetic friends of the Indians allege. . . . We have uprooted the tribe itself and have taken away from it lands which it held as a trust for posterity, and which the tribe itself had no right to give to any man. . . . Perhaps it is best that the Indians should fade away as we see them fading today. . . .

"The Indian's notion of land tenure, so distinctly primitive, could not find acceptance in . . . our civilization. . . . The communal holding of great tracts of land by Indian tribes must cease.

"I make no complaint here about the justice of driving Indians by force from lands which we need. . . . Indians, like children, have been incapable of guarding wisely their own interests in making treaties. . . . A bargain with a tribe to sell its land so that others could hold it forever and distribute it among private persons, is a transaction which no Indian mind could comprehend; . . . [In] every land cession the Indian has [agreed] to something which the mind of the primitive Indian could by no means grasp." From "Tenure of Land among the Indians," pp. 6–7, 11.

11. Donald H. Robinson, "The Glacier Moves Tortuously," *Montana: The Magazine of Western History*, 7:3 (July 1957), p. 19; Albert K. Fisher, "In Memoriam: George Bird Grinnell," *The Auk*, 56:1 (January 1939), pp. 1–12; Diettert, *Grinnell's Glacier*, pp. 57, 61–71. Grinnell's relationship with Schultz and their appreciation for the mountains is told in James Willard Schultz, *Blackfeet and Buffalo: Memories of Life among the Indians* (Norman: University of Oklahoma Press, 1962), pp. 83–109.

12. Michael F. Foley, "An Historical Analysis of the Administration of the Blackfeet Indian Reservation by the United States Government, 1855–1950," Indian Claims Commission Docket No. 279-D (1975), pp. 181–82; Muhn, "Blackfeet Cession," pp. 4–7.

13. The following works establish the importance of land in the Blackfoot religious tradition: Vest and Hansford, "Traditional Blackfeet Religion"; Bullchild, *The Sun Came Down*; Ruth F. Benedict, "The Vision in Plains Culture," *American Anthropologist*, 24 (January 1922), pp. 1–23; Carmichael, *Sacred Sites, Sacred Places*. For the role of grizzly bears, see John C. Ewers, "The Bear Cult among the Assiniboin and Their Neighbors of the Northern Plains," *Southwestern Journal of Anthropology*, 11:1 (Spring 1955), pp. 1–14; Claude E. Schaffer, *Bear Ceremonialism of the Kutenai Indians* (Browning, Montana: Museum of the Plains Indians, 1966). Information on traditional use of plants can be found in Alex Johnston, "Blackfoot Indian Utilization of the Flora of the Northwestern Great Plains," *Economic Botany*, 24:3 (1970), pp. 301–24; Richard J. Show and Danny On, *Plants of Waterton-Glacier National Parks* (Missoula, Mont.: Mountain Press, 1979); *Glacier: Great National Parks* [video] (New York: Reader's Digest Videos, 1992); Jeff Hart and Jacqueline Moore, *Montana—Native Plants and Early Peoples* (Helena: Montana Historical Society, 1976). We spoke to the following individuals about traditional uses of Glacier: Curly Bear Wagner, Earl Old

Person, Stewart Miller, Kenneth C. Eaglespeaker, Vicky Santana, and George Kicking Woman.

14. Christopher Vecsey, ed., *Handbook of American Indian Religious Freedom* (New York: Crossroad, 1991); R. Pierce Beaver, *Church, State, and the American Indian* (St. Louis: Concordia Publishing House, 1966); Howard L. Harrod, *Mission among the Blackfeet* (Norman: University of Oklahoma Press, 1971); Robert H. Keller, *American Protestantism and U.S. Indian Policy* (Lincoln: University of Nebraska Press, 1983).

15. It is impossible to determine the actual acreage purchased because the land was unsurveyed. The commission estimated the cession at 800,000 acres but believed it was significantly larger. Pollock reported that the price was "half the amount demanded by the Indians for an area considerably smaller." *Senate Document No. 118*, 54th Cong. 1st Sess., p. 7. Blackfeet oral tradition claims that tribal negotiators were misled by poor translations and perhaps liquor; it is claimed that they leased only mineral rights. Santana and Kicking Woman interviews, October 3–4, 1994.

16. *Senate Document No. 118*, p. 35.

17. Diettert, *Grinnell's Glacier*, pp. 61–71, discusses Grinnell's role in the negotiations.

18. Act of June 10, 1896, 29 Stat. 321, 353–58.

19. Christopher S. Ashby, "The Blackfeet Agreement of 1895 and Glacier National Park: A Case History," Masters thesis, University of Montana, 1985, pp. 37, 82. The original Lewis and Clark Forest Reserve was created under the Forest Act of 1897. A 1903 proclamation consolidated the Lewis and Clark with the Flathead Forest Reserve; the former included the mineral strip. Both proclamations contained clauses protecting Blackfeet rights under the 1895 agreement.

20. The Salish, Upper Pend Oreille, and Kootenai Indians of the Flathead Reservation had hunted and trapped in the northern Rocky Mountains for centuries. Some scholars believe that "Flathead" bands once lived east of the divide prior to Blackfoot expansion into the area. In 1885 Grinnell found eight Kootenai lodges camped below St. Mary River for two months; the Indians, probably from Canada, had been taking bear, moose, elk, and beaver. Grinnell also found a distinct hunting trail into the upper Swiftcurrent Valley. Hanna, *Life and Times*, pp. 138–39. Today the Salish and Kootenai claim the western half of Glacier as their homeland. Mickey Pablo interview, August 8, 1991.

21. Glacier National Park enabling legislation, May 11, 1910; Robinson, "The Glacier Moves Tortuously," p. 25; Act of August 22, 1914, 35 Stat. 699. NA: RG 79: GNP, Box 23: Solicitor's Opinion of 1916. Between 1911, when Montana relinquished jurisdiction over the park, and 1914, when the federal government finally accepted control, Congress rejected several bills on the matter. In 1912 Frederick Vreeland inquired about native rights in Glacier; he was told that they had none. Ashby, "The Blackfeet Agreement," pp. 41–42.

22. NA: RG 79: CCF: GNP: Hunting: Schoenberg to Walter Fisher, October 1911. There are numerous letters similar to Schoenberg's requesting homestead hunting rights inside the park. The secretary granted permission in a memo of December 15, 1911.

23. Jack Holterman, "The Blackfeet Agency and Glacier Park," unpublished manuscript, GNP Library.

24. NA: RG 75: BIA, 1907–1939, File 307.2, E-121: C. F. Hauke to Secretary of the Interior, January 10, 1912. While admitting that the Blackfeet had surrendered title to parklands, the BIA contended that under the 1895 agreement the tribe "expressly reserved" a right to enter Glacier Park to hunt, fish, and cut timber for agency or personal use.

25. Schultz, *Signposts of Adventure*, p. 3; Albright, *Oh, Ranger!*, pp. 87–88. Solnit in *Savage Dreams* discusses the relationship of place names to ownership; the classic work on the subject is George R. Stewart, *Names on the Land* (Boston: Houghton Mifflin, 1945).

26. NA: RG 79: CCF: GNP: E-7, Game: C. A. Jakways to J. R. Eakin, January 10, 1923. For the history of game policy, see R. Gerald Wright, *Wildlife Research and Management in the National Parks* (Urbana: University of Illinois Press, 1992).

27. NA: RG 79: CCF: GNP: Hunting: Department of the Interior to Hutchings, February 7, 1912. In spite of the hazy jurisdictional status, Interior took a firm stand in 1912: "No person, whether Indian or white man, has the right to hunt or kill game on any government or [park] lands." Interior to Chapman, June 12, 1912. But even after 1914, many Montanans believed that the state retained jurisdiction over park wildlife and continued to kill deer and elk.

28. NA: RG 79: CCF: GNP: Hunting: Peter Oscar Little Chief to Lane, November 20, 1915; Preston West to Lane, January 4, 1916.

29. NA: RG 79: CCF: GNP: Hunting: Lane to Cato Sells, January 17, 1918. Curtis W. Buchholtz, "The Historical Dichotomy of Use and Preservation in Glacier National Park," Masters thesis, University of Montana, 1969, p. 45.

30. NA: RG 79: CCF: GNP: Hunting: Albright to Lane, September 25, 1916; Lane to Sells, January 17, 1918.

31. NA: RG 79: CCF: GNP: Boundaries: W. W. Payne to Mather, December 4, 1919.

32. NA: RG 79: CCF: GNP: Boundaries: Mather to Sells, January 7, 1921; Grinnell to Cammerer, October 31, 1921.

33. NA: RG 79: CCF: GNP: Boundaries: Sells to John Barton Payne, November 23, 1920, internal NPS memo, n.d.; Mather to Sells, January 7, 1921.

34. NA: RG 79: CCF: GNP: Boundaries: Cammerer to Harvey, November 27, 1920; J. R. Eakin to Albright, July 25, 1929; D. S. Libbey to Drury, October 15, 1940.

35. NA: RG 79: CCF: GNP: Game: James P. Brooks to superintendent, December 28, 1922; Jakways to Eakin, January 10, 1923; Eakin to Jakways, January 13, 1923; Grinnell to Cammerer, March 21, 1923. NA: GNP: Box 941: superintendent to N. Drury, March 10, 1942, reports that Montana's attorney general has ruled that the state's Fish and Game Commission had no authority over wildlife on Indian reservations.

36. Grinnell reminded the NPS that Yellowstone elk had been brought north to supplement, not create, Glacier's herd. NA: RG 79: CCF: GNP: Game: Grinnell to Cammerer, March 21, 1923.

37. Ann Reagan, "The Blackfeet, the Bureaucrats, and Glacier National Park," presented to the Western Historical Association, Billings, Montana, October 1986. The NPS, still facing problems with inholders in 1929, requested another clarification of its authority over wildlife. NA: RG 79 CCF: GNP: Hunting: J. R. Eakin to Albright, November 18, 1929.

38. NA: RG 79: CCF: Box 241: Albright to Demaray, March 1, 1929; Albright to "Mr. Lewis," January 29, 1930.

39. NA: RG 79: CCF: GNP: Boundaries: Burke to Cramton, February 7, 1929.

40. NA: RG 79: CCF: GNP: Boundaries: Albright to Eakin, August 5, 1929 (telegram); Albright to Scott, February 1, 1930. GNP: Box 241, Albright to Eakin, February 3, 1930; Albright to Rhoads, January 13, 1930. Forty years later, the same approach was used in an attempt to acquire Chippewa land at Apostle Islands Lakeshore.

41. NA: RG 79: CCF: GNP: Box 241: Albright to Eakin, February 3, 1930: "Of course you will not discuss the matter with any of the Indians themselves. We do not want to get them stirred up or even mention it to them until all the necessary missionary work has been done and proper groundwork laid entering into negotiations."

42. McDonnell, *Dispossession of the American Indian*, p. 74. In 1907 the BIA and Reclamation signed an agreement authorizing the latter to construct and manage irrigation projects on Indian reservations, an arrangement that lasted until 1924, when Congress returned the task to the BIA. U.S. Senate, Committee on Indian Affairs, *Survey of Conditions of the Indians in the United States*, Hearings, parts 21–23, Browning, Mont., July 24, 1929, pp. 12, 658. NA: RG 79: CCF: GNP: Eakin to Albright, March 24, 1930; Albright to Glacier superintendent, January 20, 1933; Bureau of Reclamation to Albright, January 18, 1933; E. Scoyen to G. W. Noffsinger, April 11, 1935.

43. Reagan, "The Blackfeet," pp. 1–3, quoting A. A. Aszmann to C. L. Graves, May 14, 1938, and to D. S. Libbey, May 12, 1939. A brief discussion of the Blackfeet as tourist attractions is in William E. Farr, *The Reservation Blackfeet, 1882–1945: A Photographic History of Cultural Survival* (Seattle: University of Washington Press, 1984), pp. 192–93, 196–201. For the larger story of western tourism, see Earl

Pomeroy, *The Search for the Golden West* (New York: Alfred A. Knopf, 1957). A useful overview of railroads and parks is Runte, *Trains of Discovery*.

44. Albright, *Oh, Ranger!* p. 86.

45. Reagan, "The Blackfeet," pp. 4–5.

46. NA: RG 75: Box 1349, Meritt to Streeter, May 15, 1915.

47. Campbell is quoted in Reagan, "The Blackfeet," p. 9; for Liggett's report, see Committee on Indian Affairs, *Survey of Conditions*, pp. 12, 691. National Public Radio interview with Darnel Rides at the Door who described her grandparents' memories of Glacier Park: "Grandmother and grandfather greeted the tourists. My grandmother, she's 107 years old, she talks about it with a twinkle in her eye, with a bit of pride."

48. NA: RG 79: CCF: GNP: Hunting: Eakin to Moskey, internal memo, December 10, 1930; Albright to Leavitt, December 15, 1930; Scoyen to Cammerer, December 5, 1933; Cammerer to Scoyon, December 18, 1933; C. L. Gable to A. E. Demaray, July 16, 1939.

49. NA: RG 79: CCF: GNP: Hunting: E. C. Finney to Secretary of the Interior, June 21, 1932.

50. NA: RG 79: CCF: GNP: Hunting: Scoyen to Archer, December 31, 1932; Scoyen to Albright, April 20, 1933. After court adjourned, Scoyen and Pray discussed old times: The judge recalled how he had been responsible for guiding the Glacier legislation through the House.

51. NA: RG 79: CCF: GNP: Bison: Scoyen to Cammerer, March 28, 1934. D. S. Libbey to director, October 15, 1940. This file contains frequent memos and letters about establishing a Glacier bison herd on the reservation.

52. NA: RG 79: CCF: GNP: Bison: Scoyen to Cammerer, April 23, 1934; May 26, 1937.

53. The best analysis of the deer/predator problem in the United States is Richard Nelson, *Heart and Blood: Living with Deer in America* (New York: Alfred A. Knopf, 1997).

54. NA: RG 79: CCF: GNP: Boundaries: Boundary Status Report, March 20, 1945.

55. Buchholtz, "The Historical Dichotomy," p. 94; interview with Earl Old Person, July 29, 1991.

56. Ise, *Our National Park Policy*, pp. 598–99.

57. NARF Law Library, Boulder, Colo., file 002156, *U.S. v. Kipp*, 369 F. Supp. 774 (1974); file 002537, *U.S. v. Momberg*, 378 F. Supp. 1152 (1974).

58. NARF Library, file #002756, "Petition of the Blackfeet Tribe of Indians to the Secretary of the Interior to Approve a Conservation Agreement Providing for the Regulation of Blackfeet Reserved Rights on the Eastern Portion of Glacier," January 29, 1975; NPCA staff report, "Triple Jeopardy at Glacier National Park," *National Parks and Conservation Magazine* (September 1975), pp. 20–22.

59. Blackfeet attitudes about hunting are diverse and complex. Bill Brown, for example, has used hounds to take several mountain lions and one "Indian bear" inside the park, but he prefers to hunt on the reservation. George Kicking Woman will not hunt at all, citing religious reasons.

60. NA: RG 79: CCF: GNP: Boundaries: D. S. Libbey to Drury, October 15, 1940.

61. NA: RG 79: CCF: GNP: Boundaries: Libbey to Drury, October 15, 1940. Although the NPS failed to extend its boundary or acquire control of the Blackfeet Highway, it did hold some Blackfeet land. The East Glacier office occupies five acres on the reservation under the Congressional Act of February 10, 1912, 37 Stat. 64. Hill's railroad also benefited from this legislation, which authorized sale of Indian land at a nominal fee for a hotel and other facilities.

62. Reagan, "The Blackfeet," p. 7.

63. Reagan, "The Blackfeet," pp. 12–13, quoting J. M. Budd and C. L. Finley from the General Managers file, Great Northern Papers.

64. NPS archive, Harper's Ferry, biographical files: Guardipee. Gerald "Buzz" Cobell and Ted Hall interviews. Cobell also received a James Willard Schultz scholarship for graduate study at Montana State University. In the 1950s, Blackfeet still performed for tourists but could not find jobs in hotels or with the NPS. Gerard, Brown, and Santana interviews, October 16, 1991, and October 3, 1994. As a teenager, Santana danced at the lodges: "We loved it," she remembers, because it meant employment and money.

65. Kicking Woman and Santana interviews, October 3–4, 1994.

66. Joseph L. Sax and R. B. Keiter, "Glacier National Park and Its Neighbors: A Study of Federal Interagency Relations," *Ecology Law Quarterly*, 14:2 (1987), p. 216. To make matters more complex, the Blackfeet have internal conflicts over the mountain. Reservation land near the site is being logged; some tribal members want it designated a tribal wilderness, closed to non-Indians and with restricted logging and mining. This could be readily achieved if the tribe closed its road into the area, but in the 1990s the route remained open. Curly Bear Wagner and Stewart Miller interviews, July 30, 1991.

Chapter 5

1. Wallace Stegner, *Beyond the Hundredth Meridian: John Wesley Powell and the Second Opening of the West* (1953; reprint, Lincoln: University of Nebraska Press, 1982), pp. 119, 164; *Mormon Country* (New York: Duell, Sloan and Pearce, 1942), pp. 45–46.

2. Stegner, *Mormon Country*, p. 46.

3. John Wesley Powell, *The Exploration of the Colorado River and Its Canyons* (1895; reprint, New York: Dover Publications, 1961), pp. 298–99.

4. Powell, *The Exploration of the Colorado River*, pp. 299–300. For Paiute culture, see

the *Handbook of North American Indians: Great Basin*, vol. 11; Don D. Fowler and Catherine S. Fowler, eds., *Anthropology of the Numa: John Wesley Powell's Manuscripts on the Numic Peoples, 1868–1880*, Smithsonian Contributions to Anthropology, No. 14 (Washington, D.C.: Smithsonian Institution Press, 1971); Robert J. Franklin and Pamela A. Bunte, *The Paiute* (New York: Chelsea House Publishers, 1990); Robert C. Euler, *Southern Paiute Ethnohistory*, University of Utah Anthropological Papers No. 78 (Salt Lake City: University of Utah Press, 1966) and *The Paiute People* (Phoenix: Indian Tribal Series, 1972); Robert A. Manners, *Southern Paiute and Chemehuevi* (New York: Garland Publishing Co., 1974).

5. David Lavender, *Pipe Spring and the Arizona Strip* (Springdale, Utah: Zion Natural History Association, 1984); Howard E. Daniels, "Mormon Colonization in Northern Arizona," Masters thesis, University of Arizona, 1960; Robert W. Olson, Jr., "Pipe Spring, Arizona, and Thereabouts," *Journal of Arizona History*, 6:1 (Spring 1965), pp. 11–20; Leonard Arrington, *Great Basin Kingdom* (Cambridge: Harvard University Press, 1958).

6. In 1873 the Pipe Spring section became the Winsor Castle Stock Growing Company.

7. Fowler, *Anthropology of the Numa*, p. 22. The best account of Powell's career, and also an incisive analysis of the post–Civil War West, is Stegner's *Beyond the Hundredth Meridian*. For the Mormon ecological impact on the Kaibab Paiute, see Franklin and Bunte, *The Paiute*, ch. 3; and Richard W. Stoffle and Michael J. Evans, *Resource Competition and Population Change: A Kaibab Paiute Ethnohistorical Case* (Fredonia, Ariz.: Kaibab Paiute Tribe, 1978).

8. NA: RG 79: Pipe Spring: Mather to C. Burke, June 6, 1921.

9. "Pipe Spring National Monument: By the President of the United States: A Proclamation." May 31, 1923. A memo written for Commissioner of Indian Affairs Charles Burke six days earlier recommended that this exact language be added to Harding's proclamation, otherwise loss of the spring would be "disastrous" for the Paiutes. The writer also observed that Charles Heaton and his Pipe Spring Live Stock Co. in 1920 had sought a title confirming ownership of the spring, a request denied by Interior. NA: RG 79, Pipe Spring: BIA draft memo, May 25, 1923. Although the NPS had no objection to the insertion, it did note that "the Indians have no special need of the land." NA: RG 79, Pipe Spring, memo of May 28, 1923.

On creation of the monument, see Lavender, *Pipe Spring and the Arizona Strip*, part 3. For Mather, Albright, and the Mormons, see Jeffrey Frank, "Legacies," *Courier* (March 1988), pp. 20–22. Emerson Hough's article "The President's Forest" in the *Saturday Evening Post*, January 22, 1922, reveals conservationist interest in the Kaibab Plateau.

10. The history of the Kaibab Paiute Reservation prior to Woodrow Wilson's executive order of 1917, and why he needed to issue that order, is very unclear. To

date we have been unable to locate all the relevant government documents. The 1907 reserve was an action of Interior on October 16, 1907, but neither the BIA request nor the Interior confirmation mentions water rights. NA: RG 75, Central files, Paiute Indians, C. F. Larrabee to Secretary, October 15, 1907, and memo of T. Ryan, October 16, 1907. An executive order of May 28, 1909, is mentioned in many documents but is not in Kappler, *Indian Affairs, Laws, and Treaties*, or in the *Index to Presidential Executive Orders & Proclamations, 1789–1983*. The orders of June 11, 1913, and July 17, 1917, are in Kappler, as is the 1906 appropriation. The CIA *Annual Report* of 1907, pp. 131–32, states that the bureau had recommended that Interior withdraw an area thirty-five miles by seventy-five miles north of the Arizona/Utah boundary and adjacent to the Navajo Reservation, but does not mention the smaller area defined in the above 1907 correspondence. The CIA 1909 *Annual Report*, p. 54, refers to the May 28 order creating a reservation, adding that the area was "thought to contain valuable minerals and there has been increasing demand for permission to prospect on these lands."

11. Stegner, *Mormon Country*, p. 31.

12. NA: RG 79, Pipe Spring: Mather to C. Heaton, March 13, October 30, 1924; Mather to Burke, March 13, 1924; A. Demaray to Heber J. Grant, April 5, 1924; A. Cammerer to Mather, telegram, Blackwater, Ariz., April 12, 1924. Pipe Spring Library: Water Rights file, C. A. Engle to Burke, May 13, 1924. Only in correspondence with the BIA did Mather speak of benefits to the Indians. In a delicate position because the Union Pacific R.R., the Mormon Church, and the Heatons had each donated $1,000 toward the purchase, Mather and his staff wrote many conciliatory letters to Salt Lake City to assure the Mormon president, Heber Grant, that "necessary steps are being taken" to protect local water rights.

On special Indian water rights, see Cohen, *Handbook of Federal Indian Law*, pp. 575–604; Prucha, *The Great Father*, pp. 1179–83; William Veeder, "Water Rights: Life or Death for the American Indian," *Indian Historian*, 5 (Summer 1972), pp. 4–21; Norris Hundley, "The Dark and Bloody Ground in Indian Water Rights: Confusion Elevated to Principle," *Western Historical Quarterly*, 9 (October 1978), pp. 455–82, and "The Winters Doctrine and Indian Water Rights: A Mystery Reexamined," *Western Historical Quarterly*, 13 (January 1982), pp. 17–42; Peter Iverson, ed., *The Plains Indians of the Twentieth Century* (Norman: Oklahoma University Press, 1983), pp. 77–99; Daniel McCool, *Command of the Waters: Iron Triangles, Federal Water Development, and Indian Water* (Berkeley: University of California Press, 1987); McDonnell, *Dispossession of the American Indian*, ch. 6.

13. PSL: Water Rights file: Engle to Burke, May 13, 1924.

14. PSL: Water Rights file: Pinkley to Mather, June 13, 1924; Cammerer to Pinkley, June 20, 1924; Mather to C. Heaton, June 25, July 7, 1924; memorandum

of agreement, June 9, 1924. For Pinkley's central role in the Southwest, see Roth-man, *Preserving Different Pasts*, pp. 119–39.

15. PSL: Heaton Diary. Interview with Leonard and Edna Heaton, November 8, 1991. Lavender, *Pipe Spring and the Arizona Strip*, pp. 45–48. Personal correspondence.

16. Accusations that Leonard Heaton sought Pipe Spring water only for his family's livestock were incorrect. Other cattlemen, who owned about 75 percent of the stock using the spring, lived in Kanab, Orderville, St. George, and Cedar City.

17. NA: RG 79, Pipe Spring: Pinkley to Mather, February 27, 1926.

18. *Winters v. U.S.*, 207 U.S. 564 (1908). Later Supreme Court decisions expanded *Winters* in ways that would undermine NPS arguments against the Paiute: Indian water rights are not subject to Arizona law; it makes no difference if the reservation was created by executive order; groundwater cannot be distinguished from surface flow; future needs must be considered; and water is reserved for "beneficial" nonagricultural purposes. See *Arizona v. California*, 373 U.S. 546 (1963), *Cappaert v. U.S.*, 426 U.S. 128 (1976), and *U.S. v. New Mexico* 438 U.S. 696 (1978). The quantity of water that a tribe can claim, and retroactive adjustment of such amounts, remains a contentious issue in the West. But even in *Arizona v. California II*, 460 U.S. 605 (1983) and *Nevada v. U.S.*, 463 U.S. 110 (1983), which rejected Indian claims, the Winters Doctrine was upheld by the U.S. Supreme Court. The court divided equally on and thus upheld a Wyoming decision favoring Indian rights, *In re . . . Big Horn Water System*, 753 P.2d 76 (1988), and *Wyoming v. U.S.*, 492 U.S. 406 (1989), no opinion. See Jana L. Walker and Susan M. Williams, "Indian Reserved Water Rights," *Natural Resources & Environment*, 5:4 (Spring 1991), pp. 6–9, 49–52; Robert H. Abrams, "The Big Horn Indian Water Rights Adjudication," *Oklahoma Law Review*, 43:1 (Spring 1990), pp. 71–86; Carla J. Bennett, "Quantification of Indian Water Rights: Foresight or Folly?" *UCLA Journal of Environmental Law & Policy*, 8:2 (1989), p. 267–285; Lloyd Burton, "The American Indian Water Rights Dilemma," *UCLA Journal of Environmental Law & Policy*, 7:2 (1988), pp. 1–66; and *American Indian Water Rights and the Limits of Law* (Lawrence: University Press of Kansas, 1991); Roger Florio, "Water Rights: Enforcing the Federal-Indian Trust after *Nevada v. United States*," *American Indian Law Review*, 13 (1988), pp. 79–98; Thomas R. McGuire et al., *Indian Water in the New West* (Tucson: University of Arizona Press, 1993).

19. NA: RG 79, Pipe Spring: Mather to E. B. Meritt, February 20, 1926; Pinkley to Mather, February 27, 1926.

20. NA: RG 79, Pipe Spring: T. N. Neske to Burke, August 15, 1928. An excellent biography of Collier is Kenneth R. Philip, *John Collier's Crusade for Indian Reform, 1920–1954* (Tucson: University of Arizona Press, 1977).

21. NA: RG 79, Pipe Spring: Rhoads to Albright, August 30, September 30, 1929, April 19, May 15, 1930; Albright to Rhoads, June 21, 1930.

22. NA: RG 79, Pipe Spring: Pinkley to Albright, October 10, 1929; Pinkley to Moskey, November 28, 1930.

23. NA: RG 79, Pipe Spring: Pinkley to Moskey, November 20, 1930. Pinkley believed the BIA inserted the 1923 water clause because they lacked any rights under *Winters*; the BIA said the clause was added because of *Winters*. Rhoads to Albright, October 7, 1932.

24. NA: RG 79, Pipe Spring: E. C. Finney to Ray L. Wilbur, May 6, 1931; Rhoads to Albright, December 17, 1931.

25. NA: RG 79, Pipe Spring: J. H. Scattergood to Albright, December 27, 1932; Albright to Rhoads, February 13, 24, 1933; Albright to Heaton, February 23, 1933; Farrow to Rhoads, April 19, 1933.

26. NA: RG 79, Pipe Spring: Collier to Albright, May 9, October 13, 1933.

27. Heaton also believes that a lawsuit by his father against Farrow and the BIA had been favorably decided by the U.S. Supreme Court. No record of such a decision or filing for certiorari exists. By this time the NPS had hired Heaton as full-time caretaker at $1,020 a year.

28. NA: RG 79, Pipe Spring: Heaton to E. A. Farrow, May 26, June 5, 1933; Heaton to Albright, November 7, 1932, May 26, 1933; Pinkley to Albright, September 7, 1933; T. Parker to Albright, June 6, 1933.

29. NA: RG 79, Pipe Spring: Parker to Albright, June 6, 1933.

30. NA: RG 79, Pipe Spring: Pinkley to Albright, September 7, 1933.

31. NA: RG 79, Pipe Spring: Robert H. Rose, Report on Water Resources and Administrative Problems at the Pipe Spring National Monument, September 19, 1933, p. 52.

32. NA: RG 79, Pipe Spring: Department of the Interior, Regulations for the Division of the Waters of Pipe Spring, November 2, 1933.

33. PSL: Heaton Diary. Heaton interview, November 8, 1991. The Heatons died in 1993.

34. NA: RG 79, Pipe Spring: Joseph E. Taylor to Cammerer, December 19, 1936, April 7, 16, 1937; Cammerer to Taylor, February 11, 1937; William Zimmerman to Cammerer, March 12, 1937; A. Demaray to Taylor, March 26, May 21, 1937. PSL: Water Rights file: A. van V. Dunn to Albert L. Johnson, February 6, April 22, May 31, 1943; Charles Richey to Superintendent Zion N.P., May 27, 1943. Heaton Diary, 1936–37.

35. The Southern Paiute ICC settlements were dockets 88, 330, and 330-A, decided January 18, 1965. PSL: Water Rights file: Raymond J. Geerdes to Karl Gilbert, June 3, 1969; Gilbert to regional director, July 15, 1969; Ronald E. Cotton and William E. Fields memo, September 16, 1969.

36. PSL: Water Rights file: Agreement of April 13, 1972.

37. PSL: Water Rights file: Gilbert to director, Southwest Region, April 2, 1971, emphasis in text.

38. PSL: Water Rights file: William H. Coldiron to James Watt, November 11, 1981; William M. Herr to Tribal Council, January 16, 1984. William E. Fields, "The Kaibab-Paiute and the National Park Service," *CRM Bulletin*, 3:3 (September 1980), p. 8. Interviews, Gary Hasty, November 8, 1991; John Hiscock, December 15, 1997.

39. Western Shoshone at Battle Mountain, Nevada, in 1975 had an average income of $4,800; Paiutes living near Reno earned $6,200 a year. Martha C. Knack, "Indian Economies, 1950–1980," *Handbook of North American Indians: Great Basin*, vol. 11, p. 589.

40. Interview: November 8, 1991. Hasty added that of the many environmental groups that promised aid to the Paiutes if the tribe would reject the waste plant, only the Grand Canyon Trust had kept its word. "Threat to Pipe Spring," *National Parks* (January 1991), p. 11.

41. Fields, "Kaibab Paiute." Fields and several other NPS officials have referred to Pipe Spring as a model for tribal cooperation and took considerable pride in helping with campground construction. Art White contends that the Paiute, and most tribes, do not understand maintenance requirements. Interviews with Bill Fields, Ed Natay, John Cook, and Art White (1991).

42. Interview: November 8, 1991.

43. Hasty interview, November 8, 1991. Anthropologist Richard Stoffle, who sought to assist Paiute tourist development in the mid-1970s, blamed the jealousy of Mormon staff at the monument: "As we developed an educational hiking trail along the side of Pipe Spring, the Park Service personnel put rattlesnakes in our path each morning." Stoffle to authors, February 24, 1987. The casino opened on August 3, 1994; its staff was largely but not entirely Paiute.

44. PSL: Master Plan Development Outline, 1954.

45. PSL: Water Rights file: Geerdes to Karl T. Gilbert, July 3, 1969; Geerdes, "Ownership of Pipe Spring: A Legal and Historical Brief," to Gilbert, January 1, 1970. Geerdes found evidence in Winsor Cattle Co. records that on May 4, 1874, Pipe Spring was purchased from an "Indian Chief" for one horse. Jeffrey Frank, another NPS employee, believes that the service failed the local community as well as the Indians in not developing Pipe Spring tourism as Mather had promised in 1922. Personal correspondence, January 20, 1992.

46. Interview: Ralph Castro, November 8, 1991.

47. Interview: November 8, 1991.

48. Juanita Brooks, "Indian Relations on the Mormon Frontier," *Utah Historical Quarterly*, 12:1 (January 1944), p. 23. Also see J. Cecil Alter, comp., "The Mormons

and the Indians," ibid., pp. 49–67; and Angus M. Woodbury, "A History of Southern Utah and Its National Parks," ibid., 12:3 (July 1944), pp. 120–22.

49. Brigham Young, *Journal of Discourses*, II (Salt Lake City: Deseret Book Co., 1925), p. 264, quoted in Brooks, "Indian Relations," p. 22.

Chapter 6

1. For general introductions to the peninsula, see Ruby El Hult, *Untamed Olympics: The Story of a Peninsula* (Portland, Ore.: Binfords & Mort, 1971); Murray Morgan, *The Last Wilderness* (New York: Viking Press, 1955); Ruth Kirk, *Exploring the Olympic Peninsula* (Seattle: University of Washington Press, 1976) and *The Olympic Seashore* (Port Angeles, Wash.: Olympic Natural History Association, 1962); Bruce Brown, *Mountain in the Clouds: A Search for the Wild Salmon* (New York: Simon & Schuster, 1982); Chris Morganroth, *Footprints in the Olympics: An Autobiography* (Fairfield, Wash.: Ye Galleon Press, 1991).

2. Eric O. Bergland, *Summary Prehistory and Ethnography of Olympic National Park* (NPS: Pacific Northwest Region, 1983); James Swan, *The Northwest Coast* (1857; reprint, Seattle: University of Washington Press, 1977); Hilary Stewart, *Cedar: Tree of Life to the Northwest Coast Indians* (Seattle: University of Washington Press, 1984); Herbert C. Taylor, Jr., *Coast Salish and Western Washington Indians*, vol. 3 (New York: Garland Publishing, 1978).

3. Wickersham unsuccessfully submitted his account to Leslie's and Century publishing companies, as well as to John Wesley Powell at the Bureau of American Ethnology. Seventy years later a niece discovered the document among his papers. It was published as "A National Park in the Olympics . . . 1890" in *Living Wilderness*.

Wickersham described a nonexistent "central plateau from which flow the four large rivers." The "prairie scenery" of the interior reminded him of "the plains of Dakota." He also erred in claiming that the Solduc River's source was Mt. Olympus, a common mistake at the time.

4. Wickersham, "A National Park in the Olympics," p. 13.

5. George Pierre Castile, "The Indian Connection: Judge James Wickersham and the Indian Shakers," *Pacific Northwest Quarterly*, (October 1990), pp. 122–29. The possibility of native irony, satire, or deception of whites never seemed to occur to Wickersham and others who repeated tales about Indian fear of mountains and lakes. See Madronna Holden, "Making All the Crooked Ways Straight: The Satirical Portrait of Whites in Coast Salish Folklore," *Journal of American Folklore*, 89 (July 1976), pp. 271–93.

6. Michael G. Schene, "Only the Squeal Is Left: Conflict over Establishing Olympic National Park," *Pacific Historian*, 27:3 (Fall 1983), pp. 53–61. ONP Library files: P. Macy, "Preliminary Report," 1934. The most detailed account is Carsten

Lien, *Olympic Battleground: The Power Politics of Timber Preservation* (San Francisco: Sierra Club Books, 1991). Lien sees the Park Service as conspiring against creation of ONP and then seeking to destroy it from within.

7. ONP Library, Olympic Establishment file: Demaray to E. K. Burlew, April 18, 1938; Demaray to Ickes, September 8, 1938. The October 4, 1937, confidential minutes by O. A. Tomlinson describing Roosevelt's tour do not mention Indians, nor do maps of park proposals show reservations. Macy Papers, U. W. P. Macy to A. Cammerer, August 12, 1938, in ONP Library Administrative files, analyzes land additions under H.R.10024; it contains no reference to Indian interests. A key document in Olympic's subsequent expansion to the West was Irving Brant's twenty-page "Report on the Enlargement of Olympic National Park" (1938), ONP Library. Although Brant's recommendations would affect tribes, and although he weighed the economic costs to loggers, pulp mills, lumber mills, the state, inholders, and local communities, the report remained silent about Indian reservations. Papers of another founder of Olympic, Arthur W. Vollmer, provide no evidence he knew anything about Indians. The few early park documents that do relate to tribes are discussed below. On FDR's tour, see Frank Freidel, "Franklin D. Roosevelt in the Northwest," *Pacific Northwest Quarterly*, 76:4 (October 1985), pp. 122–31.

8. W. W. Elmendorf, "The Structure of Twana Culture," *Research Studies*, 28:3, Washington State University, 1960; George P. Castile's edition of *The Indians of Puget Sound: The Notebooks of Myron Eells* (Seattle: University of Washington Press, 1985) is the best introduction to Skokomish culture.

9. Interviews with Joseph Pavel, December 30, 1991; Russ Busch, December 23, 1991; John Aho, December 17, 1991; Paul Crawford, December 17, 1991; Joseph Tallakson, October 14, 1991. Tacoma City Light refused to provide information on these issues.

10. "Tribes Fear for Future of Dosewallips Elk Herd," Skokomish and Port Gamble press release, September 6, 1991; Crawford interview, December 17, 1991.

11. Interview, Gerald Charles, April 22, 1987. Charles's attitude reminds one of Thomas A. Aldwell, the park benefactor who thought Olympic wasted timber and should be half its size. "Our Supreme Being created our forests and their valuable crops of timber for the purpose of maintaining man as well as for the purpose of amusing him and providing for his recreation," *Conquering the Last Frontier* (Seattle: Superior Publishing Co., 1950), ch. 13.

12. ONP records: Cooperative Agreement between National Park Service and Olympic Peninsula . . . Assistance Program, August 28, 1991.

13. Carla Elofson, chairwoman, Lower Elwha Tribal Council, to Maureen Finnerty, Superintendent ONP, December 1991. Personal copy.

14. Aldwell, *Last Frontier*, pp. 78–80. Aldwell claimed that Indians feared and would not go near Lake Crescent, p. 43.

15. Washington State Library, Olympia, Wash., "A Historical Note on the Elwha River, Its Power Development and Its Industrial Diversion," unpublished manuscript.

16. Power from the Elwha provided approximately one-third of the amount needed to operate the mill; in 1984 it cost $4 a megawatt hour to produce, compared with $24 an hour from other sources. Clallam County at that time collected $28,000 a year in taxes from the power sites. The Park Service claimed no involvement; however, when the Glines dam needed a transmission line right-of-way across parkland in 1982, Crown Zellerbach paid the federal government $12.15 to lease a 2.43 acre access through the park. Charles A. McManus to Slade Gorton, April 15, 1984. Copy courtesy of Buck Adamire, Port Angeles, Wash.

17. Julie Johnson, "Building a Future for the Lower Elwha Klallam Tribe," grant application, February 15, 1991, courtesy of Joe Tallakson, Washington, D.C. Most evidence for Klallam use of the interior Olympics exists as random and undocumented oral tradition. The stories establish a pattern that lends some credence to the claim. A 1942 NPS document on early Klallam use of the Elwha was lost or misplaced sometime after 1982, according to Buck Adamire, Port Angeles. We are much indebted to Mr. Adamire for information about the Elwha dams and local history.

18. Gerald Charles interview, April 22, 1987.

19. NPCA: ONP: Polly Dyer to OPA Board of Trustees, June 9, 1986; Dyer to Al Swift, April 8, 1989.

20. Lower Elwha Tribal Council Resolution 10-89, February 8, 1989. Personal copy. Also see Johnson, "Building a Future." In 1989 the Army Corps of Engineers finally completed a flood control levee that cost $1.4 million and eliminated almost half of the tribe's land base. A thirty-minute video presenting the tribe's position on dam removal is available from the Lower Elwha Restoration Project, 1666 Lower Elwha Road, Port Angeles, Wash. 98362. In the film, NPS superintendent Maureen Finnerty states that removal is "the only way" to restore the ecosystem.

21. "Dams May Be Razed So the Salmon Can Pass," New York Times, July 15, 1990, compares Glines Canyon to the Edwards dam on Maine's Kennebec River.

22. Interview, Carsten Lien, June 2, 1987. Lien in Olympic Battleground cites the dams as an example of Park Service support of business and its timidity on environmental questions; he credits Indians with forcing the service to take a stand, pp. 348, 364.

23. NPCA: ONP: R. Chandler to Joe Mentor, February 27, 1986. U.S. Fish & Wildlife Service, "Review of and Proposed Solution to the Problem of Migrant Salmonoid Passage by the Elwah River Dams," Olympia, Wash., Office, January 1985; "Field Tests . . . for Elwha Salmonid Survival," March 1986.

24. Interviews, William J. Briggle, June 2, 1987, and Donald Jackson, April 21, 1987.

25. NPCA: ONP memo, "Background Information," August 23, 1990; *Seattle Post Intelligencer*, June 19, 1990; *Seattle Times*, July 26, 1990, p. B-1; *National Parks*, July 1991, pp. 14–16. Despite the politics, scientific support for dam removal mounted: GAO, *Hydroelectric Dams [and] Restoring Fisheries in the Elwha River*, March 1991; Department of the Interior, *The Elwha Report: Restoration of the Elwha River Ecosystem & Native Anadromous Fisheries*, January 1994.

26. The tribe's Makah Timber Enterprises program is highly controversial, the basis for efforts to recall council members in the mid-1990s. In talking with tribal foresters, one finds little difference in attitude or practice from the nearby non-Indian Merrill and Ring tree farm. Mike Duke interview, August 3, 1994.

27. Elizabeth Colson, *The Makah Indians: A Study of an Indian Tribe in Modern American Society* (Minneapolis: University of Minnesota Press, 1953), p. 45. Also see Ruth Kirk, *Hunters of the Whale* (New York: Harcourt, Brace and Jovanovich, 1974); and James G. Swan, *The Indians of Cape Flattery* (Washington, D.C.: Smithsonian Institution, 1869).

28. Kappler, *Indian Affairs, Laws, and Treaties*, vol. 2. Treaty of Neah Bay, January 31, 1855, Art. 4: "The right of taking fish and of whaling or sealing at usual and accustomed grounds is . . . secured to said Indians . . . and of erecting temporary houses for the purpose of curing, together with the privilege of hunting and gathering roots and berries on open and unclaimed lands." Section 5 of H.R.10024, creating Olympic National Park, provided that "nothing herein contained shall affect any valid existing claim . . . nor the rights reserved by treaty to the Indians of any tribes."

29. PM files: John E. Doerr, superintendent ONP, to David Parker, August 9, 1963; Bruce A. Wilkie, Makah Tribe, to BIA, Western Washington Agency, November 27, 1963; George Felshaw, superintendent BIA, to Wilkie, December 6, 1963; Doerr to Quentin Markishtum, chairman, Makah Tribe, September 22, 1964; Felshaw to Markishtum, December 30, 1964; Bennett Gale, superintendent ONP, to Wilkie, April 28, 1965.

30. Kappler, *Indian Affairs, Laws, and Treaties*, vol. 1, pp. 917–18, 920.

31. ONP: Macy Papers: Macy to O. A. Tomlinson, April 27, 1937. ONP Library: Establishment file: A. E. Demaray to Tomlinson, July 28, 1937; Cape Alava Report, 1937.

32. NPCA: Olympic file: Irving Clark to Ickes, June 21, 1939.

33. PM: Makah file: "Interest of Makah Tribe and National Park Service in Acquiring Ozette," n.d.

34. PM: Hopkins to Taholah Agency, December 27, 1946.

35. ONP: Administrative files: Orme Lewis to Hon. Jack Westland, April 27, 1953; Fletcher to Conrad Wirth, March 23, 1953; Fletcher to McKay, April 7, 1953; McKay to Fletcher, April 27, 1953.

36. PM: Petition of the Makah Indian Tribe, n.d. [c. 1956]; Gunther to Nathan Richardson, April 5, 1956.

37. PM: Resolution No. 29-69, Makah Tribal Council, October 22, 1968; Alvin J. Ziontz and Mason D. Morisset, "The Makah Tribe and the Ozette Reservation: A Legal Brief"; Statement of the Makah Tribe . . . concerning H.R.9311; Testimony of Lloyd Meeds before the House Interior Subcommittee, November 3, 1969; Statement of Harrison Loesch, House Interior Subcommittee on Indian Affairs, November 4, 1969.

38. NPCA: ONP: OPA Wilderness Plan for Olympic National Park, 1968.

39. NPCA: ONP: John Osseward to Anthony Wayne Smith, October 31, 1969.

40. PM: Philip H. Zalesky to Ziontz, May 4, 1970.

41. See John Collier, "Wilderness Now on Indian Lands," *Living Wilderness* (December 1937), pp. 3–4. In later years the tribe protected old growth and stopped development on allotments along beaches by zoning even more of its lands as wilderness. PM: Tribal Resolution 197-78, September 19, 1978; interview, Daniel Greene, December 18, 1991.

42. Interview: Alvin Ziontz, June 18, 1987.

43. PM: Makah Tribal Council Resolution 19-70.

44. Interview: Carsten Lien; Lien, *Olympic Battleground*, pp. 313–20. As in the struggle over Havasupai claims to part of the Grand Canyon, environmentalists in Olympic failed to inform themselves on Indian history and viewpoints. Lien cites no ethnographic works or interviews with tribal members, pp. 399–400.

45. ONP Library: General files: Charles W. Keller to Preston Macy, April 18, 25, May 23, 1941.

46. Ann M. Renker and Greg W. Arnold, "Exploring the Role of Education in Cultural Resource Management: The Makah Cultural and Research Center Example," *Human Organization*, 47:4 (Winter 1988), pp. 302–7. PM: Cooperative Agreement: National Park Service and Makah Indian Tribe, October 25, 1979; Roger J. Contor to Dale Johnson, chairman, Makah Tribal Council, November 7, 1979; James R. Anderson to Ziontz, November 28, 1979; Ziontz to Contor, December 26, 1979; Johnson to Contor, April 11, 1980; Contor to Johnson, April 15, 1980.

47. Washington state's release of Shi Shi surrendered the last remnant of plans for a coastal highway, a plan long promoted by politicians and peninsula boosters and, at one time, endorsed by the Makah.

48. Interviews with Daniel Greene and Kirk Wachendorf, December 18, 1991. Shi Shi had been entangled in a maze of overlapping legal jurisdictions. Besides the tribe and the Park Service, the state Parks, Game, and Fisheries Departments had an interest in the beach, as well as the U.S. Fish and Wildlife Service, the Clallam County Sheriff, Clallam County Parks, and private landowners. Testimony of Con-

gressman Don Bonker, House Subcommittee on National Parks, February 23, 1976, in Meeds Papers, Box 61, University of Washington Special Collections.

49. *Peninsula Daily News*, Port Angeles, Wash., April 9, 1991, p. 1. Interviews with Hank Warren, December 17, 1991; Donna Chapman, December 18, 1991; Kirk Wachendorf, December 18, 1991. The difficult access problems are outlined in an ONP memo to Kevin McCartney, December 16, 1983, ONP records. At the end of 1991 the Makahs applied for a $75,000 grant to purchase the private holdings of forty-three Indian landowners along the Shi Shi route. Once accomplished, the tribe would negotiate a trail maintenance agreement with the park. The Shi Shi beach trail was still closed in early 1998. In January of that year, the tribe received a $167,000 grant from the state to open the trail by that summer.

50. Records of the club are rumored to exist but could not be found. The *Seattle Post Intelligencer* of December 27, 1937, reported a meeting of Queets, Quileute, Hoh, and Quinault Indians at La Push to oppose an ocean strip and the Queets valley corridor. William Penn, their spokesman, was quoted as saying the Indians were determined to protect their rights under the treaties, which he felt expansion of the monument would violate.

51. Penn and Forlines interviews, April 11, 1987. Penn asserted that the tribe has written documents to support its claim of land stolen by the Park Service, but these, like the records of active opposition to the park's creation, are closed to outside researchers. According to Forlines, the treaty clause in the ONP enabling legislation resulted from Franklin Roosevelt's late night visit in the home of Forlines's grandfather, Samuel Sams, on the Queets River in 1937.

52. Donald Jackson, April 21, 1987, Paul Crawford, December 17, 1991, and Chris Morganroth, December 31, 1991. Park officials were delighted with an article Morganroth published in opposition to clear-cutting, *Peninsula Daily News*, November 19, 1991.

53. Jay Powell and Vickie Jensen, *Quileute: An Introduction to the Indians of La Push* (Seattle: University of Washington Press, 1976); George A. Pettitt, "The Quileute of La Push, 1775–1945," *Anthropological Records*, 14:1 (1950).

54. ONP records: internal memos, November 14, 1980, March 30, 1981, and September 25, 1984. R. Contor to Shirley Keith, April 7, 1980; Debora Juarez to Contor, April 24, 1980; Authors' files. Forlines and Morganroth interviews, April 11, 1987, and December 31, 1991.

55. ONP records: Kenneth C. Hanson, Quileute Northern Boundary Study, Quileute Tribal Council, October 31, 1980. *Peninsula Daily News*, December 7, 1981, July 1, 1990, June 27, 1991. ONP records: Daniel Tobin, regional director, to Henry M. Jackson, January 29, 1982; Russell Dickenson to Assistant Secretary of the Interior, May 12, 1982. Confusion over the extent and status of the small coastal

Indian reservations is evident in Fred J. Overly, superintendent ONP, to C. Wirth, December 19, 1952, ONP Administrative files. The tribe began to argue for restoration of parkland in 1968, when a researcher concluded that Olympic had mistakenly taken "the finest property on the Reservation." Interim Progress Report on Quileute Study, c. 1968; Kenneth Payne, chairman, Quileute Tribe, to Lloyd Meeds, November 15, 1968; Meeds to George Hartzog, November 20, 1968, in Meeds Papers, Box 7. The October 21, 1976, Quileute retrocession is under 16 USC 251.

56. Morganroth interview, December 31, 1991. Although neither the tribe nor the NPS would discuss negotiations, the latter stated that a tentative agreement had been signed as of December 1991. For the OPA's earlier response, see *Peninsula Daily News*, June 27, 1990. C. Lien on KPLU-FM, "All Things Considered," June 26, 1990. In *Olympic Battleground*, Lien describes the Quileute claim and Indian activism in general as "ominous for the future of the Olympic Strip," p. 320.

57. Mary Leitka interview, December 19, 1991; Hoh Tribal records: Susan Kay Hvalsoe to J. Tobin, December 21, 1981.

58. Hoh Tribal records: Hvalsoe to Tobin, December 21, 1981; Leitka to Hvalsoe, August 18, 1982; Leitka to William Clark, April 17, 1984; Department of the Interior to Leitka, May 29, 1984.

59. Leitka interview, December 19, 1991. H. Warren to authors, January 28, 1992. Unemployment at Hoh is 89 percent, a condition the band hopes to remedy by building a casino resort.

60. Pauline Capoeman, ed., *Land of the Quinault* (Taholah, Wash.: Quinault Indian Nation, 1990), tells the controversial story of Quinault logging practices fully and objectively. Also see Nicholas Popoff, "A Study of Management Policies and Practices of the BIA on Lands Held in Federal Trust on the Quinault Indian Reservation," Masters thesis, University of Washington, 1970. For Quinault culture, see Charles Willoughby, *Indians of the Quinault Agency, Washington Territory* (Washington, D.C.: Smithsonian Institution, 1889); and Ronald L. Olson, *The Quinault Indians*, U.W. Publications in Anthropology, vol. 6 (Seattle: University of Washington, 1936).

61. Joseph DeLaCruz interviews, March 3, April 24, 1987; October 3, 1991.

62. Interviews with Riley Lewis, October 5, 1990; H. Warren and J. Aho, December 17, 1991; DeLaCruz, October 3, 1991. *Peninsula Daily News*, May 19, 1987. The Quinault River leaves the national park several miles above Lake Quinault, where it enters tribal jurisdiction. The Queets River is protected its entire length by a park corridor until it enters the reservation a few miles from the ocean. Prior to 1953 the tribe agreed to allow extension of the corridor, but changed its stance in order to control the fishery. D. Jackson interview, April 21, 1987. The Quinault D.C. lobbyist, Joe Tallakson, agreed with DeLaCruz that Olympic has helped the tribe protect the rivers.

63. NA: RG 79, E-7, ONP Lands: General: Overly to Tomlinson, January 9, 1939; Collier ("personal") to Ickes, February 9, 1939; Demaray to Ickes, February 28, 1939. Macy Papers: Cammerer to Mrs. E. B. Ackerman, n.d. [c. 1939]. The ONP Establishment file has handwritten notes c. 1939 on Quinault timber and possible acquisition of the lake. For the scandals in Quinault allotment, see McDonnell, *Dispossession of the American Indian*, pp. 12, 21; and Capoeman, *Land of the Quinault*, pp. 172–78, especially the ownership map, p. 172.

64. Kappler, *Indian Affairs, Laws, and Treaties*, vol. 1, November 4, 1873, pp. 923–24.

65. Meeds Papers, Box 61: DeLaCruz to Don Bonker and Lloyd Meeds, July 26, 1976.

66. The U.S. Court of Claims twice decided that the BIA location of the line was mistaken: *Quinault Tribe of Indians v. U.S.*, 102 Ct. Cl. 822 (1945) and 118 Ct. Cl. 220 (1951). Native American Rights Fund Library: Northern Boundary of Quinault Reservation, February 15, 1977. NPCA: ONP: Russell Dickenson, director NPS, to H. M. Jackson, December 8, 1980. Tallakson interview, *Bellingham Herald*, October 10, 1988, p. A8. The official tribal history, *Land of the Quinault*, mentions none of the conflicts discussed here and has nothing on the park's creation; it gives a romantic and very positive view of ONP as uniquely managing peninsula lands: "Here part of our past can be pursued. [The park] provides inspiration and renewal to our spirits and a closer contact with the wild," pp. 240–44. In person, editor Pauline Capoeman regrets that most Quinault, especially young people, care little about beach protection, spotted owls, or traditional practices: Overcoming poverty is the tribe's first priority, a goal that she feels environmentalists do not understand. Interview, August 8, 1994.

67. Ise, *Our National Park Policy*, pp. 23–26, 194–95; Albright, *The Birth of the National Park Service*, pp. 69–73; Runte, *National Parks*, pp. xvii, 109, 114, 143–44, 239–40, 257. Exceptions to park rules have been made in a number of instances, such as grazing in Yosemite early in the century or, more recently, grazing and mining at Great Basin. See Gary E. Elliot, "Whose Land Is It? The Battle for the Great Basin National Park, 1957–1967," *Nevada Historical Society Quarterly*, 34:1 (Spring 1991), pp. 241–56. For the different attitudes in Alaska, see Robert Belous, "A Special Link to the Past," *CRM Bulletin*, 2:3 (September 1979), pp. 9–10; and Catton, *Inhabited Wilderness*.

68. 16 USC 255, 256. The origins of section 5 remain a mystery. The provision was discussed in none of the extensive congressional reports, committee hearings, and public debates on Olympic after 1935, nor does it appear in the two prior park creation bills sponsored by Congressman Wallgren. Not only were treaty rights not discussed, neither was the presence of Indians on the peninsula. Scores of individuals and over fifty organizations opposed the park; almost as many organizations

\

favored it. Not one person or group was native or represented Indians; no testimony mentions Indian hunting or treaty rights. Speakers expounded on manganese mines, elk protection, oil exploration, tax revenues, inholders, timber—"a contemporary preoccupation with just about every possible objection or consideration to the park, except those that might have been raised by Indians." Rebecca L. McLeod, "A Silent Record: Report on Olympic National Park Legislation on Indian Treaty Rights, 1937–38," March 21, 1984, ONP Library. McLeod also reasons that if Harold Ickes had proposed and inserted the treaty clause to allow hunting, he would have been contradicting his own statements on elk protection, probably the only issue on which all sides agreed. McLeod suggested that the lack of evidence may mean that section 5 was intended to protect native land holdings, not hunting rights. McLeod's research is convincing and supports our finding that concern for Indian rights was virtually nonexistent during the Olympic debates.

McLeod did not examine certain BIA files or have access to Wallgren's personal papers. We have checked John Collier's office records in the National Archives and the guide to his papers at Yale University, 1933–1945, finding nothing on Olympic. However the Overly letter of January 9, 1939, which proposes taking three parcels of Quinault land for the park, also recommends "reserving to them the rights of access and the privileges of hunting . . . now enjoyed." When John Collier responded by suggesting creation of an Indian forest unit, he stated that his concept would "provide a means of reserving their fishing and rights to them" and that the Quinault would not object "provided . . . their hunting and fishing rights [are] properly safeguarded." See fn. 27. There is also a statement by Ickes when he sought to reconcile Indians to the creation of Everglades National Park in 1935: "The Seminoles ought to have the right to subsistence hunting and fishing within the proposed park"; nothing connects this sentiment with Olympic. NA: RG 75: Collier office file, Box 17: Department of the Interior press release, April 2, 1935. See Harry A. Kersey, Jr., *The Florida Seminoles and the New Deal: 1933–1942* (Boca Raton: Florida Atlantic University Press, 1989), p. 109.

69. Interviews with DeLaCruz, March 3, April 24, 1987, October 3, 1991; Clay Butler, March 7, April 14, 1987, October 5, 1990, December 19, 1991; G. Charles, April 22, 1987; and Reid Jarvis, June 3, 1987. Charles and other tribal leaders no doubt had in mind the public reaction to the "Boldt Decision" ten years earlier (*Washington v. Washington State Commercial Passenger Fishing Vessel Association*, 443 U.S. 658).

70. The legal questions in *U.S. v. Hicks*, 587 F. Supp. 1162, involve whether treaty language guaranteeing hunting on "open and unclaimed land" includes a national park, and whether the treaty's "privilege" to hunt is identical with the "right" to fish, the latter having been upheld by the U.S. Supreme Court in *Commercial Passenger Fishing Vessel Association*. See H. Barry Holt, "Can Indians Hunt in National

Parks? Determinable Indian Treaty Rights and *United States v. Hicks*," in *Environmental Law*, 16 (1986), pp. 207–54; George C. Coggins and William Modrcin, "Native American Indians and Federal Wildlife Law," *Stanford Law Review*, 31 (February 1979), pp. 375–423; Edward H. Wasmuth, "Whose Wildlife Is It Anyway? Conflicts between State and Tribal Regulation . . . ," *Virginia Journal of Natural Resources Law*, 3:2 (Winter 1984), pp. 315–33.

71. *Seattle Times*, January 19, 1984. *Port Angeles Daily News*, January 20, 22, February 1, August 28, 1984. Gabrielle Elliot, "Hunting Rights and Privileges," *Seattle Weekly*, February 22, 1984. Clare Conley, "The Threatening Indian Problem," *Outdoor Life*, April 1984. "Tribes Win Hunting Rights in Olympic," *National Parks*, March 1984, p. 34. The NPCA supported Swift's bill; see NPCA Olympic file, January 19–February 7, 1984. H.R.4807, 98th Cong., 2d Sess. *Congressional Record*, 98th Cong., 2d Sess., February 8, 1984, p. E416. Al Swift to authors, December 17, 1986.

In October 1984, Hicks and Shale, who had confessed to killing the elk, were convicted, fined $500 each, and placed on two years probation.

72. *Port Angeles Daily News*, February 17, March 1, 22, August 8, 1984. Warren interview, December 17, 1991.

73. Clay Butler interview, April 24, 1987. Vi Hilbert, an Upper Skagit elder, expressed the same attitude toward North Cascades National Park, interview, March 21, 1996.

74. John Aho to authors, September 8, 1986.

75. NA: RG 79: E-7: Olympic History: Albright memo, November 8, 1929; Wirth memo, May 17, 1932. Lien, *Olympic Battleground*, p. 122.

76. Told by Mrs. Joe Samson, in Erna Gunther, *Klallam Folk Tales*, University of Washington Publications in Anthropology, vol. 1 (Seattle: University of Washington Press, 1925), p. 152.

77. Publication of popular archaeology, *Prehistoric Life on the Olympic Peninsula: The First Inhabitants of a Great American Wilderness*, in 1988, by the Pacific Northwest National Parks and Forests Association of Seattle, illustrates this change. Olympic is now a "jewel" in the Northwest Region. Other areas involving Indians and the Seattle office have been the interpretation of the Whitman Memorial, comanagement of Lake Roosevelt recreation with the Colvilles, and Muckleshoot hunting in Mt. Rainier.

78. Warren interview, December 17, 1991.

79. Crawford interview, December 17, 1991.

Chapter 7

1. One quickly learns from Earle E. Spamer's *Bibliography of the Grand Canyon and the Lower Colorado River from 1540* (Grand Canyon: Natural History Association, 1990)

just how immense canyon literature is. Excellent introductions are J. Donald Hughes, *In the House of Light and Stone: A Human History of the Grand Canyon* (Grand Canyon: Natural History Association, 1985); Robert C. Euler and Frank Tikalsky, *The Grand Canyon: Intimate Views* (Tucson: University of Arizona Press, 1992); Edwin Corle, *The Story of the Grand Canyon* (New York: Duell, Sloan and Pearce, 1951); Joseph Wood Krutch, *Grand Canyon: Today and All Its Yesterdays* (New York: William Sloane Associates, 1958); Bruce Babbitt, comp., *Grand Canyon: An Anthology* (Flagstaff, Ariz.: Northland Press, 1986); Barbara J. Morehouse, *A Place Called Grand Canyon: Contested Geographies* (Tucson: University of Arizona Press, 1996).

2. One hundred forty-six names in Byrd H. Granger, *Grand Canyon Place Names* (Tucson: University of Arizona Press, 1960), are of Anglo origin, thirteen are Spanish, and sixty-one, including such terms as Indian Gardens, refer to the region's native people. Granger's count is undoubtedly low. A 1962 park map gives at least four dozen place names derived from native languages, not counting names of rock formations.

3. Stephen J. Pyne, *Fire on the Rim: A Firefighters Season at the Grand Canyon* (New York: Weidenfeld & Nicolson, 1989), pp. 163–66.

4. The Havasupai reservation is listed as an "area" in 1932 (vol. 7) and not under "private property" (vol. 9). NA: RG 79, E-7, CCF, Grand Canyon: Development Outline file, June 30, 1932. NPS, "Mission 66 for Grand Canyon National Park and Monument," n.d., n.p.

5. George Laycock, "The Biggest Deer Drive Ever," *Outdoor Life,* 172 (October 1983), pp. 60–61, 96–98. Frank E. Weingart to authors, October 18, 1991. GCL: BIA file: Tillotson to H. Albright, March 13, 1933; W. W. Crosby to George Laben; September 14, 1922; Laben to BIA, Truxton School, September 18, 1922; Carl E. Lehnert to Chief Ranger, October 16, 1952. The BIA opposed employment of Indians in Wild West shows, which "influence them to continue their nomadic habits. . . . Indians are not to give exhibitions of dances or old time customs." The Fred Harvey Co. assured the BIA that "we handle them in the proper manner and take good care of them . . . surrounded them with every safe-guard, paid them well, etc." NA: RG 75: CCF, 1907–1939: Havasupai: H. Schweizer to A. Seligman, December 7, 1914; E. B. Meritt to Clinton West, December 14, 1914. See Prucha, *The Great Father,* vol. 2, pp. 712–15. In 1926 the agent reported that Havasupai no longer attended local fairs because they were busy working at the Grand Canyon.

6. *In and around the Grand Canyon* (Boston: Little, Brown, and Company, 1911), chs. 26–29. Roger Larson, *Controversial James: An Essay on the Life and World of George Wharton James* (San Francisco: Book Club of California, 1991), reports that NPS staff at the Grand Canyon had a low opinion of James, but Michael Harrison, himself very critical of the writer, can recall no negative reactions by rangers, except when

James spoke too long at the dedication ceremony of the national park. Harrison to authors, May 1992.

7. Dama Margaret Smith, "The Home of a *Doomed* Race," *Good Housekeeping*, 77 (September 1923), pp. 38–39, 196–205; "Thou Shalt Have No Other Gods," *Good Housekeeping*, 77 (December 1923), p. 32, 189ff.

8. Dama Margaret Smith, *I Married a Ranger* (Palo Alto, Calif.: Stanford University Press, 1930), ch. 5.

9. Smith, *I Married A Ranger*, ch. 9. In 1933, Stanford University Press published *Indian Tribes of the Southwest* by the same author, now calling herself White Mountain Smith. She described the Apache as the most handsome natives despite their "dark and sinister" history; Zuni were "always smiling and happy," and the Navajo unbreakable, the greatest of all Indians. The book devoted fifteen pages to Acoma, twenty to Zuni, and four to Havasu Canyon. The Havasupai, she remarked, with their "broad, rather stupid faces," should not be compared with happy, contented Pueblos.

10. Cammerer to Tillotson, June 10, 1938, quoted in Jacilee Wray, "Havasupai Ethnohistory on the South Rim of Grand Canyon National Park: A Case Study of Cultural Resource Management in the National Park Service," Masters thesis, Northern Arizona University, 1990, p. 74. In 1940, Cammerer rejected a park project to help the Havasupai, "because of their limited culture and unattractiveness." Cammerer to acting superintendent, April 10, 1940, quoted in Wray, "Havasupai Ethnohistory," p. 78.

11. GCL: BIA file: John M. Davis to regional superintendents, August 19, 1949.

12. NA: RG 79, E7, Grand Canyon: Boundaries: Arizona Game Protective Association to Hon. L. W. Douglas, March 31, 1930, and to W. E. S. Thompson, April 19, 1930; T. E. McCullough to Hon. Henry Ashurst, June 16, 1930.

13. NA: RG 79, E-7, Grand Canyon: Boundaries: 1923 boundary map, with a notation, "Important Stuff, NAVAJO INDIAN RESERVATION. This area is extremely valuable to the park. With water development it has the greatest possibilities as a game preserve of any point on South Rim. J. K. E."; A. Cammerer to Ashurst, April, 14, 1925; Mather to Henry Temple, May 14, 1925.

14. NA: RG 79, General Records, 1907–1939, Box 45: "Bob" to "My dear Steve," September 10, 1919. Probably written by Robert Yard, the report said that only three or four groups a year visited the area, but a road to Supai would bring prosperity. "The Indians are very simple and primitive. They are a decent people." All profits should be reaped by the Havasupai, not outsiders: "It would be a great shame to have a concessioner down there."

15. GCL: Havasupai: Cammerer to E. B. Meritt, April 22, 1927; Albright to Cammerer, May 21, 1927. Havasu Canyon excited many visitors. In 1926 Amy

Guest felt inspired to write: "Hardly anyone goes to this Canyon. There were about ten people there this year and two parties the year before. It is practically unknown, and the scenery is extraordinarily beautiful. Springs gush up from the rocks and form a beautiful mountain stream of sky-blue water which runs through a fertile valley [with] nearly a mile of cataracts and then three magnificent waterfalls. . . . It could be made one of the most beautiful spots in America. . . . It would well repay a little trouble, and become a national monument of lasting beauty." She observed the canyon's people, "very poor and ignorant, and in the past—being so remote—civilization has passed them by." NA: RG 75: CCF, 1907–1939: Havasupai: Guest to secretary of agriculture, September 29, 1926.

16. GCL: BIA file: W. W. Crosby to George Laben, March 18, 1922; F. S. Lovanskiold to J. Ross Easkin, August 22, 1924, August 28, 1925; Guy Hobgood to M. R. Tillotson, April 22, 1936; C. F. Shaffer to F. A. Kittredge, September 23, 1940; Carl E. Lehnert to chief ranger, October 16, 1952.

17. See Joseph L. Sax, "Do Communities Have Rights? The National Parks as a Laboratory of New Ideas," *University of Pittsburgh Law Review*, 45:3 (Spring 1984), pp. 499–511; Benita J. Howell, "The Anthropologist as Advocate for Local Interests in National Park Planning," in NPS, *International Perspectives on Cultural Parks* (1984), pp. 274–79; David E. Whisnut, ed., "Process, Policy, and Context: Contemporary Perspectives on Appalachian Culture," *Appalachian Journal*, 7:1–2 (Autumn/Winter, 1979–80).

18. Wray, "Havasupai Ethnohistory," pp. 22–27, 49–53; GCL: Louise M. Hinchliffe, "Origin and Development of Supai Camp," 1976 MS report; Stephen Hirst, *Havsuw 'Baaja: People of the Blue Green Water* (Supai, Ariz.: Havasupai Tribe, 1985), pp. 71–72, 91–92. Accounts differ on what Roosevelt said to the Havasupai.

19. Tillotson to Albright, October 16, 1930, quoted in Wray, "Havasupai Ethnohistory," p. 67. On NPS preference for Havasupai workers over Navajo, see U.S. Senate, *Survey of Conditions of the Indians in the United States*, 71st Cong., 3d Sess., Part 17, pp. 8737–38. The NPS employed fifty-six Havasupai between 1920 and 1939, thirty-nine between 1940 and 1959, two between 1960 and 1979, and five between 1980 and 1990. Wray, "Havasupai Ethnohistory," pp. 63–68, 94–100. Both Wray and anthropologist John Martin stress the impact of national park wages on Havasupai culture after 1920.

20. GCL: Supai Camp: diagram, November 20, 1933.

21. GCL: Havasupai file: Cammerer to Tillotson, July 22, 1936; BIA file: Brooks memo, January 23, 1936. Photos in Hinchliffe, "Origin and Development of Supai Camp."

22. GCL: BIA file: Brooks to Tillotson, May 22, 1936.

23. Wray, "Havasupai Ethnohistory," pp. 83–88; Henry F. Dobyns and Robert C. Euler, *The Havasupai People* (Phoenix: Indian Tribal Series, 1971); Hirst, *Havsuw*

'Baaja. The best account of conflict and violence in Havasu Canyon in the 1960s is John F. Martin, "Continuity and Change in Havasupai Social and Economic Organization," Ph.D. diss., University of Chicago, 1966. Personal correspondence: Robert Branges and Richard Rayner to the authors.

24. GCL: Havasupai: Carl Lehnert to chief ranger, April 13, 1953.

25. GCL: Supai Camp: John S. McLaughlin to regional director, November 2, 1955; photos of Camp, November 1955, March 1956.

26. See Philip L. Fradkin, *A River No More: The Colorado River and the West* (Tucson: University of Arizona Press, 1984). DeVoto's prophetic articles are described by Wallace Stegner in *The Uneasy Chair: A Biography of Bernard DeVoto* (Salt Lake City: Peregrine Smith Books, 1988), pp. 311–14.

27. Henry F. Dobyns and Robert C. Euler, *The Walapai People* (Phoenix, Ariz.: Indian Tribal Series, 1976); *Walapai Papers: Historical Reports, Documents, and Extracts from Publications Relating to the Walapai Indians of Arizona,* Senate Document 273, 74th Cong. 2d Sess. (1936). Hualapai life at the turn of the century is described by BIA teacher Flora Gregg Iliff in *People of the Blue Water: My Adventures among the Walapai and Havasupai Indians* (New York: Harper & Brothers, 1954).

28. Museum of Northern Arizona: Hualapai Dam: Albright to Elwood Mead, January 11, 1933. Albright did not mention Hualapai interests or BIA jurisdiction in the matter. The Bureau of Reclamation also seemed oblivious of Indians in the 1930s. A memo to the secretary of the interior arguing in favor of Bridge Canyon listed positive reasons for the dam, but failed to mention that it would be built on Hualapai land. Museum of Northern Arizona: Roy B. Williams to H. Ickes, March 24, 1938. For NPS attitudes toward reclamation projects, see Ise, *Our National Park Policy,* pp. 467–73.

29. NA: RG 79, E-7, Grand Canyon: Boundaries: Tillotson to A. Demaray, April 6, 1945.

30. H.R. 1500, 1501, 82d Cong., lst Sess. Ise, *Our National Park Policy,* p. 470.

31. With a tribal membership of one thousand, the annual fee would have provided a per capita payment of $1,000, or $4,000–$5,000 per household, roughly $40,000 in 1996 dollars. Dam construction was projected at $160 million, annual net revenue at $23 million. Dobyns and Euler, *The Walapai People,* pp. 90–97. Morris K. Udall Papers (MKU), 93d Cong., Testimony of Marshall Humprey, APA, November 12, 1973; James P. Bartlett, APA, "Summary of Arizona's Activities Directed toward Development of the Colorado River," November 12, 1973.

32. The Navajo were directly involved with the plans for Marble Canyon. The tribe first endorsed the project, then opposed it.

33. Stewart and Morris Udall Papers, University of Arizona. Both Udalls blamed Brower and the Sierra Club, but what they failed to consider in supporting the Bureau of Reclamation and the Central Arizona Project was that many Ameri-

cans had had direct personal experience with the Grand Canyon and that public perception of the park was essentially religious. Repeated over and over in the correspondence were the words "desecration," "sin," "crime," "betrayal," "human egotism," "God," "wonder," "cathedral," "Creator," "human pride." Many writers, such as a woman who claimed that the reservoir would flood Havasupai farmland, were badly misinformed.

34. Museum of Northern Arizona archives: Bureau of Reclamation to William L. Spicer, April 27, 1964; Bestor Robinson to David Brower, May 26, 1964. "U.S. Plans for Dams on Colorado," *New York Times*, March 15, 1964; *Colorado River Association Newsletter*, September 1966. Fradkin, *A River No More*, does not discuss the Hualapai. Extensive sources on the debate are given in Spamer, *Bibliography of the Grand Canyon*.

35. *Indian Affairs* (May 1966), p. 5. *Amerindian*, 15:2 (November 1966), p. 4.

36. MKU: LA: 91st Cong.: Sterling Mahone to Udall, October 10, 1969; Hualapai Tribal Council Resolution, May 3, 1969; Grand Canyon S.1296 file, 93d Cong. Lloyd H. Moss to Sam Steiger, May 1, 1974. Testimony file in the Udall papers contains much Indian support for the Hualapai. *Navajo Times*, July 19, 1973, p. 9A. NPCA: Grand Canyon: Hualapai Tribe, "Memorandum in Support of Hualapai Tribe's Opposition to S.1296" [1973].

37. NPCA: Grand Canyon file: Statement of Sterling Mahone . . . before the House Subcommittee. . . .[1973].

38. MKU: LA: 93d Cong.: Statement of Sterling Mahone, Kingman Rotary Club, April 17, 1974.

39. MKU: LC: 93d Cong., Grand Canyon: Udall to Robert L. Coshland, June 6, 1974; Mahone to Udall, March 28, 1974; Goldwater to Mahone, April 2, 1974; Goldwater to Udall, April 2, 1974. Udall wrote to Mahone on April 4 that he agreed "100 percent" with Goldwater.

40. MKU: LC: 93d Cong., Grand Canyon: Mahone to Udall, September 19, 1974. "Report from Royal Marks," *Hualapai Times* (August 1976), pp. 8–9.

41. Edgar Walema interview, November 14, 1991.

42. Jan Balsom interview, November 25, 1991. The Washington, D.C., meeting is reported in Florence Williams, "Indian Tribe Pushes for Natural River and Canyon," *High Country News*, August 26, 1991, p. 12.

43. Clay Bravo interview, November 14, 1991.

44. Walema interview, November 14, 1991.

45. Walema interview, November 14, 1991.

46. *Lesoeur v. U.S.*, 858 F.Supp. 974 (1992). U.S. District Court Records, Phoenix, Docket CIV90-1216, Complaint (#1), Plaintiff's Statement of Fact (#25), and Affidavit of Daniel Lesoeur, October 28, 1991 (#36). Grand Canyon Park Headquarters: NPS Case Incident Report by David Ashe, August 13, 1988. Interview, Jim Tuck, November 25, 1991, May 28, 1992. Hualapai trips assumed no liability for

accidents, whereas NPS concessionaires must insure against public and employee injury.

47. GCL: BIA file: Perry E. Brown to J. V. Lloyd, December 11, 1938; M. R. Tillotson to E. H. Fryer, May 18, 1938; Tillotson to L. T. Hoffman, June 8, 1938; H. C. Bryant to Navajo Indian Agency, April 10, 1947.

48. Robert Fay Schrader, *The Indian Arts & Crafts Board: An Aspect of New Deal Indian Policy* (Albuquerque: University of New Mexico Press, 1983), pp. 51–53. GCL: "Souvenirs and Native Handcraft Policy" [c. 1976]. Michael Frome in *Regreening the National Parks* (Tucson: University of Arizona Press, 1992), ch. 12, "The Silly Souvenirs They Sell," observes that since 1960 official NPS policy on concession standards has been sound, but followed "only on paper." The NPS, according to Frome, allows sale of inauthentic Indian goods if displayed separately, and he states that NPS policy restricting merchandise to items consistent with a park's purpose can be tested by visiting gift shops displaying "comic books, girlie magazines, and tawdry trinkets," p. 208. Most Indian tribes we visited complained about NPS failure to regulate crafts marketing.

49. Interviews with Butch Farrabee, March 14, 1987; Ken Miller, November 25, 1991. GCL: Beadselling, Navajo: Robert L. Miller to Gary Everhart, November 3, 1975; Miller to Paul J. Fannin, May 12, 1976; Bruce Shaw to Miller, October 10, 1975. On a "good day" in the early 1980s, vendors could make as much as $200. A four-day weekend could net $1,500; some earned over $20,000 in a season. The more organized Yellowhorse stand east of the park took in $2,000 a day on weekends. Made in homes, juniper and imported bead necklaces sold for 400 to 500 percent over cost, with no broker or traders in the middle. Roc H. Indermill, "Roadside Fever: The Social Organization of Roadside Tenure in the Context of the Navajo Beadwork Trade, 1928–1988," Masters thesis, Northern Arizona University, 1990. The penalty for bead-selling was a maximum of six months in jail and a $500 fine. Louisa R. Stark, "Navajo Bead Stands," *Courier,* 32:12 (December 1987), pp. 19, 37, ignores the conflict over NPS regulations.

50. Clarence Gorman interview, November 17, 1991.

51. Balsom interview, November 25, 1991.

52. Charles T. Wilson interview, November 6, 1991; Balsom interview, November 25, 1991. GCL: Bead selling, Navajo: Shaw to Miller, October 10, 1975, pointed out that the Navajo could sell at park borders or wholesale to Fred Harvey.

53. Leigh Jenkins interviews, April 9, June 3, 1992.

54. Interview, June 3, 1992. A good introduction to Hopi attitudes toward the Grand Canyon is Mischa Titiev, "A Hopi Salt Expedition," *American Anthropologist,* 39:2 (April 1937), pp. 244–55. For the ecological impact of Glen Canyon dam, see Steven W. Carothers and Bryan T. Brown, *The Colorado River through Grand Canyon: Natural History and Human Change* (Tucson: University of Arizona Press, 1991).

55. Balsom interview, November 25, 1991. The best example of tribal/park cooperation is the 1994 "Programmatic Agreement" on the operation of Glen Canyon dam, an effort bringing together the Bureau of Reclamation, the NPS, Arizona, the Hopi, Hualapai, Havasupai, Navajo, Zuni, and three Paiute tribes. Copy in NPS Grand Canyon files.

Chapter 8

1. James, *The Indians of the Painted Desert Region: Hopis, Navahoes, Wallapais, Havasupais* (Boston: Little, Brown, 1919), p. 246.

2. Iliff, *People of the Blue Water*, pp. 196–97.

3. Dobyns and Euler, *Havasupai People;* and E. Stephen Hirst, *Life in a Narrow Place* (New York: David McKay Co., 1976). John F. Martin, "From Judgment to Land Restoration: The Havasupai Land Claims Case," in *Irredeemable America*, ed. Imre Sutton (Albuquerque: University of New Mexico Press, 1986). Dobyns and Euler argue that the Havasupai paid a price for not resisting. Hirst's book was written from the tribe's viewpoint and republished by the Havasupai in 1985 as *Havsuw 'Baaja: People of the Blue Green Water.*

4. Quotations from Hirst, *Life in a Narrow Place*, pp. 65–67. Indian agent Henry Ewing reported in 1901 that the forest manager had halted Havasupai hunting on the plateau, causing the tribe considerable hardship. For a sympathetic yet candid assessment of the tribe's general condition, see Ewing's accounts in CIA, *Annual Reports*, 1897–1902.

5. NA: RG 75: BIA: CCF, 1907–1939: Havasupai: Captain Jim to Cato Sells, September 25, 1915; Watahomigie to Sells, September 1, 1915; Clinton West to Sells, September 1, 1915. The BIA responded that Arizona game laws were "drastically enforced" against Indians off-reservation, and that the law must be obeyed to avoid conflict. E. B. Meritt to West, September 18, 1915.

6. NA: RG 75: BIA: 1907–1937: Havasupai: C. Burke to George Leban, August 25, 1922; Agent to CIA, January 8, 1926.

7. U.S. 40 Stat. 1175. Ise, *Our National Park Policy*, pp. 233–34.

8. For negative views of the NPS, see Hirst, *Life in a Narrow Place*, and Dobyns and Euler, *Havasupai People*, pp. 29–40.

9. GCL: BIA file: M. R. Tillotson to H. Albright, October 30, 1931; H. J. Hagerman to J. Henry Scattergood, November 1, 1931; Guy Hobgood to Tillotson, October 14, 1933; BIA to J. V. Lloyd, July 6, 1938; John Herrick to Robert Holtz, July 5, 1940. U.S. Senate, *Survey of Conditions*, pp. 8747–48.

10. U.S. Senate, *Survey of Conditions*, pp. 8740–42, 8749. MKU: Legislative Assistant: 93d Cong., Havasupai: C. J. Rhoads to Patrick Hamley, June 12, 1930; Hamley

to Rhoads, October 4, 1930. GCL: BIA file: M. Tillotson to H. Albright, October 30, 1931; Hagerman to Scattergood, November 1, 1931.

11. GCL: Havasupai: H. C. Bryant to R. D. Holtz, August 19, 1939; Gordon Cox to Bryant, August 24, 1939. MKU: Legislative Assistant: 93d Cong., Havasupai: Arthur Demaray to John Collier, May 15, 1940.

12. *U.S. v. Santa Fe Pacific Railroad Company*, 314 U.S. 339.

13. MKU: 93d Cong., Havasupai: Morton Chaney to chief, USFS, May 1, 1940; Barton Greenwood to A. W. Simington, January 30, 1943; John O. Crow to John Collier, February 3, 1943. GCL: Abe Barber and Felix S. Cohen, "Examiners Report on Tribal Claims to Released Railroad Lands in Northeastern Arizona," May 1942, pp. 53–57. NA: RG 79, E-7, Grand Canyon: Boundaries: NPS internal memo, April 20, 1943; J. Collier to N. Drury, April 26, 1943; Jim Crook to John O. Crow, April 19, 1943; Walter V. Woehlke to N. Drury, May 31, 1943. A color-coded BIA map dated March 23, 1943, shows the complex ownership pattern on the plateau.

14. GCL Microfiche: Frederick Law Olmsted, H. C. Bryant, and Harold M. Ratcliff, "Report on Indian Service Proposal for Transfer of Grand Canyon National Park and Monument Lands to Indian Service as Reservation for Havasupai Indians," May 4, 1943.

15. NA: RG 79, E-7, Grand Canyon: Boundaries: Tillotson to Drury, April 6, 1945.

16. See Martin, "Continuity and Change," for a candid description of life in Supai Village. Also, Hirst, *Life in a Narrow Place*, p. 228. GCL: Martin Goodfriend, "Report of Supai, Arizona," unpublished manuscript, April 25, 1966, provides a scathing account of life at Supai: "No other Indian reservation, no Appalachian backwater, no slum or skid row anywhere" was as wretched as "these half-starved, ailing, uneducated people." Goodfriend observed that the tribe lived in constant fear of losing NPS grazing permits for pack horses, which in turn would destroy the tourist trade; he recommended building a road or tramway from Hualapai Hilltop to the village. A much more balanced account prior to the Enlargement Act is a blunt but fair report by Woodward A. Wickham to the Institute of Current World Affairs, January 1974. Alvin M. Josephy Papers: Havasupai file.

17. For travel in the canyon before it became popular, see Wallace Stegner, "A Pack Horse Paradise," in *The Sound of Mountain Water* (Lincoln: University of Nebraska Press, 1985), pp. 77–93. Joseph Wampler, in *Havasu Canyon: Gem of the Grand Canyon* (Berkeley: Howell-North Press, 1959), pp. 99–102, praised the 1957 NPS acquisition of mining patents as securing "riches of another kind" for all Americans.

18. The Havasupai and NPS disputed over guiding and use fees in the canyon. In 1964 the tribe charged hikers a $1 entrance fee. Lodging was $4 a night, and a round trip on a pack horse, $12. Martin, "Continuity and Change," pp. 80–82. Havasupai tourist income in 1964 was $30,000; it reached $200,000 by 1976. For an excellent

analysis of economic change between 1963 and 1977, see Martin, "From Judgment to Land Restoration."

19. Glenn O. Hendrix, "A Master Plan for Grand Canyon National Park," (January 1971), pp. 13–15. Hirst, *Life in a Narrow Place*, pp. 259–62. Morris Udall's staff, on learning of the strategy to acquire Havasupai land, reported that "Goldwater is furious" with the NPS and that a major controversy was in the offing. MKU: LA: 91st Cong., Grand Canyon: Dale Pontius memo, January 27, 1971.

20. Hirst, *Life in a Narrow Place*, p. 264. Hirst was strongly biased in favor of the tribe and may have misinterpreted Goldwater. A few months later the senator cautioned Mo Udall: "I am a realist, I know that we are not going to get what we are asking for, but I do think they are entitled to the hilltop and to some land where their power plant is and a little more grazing land than they are already using. . . . There is great opposition, particularly from the Sierra Club to granting them a great deal more land and I don't think this will come about." MKU: LA: 93d Cong., Grand Canyon: Goldwater to Udall, April 26, 1973. John Carter Freemuth, "The History of S.1296: The Enlargement of Grand Canyon National Park," Masters thesis, Claremont Graduate School, 1975; ch. 4 is on Barry Goldwater. For Goldwater's role in the return of Blue Lake, in which he and Richard Nixon, Morris Udall, and George McGovern collaborated, see R. C. Gordon-McCutchan, *The Taos Indians and the Battle for Blue Lake* (Santa Fe: Red Crane Books, 1991), p. 208ff. During that debate, Goldwater promised the Senate that Blue Lake would not set a precedent for further Indian land claims.

21. Some local affiliates, most notably in the Izaak Walton League and Sierra Club, broke with the parent organization. See below. The common goal of defeating S.1296 inspired alliances between environmentalists and the American Forestry Association, rod and gun clubs, the Arizona Cattle Growers Association, and the Sports Fishing Institute. Local groups opposed to the land transfer included Arizonans for a Quality Environment, Arizona Conservation Council, and the Southern Arizona Hiking Club.

22. *New York Times*, editorial, July 10, 1974. *Environmental Action*, September 28, 1974, p. 17. *Sierra Club Bulletin*, 58:7 (July 1973), p. 23. NPCA: Grand Canyon: Devereux Butcher to Anthony Wayne Smith, February 13, 1975. MKU: LA: Cong. Grand Canyon: Stephen Hirst to Jual Rodack, March 14, 1973; Jeffrey Ingram to Udall, July 10, 1974; Peggy Briney to Udall, September 20, 1974.

Letter writers on both sides often had their facts garbled. Many writers confused the Havasupai with the Hualapai and the dam issue. Some opponents of the bill claimed the Havasupai planned large tourist resorts in their own national park; one person said that S.1296 would transfer the reservation to the park. A common objection was that the bill favored a special group, but these comments remained free of racial allusions. On race, there is nothing in Udall's Enlargement Act correspondence that comes close to the response inspired by a 1969 bill to return an island in the lower Colorado River to the Quechen Indians. Local cattlemen and realtors denounced the Quechen for wasting land. Carl Self of Yuma, owner of "Southwestern Arizona's Largest Real Estate Firm," correctly noted that Indian heirship problems often made their land useless, but then added: "We know the Indian is going to be on some type of relief most of the time and the proceeds that he will get from these little parcels will not be a drop in the bucket toward his support, just about enough for a few gallons of wine." MKU papers: Legislative Correspondence (MKU: LC): 91st Cong., Self to Udall, August 7, 1969.

23. *New York Times*, July 8, 1974, p. 24. MKU: 93d Cong., S.1296: Brower to Udall, June 21, 1974.

24. National Wildlife Federation, *Conservation Report No. 24*, July 12, 1974, pp. 318–19. MKU: LA: 93d Cong.: Grand Canyon: Coalition to Save the Grand Canyon, "Grand Canyon Giveaway Opposed by Conservationists," September 12, 1974.

25. NPCA files: Grand Canyon: Toby Cooper to Joanna Carreras, June 24, 1974.

26. Martin, "From Judgment to Land Restoration," pp. 295–98, suggests that the transfer actually increased Havasupai dependence on the federal government.

27. If conservationists had read the future, they might have supported an even bigger cession, one large enough to include a uranium mine against which they and the Havasupai would join forces in the 1990s. An error that the Sierra Club and others made was to assume that any tribe would pay any price to end poverty.

28. Josephy Papers: "Statement of the Havasupai Tribe before the Subcommittee on National Parks and Recreation," November 12, 1973.

29. MKU: LC: 93d Cong., Grand Canyon: Oscar Paya to Udall, March 4, 17, 1974; Udall to Paya, March 6, 1974.

30. Fontana Papers: Henry F. Dobyns, "Help Stop the Latest U.S. Indian War!" n.d.

31. Fontana Papers: Fontana to Stewart Udall, April 30, 1974; Fontana to Robert Thomas, September 9, 1974.

32. MKU: LC: 93d Cong., S.1296: Spicer to M. Udall, April 15, 1974; H.R.5900 file: M. Udall to Stewart Udall, May 8, 1974; Havasupai resolution, July 28, 1974.

33. *Congressional Record*, 93d Cong., October 10, 1974, pp. 35191–206.

34. Hirst, *Life in a Narrow Place*, p. 281; *Havsuw 'Baaja*, pp. 231–35.

35. Kendra Shawne McNally, "The Grand Canyon National Park Enlargement Act: Perspectives on Protection of a National Resource," *Arizona Law Review*, 18 (1976), pp. 232–75. John Hough, "Indigenous People and the Grand Canyon National Park," draft in the GCL, later published as "The Grand Canyon National Park and the Havasupai People: Cooperation and Conflict," in West and Brechin, *Resident Peoples and National Parks*, pp. 215–30. Interview with Robert Euler, June 19,

1992, and his "Havasupai of the Grand Canyon," *American West*, 16:3 (May 1979), pp. 12–17, 65. Euler's incomplete manuscript, "Cultural Patterns in the Havasupai Use Lands" (1976), is in the GCL. By far the best analyses of NPS/Havasupai relations are in Martin, "From Judgment to Land Restoration."

36. GCL: Havasupai file: "Working Draft of Proposal for Secretarial Land Use Plan for Addition to Havasupai Indian Reservation," October 30, 1975; Leon Rogers to Merle Stitt, November 3, 1975.

37. Interviews, Robert Euler, June 19, 1992; Doug Brown, November 25, 1991. Euler, "Cultural Patterns." Barbara Morehouse has observed that none of the original "zones of influence" survived in Congress, except that a "zone of influence" was created for the Havasupai in the park. Morehouse has important insights into the fluidity of park boundaries and multiple definitions of space. Morehouse, *A Place Called Grand Canyon*. A balanced treatment of post-1976 relations is John Hough, "The Grand Canyon National Park and the Havasupai People: Cooperation and Conflict," in West and Brechin, *Resident Peoples and National Parks*, ch. 19.

38. Michael Harrison interview, December 16, 1991. Harrison says the camp served Havasupai labor crews in the 1920s and created no problem. Rangers and staff "paid damn little attention to it; they were nice people, they were peaceful, they never caused any trouble. I don't recall a single instance of a drunk Havasupai Indian."

39. GCL: Hinchliffe, "Origin and Development of Supai Camp." Wray, "Havasupai Ethnohistory." The oral tradition about Big Jim and Roosevelt is recorded in Woodward Wickham's 1974 report, part III, p. 4, Josephy Papers: Havasupai.

40. "Indian Village," architect's draft, November 20, 1933, recommended by Tillotson and approved by Cammerer, in Grand Canyon Library: Supai Camp. For Tillotson's generally positive attitude toward the Havasupai, see his *Grand Canyon Country*, ch. 3.

41. Photos in Hinchliffe, "Origin and Development of Supai Camp."

42. GCL: BIA: James P. Brooks to M. Tillotson, January 23, May 22, 1936.

43. Euler interview, June 19, 1992. Hinchliffe, "Origin and Development of Supai Camp"; Wray, "Havasupai Ethnohistory," pp. 80–88; GCL: Havasupai: Supai Camp: Meritt Barton to superintendent, January 8, 1954.

44. GCL: Havasupai: Supai Camp: Gary Howe, "Supai Camp—Where Do We Go?" April 22, 1971.

45. GCL: Havasupai: Supai Camp: Babbitt to Stitt, July 30, 1976; Jack to Everhardt, September 14, 1976.

46. Wray, "Havasupai Ethnohistory," pp. 115–23; GCL: Grand Canyon National Park Special Use Permit, August 24, 1989; interview with Jim Tuck, January 10, 1992; personal correspondence, 1991, Richard S. Rayner and Robert Branges.

47. Hough, "The Grand Canyon National Park," pp. 222–24; interviews with Jan Balsom and Doug Brown, November 25, 1991.

48. Interviews with Doug Brown, Jan Balsom, Robert Chandler, and Ken Miller, November 25–26, 1991.

49. Chandler interview, November 26, 1991; NPS, *Grand Canyon Management Plan*, 1984. NPS historian Merrill Beal's book on the Canyon virtually ignored Indians; it related that "Canyon country is Indian country" and then disposed of the entire subject in two hundred words, telling the reader more about Havasu Falls than about the Havasupai. *Grand Canyon: The Story Behind the Scenery* (Las Vegas: KC Publications, 1989), pp. 53–54. A 1990 NPS brochure colored the Hualapai Reservation pink, yet did not identify the tribe by name. The 1995 *Draft General Management Plan*, even though it recognized traditionalist native views about the canyon (pp. 141–46), still paid much more attention to archaeological sites than to contemporary relations.

50. Wayne Sinyella, "Native Americans Cannot Celebrate Stealers of Land," *Navajo-Hopi Observer*, October 30, 1991, p. 5.

51. Theodore Roosevelt, "Remarks to the People of Arizona," in, *The Grand Canyon: Early Impressions*, ed. Paul Schullery (Boulder: Colorado Associated University Press, 1981), pp. 101–2. The same collection has quasi-mystical writing by John Muir, Zane Grey, and John Burroughs; similar selections by Clarence Dutton, John Van Dyke, Irvin Cobb, and Haniel Long are in Bruce Babbitt, comp., *Grand Canyon: An Anthology* (Flagstaff, Ariz.: Northland Press, 1986). Two compelling expressions of the same sentiment are Francis and Helen Line, *Grand Canyon Love Story* (West Allis, Wisc.: Pine Mountain Press, 1984), pp. 284–85; and Diane Sylvain's eloquent "Night Visions of a Wild and Strange Place," *High Country News*, 23:3 (February 25, 1991), p. 15.

52. For the Indian as local color, see Horace M. Albright, *Oh, Ranger!* pp. 82–84. M. Tillotson's *Grand Canyon Country* was somewhat less paternalistic. For midcentury romantic views of the Havasupai, Philip Ferry's "Canyon Utopia" in *Natural History*, 59:2 (February 1950), pp. 72–79, is replete with allusions to the Garden of Eden, the Grand Llama, and Mecca. Donald Janson idealized Havasupai as living "in their little paradise . . . in peace with nature for perhaps a thousand years." "People of the Blue Green Waters," *Audubon*, 68:6 (November 1966), pp. 464–69.

53. Popular expressions of the larger myth are Kirkpatrick Sale, *The Conquest of Paradise* (New York: A. A. Knopf, 1990); Jerry Mander, *In the Absence of the Sacred* (San Francisco: Sierra Club Books, 1991); Susan Jeffers, *Brother Eagle, Sister Sky: A Message from Chief Seattle* (New York: Dial Books, 1991); Alan Ereira, "Words of Warning: A Message from the Elder Brothers," *Buzzworm: The Environmental Journal*, 4:2 (April 1992), pp. 40–45; and the Oscar-winning film *Dances with Wolves*. Origins of positive

stereotyping have been traced by Hoxie N. Fairchild, *The Noble Savage: A Study in Romantic Naturalism* (New York: Columbia University Press, 1928); Leslie A. Fiedler, *The Return of the Vanishing American* (New York: Stein and Day, 1968); Robert F. Berkhofer, Jr., *The White Man's Indian: Images of the Indian from Columbus to the Present* (New York: Alfred A. Knopf, 1978); and Gill, *Mother Earth.* Doubts about Indians as stewards of wilderness can be found in John Collier, *From Every Zenith* (Denver: Sage Books, 1963). For critical assessments, see Calvin Martin, *Keepers of the Game* (Berkeley: University of California Press, 1978) and "The American Indian as Miscast Ecologist," *History Teacher,* 14:2 (February 1981), pp. 243–52; Thomas W. Overholt, "American Indians as 'Natural Ecologists,'" *American Indian Journal* (September 1979), pp. 9–16; Richard White, "Native Americans and the Environment," in W. R. Swagerty, ed., *Scholars and the Indian Experience* (Bloomington: Indiana University Press, 1984), pp. 179–204; O. Douglas Schwartz, "Indian Rights and Environmental Ethics," *Environmental Ethics,* 9 (Winter 1987), pp. 291–302; J. Baird Callicott, "American Indian Land Wisdom," *Journal of Forest History,* 33:1 (January 1989), pp. 35–42; and James A. Clifton, ed., *The Invented Indian: Cultural Fictions and Government Policies* (New Brunswick, N.J.: Transaction Publishers, 1990). An incisive radio program, "Isinamowin: The White Man's Indian," may be obtained from CBC Radio, P.O. Box 500, Station A, Toronto, Ontario, M5W 1E6.

For the history of Chief Seattle's speech, especially its 1971 environmental version by Ted Perry, see Rudolph Kaiser, "Chief Seattle's Speech: The 5th Gospel," in Christian Feest, ed., *Indians and Europe* (Aachen: Rader Verlag, 1987), pp. 505–26; Jerry Clark, "Thus Spoke Chief Seattle," *Prologue,* 17:1 (Spring 1985), pp. 58–65; Fergus M. Bordewich, *Killing the White Man's Indian* (New York: Anchor, 1996), ch. 4; and Albert Furtwangler, *Answering Chief Seattle* (Seattle: University of Washington Press, 1997). For a lucid argument against environmental exploitation of the speech, see Randy Adams, "Chief Seattle & the Puget Sound Buffalo Wallow," *Borealis,* 5:1 (Spring 1994), pp. 51–54. The reluctance of scholars to relinquish myths they love is apparent in Theodore Rozak's treatment of Seattle's speech, *The Voice of the Earth: An Exploration of Ecopsychology* (New York: Simon & Schuster, 1992), pp. 50, 71, 338–39.

54. MKU: 93d Cong.: Grand Canyon: Dan Langmade to Udall, n.d.; J. Kuncl to James Haley, n.d.; W. B. Hicks to Udall, April 6, 1973; Peter Wild to Roy Taylor, July 2, 1974; Jeff Ingram to Udall, July 10, 1974; M. Sharpe to Haley, July 22, 1974; Dwight Rettie to Haley, July 30, 1974; Coalition to Save the Grand Canyon to Udall, September 12, 1974; Peggy Briney to Roy Taylor, September 20, 1974; Janet Moench to Udall, September 27, 1974; Larry Hart to Udall, October 28, 1974.

Arguments against the transfer are in the *National Wildlife Conservation Reports,* pp. 23–35 (1975); "Grand Canyon Up for Grabs," *Environmental Action,* September 28, 1974, p. 7; "Threat to Grand Canyon," *Bioscience,* 24 (December 1974), p. 743; "Grand Canyon Raid," *New York Times* editorial, July 10, 1974.

The Native American Religious Freedom Act, which provided feeble congressional support for claims to sacred places, would pass in 1978 (P.L. 95-341). A series of
lawsuits over conflicting land claims followed. See Vecsey, *Handbook.*

55. Fifty-eight NPS sites totaling 270,000 acres in twenty-seven states had been
abolished by 1975, including at least eight clearly related to native history: Mack-
inac, New Echota, Custer Park (South Dakota), Old Kasaan, Papago-Saguaro,
Shoshone Caverns, Sully's Hill, and St. Croix. Rettie, *Our National Park System*, pp.
245–49.

56. Josephy Papers: Havasupai file: Statement by Havasupai Tribe, November 12, 1973. For public resentment toward environmental organizations, see letters
in *The Living Wilderness*, 1974–75, pp. 58–59; "Another Indian Land Grab," *Nation*,
April 29, 1974, p. 485; "Indians and the Canyon," *Time*, August 12, 1974; MKU: LC:
93d Cong.: B. Fontana to Stewart Udall, April 30, 1974; F. and V. Sveslosky to
M. Udall, December 5, 1974; Kenneth Kerr to M. Udall, December 3, 1974; Joyce
Stripe to M. Udall, December 5, 1974; Michael Collier to M. Udall, December 9,
1974.

57. *Congressional Record*, 93d Cong., October 10, 1974, pp. 35191–206. "Mo's
attitude was that unless environmentalists can show very, very clearly that Indian
rights are detrimental to some critically environmental need, in most cases he would
come down on the Indian side." Interview with Frank Ducheneaux, legislative assistant to Udall, 1975–1990, October 16, 1991.

58. MKU: 93d Cong.: Grand Canyon: Havasupai Tribal Council Resolution, July
28, 1974. Sierra Club lobbyist Jeff Ingram gives tribal attorney Sparks primary
credit for the bill's passage: "That period in March was a brilliant campaign; whatever Sparks was paid, he deserved it because he orchestrated it and essentially
turned the whole question right around." Ingram interview, June 16, 1992. Considerable credit is due Byler of the American Association on Indian Affairs for mobiliz-
ing public and native support.

59. Josephy Papers: W. Wickham Report, pt. 3, pp. 9–12.

60. NPCA Papers: Grand Canyon: Toby Cooper testimony before House committee, n.d.; C. Harris to NPCA, May 19, 1974; J. Carreras to E. Connally, May 30,
1974; R. L. Coshland to T. Cooper, June 11, 1974; T. Cooper to J. Carreras, June 24,
1974; Anthony Wayne Smith to R. Scurlock, October 31, 1974; Devereux Butcher
to A. W. Smith, February 13, 1975. MKU: 93d Cong., Grand Canyon: A. W. Smith to
James Haley, May 14, 1974.

61. MKU: LC: 93d Cong.: Grand Canyon: Brower to Udall, June 21, 1974; Tom
Garrett telegram to Udall, June 24, 1974; Udall to Brower, June 27, 1974; Tom
Wright to Udall, September 14, 1974; Udall to Wright, September 20, 1974; Ann
Roosevelt, "The Grand Canyon Giveaway," *Not Man Apart*, 4:16 (November 1974),
p. 6. "They're After the Grand Canyon Again: The Grand Canyon!" advertisement

ran in the *New York Times*, July 8, 1974. For context, this was the era of AIM's occupation of Wounded Knee and of successful Indian land claim tactics in Maine. See Stan Steiner, *The New Indians* (New York: Dell Publishing Co., 1968); Alvin M. Josephy, Jr., *Red Power* (New York: McGraw-Hill, 1971) and *Now That the Buffalo's Gone* (New York: Alfred A. Knopf, 1982); Vine Deloria, Jr., *Behind the Trail of Broken Treaties* (New York: Delacorte Press, 1974); and Peter Matthiessen, *In the Spirit of Crazy Horse* (New York: Viking Press, 1983). For land claims litigation, consult Paul Brodeur, *Restitution: The Land Claims of the Mashpee, Passamaquoddy, and Penobscot Indians of New England* (Boston: Northeastern University Press, 1985); and Francis G. Hutchins, *Mashpee* (West Franklin, N.H.: Amarta Press, 1979). John McPhee's *Encounters with the Archdruid* (New York: Farrar, Straus and Giroux, 1971) provides insight into Brower's tactics.

62. "Navajos Join Rainbow Bridge Suit," and "White Man Speak with Forked Highway," *Not Man Apart*, April 1974, p. 5; May 1974, p. 6.

63. Wallace Stegner interview, December 11, 1991; *Congressional Record*, 93d Cong., August 2, 1973, p. S15486, for Goldwater's attack on Sierra Club extremism. In *Time*, Goldwater described the club as "a closed society, a self-centered, selfish group, who care for nothing but . . . their personal conceptions of the way everyone else should be compelled to live." August 12, 1974, p. 65. See Freemuth, "History of S.1296," ch. 4, for the relationship between Goldwater and the Sierra Club. We are grateful to Edgar Wayburn for providing club policy statements of May 7 and August 21, 1966.

64. Edgar Wayburn interview, December 13, 1991; Ingram interview, June 16, 1992; Stegner interview, December 11, 1991; Sierra Club policy adopted February 13, 1970, and May 6, 1972; Ingram and Brock Evans quoted in *Time*, August 12, 1974; John McComb, "Grand Canyon Giveaway," and B. Evans, "Let's Not Give Up the Canyon," in the *Sierra Club Bulletin*, July 1973 and September 1974; T. H. Watkins, "Ancient Wrongs and Public Rights," *Sierra Club Bulletin*, 59:8 (September 1974), pp. 15–16, 37–39; Brock Evans to authors, December 3, 10, 1991.

65. Ingram interview, June 16, 1992. Fontana Papers: "Statement of Position of the National Native American Issues Committee of the Sierra Club," March 30, 1974. Josephy Papers: Havasupai Tribal Council flyers, March 1973. MKU: Grand Canyon Correspondence: Stephen Hirst to Margot Garcia, December 5, 1973; Leslie Albee to Sam Steiger, April 19, 1974; Michael McCloskey telegram to M. Udall, April 25, 1974; Martin Litton to *Los Angeles Times*, June 12, 1974. *Canyon Shadows: The Voice of the Havasupai People* (newsletter), February 3, 1974. Hirst, *Life in a Narrow Place*, pp. 264–73.

66. MKU: LC: 93d Cong.: Grand Canyon: Edward H. Spicer to Udall, April 15, 1974. The *Sierra Club Bulletin* never presented the Indian side. Brock Evans's final report in the *Bulletin*, "House Gives Havasupai Grand Canyon Lands," November

1974, p. 21, says only that Congress set a dangerous precedent. Of course environmentalists were not unique in thinking they knew what was best for Indians; John Collier, one of the great champions of native people in the twentieth century, held romantic ideas about Indians, often did not understand the actual people he was trying to save, and could use coercion to promote BIA programs. Philip, *John Collier's Crusade*, p. 239.

67. Alvin M. Josephy, Jr., "Indians and Environmentalists," *New York Times*, November 27, 1975, p. 33. Josephy Papers: Josephy, Susanne Anderson, and Tom Mudd to Michael McCloskey, April 16, 1975.

68. Ingram interview, June 16, 1992; Euler interview, June 19, 1992; Balsom interview, November 25, 1991. William Byler remains angry about the events. Evans recalls that fear of economic development in the canyon motivated him in 1973–74: "We had to oppose environmentally destructive [Indian] actions the same as we would oppose those of any white corporation. . . . The Grand Canyon, in its entirety, is as sacred to the Sierra Club as religious sites are to many native peoples, and for the same reason. . . . I call myself 'pro-environment' and am willing to criticize *anyone* who seeks to destroy our earth." Evans to authors, November 19, 1991. Both Ingram and Edgar Wayburn pointed out that in the 1970s the Sierra Club's main concern was not Arizona but Alaska.

69. Craig Bates, "Native Americans: Perpetuating a Wealth of Cultures in the Parks," *National Parks*, 59 (September 1985), pp. 12–15; James Bruggers, "The Salish-Kootenai Comeback," *Sierra* (August 1987), pp. 22–26; Marjane Ambler, "The Lands the Feds Forgot," and Martha Peale, "Beating the Drum for Caribou," *Sierra* (June 1989), pp. 32–40, 44–48; Michael Tennesen, "Poaching, Ancient Traditions, and the Law," and Paul Schneider, "Other People's Trash," *Audubon* (July 1991), pp. 90–97, 108–119; Harry Thuston, "Power in a Land of Remembrance," *Audubon* (December 1991), pp. 53–59; David J. Simon, "Healing the Sacred Hoop: Lakota and the National Park Service," *National Parks*, 65:9 (September 1991), pp. 24–29; "Travelers between Two Worlds," *Sierra* (May 1992), pp. 106–13; Rebecca Solnit, "Up the River of Mercy," *Sierra* (December 1992), pp. 50–57, 78–84; Margaret K. Knox, "Their Mother's Keeper," *Sierra* (April 1993), pp. 52–57, 81–84; "A Place at the Table," *Sierra* (June 1993), pp. 51–58, 90–91; "Curly Bear's Prayer," *Audubon* (April 1993), pp. 114–19; Todd Wilkinson, "Ancestral Lands," *National Parks*, 67:7 (August 1993), pp. 31–35; Robin Winks, "Sites of Shame," *National Parks*, 68:3 (March 1994), pp. 22–23; Elizabeth Hedstrom, "Scenes from the Indian Wars," *National Parks*, 69:1 (January 1995), pp. 44–46; and Winona LaDuke, "Like Tributaries to a River," *Sierra* (December 1996), pp. 38–58. A full-page advertisement for the collector's plate "Prayer to the Great Spirit" runs frequently in environmental magazines; it shows a traditional Sioux warrior "in perfect harmony with the forces of nature." *Audubon* (April 1993), p. 103.

70. Comments of Brock Evans at the Native American/Environmental Round-table, November 7, 1991.

Chapter 9

1. Balsom interview, October 18, 1994; Stephanie R. Dubois, Glen Canyon National Recreation Area, to authors, March 3, 1995.

2. Paul G. Zolbrod, *Diné bahané: The Navajo Creation Story* (Albuquerque: University of New Mexico Press, 1984), pp. 316, 331.

3. Window Rock: Navajo Tribal Law Library: Navajo Tribal Code, 1977, Title 19; Tribal Council Resolutions, 1922–1951, p. 156, July 12, 1934, and CAU-48-64, August 28, 1964. The other tribal parks were Tsegi Canyon (1960), Lake Powell and Little Colorado (1962), Tse Bonito and Window Rock (1963), Kinlichee (1964), and Marble Canyon (1966). A brief introduction to Navajo/NPS history is David Brugge, "The National Park Service and the Navajo Nation," *CRM Bulletin*, 3:3 (September 1980), pp. 6–7.

4. Courtney Reeder Jones, *Letters from Wupatki* (Tucson: University of Arizona Press, 1995).

5. Clarence Gorman interview, November 7, 1991; Alexandra Roberts, "Navajo Ethno-History and Archeology," *The Wupatki Archeological Inventory Survey Project Final Report* (Santa Fe: NPS, 1990), pp. 20–24.

6. The term arises from the pattern of land owned (sections or larger) by Navajos, private parties, railroads, or state and federal governments. The Checkerboard Area is under the BIA's Eastern Navajo Agency; today, two-thirds of the land belongs to the Navajo. See James M. Goodman, *The Navajo Atlas* (Norman: University of Oklahoma Press, 1982), pp. 56–57; for parks and sacred sites, see pp. 88–90.

7. David Grant Noble, *New Light on Chaco Canyon* (Santa Fe, N.Mex.: School of American Research, 1984).

8. Archaeological research and evidence of prehistoric Navajo occupation is minimal. See David M. Brugge, *Tsegai: An Archeological Ethnohistory of the Chaco Region* (Washington, D.C.: National Park Service, 1986), pp. 1–4; interview with David Brugge, December 8, 1991.

9. Kappler, *Indian Affairs, Laws, and Treaties*, Treaty of Fort Sumner, June 1, 1868, art. 13: The Navajo agreed to make the reservation a "permanent home, and they will not as a tribe make any permanent settlement elsewhere, reserving the right to hunt on lands adjoining said reservation. . . . If any Navajo Indian shall leave the reservation to settle elsewhere, he or they shall forfeit all the rights, privileges, and annuities conferred by the terms of this treaty." This provision contradicts the record of treaty negotiations in which William T. Sherman promised Navajo that they could settle vacant land off the reserve. David M. Brugge, *A History of the Chaco*

Navajo (Washington, D.C.: National Park Service, 1974), pp. 49, 79n. For the history of broken treaties, see Ruth M. Underhill, *The Navajos* (Norman: University of Oklahoma Press, 1956), pp. 87–92, 113.

10. The complex story of Navajo expansion is described in Lawrence C. Kelly, *The Navajo Indians and Federal Indian Policy, 1900–1935* (Tucson: University of Arizona Press, 1968).

11. Robert H. Lister, "Chaco Canyon Archaeology through Time," in Noble, *New Light on Chaco Canyon;* McNitt, *Richard Wetherill, Anasazi.*

12. S. J. Holsinger, *Report on Ruins of Chaco Canyon,* quoted in Brugge, *A History of the Chaco Navajo,* p. 171.

13. Brugge, "The Chaco Navajos," in Noble, *New Light on Chaco Canyon,* and *A History of the Chaco Navajo.*

14. NA: RG 79, E-7: Chaco Boundaries: J. Nusbaum to Horace Albright, August 1, 1929. Brugge, *A History of the Chaco Navajo,* p. 418.

15. NA: RG 79, E-7: Chaco Boundaries: Pinkley to Stacher, September 9, 1927; A. Demaray to N. Judd, July 19, 1929; A. Cammerer to BIA, April 23, 1930; Stacher to NPS, December 27, 1930. The sale failed when the NPS could not meet the $300 price. In 1947 Indians still had title to part of the land. M. Tillotson to N. Drury, March 21, 1947. NPS and BIA cooperation on securing land is fully discussed in Brugge, *A History of the Chaco Navajo,* pp. 365, 384, 396. For context, NPS efforts to acquire Navajo land were a small part of a larger struggle involving the Park Service aligned with the Smithsonian and National Geographic Society against the state of New Mexico, the University of New Mexico, the School of American Research, Edgar Hewett, and white landowners including Gus Griffin, the monument's first NPS custodian. "The chief problem is the Griffin homestead and Griffin himself. They must be eliminated." H. Albright internal memo, December 3, 1931; Hewitt to Albert Simms, June 11, 1930; Pinkley to Albright, April 27, 1932.

16. Julian to A. Cammerer, August 19, 1933, quoted in Brugge, *A History of the Chaco Navajo,* p. 424.

17. U.S. Senate, *Survey of Conditions,* Part 34, p. 17.

18. Robert P. Powers, William B. Gillespie, and Stephen H. Lekson, *The Outlier Survey: A Regional View of Settlement in the San Juan Basin,* 5 vols. (Albuquerque: Chaco Center, NPS, 1983). Interview with Charles Voll, December 6, 1991. NPCA files: Chaco: list of outliers; Mark Michel to Robert I. Kerr, April 14, 1983; Michel to Bill Richardson, February 8, 1985. Public Law 96–550 (1980) and H.R.3685, 99th Cong. 1st Sess. (1986).

19. Interview with Leo Watchman, Jr., November 4, 1991.

20. The NPS recognized interpretive shortcomings at Chaco and by the 1990s had resolved to include the Navajo story. Ed Natay interview, S.W. Regional Office, December 6, 1991. For contrast, at a monument that has had harsh disputes with the

NPS, the Wupatki visitor's center offered six videos and eighty-five different books screened by a Navajo ranger, Inez Paddock. The books included accounts of the Long Walk, political controversy, the Smithsonian *Handbook*, problems of culture change, stories of Navajo warriors, and women and children. Wupatki also had a Two Gray Hills loom with the name of the weaver and a display showing modern Navajo "moving forward with great strides." Paddock interview, April 20, 1992.

21. Interview with Clarence Gorman, November 7, 1991.

22. Hal K. Rothman, *Navajo National Monument: A Place and Its People* (Santa Fe, N.Mex.: Southwest Regional Office, NPS, 1991), pp. 73–74, 77, 88–91.

23. NA: RG 79, E-7: Navajo, Box 2300: Pinkley to A. Cammerer, June 30, 1934.

24. Rothman, *Navajo National Monument*, pp. 61–63. White, for example, took time to learn silversmithing from the Navajo. Trained in anthropology, he made special efforts to hire local people at pay equal to that of white employees. Bob Black worked at the monument for thirty-one years; Delbert Smallcanyon was a native stonemason responsible for much of the remarkable trail work near Betatakin. Interview with Art White, January 20, 1992.

25. NPS, *Statement for Management: Navajo National Park*, 1987, pp. 27–30. Rothman, *Navajo National Monument*, pp. 91–106. NA: RG 79, E-7, CCF: Navajo: John Wetherill to F. W. Griffith, August 18, 1917; J. W. Brewer to N. Drury, June 28, 1946; Hugh Miller Report, July 27, 1937; C. Wirth memo, October 22, 1937. Gorman interview, November 17, 1991.

26. NA: RG 79, E-7: Navajo, Box 2300: Vreeland to A. Cammerer, April 29, 1934; Vreeland to F. Pinkley, April 29, 1934. Emphasis in text. Frederick K. Vreeland (1874–1964) of Montclair, N.J., owned the Vreeland Apparatus Co. of New York City and held numerous patents for radio and telephone devices; he published *Maxwell's Theory and Wireless Telegraphy* (New York: McGraw Publishing, 1904), plus many scientific articles. Mt. Vreeland in the Canadian Rockies is named for him.

27. NA: RG 79, E-7: Navajo: Pinkley to Vreeland, April 28, 1934. (Pinkley or Vreeland's letter is incorrectly dated.)

28. Memorandum of Agreement, May 8, 1962, art. 7–8; copy in NPS, *Statement for Management*, 1987.

29. Navajo Nation and National Park Service, *Antelope Point: Final Development Concept Plan*, March 1986. 1970 Memo of Agreement, reprinted in ibid., pp. 155–65; and Lorraine Mintzmeyer, "Finding of Environmental Non-significance," ibid., pp. 143–44. Navajo Nation, BIA and NPS Memorandum of Understanding, 1994. Bill Donovan, "Resort Plans Still a Dream," and Karin Schill, "This Time Folks, It Just Might Be for Real!" *Navajo Times*, May 14, 1992, and October 13, 1994. Liquor is allowed within NPS jurisdictions but prohibited on the Navajo Reservation. The Le Chee Chapter (Page, Ariz.) recommends alcohol sales to provide jobs and revenue: "It's not good," conceded Jess Biakiddy at a public hearing, "but we ought to allow

the sales at the point. . . . We got millionaires coming from all over to enjoy the lake, if they want to drink the stuff, let's pour it into them. Let them have it, we want their money." *Antelope Point Concept Plan*, pp. 133, 189–90.

30. S. Udall Papers (SU): C. Wirth to Udall, January 24, 1961, includes a copy of Richard A. Ballinger to Taft, May 27, 1910, advising that the site was on tribal land.

The actual discovery of Rainbow Bridge is credited to Mike James, a Paiute called "Mike's Boy," who was still alive sixty years later when Art White located him on Finger Mesa, Utah. As a publicity stunt, White brought James, the superintendent of Glen Canyon, and the regional director together for a photo just before water reached the base of the bridge: "I thought, 'I'll never get this old boy up there on Rainbow Bridge, he can't walk.' So we ended up hauling him in a folding lawn chair. I had to wake him up early one morning, get him on his horse, into the car and down to the crossing and on a boat—thank God, the boats could get up pretty close by then. We hauled him into Rainbow Bridge at high noon, by golly, and presented him with a check for fifty bucks and a new Pendleton blanket, and said, 'Thanks.' Then we took him back home." Art White interview, January 20, 1992.

31. Rothman, *Navajo National Monument*, pp. 24–25, 79; Fradkin, *A River No More*, pp. 192–97.

32. MKU: Administrative. Corr., 93d Cong., Rainbow Bridge: Citizens Committee to M. Udall, June 14, 1961.

33. SU: Udall to Wayne N. Aspinall, August 27, 1960. Stewart Udall interview, January 18, 1991.

34. SU: Box 160, file 3: minutes of meeting, January 30, 1961. The BIA was not present. The file contains a large marked map, "Rainbow Bridge Study," April 1961.

35. SU: Anthony Wayne to Udall, October 4, 1961; Udall to Paul Jones, December 1, 26, 1961; Jones to Udall, December 18, 1961; Udall to Wirth, September 19, 1961; Udall to R. Bennett and G. Hartzog, September 12, 1967. Navajo Law Library: Tribal Council Resolution of July 16, 1956. *New York Times*, February 8, 1961; *Washington Post*, February 8, 1961; *Tucson Daily Citizen*, February 9, 1961, December 14, 1961; Phoenix Gazette, December 7, 1961. For the Udall-Littell feud, see Peter Iverson, *The Navajo Nation* (Albuquerque: University of New Mexico Press, 1981), pp. 83–89.

36. SU: Box 160, file 3, Minutes; Wirth to Udall, January 24, 1961, surmised that "Indians regarded the bridge with superstitious awe." *Badoni v. Higginson*, 638 F.2d 172 (1980).

37. *Badoni v. Higginson*, 638 F.2d at 179. For an argument that the courts are actively hostile to the practice of native and other unconventional religions, see Stephen L. Carter, *The Culture of Disbelief* (New York: Anchor Books, 1993), pp. 126–35. Also see Sarah B. Gordon, "Indian Religious Freedom and Governmental Development of Public Lands," *Yale Law Journal*, 94:1427 (1985), pp. 1447–71.

38. S. Udall and A. White interviews, January 18, 20, 1992.

39. Interview with Marian Albright Schenck, December 5, 1991.

40. Ise, *Our National Park Policy*, pp. 212, 268, 285, 352; Shankland, *Steve Mather of the National Parks*; Swain, *Wilderness Defender*. An excellent historical analysis of NPS ideology is Susan R. Schrepfer, *The Fight to Save the Redwoods* (Madison: University of Wisconsin Press, 1983). Schrepfer quotes Herbert Hoover on how "self perpetuation, expansion, and an insistent demand for more power" are inherent in bureaucracies, pp. 59–60, 70. See also Clarke and McCool, *Staking Out the Terrain*. Accounts of how these struggles affected the Navajo may be found in Kelly's *The Navajo Indians and Federal Indian Policy*; Parman's *Navajos and the New Deal* (New Haven: Yale University Press, 1976); and Richard White, *The Roots of Dependency* (Lincoln: University of Nebraska Press, 1983).

41. NA: RG 79, E-7: Navajo: Vreeland to A. Cammerer, April 4, 1934.

42. NA: RG 75, 1907–1939: General Services: Minutes of Navajo Tribal Council, Fort Wingate, July 6–7, 1930. The tribe sought the strip for the reservation, leading Chee Dodge and other Navajos to wonder why an old friend like Wetherill had turned against them.

43. NA: RG 79, E-7: Pipe Spring: Toll to Albright, April 28, 1931, photo book and letter.

44. NA: RG 79, E-7: Navajo: Albright to Charles J. Rhoads, December 5, 1931; C. Wirth to Albright, January 23, 1933; Wirth to Harold C. Bryant, April 24, 1933; Albright to Wetherill, February 13, 1933. Marian Albright Schenck interview, December 5, 1991.

45. NA: RG 79, E-7: Navajo: Draft legislation, April, 1933.

46. NA: RG 79, E-7: Navajo: Albright to Wetherill, March 27, 1933; Albright to Toll, April 6, 1933; Toll to Albright, April 11, 1933; C. Wirth memo, n.d. [c. April 1933]; Collier to Albright, June 21, 1933. Harpers Ferry Library, NPS, file L-60: Ansel F. Hall, *General Report of the Rainbow Bridge-Monument Valley Expedition of 1933*. Schenck interview, December 5, 1991.

47. NA: RG 75, CF, 1907–1939: Navajo: Tribal Council Minutes, Tuba City, Arizona, October 30–November 1, 1933. NA: RG 79, E-7: Navajo: Collier to Cammerer, August 30, 1933.

48. NA: RG 79, E-7: Navajo: Donald B. Alexander to C. Wirth, March 8, 1934; F. Kittredge to Cammerer, June 4, 1934; A. Demaray to Kittredge, June 16, 1934.

49. NA: RG 75, CF, 1907–1939: Navajo: Minutes of the Meeting of the Tribal Council, Keams Canyon, Arizona, July 10–12, 1934.

50. NA: RG 75, CCF, 1907–1939: NPS Correspondence: A. Cammerer to M. Tillotson, November 2, 1934; Cammerer to F. Pinkley, November 3, 1934. NA: RG 75: CF, 1907–1939, A. Cammerer to J. Collier, November 9, 1934; Collier to T. Dodge, September 10, 1935; and Dodge to Collier, September 14, 1935, suggest

that the Navajo considered the idea for another year. NA: RG 79, E-7: Navajo: F. Kittredge to Cammerer, October 21, 1936; E. Gammeter to A. Cammerer, February 1, 1935; Gammeter to H. Ickes, April 8, 1935; Gammeter to Cammerer, April 4, 1939; A. Demaray to Gammeter, February 12, 1935; C. Wirth to Gammeter, April 19, 1939. Escalante is mentioned in the secretary of the interior *Annual Reports,* 1933–1940. According to Ise, it was still a goal in the 1950s, although power development in the region made it impossible. *Our National Park Policy,* pp. 527–28.

51. Collier's order was published in *Living Wilderness* (December 1937), pp. 3–4. For a criticism of Collier's attempt to preserve wilderness, see Philip, *John Collier's Crusade,* p. 185. Interview with Fred White, November 4, 1991.

52. Schenck and Udall interviews, December 5, 1991; January 18, 1992. Also see Freemuth, *Islands under Siege,* p. 38.

53. Schenck interview, December 5, 1991. At least one map, drawn by T. L. Mayes in the spring of 1933, did survive. It is in the NPS records, NA: RG 79, CCF, 1933–1949: Navajo, 0-32-900-02, Box 2301. Albright does not mention Escalante in his *Birth of the National Park Service.*

54. Interview with Michael Harrison, December 16, 1991.

55. NA: RG 75, E-7: Navajo: Vreeland to A. Cammerer, June 23, 1934.

56. NA: RG 79, E-7: Pipe Spring: A. Cammerer to H. Clarkson, January 12, 1924. David M. Brugge and Raymond Wilson, *Administrative History: Canyon de Chelly National Monument, Arizona* (Santa Fe, N.Mex.: National Park Service, 1976), p. 7.

57. NA: RG 75: General Services document 054-1925: Minutes of the Tribal Council, July 7, 1925. NA: RG 75: CF, 1907–1939, Navajo: Hagerman to Charles Burke, July 11, 1925.

58. Public Law 667, 71st Cong. (H.R.15987).

59. NA: RG 75: General Services document 054-1930-24619: Minutes of the Navajo Tribal Council held at Fort Wingate, July 7–8, 1930.

60. John Cook credits the Lands Group idea to Director George Hertzog during a visit to Arizona. Interview with John Cook, December 4, 1991.

61. NA: RG 79, E-7: Canyon de Chelly: Rules and Regulations, 1936. Brugge and Wilson, *Administrative History,* pp. 143–81. John Cook, Arthur White, Herb Yahze, William Fields, and Meredith Guillet interviews. The climbs of Spider Rock involved Sierra Club outings that were especially irritating to people living in the canyon. The NPS controlled the problem at de Chelly, but at Devil's Tower in Wyoming matters proved difficult in mediating between Lakota Sioux, who claimed the monument as a sacred site, and thousands of rock climbers for whom it was a unique ascent. See Charles Levendosky, "Group Sues to Stamp Out Tolerance," *High Country News,* 28:7 (April 15, 1996), p. 17.

62. NA: RG 75: John Collier office files: NPS: H. Burnett to Collier, October 21, 1934. NA: RG 79, CCF, 1933–1949: Canyon de Chelly History: F. Vreeland to

H. Ickes, April 27, 1935; Ickes to Collier, May 13, 1936; Cammerer to Pinkley, June 29, 1936; J. Stewart to Collier, February 29, 1936; Pinkley to Cammerer, April 10, 1936; Demaray to Ickes, April 11, 12, 1936. The BIA and NPS later cooperated on fire control, watershed management, road repair, power, and water systems. Brugge and Wilson, *Administrative History*, pp. 114, 120, 134, 140, 212, 248.

63. Guillet, A. White, Brugge, and Charles Voll interviews. Brugge and Wilson, *Administrative History*, pp. 91, 116–17, 122, 125, 215, 228–29.

64. NPS: Southwest Regional Library: Canyon de Chelly: "Review of the Relationship between the National Park Service and the Navajo Tribe," November 17, 1958, by Paul Berger, Meredith Guillet, and Arthur White.

65. White, Guillet, and Voll interviews. NPS "Review of the Relationship," pp. 7–10. Southwest Regional Library: Canyon de Chelly: Guillet to G. Hartzog, December 11, 1964. Jeffrey Mark Sanders, "Tribal and National Parks on American Indian Land," Ph.D. diss., University of Arizona, 1990.

66. Tara Travis, "Canyon de Chelly National Monument: Interpreting a Dynamic Cultural System," *CRM*, 17:7 (1994), pp. 19–22. The grim story of Kit Carson and Navajo evacuation in 1863 is told in the NPS publication *Canyon de Chelly: The Story of Its Ruins and People* (1973) by Zorro A. Bradley. When asked about dogs at de Chelly, Charles Voll exclaimed, "Oh, dogs. Yes, yes, yes, yes, yes! The packs of dogs were potentially dangerous, but John Cook told me not to shoot dogs in the campground. It seems a year or two before some park ranger pulled out a gun and shot this dog, put a bullet straight through it. It ran through the campground bleeding. Tourists don't like that." Voll interview, December 6, 1991.

67. Interviews with Charles Voll, Herb Yahze, Wilson Hunter, and Charles Wilson.

68. Interviews with Theodore Evans, November 5, 1991, and Deswood Bitsoi, November 6, 1991.

69. Tracy J. Andrews, "Navajo Land Use and Settlement Variability in Canyon de Chelly and Canyon del Muerto," unpublished manuscript, 1991. Joan Mitchell, "Planning at Canyon de Chelly National Monument," *CRM*, 10:1 (February 1987), pp. 19–21, 30; Jim Cowley, "Canyon De Chelly—An Ethnographic Landscape," *CRM*, 14:6 (1991), pp. 10–11; Mark Shaffer, "Soul of Navajos under Siege" and "Gorge's Path Looks Like Eden," *Arizona Republic*, June 8, 1986. *Gallup Independent*, May 1, 1986, on power lines. Joanne Simonelli, "Tradition and Tourism at Canyon de Chelly"; and Lupita Johnson, "Living in Canyon de Chelly," *Winds of Change* (Winter 1992), pp. 13–22. *Canyon Overlook*, visitor's guide, 1991. NPS and Navajo Nation *Statement for Management: Canyon de Chelly*, 1986; and *Joint Management Plan*, 1990. NPCA Papers: Canyon de Chelly: Laura L. Beaty to Roger Siglin, August 5, 1985.

The 1986 and 1990 joint NPS/Navajo/BIA reports listed all the problems at de

Chelly, but offered few solutions beyond moving toward comanagement and a commitment to modernize visitor center interpretation.

70. Brugge and Wilson, *Administrative History*, pp. 257–64, provides an excellent analysis of the problems.

71. Navajo Law Library: Tribal Council Resolutions, December 6, 1962; Tribal Code, title 19. It is difficult to obtain a definitive list of tribal parks today. A 1992 publication omitted Marble Canyon, Lake Powell, and Tsegi, but listed parks at Great Falls, Four Corners, Wheatfield Lake, and Assayi Lake. Some are considered "paper parks."

72. Interviews with Fred White, Herb Yahze, Wilson Davis, Charley John, Wilson Hunter, and Clarence Gorman, November, 1991; Tony Skrelunas interview by Barbara Morehouse, May 12, 1992. Gorman became director of the Navajo tribal parks in 1993.

73. Sanders, "Tribal and National Parks," pp. 69–70, 98ff. According to Art White, in 1974 the tribe tried to give Monument Valley to the NPS, which, by that time, did not want it. Some NPS staff are skeptical about the tribe's commitment to operating parks: "Sure, you can say, 'Look at Monument Valley.' Well, go ahead and look at it—with a Buick on top of every butte." A. White and C. Voll interviews, January 20, 1992; April 4, December 6, 1991.

74. Interviews with Fred White, Lee Cly, November 7, 1991; Wilson Davis, October 14, 1994.

75. Monument Valley relies on untrained tour guides to tell the legends and history; some do, some don't, and some garble the message. A white pin-up girl on one tour guide's trailer challenges visitor sentimentalism. Recreation Resources Department, Navajo Tribe, and SW Regional Office, NPS, *Monument Valley Navajo Tribal Park Master Plan*, 1983.

76. See Lowry, *A Capacity for Wonder*, pp. 43–51, 57–60.

Chapter 10

1. Marjory Stoneman Douglas, *The Everglades: River of Grass* (St. Simons Island, Ga.: Mockingbird Books, 1974). European explorers were unimpressed by the beauty and biological diversity of the grasslands, describing south Florida as "a series of vast, miasmic swamps, poisonous lagoons, dismal marshes, a rotting shallow, inland sea malignant with tropical fevers and malarias, evil to the white man." Not until the late eighteenth century could someone like the naturalist William Bartram in his *Travels* begin to praise this environment; another century passed before John Muir in his *Thousand Mile Walk to the Gulf* extolled wetland beauty and fecundity. The term Everglades itself is less than two centuries old: British surveyor

Gerard de Brahm, sailing along the coast in the early 1700s, referred to the "River Glades": later English maps cited "Ever Glades."

2. Much has been written about the Seminole and Miccosukee. See Harry A. Kersey, Jr., *The Seminole and Miccosukee Tribes: A Critical Bibliography* (Bloomington: Indiana University Press, 1987). Perhaps the best general study is James W. Covington, *The Seminoles of Florida* (Gainesville: University Press of Florida, 1993). Covington's "Trail Indians of Florida," *Florida Historical Quarterly*, 58 (1979), pp. 37–57, discusses Miccosukee history. We conform to the spelling used by the tribe, Miccosukee, instead of the usage of anthropologists and linguists, Mikasuki. A good brief study is Merwyn S. Garbarino, *The Seminole* (New York: Chelsea House, 1989). Charlton W. Tebeau's *Man in the Everglades: 2000 Years of Human History in the Everglades National Park* (Coral Gables, Fla.: University of Miami Press, 1990), pp. 17–79, discusses prehistory. Tebeau's *Florida's Last Frontier: The History of Collier County* (Coral Gables, Fla.: University of Miami Press, 1957) is a significant work. Seminoles also absorbed remnant Yamassee, Yuchi, and Calusa people, as well as free blacks and runaway slaves. For the eighteenth century colonial background, see Allan Gallay, *The Formation of a Planter Elite* (Athens: University of Georgia Press, 1989).

3. John K. Mahon, *History of the Second Seminole War, 1835–1842* (Gainesville: University of Florida Press, 1967), and "Indian-United States Military Situation, 1775–1848," *Handbook of North American Indians*, vol. 4, pp. 144–62; Virginia Bergman, *The Florida Wars* (Hamden, Conn.: Archon Books, 1979); Ronald N. Satz, *American Indian Policy in the Jacksonian Era* (Lincoln: University of Nebraska Press, 1975). Leitch J. Wright, Jr., "Blacks in British East Florida," *Florida Historical Quarterly*, 54 (1971), pp. 425–42, discusses the large number of blacks who joined the Seminoles rather than stay in the American colonies, and Wright's "A Note on the First Seminole War as Seen by the Indians, Negroes, and Their English Advisors," *Journal of Southern History*, 34 (1968), pp. 565–75, provides further background. Kenneth W. Porter's "Negroes and the Seminole War, 1817–1818," *Journal of Negro History*, 36 (1951), supports the theory that Andrew Jackson's assault on the tribe was inspired in part by the presence of blacks.

4. Harry A. Kersey, Jr., *Pelts, Plumes, and Hides: White Traders among the Seminole Indians, 1870–1930* (Gainesville: University Presses of Florida, 1975).

5. NA: RG 75: Seminole Indians: file 426-12: Lucien Allen Spencer to Robert G. Valentine, February 29, 1912. Spencer describes conditions prevailing among the Seminoles after several canals had lowered the water level on large tracts of their territory, destroying alligator and otter grounds. He reported that Seminoles provided only a third of all hides traded at the Protestant Mission seventy miles southeast of Ft. Myers. On further inquiry, he found the same conditions at all trading posts in southern Florida. Spencer concluded that "the great need at the present time is for a game reservation . . . set aside as an Indian reservation." The file also

contains numerous items expressing concern, including a "Plea for the Seminole as Part of Conservation," *Kissimmee Valley Gazette,* by Minnie Moore-Willson (1913). Moore-Willson questioned the need for draining the swamps of south Florida and called for justice in dealing with Indians: "In this legislative drainage act, Florida forgot her duty to . . . peaceable Seminole Indians, who are the only Americans who have a genuine right to this location. . . . There is today more than enough land in Florida for both races."

6. For the park standards issue, see Miles, *Guardians of the Parks,* pp. 71–95; and Rettie, *Our National Park System,* pp. 73–85. The biologic reform is discussed in Schrepfer, *The Fight to Save the Redwoods;* and Wright, *Wildlife Research and Management.*

7. NA: RG 75: Seminole Indians, file 11055, 1930: Albright to Rhoads, March 1, 1930; Rhoads to Albright, March 10, 1930; Cammerer to Rhoads, August 20, 1930. Cammerer also observed that "if the reservation is affected, it would not be a serious disadvantage, since the Indians may be used in connection with the operation of the park. There are, however, some complications of jurisdiction."

8. NA: RG 75: Seminole Indians, file 11055: Nash to Rhoads, December 4, 1930. U.S. Senate, *Survey of the Seminole Indians of Florida,* pp. 20–59, 86. Nash's map is in this document facing p. 1.

9. NA: RG 79: Everglades N.P., Box 233: Narrative of a Trip into the Everglades by Augustus Houghton, February 9–12, 1932.

10. 73d Cong. 2d Sess. Chapter 371, May 30, 1934, pp. 20–59, 86, *An Act to Provide for the Establishment of the Everglades National Park in the State of Florida.*

11. "Oil Leases to Help the Poor Seminole!" *American Eagle* of Estero, Florida, May 28, 1931. The story tells of a bill in the state legislature to allow oil exploration on the reservation. Supporters claimed that the Seminoles supported drilling in view of future lease fees. Opponents protested that oil companies were using the Indians: "Aside from being of doubtful benefit to the Seminole Indians . . . oil leases . . . would tend to impede immeasurably the . . . proposed Tropic Everglades National Park." NA: RG 79: Everglades, 1928–1931, Box 234: Coe to Henry R. Cloud, December 8, 1931.

12. Dorothy Downs, "Coppinger's Tropical Gardens: The First Commercial Indian Village in Florida"; and Patsy West, "The Miami Indian Tourist Attractions: A History and Analysis of a Traditional Mikasuki Seminole Environment," *Florida Anthropologist,* 34:4 (December 1981), pp. 200–224, 225–31. Frederick W. Sleight, "Kunti, A Food Staple of Florida Indians," ibid. 6 (1953), pp. 46–52.

13. NA: RG 79: Everglades, Box 914: E. Coe to J. Collier, May 13, 1936; Coe to Sholtz, August 3, 1936; Coe to Cammerer, August 3, 1936. West, "The Miami Indian Tourist Attractions." In his report to Congress, Nash discussed the problem of jurisdiction over Seminole villages, a "foci of venereal infection," inside the city limits of Miami and St. Petersburg. U.S. Senate, *Survey of the Seminole Indians,* p. 44.

14. NA: RG 79: Everglades: General, 1933–1949, Box 911. Department of the Interior press memorandum, March 31, 1935: text of Ickes's radio address, "Visit Your National Parks." Press memorandum, April 2, 1935. U.S. Senate *Reports*, 95th Cong., 2d Sess., Committee on Indian Affairs, *Distribution of Seminole Judgment Funds: Hearings . . . on Indian Affairs on S.2000 and S.2188.* This document also contains the Indian Law Resource Center *Report to Congress: Seminole Land Rights in Florida*, Exhibit 5, pp. 134–35. For insightful analysis of the tribe's experience under Ickes, see Kersey, *The Florida Seminoles and the New Deal.* Background on Ickes's commitment to conservation and Indians is in T. H. Watkins, *Righteous Pilgrim: The Life and Times of Harold L. Ickes, 1874–1952* (New York: Henry Holt & Co., 1990). Watkins leaves little doubt that Ickes was deeply influenced on these issues by his first wife, Anna Wilmarth Ickes. For the Osceola story, see Alvin M. Josephy, Jr., *The Patriot Chiefs: A Chronicle of American Indian Resistance* (New York: Viking Press, 1969), pp. 176–208.

15. John Collier, "With Secretary Ickes and the Seminoles," *Harlow's Weekly,* April 20, 1935, pp. 7–8. "Seminole Group Promised Lands at Parley," *Palm Beach Post,* March 21, 1935, p. 1. NA: RG 75: Collier Papers, Office file, Box 17: Seminole petition, March 20, 1935; Interior press release, April 2, 1935.

16. NA: RG 79: Everglades: Box 903: Cammerer to Burlew, March 13, 1934. Gene Stirling, "Report on the Seminole Indians of Florida," 1935, in Indian Law Resource Center, *Seminole Land Rights,* pp. 177–89, cited above.

17. NA: RG 79: Everglades, general, 1933–1949, Box 903: Coe to Ickes, July 5, 1935, August 3, 1936; Coe to Collier, May 13, August 3, 1936; Coe to Cammerer, August 3, 1936; Coe to Walters, August 19, 1936. Ernest Coe's rhetoric grew increasingly shrill: "We all realize that the Seminole is a pathetic spectacle."

18. NA: RG 79: Everglades, general, Box 911: Cammerer to Coe, April 18, 1935.

19. NA: RG 79: Everglades, general: Box 913: J. J. Cameron, "The Seminole Problem," NPS report, 1938. Coe to Collier, May 6, 1936; Ickes to David Holtz, March 20, 1936; F. J. Scott to Collier, April 4, 1936. Many of these documents are reproduced in Indian Law Resource Center, *Seminole Land Rights.*

20. "Seminoles Prepare to Fight Eviction from Glades Park," *Fort Myers News,* April 11, 1937.

21. NA: RG 79: Everglades: J. J. Cameron, "The Seminole Problem," 1938.

22. NA: RG 79: Everglades, general, Box 911: N. Drury to Chapman, August 12, 1938. Box 912: Coe to Paul Bartsch, May 22, 1943.

23. NA: RG 79: Everglades, general, 1933–1949: Box 913. Beard to NPS regional director, May 8, 1947.

24. Ibid.

25. NA: RG 79: Everglades, Box 907: Beard to regional director, Fish & Wildlife Service, March 26, 1947.

26. NA: RG 79: Everglades, general, 1933–1949, Box 913: Marmon to Beard, April 24, 1947; Thomas J. Allen to Marmon, May 13, 1947.

27. NA: RG 79: Everglades, 1933–1949: Box 907: Beard to James Silver, May 30, 1947; director of USFWS to commissioner of Indian affairs, June 10, 1947. Box 902: news release of Truman speech, December 5, 1947, plus clippings and invitation list. Box 913: Charles A. Richey to regional director, region one, February 28, 1949. Also see Peter Matthiessen, *Indian Country* (New York: Viking Press, 1984), p. 34.

28. John C. Paige and Lawrence F. Van Horn, *An Ethnohistory of Big Cypress National Preserve* (Denver, Colo.: NPS, 1982), pp. 110–14, discusses Miccosukee claims based on 1839–1845 treaties that granted Seminoles most of southern Florida. Indian Law Resource Center, *Seminole Land Rights*, pp. 286–89.

29. *Seminole Land Rights*, "Report on the Florida Seminoles," December 1954, p. 272.

30. Billy Cypress to Robert Chandler, May 14, 1990. Authors' copy.

31. Robert Chandler interview, November 26, 1991. "Take Two Panther Claws . . . ," *Science*, 84 (October 1984), p. 82; Ken Slocum, "Indian Hunters Come under Fire," *Wall Street Journal*, October 15, 1987, pp. 1, 27.

32. Interview with Robert Chandler, November 26, 1991. In the 1960s, rangers suspected Seminoles of setting fires in the park to create jobs; Robert Branges to authors, November 1991. The NPS is also under constant scrutiny and legal pressure from environmental groups, as is evident in the NPCA Everglades and Big Cypress files.

33. Cypress to Chandler, May 14, 1990. Interviews with Bruce Hoffman, Steve Terry, Billy Cypress (Miccosukee), Billy Cypress (Seminole), Fred Tiger, Buffalo Tiger, April 1991; meeting of the NPS, Army Corps of Engineers, and "Trail Seminoles," April 19, 1991.

Chapter 11

1. Albright, *Oh, Ranger!*, pp. 81–96.

2. William Cronon, ed., "The Trouble with Wilderness," in *Uncommon Ground: Toward Reinventing Nature* (New York: W. W. Norton, 1995), pp. 69–90.

3. For Mather's and Albright's aggressive expansionism, see Foresta, *America's National Parks and Their Keepers* (Washington, D.C.: Resources for the Future, 1985), pp. 18–47; Susan Schrepfer, *The Fight to Save the Redwoods*, pp. 59–60, 70; Ise, *Our National Park Policy*, pp. 212, 267–69, 322.

4. *Federal Register*, September 22, 1987, pp. 35673–78.

5. NA: RG 79: E-7, Navajo, Box 2300: Chatelain to Cammerer, June 20, 1934. Evolution of the 1987 policy can be traced through the service's *CRM Bulletin* begin-

ning in 1978 with Jackson W. Moore, "The National Park Service's Native American Policy: A Status Report," 1:3 (September 1978), pp. 1, 5, 8; Forrest J. Gerard, "The Indian in America," 2:2 (June 1979), and "Being Good Neighbors with First Americans in the Western Region," 3:3 (September 1980), pp. 1–3. Muriel Crespi, "Native American Relationships: An Evolving Script," Courier, 32:12 (December 1987), pp. 38–39.

6. Schrepfer, The Fight to Save the Redwoods, p. 241.

7. Freeman Tilden, The National Parks (New York: Alfred A. Knopf, 1968), foreword by George B. Hartzog. A useful booklet, The National Park Service (Las Vegas: KC Publications, 1987), by Horace Albright, Russell Dickenson, and William Penn Mott, unfortunately refers to no Indians except ancient ones and its map of the system omits Pipe Spring and Apostle Islands. NPS historian Merrill Beal, although he wrote extensively about Indians in his earlier book on Yellowstone, virtually ignored them in Grand Canyon (Las Vegas: KC Publications, 1989). Despite recognizing that "Canyon country is Indian country," Beal had more to say about Havasu creek and its waterfalls than about the tribe. A public relations piece may not reflect the knowledge and feelings of an author; Dickenson, for example, in his keynote address to a world parks conference at Mesa Verde in 1984 made a powerful plea for honoring diverse cultures and called for "permanent working relationships" between government, native communities, and environmental groups. NPS, International Perspectives on Cultural Parks, pp. 1–4; Dickenson interview, March 22, 1996.

8. Examples of an enlightened approach in NPS internal publications is Raymond H. Thompson, "Desert Archaeology: A Neglected Interpretive Resource," CRM, 13:3 (1990), pp. 8–11; Dean B. Suagee and Karen J. Funk, "Reconfiguring the Cultural Mission: Tribal Historic Preservation Programs," CRM, 13:4 (1990), pp. 21–24; Leland M. Roth, "Living Architecture: Differing Native and Anglo Perceptions of Preservation," CRM, 18:5 (1995), pp. 33–40.

9. Patricia Nelson Limerick, The Legacy of Conquest: The Unbroken Past of the American West (New York: W.W. Norton & Co., 1987), p. 190.

10. Interviews with William Briggle, June 3, 1987, and Muriel Crespi, November 23, 1987. Crespi, an anthropologist in the Washington, D.C., office who considered it her "great mission" to enlighten the NPS about Indians, pushed through the 1987 policy. Directives from above, however, may have little effect throughout the NPS and often disappear in the field, as this one did in many regions. Rettie, Our National Park System, is excellent on the internal management of the service; see pp. 136–40.

11. Ed Natay, "NPS Closely Bound to Native Americans in Southwest," Courier, 32:12 (December 1987); John E. Cook, "The Cultural Legacy of America's National Parklands"; and Tanna Chattin, "John E. Cook: Profile of Leadership in NPS-American Indian Relationships," CRM, 14:5 (1991), pp. 38–43.

12. Sax, "Do Communities Have Rights?" pp. 499–511. Sax's critique of the NPS at Buffalo River, Boxley Valley, Stehekin, and the Cuyahoga Valley also applies to reservations.

13. West and Brechin, *Resident Peoples and National Parks*, part 7. A penetrating essay is Robert Goodland's "Prerequisites for Ethnic Identity and Survival," ch. 19, ibid. Goodland lists recognition of territory, protection from disease, time for change, and self-determination as essential. Similar analysis may be found in H. Paul Friesema, "American Indians and the National Parks of the Southwest," NPS, *International Perspectives*, pp. 286–90. On "partnership parks," see Rettie, *Our National Park System*, pp. 39, n.38; 56.

14. Statement of Horace M. Albright, 1933, Marian Albright Schenck Papers.

15. Charles Riggins interview, March 30, 1992. This employment rate of 2 percent, four times the Indian population, is low only if one postulates special Indian ties with parklands. Furthermore, the small population of many reserves limits NPS procurement programs. The Havasupai have five hundred members, the Miccosukee four hundred, the Kaibab Paiute and Hoh just over two hundred. A community of four hundred will have no more than one hundred employable adults, some of whom are needed for tribal government and many of whom will lack the minimal education and skills for park jobs. Young Indians who leave to gain those skills often do not return, and if they do, they may be resented by their own people. Employment problems, even in areas of high native population such as southeast Alaska and the Yukon in Canada, are discussed in Paul G. Sneed, "National Parklands, Northern Homelands," Ph.D. diss., University of Hawaii, 1993.

16. NA: RG 79, E-7, CCF, 1933–1949, Canyon de Chelly: Pinkley to Cammerer, December 31, 1935. Indians repeatedly made this point in our interviews—for example, Clay Butler, Jerry Charles, and Fred White. For a discussion of NPS problems in hiring minorities and women, see Rettie, *Our National Park System*, pp. 121, n.4; 148, n. 16; 155.

17. Dickenson interview, March 22, 1996.

18. NA: RG 75: BIA general services, 054-1930-24619: Navajo Tribal Council Minutes, 1930. The 1958 report of Art White and Meredith Guillet made the same point: "Navajo will work with one man and eventually gain confidence in a particular individual. Rapid shifting of monument personnel throughout the years has not allowed the local Navajo to build confidence through long association with any one individual." Thirty years later regional director John Cook agreed, claiming that NPS staff "move around too much." Cook interview, December 4, 1991. Jan Balsom at the Grand Canyon, Russell Dickenson, and many other park personnel concur. On the "fairly low tolerance for homesteaders" in the NPS, see Everhart, *The National Park Service*, p. 2.

19. Demaray to Ickes, August 14, 1934, quoted in Brugge and Wilson, *Admin-*

istrative History, p. 50. Lane memo of May 13, 1918, in Dilsaver, *America's National Park System: The Critical Documents,* pp. 48–52. For a balanced analysis of NPS responsibility to the general public, see Foresta, *America's National Parks.*

20. Rettie, *Our National Park System,* p. 213.

21. For example, the conceptual confusion in *Lyng v. Northwest Indian Cemetery Protective Association,* 485 U.S. 439 (1988) and *Employment Division v. Smith,* 494 U.S. 872 (1990). See Carter, *The Culture of Disbelief,* pp. 126–32. On the difficulty of resolving native claims, see Sarah B. Gordon, "Indian Religious Freedom and Governmental Development of Public Lands," *Yale Law Journal,* 94 (1985), pp. 1447–71. The statement about general NPS staff attitudes is based on our 1991 survey of thirty-seven retired NPS administrators and our interviews with NPS leaders such as Howard Chapman who have a sophisticated grasp of Indian/park relations. Chapman sees the service as having responsibility without control, often caught between a mandate to protect parks and the public's emotional responses to native demands. Interview, May 8, 1992.

22. See Sanders, "Tribal and National Parks." Since 1990 the NPS grants to Indian tribes has totaled over $7.3 million. *CRM,* 18:6 (1995), pp. 18–23. The origin of Keepers of the Treasures is described in *CRM,* 14:1 (1991), p. 14; see Patricia L. Parker, *Keepers of the Treasures: Protecting Historic Properties and Cultural Traditions on Indian Lands* (Washington, D.C.: NPS, 1990). The NPS is also the agency charged by Congress with administering "repatriation," the return of human remains and native artifacts from museums. On the emotional issue of human remains, see Bruce Craig, "Bones of Contention: The Controversy over Digging Up Human Remains in Parks," *National Parks* (July 1990), pp. 16–17.

23. "Twelve Tribes Become Full Partners in the National Historic Preservation Program," *CRM Bulletin,* 7 (1996), pp. 5–6, 39–40. "Native Alliance," *Masinaigan,* NCAI (Winter 1996), p. 25. Members of the alliance included the Hualapai, Navajo, Timbisha, and Miccosukee.

24. Gary Hasty interview, November 8, 1991. The Grand Canyon Trust has made a consistent effort and gained respect by working with tribes on the Colorado Plateau; Tony Skrelunas interview with Barbara Morehouse, May 12, 1992. Also see Peter Poole, "Developing a Partnership of Indigenous Peoples, Conservationists, and Land Use Planners," Working Paper, World Bank, 1989.

25. Chase, *Playing God in Yellowstone,* p. 113.

26. See Goodland, "Prerequisites," in West and Brechin, *Resident Peoples and National Parks;* and Wilkinson, *American Indians, Time, and the Law,* pp. 68–76, 186–88; Runte, *National Parks,* pp. 110–11.

27. Schama, *Landscape and Memory,* pp. 7, 574.

INDEX

Evans, Brock, 183–84, 293n. 68
Evans, Daniel, 194
Evans, Theodore, 211–12
Everglades National Park, 221–22: ab-
    original cultures, 217–19; creation of,
    222–23, 227; logging in, 220, 230; and
    the Spanish, 217; tourism, 220, 221,
    223–25, 228. *See also* employment;
    Miccosukee; minerals; Seminole
Everhardt, Gary, 175
Ewing, Henry, 157–58, 163, 168, 284n. 4

Fall, Albert, 27, 29
Farrow, E. A., 74–75, 77, 79
Federal Energy Regulatory Commission,
    U.S., 97, 102, 105
federal government, U.S.: Indian policy,
    18–19; land policy, 50–51; national
    lakeshores, 4–5, 245n. 8; in the West,
    27–28. *See also specific bureaus and depart-
    ments*
Fields, Bill, 234
filmmaking, 62, 213–14
Finnerty, Maureen, 98, 100, 108, 128
Fish and Wildlife Service, U.S., 105–6,
    227, 229
fishing, 25. *See also* Glacier; Olympic Na-
    tional Park; *and specific tribes*
Fletcher, Lena, 111
Florida, state of, 220–22, 227
Fontana, Bernard, 169–70
Ford, Gerald, 156, 164
Forest Reserve Act of 1891, 93
forests. *See specific parks*
Forest Service, U.S., 27, 35, 50, 122, 200:
    and Grand Canyon, 136–37, 138,
    158–59, 160–61, 163–64, 182
Forlines, David, 116–18, 126–27
Fred Harvey Company, 134, 141, 148–
    52, 174, 206
Friends of the Earth, 103, 164–70, 179–81

Gammeter, Emil, 203
Geerdes, Raymond, 83, 87

Glacier National Park: aboriginal cul-
    tures, 44; Blackfeet Highway, 54, 61–
    62; boundary disputes, 53–56, 59–60;
    creation of, 44, 47–51, 258n. 15; fish-
    ing in, 58–59; forests, 48, 49–50, 55,
    60–61; tourism, 54, 57–58, 61–64. *See
    also* Blackfeet; Grinnell; minerals;
    Salish-Kootenai
Glen Canyon, 141–42, 146–47, 154,
    185–86, 195–99, 201–2, 204
Goldwater, Barry, 145, 163, 164–66, 170,
    175, 178, 181–82, 286n. 20, 292n. 63
Gorman, Clarence, 150, 192–93, *193*, 199
Gorton, Slade, 106
Grand Canyon Enlargement Act (1975),
    144, 156–84: and media, 169; opposi-
    tion to, 165–67, 178–79; support for,
    167–70, 179–80. *See also* Havasupai
Grand Canyon National Park: boundary
    issues, 136–37, 147–49, 153, 179; cre-
    ation of, 133, 158; dams, 141–46; fed-
    eral policy and, 162–63; logging in,
    165; as national monument, 133–34,
    142; pre-contact cultures, 132–33;
    tourism, 146–53, 159, 162–63, 165–
    66, 171–72. *See also* employment; Grand
    Canyon Enlargement Act; Grand Can-
    yon Village; grazing; Havasupai; Hopi;
    Hualapai; minerals; Navajo
Grand Canyon Village, 138, 140, 159,
    168–69, 172, 173, 179, 184
Grand Teton National Park, 60, 122
Grant, Heber, 86, *86*, 264n. 12
Grant, Ulysses S., 23, 109, 121
Grayhair, Ninie, 149
grazing: and Blackfeet, 46, 48, 64; in
    Grand Canyon, 159–61, 167, 172,
    179; at Pipe Spring, 69–70, 72–74. *See
    also* Navajo
Great Northern Railway, 56–59
Great Thumb Mesa, 137, 160–61, 171–
    72, 184
Grey, Carl, *86*

ABOUT THE AUTHORS

Robert H. Keller is a graduate of the University of Chicago. He recently retired from Fairhaven College, Western Washington University, where he taught federal Indian policy and law and received a distinguished teaching award. Dr. Keller has been a frequent visiting scholar at the Arizona State Museum and the University of Arizona, where much of the research for this book was completed. He has published and lectured widely on Indian history. His works include *American Protestantism and U.S. Indian Policy*. He is also the editor of *In Honor of Justice Douglas*. Dr. Keller currently works with the Whatcom Land Trust.

Michael F. Turek is an Air Force veteran and a graduate of Fairhaven College. He has worked for the National Park Service, U.S. Forest Service, Native American Fish and Wildlife Society, Yakama Indian Nation, and InterTribal Bison Cooperative. He is currently employed by the Alaska Department of Fish and Game as a subsistence resource specialist. Mr. Turek, who lives in Juneau, has traveled extensively in Greenland and Asia.